MILK PROCESSING & DAIRY PRODUCTS INDUSTRIES

LIST OF PUBLICATIONS/BOOKS PUBLISHED BY

ENGINEERS INDIA RESEARCH INSTITUTE 4449, NAI SARAK, MAIN ROAD, DELHI - 6 (INDIA)

CHEMICALS/DYES/PETRO CHEMICALS/LUBRICANT/ ELECTROPLATING

Name of Books	₹	US$
* Hand Book of Lubricants, Grease and Petrochemical Technology	750/-	75
* Small Medium & Large Scale Chemical Industries	375/-	40
* Industrial Chemicals Technology Hand Book	1100/-	110
* Project Ideas on All Chemicals & Allied Industries	1300/-	130
* Electroplating, Anodizing & Surface Finishing Technology	750/-	75
* Agro Chemical Industries (Insecticide & Pesticides)	900/-	90
* Technology of Synthetic Dyes, Pigments Intermediates	1100/-	110
* Petrochemicals, Lubricants, Greases & Petroleum Refining	900/-	90
* Modern Technology of Organic & Inorganic Chemicals	1400-	140

GUMS, ADHESIVES & SEALANTS

Name of Books	₹	US$
* Technology of Gums, Adhesives & Sealants with Formulations	950/-	95
* Hand Book of Adhesives with their Formulae	650/-	65
* Adhesives Technology & Formulations Hand Book	975/-	100

SMALL SCALE INDUSTRIES/ STATIONERY/PAPER/INKS/ CANDLES & EXPORT BUSINESS

Name of Books	₹	US$
* Start Your Own Export Business (How To Export)	350/-	35
* Start Your Own Small Business and Industry	350/-	35
* Candle Making Processes & Formulations Hand-Book	380/-	38
* Stationery, Paper Converting & Packaging Industries	400/-	40
* Profitable Businesses to Start for Entrepreneurs	400/-	40
* Modern Small and Cottage Scale Industries	650/-	65
* Profitable Small Cottage Tiny & Home Industries	650/-	65

OFFSET PRINTING, SCREEN PRINTING & PACKAGING PRINTING INKS

Name of Books	₹	US$
* Printing Processes Technologies & Industries	375/-	40
* Hand Book of Printing Technology (Offset, Screen, Flexo, Gravure, Inkjet & Digital)	975/-	100
* Hand Book of Offset Printing Tech.	500/-	50
* Screen Printing with Processes & Technology	350/-	35
* Hand Book of Packaging Industries	1300/-	130
* Hand Book of Packaging Technology	900/-	90
* Modern Inks Formulaes & Manufacturing Industries	325/-	33
* Modern Technology of Printing Inks.	1150/-	115
* Modern Packaging Technology for Food Products	600/-	60
* Hand Book of Food Packaging Technology	900/-	90
* Hand Book of Pre Press	800/-	80

WOOD, VENEER, FOREST BASED

Name of Books	₹	US$
* Modern Technology of Wood, Veneer, Plywood, Particle Board, Fibre Board, Bamboo and Forest Products	1600/-	160

PAINT, VARNISH, COATING AND LACQUERS

Name of Books	₹	US$
* Paint Pigment Varnish & Lacquer Manufacturing	450/-	45
* Paint Varnish Solvents & Coating Technology	800/-	80
* Technology of Coatings, Resins, Pigments & Inks Industries	975/-	100
* Paint, Pigment, Solvent, Coating, Emulsion, Paint Additives and Formulation	900/-	90
* Mfg. Tech. & Formulations H.B on Thinners, Putty, Wall & Industrial Finishes & Synthetic Resins	900/-	100

PLASTIC/POLYMER PROCESSING, COMPOUNDING, MOULDS, PET, RESINS & RUBBER INDUSTRIES

Name of Books	₹	US$
* Injection Moulding of Plastics	750/-	75
* Moulds Design & Processing Hand Book	495/-	50
* Plastic Processing & Packaging Industries	975/-	100
* Hand Book of Plastic Projects (Hi-Tech Plastic Projects)	1300/-	130
* Synthetic Resins Technology with Formulations	800/-	80
* Technology of PET Bottles, Preform & PET Recycling	850/-	85
* Plastic Compounding, Masterbatches, PET & Other Plastics	750/-	75
* Technology of PVC Compounding and Its Applications	900/-	90
* Hand Book of Polymer and Plastic Technology	950/-	90
* Plastic Water Recycling Technology	750/-	75
* Hand Book Plastic Materials & Processing Technology	750/-	75
* Technology of Plastic Films	650/-	65
* Rotational Moulding Technology	450/-	45
* Hand Book of Fiber Glass Moulding	450/-	50
* Technology of Reinforced Plastics	750/-	75
* Modern Technology of Extrusion and Extruded Products	800/-	80
* Technology of Synthetic Resins and Emulsion Polymers	975/-	100

BAKERY & CONFECTIONERY

Name of Books	₹	US$
* Hand Book of Bakery Industries	350/-	35
* Hand Book of Confectionery with Formulations	600/-	60
* Hand Book of Modern Bakery Prod.	750/-	75
* Modern Bakery Tech. & Fermented Cereal Products with Formulae	1250/-	130
* Breakfast, Dietary Food, Pasta, Cereal Product Technology	1150/-	115

REAL ESTATE/HOTEL

Name of Books	₹	US$
* Real Estate Plazas, Hotel, Hospital & Commercial Complexes	1300/-	130

BIO-TECHNOLOGY

Name of Books	₹	US$
* Model Technology of Bio-Proccessing	1475/-	150
* Technology of Bio-Fuel (Ethamel & Biodiesel	975/-	100

E-Mail: eiribooks@yahoo.com, eiriprojects@gmail.com

Website : www.eiriindia.org, www.eiribooksandprojectreports.com, www.eiri.in

MILK PROCESSING & DAIRY PRODUCTS INDUSTRIES

Written By

EIRI BOARD OF CONSULTANTS & ENGINEERS

ENGINEERS INDIA RESEARCH INSTITUTE

4449, Nai Sarak, Main Road, Delhi - 110006 (India)
Ph: 91-11-23918117, 23916431, 45120361
* E-Mail: eiribooks@yahoo.com, eiriprojects@gmail.com
*Website: www.eiriindia.org, www.eiribooksandprojectreports.com

PRINTED & PUBLISHED BY

ENGINEERS INDIA RESEARCH INSTITUTE

4449, Nai Sarak, Main Road, Delhi - 110006 (India)
Ph: 91-11-23918117, 23916431, 45120361
* E-Mail: eiribooks@yahoo.com, eiriprojects@gmail.com
*Website: www.eiriindia.org, www.eiribooksandprojectreports.com

Sole Distributors:

EIRI PROJECT CONSULTANTS AND PUBLISHERS
4/54 Roop Nagar, Delhi-110007

2nd Edition

ISBN: 9788186732472

Printed in New Delhi (INDIA)

Rs. 950/-

Printed & Published by Sudhir Gupta for "Engineers India Research Institute", 4449 Nai Sarak, Main Road, New Delhi -110006

Preface

The book **'MILK PROCESSING AND DAIRY PRODUCTS INDUSTRIES'** covers almost all the basic and advanced details to setup own milk processing unit. The Book covers following Contents : Known Indian Milk Products, Cheese, Butter, Yoghurt, Evaporated and Condensed Milks, Dried Milk/Milk Powder, Ice-Cream, Some Dried Dairy Products, Market Dahi and Pure Culture Dahi, Packaging of Milk, Packaging of Milk and Milk Products In India, Packaging Trends for Cheese and other Dairy Products, Milk-Based Soft Drink With Longer Shelf-Life, Fermented Milk Products-Flavour & Bio-technolgoy, Losses and their Possible Management In Dairy Industry, Cultured Milk Products in Human Nutrition, Freeze-Dried Starter Cultures In Fermented Dairy Products Manufacture, Dairy Products, Products Diversification In Dairy Industry, Coffee Complete, Paneer, Cheese from Buffalo Milk, Whey Protein Concentrate, Production of Yoghurt, Tea Complete, Casein from Milk, Dairy Farm, Flavoured Milk, Dairy Farm to Produce Milk, Ice Cream & Ice-Candy, Processed Cheese, Milk Powder & Ghee, Soya Milk and Paneer, Lactose and By Products Processing from Milk, Condensed Milk (Sweetened), Butter Milk, Toned Milk, Dairy Products and Milk Packaging in Pouches, Soya Milk and Tofu, Details of Machineries Used in Dairy Farms and Products, Suppliers of Plant and Machineries.

Frankly speaking- the book is also quite indispensable for those who have also setup their industry.

The book has been written for the benefit and to prove an asset and a handy reference guide in the hands of new entrepreneurs & well established industrialists.

Director
ENGINEERS INDIA RESEARCH INSTITUTE
Nai Sarak, New Delhi (INDIA)
E-Mail : eirisidi@bol.net.in

Contents and Subject Index

Chapters	Page No.

Chapter 41

Chapter 1

KNOWN INDIAN MILK PRODUCTS

Some dairy products are popular throughout the country whereas some are region specific. The Indian dairy products conserves the precious milk solids for relatively long storage period. Traditionally, Indian Dairy Products have been manufactured by individual halwais (sweet makers) and some of entrepreneurs. Recently a few organised dairies have started production of some of the products on a large scale, but the contribution of the organised dairy industry is far less significant.

An impressive range of Indian Dairy Products most of which have a region specific complexion, have been evolved in the country over the years. Apart from their significant nutritional roles, many of them have social and ceremonial connotations. The products may be classified on the basis of the processing employed for the manufacture as follows :

A Fermented products : a) Dahi - a popular item of Indian diet, b) *Misti Doi* - from concentrated sweetened milk popular in Eastern India, c) *Srikhand*, whey drained dahi, sweetened with sugar with spices and nuts, popular in western and central India, and d) Lassi a whisked dahi with or without sugar, popular all over India.

B Fat-rich products : a) Makkan, prepared by churning dahi and the butter is used as intermediate for making ghee by the traditional method, b) Ghee, a heat clarified butterfat with rich aroma, and widely used all over India as a cooking medium and for garnishing cooked rice and chappatis.

C Heat desiccated milk products : a) Khoa is a partially heat desiccated milk product traditionally made in a shallow iron karhai with direct heat and constant agitation. It is an intermediate product for making sweets such as burfi or peda. It is popular in North, central and western region, **b)** ***Rabri*** is concentrated and sweetened product having several layers of clotted cream. It is popular in northern and eastern regions of the country. It is used for direct consumption, **c)** ***Kurchan*** is concentrated wholemilk product prepared by simmering milk in open vessel without stirring. It is popular in north and central region. It is directly consumed. **d)** ***Pyothi*** is concentrated milk with sugar and aromatic spices. It is popular in western and southern regions.

D Heat and acid coagulated products : a) Panir is white and spongy with mildy acidic flavour. It is used in culinary dishes and snacks. Buffalo milk is commonly used. It is popular in North, western and Central regions. Chhanna is white with yellowish tinge, spongy with mildly acid flavour mostly prepared from cow milk. It is an important base for a large variety of sweets mostly in Eastern India.

E Cereal based products : Kheet and payasum are thickened milk, with caramal flavour, sweetened besides containing aromatic spices and flavourings.

DAHI : Next to milk, dahi is the most popular milk product utilising about 8% of the total milk production in India. This fermented product is obtained from both cow and buffalo milk. It is known for its palatability, refreshing taste and therapeutic importance. This is prescribed by physicians for combating gastro intestinal disorders.

The different types of dahi consumed throughout India have been categorized as follows :

North zone	:	Dahi, lassi.
South zone	:	Dahi, buttermilk (matha)
Eastern zone	:	Payodhi (lal-dahi) or Misti dahi.
Western zone	:	Srikhand.

The ISI Standards (BS-9617 ; 1980) for Dahi are as follows :

Characteristic	*Sweet dahi*	*Sour Dahi*
Acidity % lactic	0.7	1.0
Yeast/moulds/g max	100	100
Coliform/g max	10	10
Phosphatase test	-ve	-ve

According to BIS, dahi shall be plain or flavoured and the following cultures shall be used in preparing dahi a) *Lactococcus lactis* sub sp *bivar diacetyilactis*, single or in combination with Leconostoc species, b) also as above along with *L. delbruckeii* subsp *bulgaricus, L acidophilus,* and *L casei* and *str salvarius* subsp *thermophilus.* Buffalo milk produces a higher rate of acid production than cow milk. The firmness is also better in dahi made from buffalo milk. Good manufacturing practices and sound hygiene assures good product.

Before incubation, carbonation of the product at very low pressure for a min. before crown corking provides a firm curd with no ga holes when stored at ambient temperature for nearly 2 weeks.

Dahi is used for direct consumption with or without salt/sugar or for preparing makkan or srikhand.

Srikhand is a semi soft, sweetish sour whole milk product made from lactic fermentation of curd. It is a curd preparation with added sugar, flavoring agents (saffron/camphor), fruits and nuts and is popular in the states of Gujarat, Maharashtra and part of Karnataka. It is heavily consumed in summer season.

It is made as follows : Skim milk is pasteurized at 80°C/15s, cooled and inoculated with dahi culture at 0.5% and incubated for 8 h at ambient temperature to develop around 0.8 - 1.0% lactic acid. The curd is fed to basket centrifuge and worked at 1000 rpm, worked with 80% cream, powdered sugar (equal to the weight of chakka) cardomom and other spices for around 2 min. to get homogenous consistency. The product is packed in 100/500 g containers for sale. Storage life 15 days under refrigeration. The chakka in the basket is unloaded to planetary mixer, stored in refrigerated cabinet.

The total period required for Srikhand could be reduced from 24 h to 6 h by reducing curd setting time from 10-12 h to 4 h by a) using 6% incoculum and b) accelerating the whey expulsion rate from 2.5 and 2 h by heating the dahi to about 60-70°C for 10 min.

The % composition of Srikhand is given below :

Product	*Moisture*	*Fat*	*Sugar*	*Protein*
Market	35-36	1.9-5.5	53-54	5.3-6.1
Baroda dairy	40-43	5-6	45	10

The Bureau of Indian standards have given the following % standards for Srikhand.

Total solids min	58.0	Sucrose (dry) max	72.5
Milkfat (dry) min	5.0	Total ash (dry) max	0.9
Milk Protein (dry) min	10.5	Coliform/g max	10
Titratable acidity % l.a. max	1.4	Yeast/mould/g	50

Sweetened Dahi : (misti dahi, lal-dahi, payodhi) is made in the Eastern region of the country. It is brown in colour with caramalized flavour and firm body. Nearly 6.25% cane sugar (or jaggery) is added to milk before boiling or at setting. The volume is reduced to 75%. It is than cooled, inoculated with previous day's product at 1%, set in earthern basins and the product is ready after 16h.

Makkan : is desi butter normally obtained by churning whole milk curd (dahi) using crude indigenous devices. According to PFA Rules (1976) it should contain not less than 76% milkfat by weight. It should be free from other animal fats, mineral oils, and vegetable oils and fats. Standard quality makkan may analyse moisture 18-20%, butterfat 78-81% non-fatty solids 1.5%, lactic acid not more than 0.2%.

The village method of making butter suffers several drawbacks. Use of unprocessed milk, self soured starter, setting for long periods, uncontrolled agitation with no proper temperature control leading to lumpy butter not suited for proper washing causing more fat loss in buttermilk leads to poor quality and low outrun. Further, storage of butter in porous mud pots or rusty tin containers accelerates deterioration. Some of these conditions can be rectified to get the better quality butter. Approximate yield of makkan with different types of milk is given below :

Type of milk	Fat%	Yield/100 kg milk (kg)	Milk needed to produce 1 kg. makkan (kg)
Cow	4.5	4.5	22
Mixed	5.8	5.8	18
Buffalo	7.0	7.0	14

Makkan is used for conversion into ghee, for direct use on chappaties, medicinal use and as a sacrificial offering.

Ghee is clarified butterfat prepared from cow or buffalo milk. Among the milk products ghee occupies a pri-eminet position in India. An average sample of ghee is over 99.5% milkfat. The rest of it is made up of largely of moisture and very small amounts of MSNF and extraneous matter. A good ghee has its characteristic aroma, flavour, and taste which are essential attributes for consumer acceptance. There is also considerable emphasis for proper body and fixture. A good ghee should have well developed granules dispersed fairly thickly and uniformly over the entire mass. Normally nothing should be added to already made ghee to augment and/or preserve its preferred attributes. The PFA permit addition of only BHA and BHT, either singly or in combination upto a maximum of 0.12% by weight of ghee, as an anti-oxidant.

Typical ghee has the following composition.

	Cow	Buffalo
Milkfat %	99-99.5	99-99.5
Moisture %	0.2-0.5	0.2-0.5

(Cont'd)

Carotene mg/g	3.2-7.4	-
Vitamin A IU/g	19-34	17-38
Tocopherol mg/g	26-48	18-37
Free fatty acid (% oleic)	1.3	1.3

Ghee for export should meet the following legal requirement in India.

Butyro refractometer reading at 400C	40-45 depending on the region.
R M Value	21-28 depending on the region.
Free fatty acids % oleic (max)	3.0
Moisture % (max)	0.5

Ghee is the richest source of milkfat of all Indian dairy products. It i an essential source of energy for the body. It contains fatty acids like linoleic linolenic and arachidonic which is regarded as essential fatty acids. Ghe contains about 5 times the level of conjugated Linoleic acids (CLA) thai what is present in original milkfat. CLA is known to be anti carcinogeni agent. CLA are also known to be potent anti-oxidants contributing to lon keeping quality of ghee at ambient temperature. It is a vehicle for carryin vitamins A, D, E and K. It is highly digestible than any other natural fats tha is included in the human diet. The % utilization in the body of the tota ingested (milk) fat is 97.

The principles of production entail a) fermentation process of milk or cream, b) mechanical process to gather milkfat is concentrated from. c) a physico-chemical process of heating at a specified range of temperature to remove moisture and to induce interaction of milkfat with the fermented residue fo SNF of the serum which occurs in the concentrated milkfat providing characteristic aroma, flavour and taste of ghee in processes a and c.

Method of manufacture :

Indigenous method : Whole milk is the primary raw material which is allowed to curdle. The curd is broken up with a pole-paddle initially and later by the addition of cold water. Butter separating in lumps is gathered and finally clarified by heating in a pan over direct fire. The method is most suited for handling small quantities of butter. The disadvantages of this technique are : a) lack of cleanliness in handling milk, b) uncontrolled fermentation, c) inherent defects of churns and inefficient working, d) storage of butter exposed to microbial attack, e) uncontrolled heating and, f) use of undesirable pots and pans for production and storage of butter and ghee. For large scale production this method is unsuitable (needing 20 Kg. milk/ Kg. of ghee scale production this method is unsuitable (needing 20 Kg. milk/Kg. of ghee production). The fat recovery may be 83% with cow milk and 88% with buffalo milk. Still indigenous production is enormous in the country.

Creamery method *:* is used in almost all organised dairies where raw material is *unsalted creamery* butter. The butter is heated in improved ghee boiler which consists of stainless steel jacketed pan having a manual stirrer and provision for movable stainless steel tube at the bottom of the pan for emptying the contents of the pan when required. It is also provided with steam control valve, pressure and temperature indicator. Butter is melted in the pan and most of the moisture gets removed at 90°C. The contents are constantly agitated. The scum which gathers on the surface is removed from time to time by a ladle. There is a profuse effervescence accompanied by cracking sound in the early stages of boiling but both decrease when moisture content is reduced. When all the moisture is driven out, the temperature of the liquid mass suddenly shoots up and heating at this stage needs careful control. The effervescence becoming finer and curd particles becoming browner when ghee flavour emanates. The final temperature usually ranges from 110-120°C depending on the region. After cooling and sedimentation, the ghee is filtered through muslin cloth to separate ghee residue. It then goes for granulation and packaging. The recovery of fat from cow and buffalo milk is 91 and 93% respectively.

Prestratification method *:* When butter is left undisturbed at around 80-85°C for 15-30 min., it stratifies into 3 distinct layers, viz., a top layer of floating denatured particles of curd, a middle layer of fat and a bottom layer of buttermilk. The bottom layer contains 60-70% of SNF and also 80% moisture originally present in butter. The buttermilk is carefully removed and the remaining 2 layers are raised to usual clarification temperature of 110-120°C. This method saves fuel and produces ghee with lower acidity with long shelf life.

Direct cream method *:* Fresh milk is separated to give a high fat percentage of 60% fat. The cream is diluted with twice the amount of clean water and reseparated. This separation removes most of the casein and other impurities. This helps in better fat recovery. The cream is then inoculated with good starter culture and ripened for 6-8h to obtain fine flavour. The cream is then clarified into ghee using ghee pan as in creamery butter method. There is overall labour economy (Procedure of butter is eliminated). The recovery of fat is 91% with cow milk and 87% with buffalo milk.

Granulation in ghee : Granularity is an important criterion of quality and even purity. The partly granular form assumed by ghee is due to certain contents of glycerides of higher melting saturated fatty acids especially palmitic and stearic acids. In this regard, buffalo ghee is usually more saturated, crystallizes more effectively than cow ghee. The desi ghee also produces large crystals in ghee. On the other hand, the ghee obtained by creamery butter or direct cream process need necessarily have large crystals. Heating ghee to 60°C followed by rapid cooling produce small grains in ghee. If the ghee is held 1° above the melting point of ghee (cow 29°C, buffalo 31°C) big grains in large numbers are formed.

Packaging and storage : The containers should be light proof, preferably with minimum tin coating to 50 ETP (electrolytic tin plate). Packing in large containers causes moisture to gravitate downwards. Smaller containers are preferable (0.5, 1.0 and 5 kg.). Ghee is filled to the brim allowed to stand for 6-8h, the contraction in volume made up with liquid ghee before sealing, Cool, dry storage is preferable for ghee.

Legal standards : To protect consumer interest and check adulteration the Government have fixed legal standards for ghee. The market receives ghee which high moisture or indifferently made with high acidity. Both these affect the keeping quality. Sometimes due to limited availability of milk, production of ghee is not commensurate with the demand. This leads to adulteration on a fairly large scale, with animal fats or Vanaspathi, Although, Food laws are sufficiently comprehensive, application of laws become inefficient due to the absence of easy, quick and fool proof method for detection of adulteration. For various reasons presumptive tests are of limited value. It is only in this context seasamol Baudouin Test has been devised to find out adulteration of ghee with Vanaspathi. This is a qualitative test based on the principle that Vanaspathi manufacturers should add 1% sesame oil before final packing of Vanaspathi. The sesame oil can be detected by simple test.

Agmark Grading : To counter the spurious practice of adulteration, Government of India, through its Directorate of marketing and Inspection have introduced Grading scheme under the Agricultural produce (Grading and Marketing) Act 1937 and market it under lable AGMARK affixed on containers of tested ghee so as to assist consumers in getting pure and quality product. The AGMARK label for marketing requires the ghee to conform to certain physico chemical specifications. Grading under the scheme is voluntary.

The traders should apply to the State Marketing officer and if party is considered suitable, licence is granted. The manufacturer should have adequate facilities for testing refinery and spacious godown. Three samples are taken from each lot : one for analysis, one for check analysis in control laboratory and the third sealed and kept with packer for future reference. Agmark ghee is packed as special and General grade depending on maximum limit of free fatty acids in ghee. The tin containers may have capacities of 100 g., 250 g., 1 kg., 2 kg., 4 kg., 8 kg. and 17 kg.

The AGMARK specifications are :

Tests	*All India*	*Winter**	*Summer**
Baudouin	-ve	-ve	-ve
Phytosterol acetate test	-ve	-ve	-ve
BR Reading 40°C	40-43	41-44	42.5-45.0
RM Value NLT	28	23	21
Polenske value	1.5-2.0	0.5-1.2	0.5-1.0
Moisture % NMT	0.3	0.3	0.3
Free fatty acids % oleic			
Special grade (Red lable) NMT	1.4	1.4	1.4
General grade (Green label) NMT	2.5	2.5	2.5

NMT : Not more than. NLT : Not less than.

*Where cottonseed is fed extensively to milch animals.

Fat recovery in ghee made by different methods :

The yield of ghee by following different methods of ghee making is given below. The fat % in cream is directly proportional to the yield of ghee and inversely proportional to the yield of ghee residue as shown below :

Raw material kg. %		% fat recovered in ghee	Ghee residue in kg. %
Cream	40 ± 2	85.0	10.4
	50 ± 2	90.0	8.3
	60 ± 2	93.7	6.7
	70 ± 2	94.7	5.5
	80 ± 2	96.6	3.0
Butter	83 ± 2	98.3	1.6

Deterioration : Higher storage temperature, moisture content, storage temperature, acidity, presence of Cu and Fe as well as more head space in container increases spoilage in ghee. Ghee residue acts as a good antioxident in ghee. An estimation of the induction period gives an indication of the keeping quality of ghee. About 20 h. induction corresponds to a market life of 6 mo. in ghee. Normally ghee prepared from direct sweet cream or sweet cream butter packed to the brim in good containers and sealed is expected to have a storage life of 6-12 mo. at 21°C.

Renovation : Old and rancid ghee of second quality can be renovated by reheating, blending with superior quality ghee or neutralising high acidity.

Defects in ghee : The flavour defects include, smoky, cooked, burnt, rancid, oxidised/metallic; the texture defects are greasy condition and sediment may be high or burnt.

Uses of ghee : Ghee is used as a cooking or frying medium in confectionery, direct consumption with chappaties or rice and for medicinal use. The ghee residue is consumed with chappaties/rice in household, for toffees, for sandwich spreads and burfi like sweet.

Lassi : It is traditionally prepared by stirring whole milk curd into a delicate drink to which sugar or salt are added. To make the product flowable a small amount of cold water is added. Lassi has a low keeping quality and it very quickly separates into a watery layer on the top and thick proteinous layer at the bottom. The composition varies considerably depending on the composition of dahi, the extent to which diluted when churning and efficiency of fat removal. It contains appreciable amounts of milk proteins phospholipids and an excellent bevarage for quenching thirst due to lactic acidity. The composition is fat 0.8%, SNF 3.0%, proteins 1.3%, lactose 1.2%, ash 0.4% and lactic acidity 0.44%.

A long life UHT lassi is also manufactured. The process involves lowering the pH to a level at which some of the coagulated milk proteins tend to go back into the liquid phase. While the higher fat content of lassi helps to keep the milk proteins in suspension the higher SNF tends to precipitate the milk proteins. A delicate balance of fat and SNF at right pH ensures stability of the product at room temperature for about 3 mo. The product shows lot of promise. Lassi is viscous fluid with creamy mouthfeel, rich aroma predominantly of diacetyl and mildly to highly acidic.

Khoa : In the unorganised sector of the dairy industry Khoa manufacture is a major activity. It is estimated that about 322-000 tons of Khoa representing 7% of the total milk production is produced annually in India. Khoa is an intermediate product and forms base for a large number of sweets such as burfi, peda, milk sweets, kalakhand and gulabjamun. Normally buffalo milk in 4-6 1 lots is simmered with vigorous scraping in a shallow iron pan over direct fire till a semi solid mass is formed. Lot of free fat is released towards the finishing stage and the mass becomes almost non-sticky on the heating surface. Each lot takes 5-10 min. to finish. In the commerce 3 grades of khoa are identified. *Pindi* is characterised as a circular ball of hemispherical pat with smooth homogenous body and texture. It is used for preparation of burfi and peda. *Danedar* is characterized by granular texture and uneven body. Usually 0.1% citric acid (on product basis) is added during desiccation. This forms base for kalakhand granular burfi, milk cake and granular milk sweets. *Dhap* has loose and sticky body and smooth texture due to less intense heat treatment. It is suited for gulabjamun as it permits formation of uniform balls suitable for frying and absorption of sugar syrup. The approximate composition is given below :

Type	*Fat %*	*Moisture %*
Pindi	21-26	31-33
Dhap	20-23	37-44
Danedar	20-25	35-40

The average % chemical composition of Khoa is given below :

Type of milk	*moisture*	*fat*	*protein*	*lactose*	*ashiron**	*mg/kg.*
Cow	25.6	25.7	19.2	25.5	38	103
Buffalo	19.2	37.1	17.8	22.1	36	101

The initial fat content of cow milk was 4.8% and that in buffalo milk 7.8%. The ratio of concentration is 5.4 for cow milk and 4.5 for buffalo milk.

In the prepration, milk is boiled in karahi over brisk fire. Milk stirred vigorously with circular motion. The milk contact surfaces should be scraped to milk being scorched. At certain concentration milk coagulates, the colour changes. When viscous mass reaches a semisolid pasty consistency, the product is ready when iron pan is removed from fire, khoa pat is made to a single compact mass. Continuous khoa making, avoiding drudgery for large scale production of khoa are also available though not yet popular.

Several heat induced changes takes place. Whey proteins get denatured. Casein gets irreversibly denatured. Almost half the globular fat is released as free fat (44-62% of fat appears as free fat in khoa). Lactose remains in supersaturated solution disperesed in fine droplets. pH decreases from 6.60 to 6.35% soluble N, free fatty acids and peroxide value increase. Shelf life is about 3 days at ambient temperature and 3 weeks under refrigeration.

Delhi is the biggest khoa marketing centre in the country. According to PFA Rules khoa from cow, buffalo, goat or sheep milk should contain not less than 20% of fat in the finished product. As per IS:4883-1968 Moisture (max) is specified as 28% and fat on dry basis (min) 26.0%. In organised sector modern packaging methods use vegetable parchment wrappers and laminated pouches of capacity 50, 100 and 200g. sizes. In spite of high heat treatment, the microbiological quality of khoa varies considerably, viz. acid formers 3.2 to 33.0 x 10^3 cfu/g. proteolytic type 2.5 to 21.3 x 10^3 / cfu/g and spore formers 200/g perhaps due to post heat contamination.

The yield depends on type and quality of milk used, the % moisture retained and loses in handling. On an average the yield of khoa ranges from 15 - 19% with cow milk and 21 - 23% with buffalo milk.

Quality of khoa : The physical quality of khoa is given below :

Particulars	*Buffalo*	*Cow*
Colour (with brown tinge)	White	Straw yellow
Appearance	Oily greasy surface	Moist
Body	Soft	Slightly hard
Texture	Smooth/granular	Little sandy
Smell	Rich/nutty	Rich/nutty
Taste	Little sweet	Little saltish
For sweets	Highly suitable	Suitable

The common defects in khoa are :

Flavour : Smoky, high acid, rancid and stale.

Body and texture : Excessive hardness and acidity (low fat) gritty due to large lactose crystals.

Colour and appearance : Dry surface, visible dirt, burnt particles, mouldy surface, fat or moisture leakage (incorrect method in preparation).

Rabri : is a heat desicated, thickened milk sweet from mostly buffalo milk. It is favoured dessert in rural and urban parts of Central and North India. Buffalo milk is simmered in shallow pans with frequent scraping of the heating surface to resuspend the clots into the thickened milk. When clots are well formed, sugar is added with continued stirring till clots become firm with desired consistency. The product is pale yellow to light brown with sweetish, nutty caramel flavour. Visible caramlised clots and creamy viscous body can be seen. It analyses 20% fat 13% protein, 16% lactose, 15% sugar, 3.5% ash and 35% moisture. Under refrigeration the product has a shelf life of 5-7 days. It is used for direct consumption.

Kurchan : is a heat desiccated clotted milk sweet made from buffalo milk. It is much relished in Central and Northern parts of India. Milk is simmered in shallow vessel with controlled stirring to prevent scaling and permit formation of thick skin on the surface of milk. The skin formed is scooped off and placed on the peripheral edges of the vessel to control evaporation and formation of clotted mass. Sugar is finally mixed in layers and stacked lightly over each other. It is light brown in colour with clotted semi solid body and creamy consistency. It is roughly a five fold concentrated milk. It analyses fat 23%, protein 15%, lactose 15%, sugar 15%, ash 3%

with moisture 28%. The shelf life at 5-10°C is about 5-7 days. It is used for direct consumption.

Chhana is a heat-acid coagulated milk product which forms the base of several popular Indian sweets like rasagolla, sandesh, chum-chum etc. It has been estimated that about 4% of the total milk produced in the country is converted into Chhana. It originated in Eastern states, but is now popular in north, north-western regions of India. According to PFA Rules chhana is the product obtained form cow or buffalo milk or a combination thereof by precipitation with sour milk, citric or lactic acids. It should not contain more than 70% moisture, and the milkfat content should not be less than 50% of the dry matter.

The specification IS : 5162-1980 is given below :

characteristics	*skim milk chhana*	*wholemilk chhana*
Moisture % max	60	65
Milkfat % dry basis	5 (max)	50 (min)
Protein % dry basis min*	30	25
Ash % dry matter max	5	5

The % chemical composition of chhana is given below :

*Type of milk**	*Moisture*	*Fat*	*Protein*	*Lactose*	*Ash*
Cow	53.4	24.8	17.4	2.1	2.1
Buffalo	51.6	29.9	14.4	2.3	2.0

*The average composition of cow milk used was fat 4.5% and TS 13.0% buffalo milkfat 8.4% and TS 17.9%. The chhana is a rich source of fat, protein, minerals and fat soluble vitamins.

The preparation consists in taking cow milk in a boiling pan (2-40 1/ batch) and is coagulated at 82°C using sour whey, or organic acids. The whey is drained off by straining through muslin cloth. Normally 2.5 g. citric/ lactic acid (in solution) is required to coagulate 1 kg. of fresh sweet milk. Cow milk is normally preferred as it yields smooth-textured product. In chhana markets the wet chhana is generally wrapped in cloth. On arrival it is pressed between two circular stone weights to remove excess whey before offered for sale. Large scale continuous machines for making chhana are also available.

The yield of chhana with 54% moisture ranges from 16-18% for cow milk and from 22-24% for buffalo milk.

Hardly any chhana is sold in the market in satisfactory package.

Chhana is transported overnight in bamboo baskets with leaf linings. The keeping quality under ordinary packaging is 2, 3 and 7 days at 37°C, 24°C and 7°C respectively.

The physical quality of chhana is given below :

Particulars	*Buffalo*	*Cow*
Colour	Whitish	Light Yellow
Appearance	Greasy	Moist
Body	Slightly hard	Soft
Texture	Coarse	Smooth
Flavour	Mildly acid	Mildly acid
For sweets	Not suitable	suitable

A minimum of 4.0% fat in cow milk and 5.0% in buffalo milk is suited for desireable body and texture in chhana for sweets. For short journey no packaging is done. Mould growth is common at low temperature. Chhana forms a base and filler for milk sweets such as rasagolla, sandesh and pantooa. It is also consumed with sugar or salt. The common defects are smoky, sour, rancid and stale flavour, hard body, coarse texture dry surface; and mouldy surface.

Chhana spread : Since butter spread is a high fat product whereas chhana spread is almost a perfect food. The process involved is to make use of semi-soft mass of chhana from cow/buffalo milk as a base for the cheese spread. Chhana is broken in domestic mixer with little water. (10-20 ml/100 g chhana) to facilitate mixing and spreadability. Salt at 1.0% is added during grinding together with 1 part of citric acid dissolved in 1 part of water at 0.8 - 1.0 ml/100 g spread to lower the pH to around 5.0. The product is then packed in plastic cups. It has storage life of 8-10 days under refrigeration. Addition of chakka enhances the flavour. For this milk is heated to 90°C/30 min cooled to 42°C and ripened with mixed starter culture *(str. salvarius subsp thermophilus + Lac delbruckeii sub sp. bulgaricus; 1:1)* at 1% level. After setting whey is drained and chakka is used. To 70 g chhana 30 g chkka is added mixed with salt and acidifying agent. This improves the flavour. The % composition of chhana spread is given below :

Spread	*moisture*	*fat*	*protein*	*lactose*	*ash*	*pH*
Chhana cow	62.5	15.9	17.5	2.2	1.9	5.0
Chhana + Chakka 70 : 30	61.5	16.5	18.2	1.9	1.6	5.2

KACHAGOLLA : On ceremonial occasion milk sweets are available in West bengal. Various types of Sandesh are sold in the market and these are classified as Kachagolla (high moisture grade) narampak (medium moisture grade and karepek low moisture grade) the origion of kachagolla is the oldest chhana is prepared from cow milk. It is kneaded with cane sugar at the rate of 30-35% by weight of chhana in an open iron karhai and cooked under controlled heating in a low flame with continuous stirring and scraping with a ladle. The mixture develops characteristic sticky granular texture and aroma. The product analyses moisture 25%, fat 6%, protein 10%, sucrose 30%, ash 1.0%, acidity % lactic 0.51%, free fat as % of total fat 26%. The samples are highly contaminated with staphylococci. It is placed in trays in lumps or balls on racks for display to consumers. On sale it is packed in paper board or earthern pots. The shelf life is 1-2 days at room temperature and 3-5 days under refrigeration.

Panir is an important indigenous soft cheese which forms a base for a variety of culinary dishes, stuffing material for various vegetable dishes, snacks and sweets meats. About 4-5% of the total milk produced in India is converted into panir. It is mostly made in unorganised sector. Buffalo milk is standardized to 55% fat and boiled in a vat. It is coagulated with citric acid at 70-80°C. Whey is drained off and pressed in hoops. It is firmed by keeping in chilled water. They are then cut into pieces for retail sale in polythene bags. It is white, spongy, close knit with nutty flavour. The average composition is moisture 55-70%, fat 22-26%, lactose 2.0-2.5% and ash 2.0-2.2%. Under parchment paper it has storage life of 8 days under refrigeration. Dipping in sorbic acid 1000 mg/or rubbing with 0.25% scorbic acid is effective against spoilage by moulds. Panir from cow milk is weak, soft and fragile.

Frozen Milk products :

Kulfi is a frozen dessert prepared from concentrated milk/khoa. It has typical ice texture with caramal flavour. It is prepared usually in the northern, central and western parts of India. Milk is thickened in a shallow pan with constant agitation. Sugar, nuts, essence and colour are added towards the finishing stages. The concentrated mass is poured into metallic moulds and frozen in a mixture of ice and salt. It is white with brownish appearance with compact body, ice texture with nutty caramal flavour.

Malai ka baraf is a popular in northern and western parts of India. It is prepared by freezing a mixture of malai (heat desiccated/clotted milk) sugar, nuts and essence. It has plastic body, with crunchy texture and delicate nutty and caramel flavour.

Cereal based product :

Payasum : is thickened milk, cooked with cereals with pleasing rich caramal flavour, sweetened and with aromatic spices and flavourings.

Kheer : Rice is cooked in milk and thickend with slow simmering, sweetened, served hot or chilled with a dash of nuts and aromatic spices.

Kleech : is cereal based indigenous milk produce prepared during festival season in Rajasthan. It is prepared by boiling debraned gelatinized wheat in milk. One hundred g of wheat is soaked in water for 30 min. and the bran is removed by grinding and mechanical force. It is then cooked in a pressure cooker/180g + 72 ml water). Warm whole milk is added 3 1 testing 4.2% fat and 8.6% SNF. The mixture is heated with stirring till viscous product is obtained. Powdered sugar is added at the rate 12% and further heated to get desired consistency. it is cooled to room temperature and cardamom powder is added at 0.5g/100g of the product. The product can be stored at 15-20°C for more than 6 days. Shelf life is improved under refrigeration. The sample analyses protein 4.3%, fat 5%, total solids 32% and ash 1.8%. Instead of sugar jaggery can also be added.

Milk sweet recipes : It is difficult to give specific receipes for various milk sweets, because practices with respect to some of them differ widely. The directions given is therefore merely a general guide.

Cake without egg :

Ingredients : Condensed milk 180 g (12 teaspoon); butter 210 g (7 tsp) milk 100ml (3/4 cup), sugar 30 g (1/4 cup); Maida 95 g (1 cup), almond 10; yellow colour 2-3 drops; baking powder 25 g; soda bi-carb 35 g; almond flavour 2-3 drops.

Procedure : Beat melted butter, condensed milk, yellow colour, milk, sugar and flavour, using egg beater. Mix flour, baking powder and soda bi-carb to get smooth texture. Mix crushed almond. Grease baking dish and pour the butter. Bak 40-50 min. moderate heat in oven.

Chhana-kheer :

Ingredients : Milk 1 kg., chhana 150 g., sugar 40 g., flavour few drops, dry nuts few.

Procedure : Cut chhana to pieces. Boil milk and reduce to half volume. Add sugar boil further to 1/3 original. Add chhana and heat gently till sugar penetrates to chhana cubes. Cool. Sprinkle flavour. Decorate with dry nuts.

Chhana Murki :

Ingredients : Chhana 250 g; sugar 125 g; flavour few drops, water 45 g' Dry nuts few.

Procedure : Dissolve sugar in water and boil till it becomes stringly. Add 4 tsp of milk to clear sugar from dirt. Cut chhana into cubes and put in syrup in karhai. Boil with gentle stirring for 5 min. Remove from fire and allow to cool. Stir cubes till entire sugar is coated around them. Sprinkle flavour. Decorate with dry nut flakes.

Chocolate burfi :

Ingredients : Milk 1.5 kg; cocoa powder 12.5 g; sugar 90 g; silver paper 1; Ghee 0.5 tsp. pista few.

Procedure : Boil milk in karhai on brisk flame with stirring. Scrap all parts of the pan with which milk comes in contact. Stir the viscous product. Add ghee on the sides and stir well. Add sugar with stirring. Separate 1/3 of pan contents and mix with silver paper and sliced pista. Cut to size.

The IS : 550-1970 specification for Mawa burfi is moisture max 15% sucrose max 48%, milkfat min 12.5, lactose min 15.0, acidity lactic % 0.35, SPC/g max 30,000, yeast and mould count/g 10.

Chocolate cream fingers :

Ingredients : Butter 85 g, cocoa 30 g, flour 140 g, sugar 85 g, egg 1, Vanilla few drops, little milk, cream butter 85 g, icing sugar 45 g.

Procedure : Sieve flour and cocoa twice. Add cream butter and sugar. Add beaten egg and heat. Add flour cocoa mixture gradually beating all the time to smooth paste.

Chocolate mould :

Ingredients : Milk 500 g, cocoa 5 g, corn flour 45 g, sugar 45 g, Vanilla few drops; cream cherry to decorate.

Procedure : Boil the milk. Mix 45 g. corn flour in 1/2 cup water. Mix the mix when it boils and add corn flour with stirring. At proper consistency add cocoa and boil. Add flavour etc., wet jelly mould and pour out the whole mix into it. Decorate with cream and cherry and keep in refrigerator.

Coconut balls :

Ingredients : Condensed milk 400 g (1 tin); coconut dust 0.5 kg., colour and flavour.

Procedure : Pour condensed milk in a vessel. Mix 470 g. coconut dust. The remaining coconut is divided into 3 parts for different flavour and colour. Maket to any shape and dip in dyed coconut dust till it gets coated. Keep at room temperature.

Coconut bun :

Ingredients : Butter 45 g; sugar 55 g; egg 1; baking powder 0.25 tsp, flavour 85 g; desiccated coconut 35 g; little milk; paper cups 15.

Procedure : Sieve flour, baking powder and sugar. Add butter. Beat in egg; mix coconut using little milk. Half fill paper cups and bake at 200°C/15-20 min.

Coconut burfi ;

Ingredients : Khoa 275 g; sugar 135 g; grated coconut 35 g; silver paper one; colour few drops.

Procedure : Mix sugar and Khoa in karhai over gentle heat with stirring. When it forms balls remove from fire. Add coconut with fingers and stir well. Spread in tray. Mix colour. Put back on fire. Cook till creamy. Spread on top of first layer. Cool. Decorate with silver paper. Cut to size for serving.

Cottage cheese cake :

Ingredients : Butter 2 tsp, Zwieback crumbs 2 cup; sugar 2 tsp; Dry cottage cheese 2 cups; cream 1.5 cups; flour 1 tsp, lemon extract 0.25 tsp, sugar 1 cup; salt 0.5 tsp, nutmag 1 tsp, egg 8, Vanilla 1 tsp; separated grated rind of half lemon 3 Nos.

Procedure : Blend zwieback with softened butter and 2 tsp. sugar and press in pan. Press dry cottage cheese through sieve.

Combine cheese with remaining ingredients except egg and mix well. Beat stiff into butter. Pour in pan. Sprinkle with zwieback crumb. Bake moderately for 1 h. till custard is set in centre and browned.

Gulab Jamun :

Ingredients : Khoa 300 g; maida 35 g; baking powder 1/2 tsp ; sugar 1 kg; Water 1 g., ghee 500 g.

Procedure : Break khoa in bits. Mix baking powder and maida separately. Add the mix to khoa and knead with little water till dough is obtained. The consistency should form small balls. Dissolve all sugar in water and boil till 2 string consistency is obtained. Add 4 tsp of milk and ladle out scum. Test fry balls in ghee in shallow pan. Colour should become deep brown. Cut one and examine for porosity. If suitable, fry whole lot, Remove balls and put in syrup. Keep at room temperature for 10-12 h. before serving.

Kalakhand :

Ingredients : Milk 1 kg; sugar 60 g; Pista few; silver paper 1 No.; Cardamom few.

Procedure : Boil milk in karhai in non smoky flame. Stir for 15 min. Add citric acid as solution; partial coagulation takes place. Stir vigorously. At semi solid stage add sugar with stirring. Add crushed cardamom. Remove from fire. Set in greasy tray and allow to cool. Cut to shape and decorate with silver paper and pista.

Orange pastry :

Ingredients : flour 4 cups; butter 7 tsp; condensed milk 1 tsp; yellow colour 1/4 tsp; flavour orange 1/2 tsp; milk 150 ml. Baking powder 3/4 tsp. soda bicarb 1/4 tsp.

Procedure : Beat butter condensed milk, milk, orange flavour and yellow colour. Add flour, baking powder and soda bicarb. Mix. Pour in pastry mould. Bake at 82°C/30-35 min.

For decoration beat 1.5 cup cream with 1/2 tsp. orange flavour and 1/2 cup icing sugar till it becomes thick. Spread as a layer on the top of pastry. To the rest of the cream add orange colour and beat the cream. Pour this on the first layer. Decorate with orange colour.

Pantooa :

Ingredients : Khoa 300 g, chhana 300 g; baking powder 1/2 tsp, Maida 35 g; sugar 1 Kg; water 1 Kg; ghee 500 g.

Procedure : Break khoa and chhana into bits. Mix baking powder to maida separately. Add this to khoa and mix. Knead with small quantities of water till dough is obtained. Then proceed as for Gulab Jamun.

Peda :

Ingredients : Khoa 225 g, Sugar 75 g, Pista few, silver paper 1, cardomom few.

Procedure : Break khoa into bits. Mix ground sugar. Put in Karhai and cook on low flame with stirring. Add cardamom. Pour into trays and cool. Decorate with silver paper and sliced pista. Cut to size and serve.

Rasagolla :

Ingredients : Soft chhana 250 g; Maida 8 g; sugar 250 g; water 1 kg; Rose flavour few drops.

Procedure : Break chhana into bits and keep it cool. Maida may be added to avoid cracks in finished product. Dissolve all sugar in water and boil with 2 tsp of milk and ladle out the scum. Make balls of chhana and put them into boiling syrup. Avoid over crowding. Close balls will swell. If conditions are proper there will be no cracks. The finished product is ready in 20-25 min. The syrup will have 1 string consistency, sprinkle rose to serve. In each balls sugar coated elaichidana may be put in the centre of each ball.

Canned Rasagolla : The procedure is cow milk - boiling - cooling to 60°C Coagulation (0.5% citric acid) - straining - chhana - kneading - preparation of balls - cooking in clarified sugar syrup. (60 brix/25 min) - dipping in sugar syrup 50 brix - canning - steaming in presterilized cans with lids - storage. The types of rasagollas sold are ordinary, sponge, canned and diabetic use.

The chemical composition is given below :

Constituents %	*Spongy*	*Ordinary*	*IS 4079 - 1967*
Moisture	50.0	38.2	55 max
Sucrose	37.0	43.6	45 max
Fat	5.3	7.3	5.0 min
Protein	5.5	6.4	5.0 min

Sandesh :

Ingredients : Chhana 250 g; Sugar 75 g; Pista 10 g; Cardamom few No. Silver paper one.

Procedure : Break fresh chhana into bits Mix ground sugar. Put in karhai and cook on slow fire with strring. Add crushed cardamom towards the end. When moisture is ready (balls) when tested) pour into tray for cooling. Cut to desired size, decorate with pista and silver paper.

Chapter 2

CHEESE

What is Cheese : Cheese is a fresh or ripened concentrated nutritious solid or semi-solid product. It is obtained by the coagulation of milk, cream or skimmilk of domestic animals with or without the use of rennet or organic acids. It is primarily a long term storage product to provide food throughout the year. Cheeses may have varying ratios of protein, fat, lactose and moisture. The extent to which the whey is retained in the cheese determines the amount of soluble nutrients left in the finished cheese. The cheese may have ripening agents and enzyme systems. It may have varying number of select micro organisms, yeast or mould which contribute to the texture, aroma and flavour.

Functions of milk constituents in cheese making

1 **Milkfat** : The aim of the cheese maker is to retain as much milkfat as possible in cheese and losing the smallest posible amount in whey. Milkfat influences (1) yield of cheese, (2) quality of cheese, (3) imparts a slight yellow colour to cheese, (4) provides mellowness of body and smoothness of feeling, besides (5) richness and delicacy of taste.

2 **Casein** : It is of special importance in cheese making. It has the property of reacting with rennet which makes possible the preparation of cheese. During coagulation, it holds the fat globules in the curd and continues to hold them as firmly as possible throughout the process of cheesemaking. It retains whey in the curd in required amounts and permits excess whey to escape. It acts like a sponge in holding whey. One kg. of casein holds about 1 to 1.25 kg. of water. In finished cheese, it gives firmness and solidity of body. It provides peculiar cheese flavour, and gets converted into soluble nutritious compounds.

Casein in milk is present in combination with calcium as calcium caseinate. It is in suspension. During souring it separates as heavy solid white mass due to the action of lactic acid. This acid acts on calcium caseinate, forms calcium lactate and sets free the casein. These casein particles come together causing coagulation or precipitation. Rennet reacts on calcium caseinate and produces a casein rich in calcium. Ca caseinate

+ rennet = Ca para caseinate (uncoagulated). Ca para caseinate + soluble Ca salt = Coagulated Ca para caseinate. Thus, the reactions of rennet and acid on casin in milk are quite diferent.

3 **Water** : It is the most prominent constituent in amount. It influences the yield of cheese and can be obtained free of cost. The legal limitations and keeping quality of cheese forces the cheese maker to control the moisture. It influences the character of the body in cheese by giving smoothness and mellowness. It supplements the function of fat but does not give richness or delicacy of taste. In skimmik cheese, unless moisture is 50%, the cheese will be hard tough and unpalatable. In hard cheese, if moisture is less than 30%, the body becomes dry and crumbly. In a good cheese, the higher the fat, the lower the amount of moisture that can be retained. It gies favourable conditions for the work of the agents which change insoluble cheese protein into soluble forms. If moisture is below 25%, the cheese fails to ripen.

*4 **Milk sugar** :* Lactic acid is produced from lactose. The soluble calcium salts formed favour the rapidity and completeness of rennet action in curdling milk. This is the immediate object of ripening milk in cheese making, Soluble calcium salts assists in the contraction of curd. The Ca salt causes some changes in curd during cheddaring, when texture changes - resembling the fibre of cooked meat of a chicken's breast. The curd form long silky strings on a hot iron. In cheddar cheese there is no free lactic acid. There is always excess calcium to combine with this acid. More whey in curd means more soluble calcium salt leading to "acid or sour cheese". It prevents the growth of other microorganisms producing undesirable gases and ill smelling compounds.

*5. **Minerals in milk** :* This is connected with the functions of milk sugar. The insoluble calcium salts are converted into soluble salts. Cheese contains appreciable amount of calcium lactate.

Cheese making basics : The basic processes in the preparation of all cheese varieties from milk involve, a) concentration or coagulation of some of the valuable milk solids, b) preservation of solids as curds and c) ripening of the curd to get desirable characteristics in the end product. The major variables include a) input variables - milk quality, type of organisms, enzymes added, b) treatment variables - standardization, heat treatment, homogenization, c) manufacturing variables - setting time and temperature, size and uniformity of the curd, cooking, draining and washing practices, quantity and method of salting, hooping and pressing practices, d) ripening time, temperature, relative humidity, treatment of cheese surfaces and package.

Concentration is aided by enzyme or organic acid. Both types of coagulum can control and release whey. The rennet coagulum is more or less firm and elastic. The acid curd is less cohesive. Whey expulsion inrennet curd is accelerated by cutting and controlled application of heat to shape the curd. Such a concentration can also be done by ultrafiltration which is treated separately in the text. Preservation is effected by hygienic milk production, product production hygiene and controlling the adverse effect of microorganisms. Ripening refers to storage of cheese at suitable conditions for different mo. for the development of texture, aroma and flavour by microorganisms and enzymes.

Thermisation : In modern milk handling, it is often necessary to store cheese milk at 3-7°C for one or 2 days over week end between reception and commencement of cheese making. If the bacterial quality of milk is poor, the psychrotrophic organisms develop thermoduric lipases and proteases which may cause off flavour during the ripening of cheese. In such cases, it is safer to thermise the milk at 65°C/15/s. Thermisation is a milder heat treatment than pasteurisation. The purpose of this is to reduce the bacterial load of milk. This treatment kills most of the psychrotrophic bacteria and prevent production of lipases and proteases during storage. Thermisation is not a legal process and is not a substitute for pasteurization.

Homogenization : For some cheeses like Blue, Feta and Danablu, the milk is homogenized to a) reduce whey exudation from the coagulum, b) make cheese appear white c) promote hydrolysis of fat because it provides increased surface area for fat globules and d) adds to the smoothness of cheese. In blue varieties, it provides greater access of lipase to fat, allowing faster fat hydrolysis which is necessary for typical cheese flavour. The effect increases with higher homogenizing pressure. It may be done in one or two stages (140 kg/cm^2 and 35 kg/cm^2).

Clarification : The milk receive, may contain dirt particles and high somatic cells which produce inferior coagulum and in Swiss cheese abnormal holes. To remove unwanted debris the centrifugal removal is effective.

Bactofugation : is the process of centrifugal removal of microorganisms from milk. The objective is to remove bacteria as well as spores and to avoid the effects of heat on the functional properties of milk including certain enzymes that assist in the ripening process. However, at its best, it removes only about 99% of the bacteria in milk. It cannot be relied upon to remove all pathogens and viruses. Force exerted on milk is around 9000 times to the force of gravity. When milk preheated at 54°C is fed to the machine, the heavy microflora and debris are thrown out to the periphery of the bowl.

The Partial partitioning of milk effected by rennet causes a coagulum having major protein, fat, mineral salts and all microorganisms entrapped in it and separation of liquid whey. The retention of milk fat, protein, lactose and ash constituents amount to approximately 92, 75, 4 and 40% respectively. The % distribution of milk constituents in cheddar cheese and whey is ;

Milk constitutents	Cheese	Whey
Fat	92.5	7.5
Protein	76.6	23.4
Casein	96.0	4.0
B Lactoglobulin	7.1	92.9
Lactose	3.9	96.1
Salts	51.5	48.5

The quality of cheese milk : The necessity for the great care in the production of milk for cheese manufacture need not be over emphasised. The deterioration in milk quality is very rapid unless every care is exercised in hygienic production and handling. A good quality cheese cannot be made from low quality milk. It should be understood that the growth conditions for the harmful microorganisms is very favourable in the cheese making process. The bacterial count of raw milk must be low to avoid development of unwanted flavours and enzymes since they may survive pasteurization and cause faults in cheese. Apart from the total bacterial count, a knowledge of the bacterial flora is also of importance.

The milk should contain very few butyricacid forming bacteria and spores. The spores are not destroyed by pasteurization and they may cause serious damage by developing large volumes of hydrogen and unwanted flavour and ruin the cheese. Some cheeses like Emmental and Gruyere are often made from selected *unpasteurized* milk to preserve their characteristic aroma and flavour. The spores can come from poor quality silage feeding to animals which is likely to introduce *Clostridium butyricum* in milk at milking time. For example, in Switzerland silage feeding is prohibited in areas where Emmental cheese is made. This cheese is only mildly acidified and salted and stored at high temperature and butyric acid fermentation may damage the cheese along with some casein. Around 25% of milk is removed as sludge in bactofugation. This results in significant loss in cheese yield. Sterilization of the sludge before adding it back into cheese milk prevents casein loss. This process is useful where the spore counts are high in raw cheese milk and useful tor large scale handling of milk.

Potassium nitrate : The most serious and economically most important defect in milk product is the phenomenon of late blowing of brine salted semi-hard and hard cheeses like Gouda, Edam, Tilsit, Gruyere and Emmental during ripening. This is caused by the butyric acid bacteria which transforms lactate to butyric acid, acetic acid, Co^2 hydrogen and bad taste. Dutch and Swiss cheeses are very sensitive to butyric acid fermentation (BAF) whereas cheddar and other dry salted cheeses are not. Several methods are available to prevent BAF in cheese at the plant. Addition of inhibitory salt like KNO_3

not exceeding 15g/100 / cheese milk is advocated. In fact nitrate is not toxic. It is reduced to nitrite by either coliforms or enzymes (Xanthine Oxidase). The nitrite which is toxic prevents the growth of undersirable organisms. Only limited quantity of nitrate can be added since the salt is inhibitive to the growth of propionic acid organisms necessary for the development of eyes. Large amounts of nitrate can be added since the salt is inhibitive to the growth of propionic acid organisms necessary for the development of eyes. Large amounts of nitrates create reddish brown colour and bitter flavour in cheese due to reaction of tyrosine with nitrite. Nitrite can form nitrosamines which is carcinogenic. This has caused limitation on the use of nitrates although levels of nitrate or nitrites are very low in about 12 weeks storage of cheese (Fig.3-1). Hence, the use of salt petre is not likely to influence the formation of nitrosamine. Bactofugation is another alternate to mitigate the adverse influence of BAF. A third alternative, is the use of lysozyme (from egg yolk) at 2.5g/100 cheese milk. Lysozyme damages the cell walls of bacteria and generating spores. If lysozyme concentration is too much, growth of lactic acid bacteria may also be inhibited. Lysozyme is stable in cheese curd and can replace KNO_3 for preventing late blowing of brine ripened cheeses.

Enzymes in cheese making : Enzymes are used for a) clotting of milk, flavour and texture development, b) flavour enhancement, c) accelerated ripening, d) protection of cheese quality by preventing BAF and e) destruction of H_2O_2 added to bleach cheese milk.

Clotting of milk, texture/flavour development of all varieties of cheese, enzymes used are calf rennet (chymosin); Brine rennet containing Pepsin-A and B; Pig pepsin A; Proprietory blends of two or more animal derived

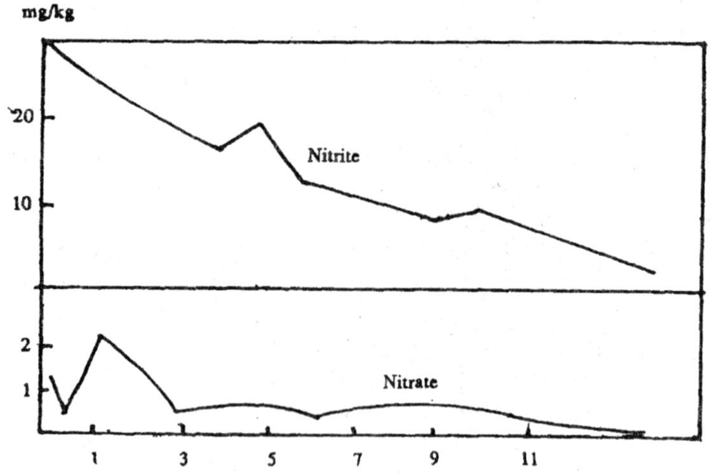

Fig 3-1 Changes in nitrate and nitrite during ripening of Gouda cheese

enzymes; Proprietory blends of animal derived + microbial derived enzymes; Microbial coagulant-carboxy proteinases of *Mucor miehei, Micor pusilus* Lindt and *Endothea parasitice* origin.

Chymogen is produced via controlled fermentation of *Aspergillus niger* var *awamori*. As a result of recombined RNA technique fermentation produced chymogen are available for preparing a number of cheese types.

For flavour enhancement mostly for italian types of Feta/Blue veined cheese carboxyl esterases from pregastric and pancreatic tissues; lipase from edible fore stomach tissues of calf/kid/lamb; microbial lipase of *Aspergillus niger,* Aspergillus *oryzae* and *mucor miehei* are used.

For accelerated cheese ripening : Lipase from edible fore stomach tissues of calf/kid/lamb; microbial lipase from *Aspergillus niger, Aspergillus* oryzae and Mucor miehei; microbial proteinases from *B. subtilis* and *Aspergillus* oryzae for spray dried cheese; proteinase from *P. camemberti* and micrococcus *caseolyticus* for soft, firm and hard pressed cheeses; *Carboxylester hydrolysase* of pancreatic tissue for Italian/blue cheeses; proteinases from *Aspergillus* niger for processed cheese and cheese spreads are used.

All enzymes must conform to levels of arsenic, lead, heavy metal, mycotoxin, antibacterial activity, coliform, salmonella, coliform and total viable counts.

Calf rennet is a highly potent milk clotting enzyme. It is used for a) coagulation of milk and provide conditions for whey expulsion in the curd and b) break down protein during ripening. It is made from the 4th stomach of young suckling calves. The washed stomach is tied at both ends and inflated and suspended in a ventilated cool place. It can also be dry salted. The dried stomachs are folded, packed and sent to factory for extraction. The stomachs are sliced into strips and extracted in a slightly-salt solution, filtered and purified by salting out. The coagulating activity is due to the enzyme chymosin and partly due to pepsin. The extract from older calves contain more pepsin.

	Rennin (activity %)	**Pepsin (activity %)**	**pH (max activity)**
From young calves	88-93	6-12	6.2-6.6
From older calves	6-10	90-94	1.7-2.3

To get best possible preservation the pH of calf rennet is adjusted to 5.5 and slat concentration 15-20%. Rennet is a dark amber coloured liquid with fleshy smell. Five % of glycerine is used as preservative, if whey has to be used for human consumption. Boric acid and benzoic acids are other preservatives. It is sensitive to light and hence stored in coloured bottle at low temperature (10°C). It loses its strength by 1%/mo (The strength is reduced on dilution and storage). Alkali and strong acids destroy its power. It is unstable to heat. It is available in liquid, powder and tablet forms. It is a sulphur containing protein. Albumin and globulin retard coagulation. Boiling of milk resulting in denaturation of proteins removes the inhibitory effect. animal rennet is prohibited for use in India. For the last 2 decades, too few calves have been slaughtered World wide to satisfy the demand for rennet. Consequently, extracts from the stomachs of more mature bovines are offered commercially. In these upto 100% of the clotting activity may be due to pepsin.

Due to commercial pressure to produce adequate supplies of standard rennet at a realistic price there has been a tendency for the past two decades to supply product with reduced proportion of chymosin, (80% chymosin; 50% chymosin + 50% bovin rennet; 25% chymosin + 75% bovine rennet. This pressure led to the development of fungal-derived microbial rennet enzymes. The majority of the available rennets on the market are derived from the fungi. They have proteolytic specificity to chymosin. In 1981, more than one third of all cheese produced world-wide utilised microbial rennets. They have found exclusive use for vegetarians.

Source	Name	Source	Name
Micor miehie	Renilase	Bacillus subtlis	Microzyme
Micor miehie	Fromaase	Micor pusillus	Emporase
Micor miehie	Marzyme	Endothea parasitica	Sure curd

The residual coagulant activity in whey, when it is for use in formulated dairy products, baby foods and dietary aids may cause proteolysis during whey processing causing off-flavour development or even coagulation of milk containing foods.

Vegetable rennet : The plants providing extracts for milk clotting are Fig. tree *(Ficus carica)* and Withania berries *(Withania coaagulans)*. Some of the extracts from *Caarica papaya* (papain), Annas *saliva* (bromelin) are highly proteolytic.

Rennet activity is expressed as the quantity of fresh milk that can be coagulated by one ml. of rennet in the course of 40 min at 35°C. The activity of standard liquid rennet is generally 12,000-15,000. Rennet in tablet form are less bulky for transport and they maintain their activity for many months. They keep sterile without necessity of presevatives. A tablet may be enough for 50 / of milk.

Temperature : The activity of rennet enzyme is highest at 42°C. However, at 30°C coagulation takes 2-3 times longer than at 42°C. In cheese making since activity of lactic acid bacteria is around 30°C renneting is not done at the optimum temperature for the enzyme rennet. The temperature at which the curd takes to firm will make the point clear.

Temperature °C	21-27	30	32-36	Over 50
Type of curd	Soft Jelly like	Firm	Tough rubbery	Hard

Rennetability is poor in cold stored milk as well as with rennet of microbial origin (Fig.3-2). The rate of clotting depends on pH of milk.

Calcium ion concentration : The casein comprises of 4 moities alpha, beta gama and kappa. It is the Kappa-casein which exerts a stablising influence on coagulation. The rennet enzyme releases the kappa casein which destabilises the casein complex. It is a 2 stage process, the first being enzymic.

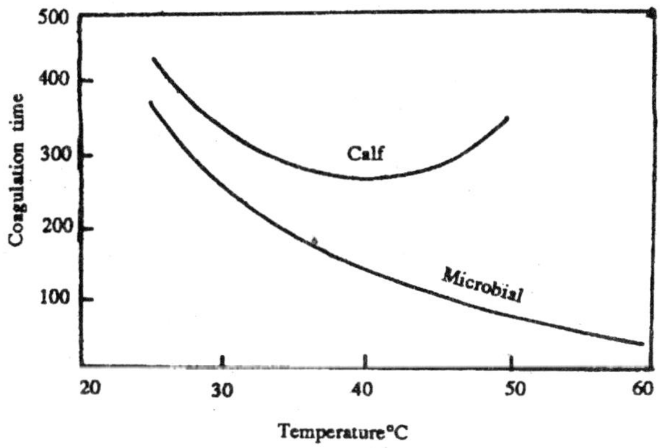

Fig 3-2 Comparison of calf and microbial rennet

$$\text{Kappa casein} \xrightarrow{\text{enzyme}} \text{para-k casein} + \text{macro peptide}$$

In the concurrent non-enzymic stage

$$\text{Para-k-casein} \xrightarrow{\text{enzyme}} \text{para-k-casein} + \text{maecro peptide}$$

In the concurrent non-enzymic stage

$$\text{Para-k-casein} \xrightarrow[\text{pH 6.0-6.4}]{\text{Ca}} \text{dicalcium para-k-casein}$$

In the first phase, coagulation with rennet, kappa casein is released and for the precipitation of para casein fre Ca ions are necessary. At 30°C using 15 ml rennet/100 ml milk, the first phase lasts for 10 min and the second phase only one min. The speed of the first phase depends on the quantity of enzyme, the second phase is independent of the quantity of enzyme. The coagulation soft and weak becomes gruadully firmer and cohesive and in about 20 min from the first sign of coagulation becomes ready for cutting.

When cheese milk is of poor quality, the coagulum may become loose and make heavy fat loss. In such cases, calcium chloride is used to improve rennettability of the milk. The maximum permissible amount is 20 g/ 100 / milk. One ml saturated solution (40% $CaCl_2$) may provide 0.6 g $Cacl_2$.

Poor coagulation of milk may may be due to a) low colloidal Ca phosphatecitrate, b) low total citrate and soluble Ca, c) low casein and Ca, high pH Na+ and chloride, d) high soluble citrate-phosphate and low soluble Ca and Mg; high proportion of alpha S_1, casein, low casein bound Ca.

Proceeding aid means a substance not consumed as a foodtingredient by itself, intentionally used in the processing of raw material, foods or other ingredients to fulfil in certain technological purpose during treatment or processing and which may result in non-intentional but unavoidable presence of residue or derivative as in the final product. There is only a slight difference between processing aids and food additives.

Enzymes, KNO_3, food colours, and other indigenous inorganic salts, organic acids are used as processing aids in cheese making.

Inhibitory salts : In order to reduce the acidity by lactic acid bacteria, salts like $NaHCO_3$ and $CaCO_3$ mixtures are added along with salt at the rate of 30 g/kg of curd like Quark. Some strain of S.lactis which is capable of producing nisin (antibiotic) curbs the activity of gas forming bacteria in processed cheese. Nisin is also added at concentration not more than 0.25% w/w in cheese.

Organic acids : Although lactic acid is produced in *situ* by lactic acid bacteria in milk/curd, lactic or acetic acids are used as acidulants in Ricotta cheese; vinegar (0.03%) in making Quesco Blanco cheese, besides lemon juice in making cottage cheese or indigenous *paneer.*

Antibiotics are used singly or in combination for the treatment of udder diseases. They may be slowly released into the milk and curb the activity of starter organisms.This requires continuous vigilence in testing incoming milk supplies.

Cheese Colour : The colour of cheese is important for consumer appeal. To maintain all the year round uniformity annato or Beta carotene are used particularly in chedar cheese. Annato is a colour extracted from the seeds of *Bixa Orellena* with NaOH. The pigment is acid bixin which in alkaline form becomes nor-bixin. The colour is composed of yellowish and red tints. In cheese the dye gets attached to casein. The colour is generally 20 mg/kg cheese; that for Beta carotene 40 mg/kg. Since cheeses from buffalo and goat milk are snow white artificial whitening of cheese came into use to make cheeses from Cow milk with yellow colour. For Mozzarella and Feta cheeses, chlorophyll is used (15 mg/kg) as masking agent. Chlorophyll is a green dye the colour of which is complimentary to the deep

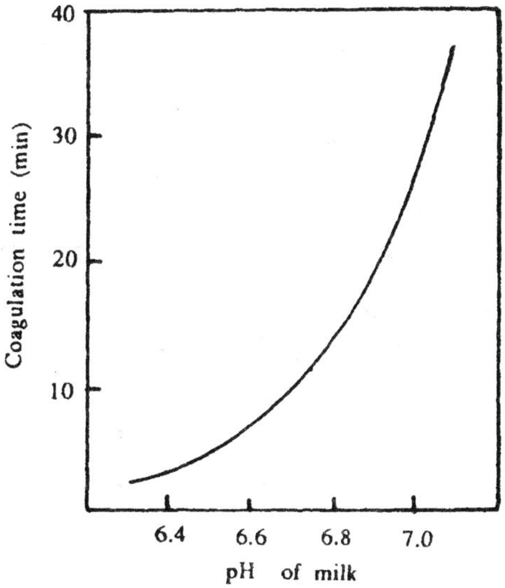

Fig 3-3 pH and rate of clotting of milk

yellow orange colour of carotene. The dyes in right proportion may appear white in cheese. In some cases benzoyl peroxide (pigment white) is used at low concentration (0.001%) to bleach the beta carotene colour of cheese in Blue cheeses. Since carotene is lost supplementation with vitamin A is necessary. For Mozzarella, if white colour is needed, titanium oxide (Lucidal-88) can be used wherever permissile to mask yellow colour.

Titanium oxide is an inert powder 0.002% by weight/kg cheese can be used.

Standardisation of milk ; Milk varies in composition from season to season as well as from breed to breed (Fig 3-4). Because of this, the cheese produced in some months of the year suffer from imbalance in the protein/

fat ratio. This is amplified below :

% fat In milk	%casein In milk	kg cheese/ 100 kg milk	kg cheese/ kg fat	Fat/casein ratio
3.00	2.1	8.30	2.73	0.700
3.25	2.2	8.88	2.63	0.677
3.50	2.3	9.45	2.70	0.650
3.75	2.4	10.03	2.67	0.640
4.00	2.5	10.60	2.65	0.625
4.25	2.6	11.17	2.63	0.612
4.50	2.7	11.94	2.61	0.600
5.00	2.9	12.90	2.58	0.580

The yield of cheese increases with fat % in milk, whereas the yield of cheese/kg fat and fat/casein ratio decreases. When the fat/casein ratio is out of balance the body and texture of cheese may either be soft or too hard unless the balance is adjusted (Fig 3-5, 3-6).With milk low in casein, the

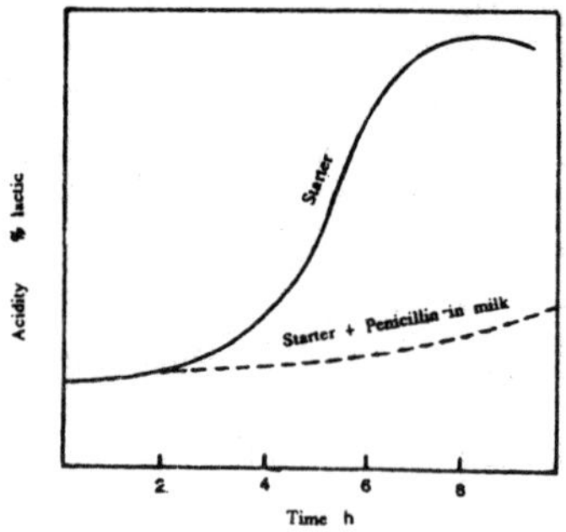

Fig 3-4 Effect of penicillin on acid production in milk

yield of cheese is naturally low because casein forms a structure inside which all the components are trapped or to which they are adsorbed. The optimum level of fat/casein ratio to provide maximum yield of high quality cheese is 1.0:0.7.

The standardization is done by using Pearson square by abstraction of skim milk to adjust the standard or by separation process which will provide the required fat % in the milk. The cream available can be used for butter making. It is rarely that cream needs to be added to the milk.

The aim of the cheese maker is to standardise the cheese milk to, a) produce cheese which has a composition which complies to the legal

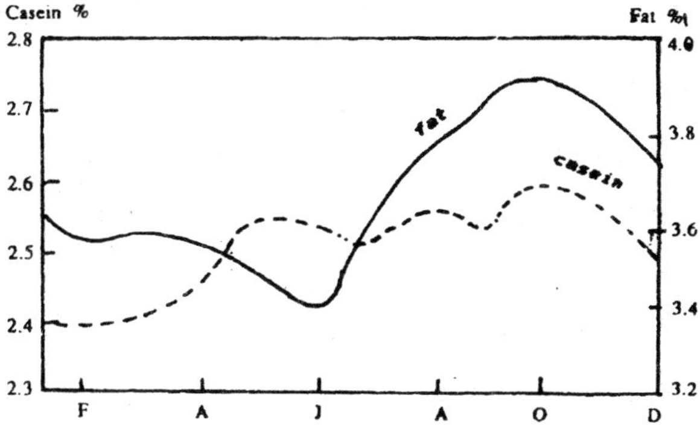

Fig 3-5 Variation in fat and casein percent in milk

standards and b) to make most economical use of the milk components having *max* amount of moisture with minimum *fat* besides a product having consumer acceptance.

Pasteurization/heat treatment

a) Destruction of bacteria and enzymes : Cheese made from raw milk is considered to have better flavour and aroma but the quality of milk is seldom good that one can take the risk of not pasteurizing it. Pasteurization process kills nearly 98-99% of bacteria in milk. Coliform organisms which produce larges amount of gas and undesirable pathogens are destroyed with certainty. Butyric acid bacteria cannot be killed, propionic acid bacteria cannot all be killed. Bacteriophages require higher heat treatment for destruction. The pasteurized milk must be protected against recontamination by hygienic handling of all equipment. Although lipases present in milk are inactivated, the lipases and proteases produced by psychrotrophic organisms are not inactivated.

b) Protein denaturation : Whey proteins are denatured by heat and they get precipitated with caseins during both rennet and acid precipitation. Because of the higher water binding capacity of these proteins, pasteurization leads to a slightly higher outturn.

c) Change in rennetability : Pasteurization reduces rennetability and causes weaker coagulum and slow expulsion of whey from the curd.

d) Pasteurization at 72°C/15 s is desireable. Minimal heat treatment (65°C) with or without holding time is used by some cheese makers to preserve milk enzymes (lipase/protease) and hasten ripening process. If whey cream is added to cheese milk to increase fat content, it is necessary to heat cream drastically (90°C/30 min) to destroy the bacteriophage in cream. Cheese sold in USA that are made from *unpasteurized* milk must be ripened for atleast 60 days by which time all the pathogens die and cheese is made safe for consumption. Hydrogen peroxide catalase method can be used to destroy unwanted organisms from cheese milk. Hydrogen peroxide is a bacteriostatic agent which has some possibility in small cheese plants. The treatment with peroxide is suited for Swiss cheese making. It calls for the addition of 0.05% *food grade* H_2O_2 and heating to 56°/15 s and cooling it to the setting temperature in cheese vat. Catalase is added to deactivate residual H_2O_2 prior to addition of bacterial starter. This method selectively destroys coliforms, vegetative cells of Clostridium, staphylococci and other microorganisms that can cause defects in cheese. With this treatment, cheese ripens faster than when made from pasteurized milk. Wherever Regulations/Acts permit, it can be used with advantage.

Some of the factors governing manufacture of Cheese are :

1 *Influence of microorganisms :* Lactic acid formed by starter culture promotes a) effect on rennin enzyme, b) whey exudation and contraction of curd grains, c) inhibits growth of harmful microorganisms, d) controls the consistency of cheese, e) controls the effect of ripening enzymes and f) directly influence the flavour of cheese.

Acid development : Strong acidification makes the curd brittle and weak acidification makes it rubbery. For a semi-hard cheese the pH of the finished cheese should be around 5.2, if the consistency of final cheese after 3-4 mo of ripening is to be pliable and sliceable.

CO_2 and aroma formation : The aroma bacteria ferments lactose and citric acid to lactic acid, acetic acid, CO_2 diacetyl and CO_2. The higher the aroma bacteria in starter the faster the citric acid will ferment. Too rapid formation of citric acid and CO_2 formation in closer textured cheese with round holes is undesirable because it may cause much time is available for CO_2 to diffuse from cheese.

Vitality : If the vitality of bacteria and its ability to develop acid in milk are constant, a constant pre-ripening time will give a constant degree of pre-ripening. The degree of pre-ripening time is controlled by pH. The amount of inoculum and pre-ripening time depends on the composition of milk, the cheese making process and characteristics that are required in the final cheese. The amount of inoculum should be kept constant unless changes are desired. The same applies to the ripening time (period of time between addition of starter and addition of rennet. The normal amount of inoculum s 0.5-2.0% The pre-ripening time is usually 30 to 60 min.

Lactose/protein ratio : The pH value of cheese is not only determined by the amount of acid alone. The pH value provides information of ratio of acid and buffers. In milk and cheese the most important buffers are protein and phosphares. In milk the ratio of lactose/proteins (46 g lactose/100 kg)/(34 g of protein/100 kg) = 1.35 whereas in cheese the ratio is very low, (17 g lactose/kg cheese)/(234 g protein/kg cheese) = 0.08. Therefore, in cheese curd the content of buffers binding H-ions from lactic acid is much higher than in milk. That is why lactic acid without concentration of H-ions becoming as high (pH becoming too low) as in acidification of milk. Therefore, the whey content of cheese can become decisive for the pH value that can be reached during acidification of cheese pH minimum or lowest pH in cheese). Acidification is usually complete in about 48 h and the pH value that is reached during the period is decisive factor for consistency, keeping quality and flavour for maturing of cheese. To a large extent the distinguishing features of different cheese varieties are caused by different pH minima and many cause cheese faults that can be traced back to the pH minimum.

If water is added to cheese milk or whey the lactose content of the cheese becomes relatively lower. This means addition of water makes it possible to make cheese with relatively higher mositure without becoming too acid. The rate of acid development in cheese is faster (low pH at the end of stirring) more Ca and P will be released with more acid whey and as phosphate is a buffer, the buffering capacity will be reduced. This means that the pH value will be lowered further at a given degree of the lactic acid fermentation after the end of whey drainage.

2 Control of moisture in cheese : Acid treatment promotes control of casein network leading to whey exudation. Contraction is promoted by cutting the curd to small pieces and makes the travel distance of whey short. Cutting provides larger surface area from which whey can escape and contraction is promoted by acid development in the curd. Contraction can also be hastened by increasing the temperature (scalding), when the water binding capacity of casein decreases. Stirring promotes control of temperature to expose the curd surfaces and promotes whey escape. Profuse development of microorganisms takes place inside the curd grain. The cutting time is judged when coagulum is firm to cut as judged by lifting the coagulum. to break. A clean cut surface will give clear whey separation. The grain size for cheddar is 5.7 mm, for dipped cheese 10-12 mm when fusion becomes less.

Pre-stirring : In kneaded/dipped cheese, the curd is kept undisturbed for 15-20 min to make curd firm and drain with stirring to avoid lumps. The moisture content of cheese must be controlled so that the legal limits are not exceeded. More than moisture in cheese, the assessment of water in fat free substance (wffs) is very useful % wffs = (% of moisture in cheese x 100) / (100-%fat in cheese). Suppose a cheese is having 44% moisture and 27% fat, the % wffs = (44x100)/(100-27)=60. This assessment is useful because there is a clear relation between % wffs and firmness of cheese than between % moisture and firmness, because the fat does not bind water in cheese just like casein. Suppose there are 2 cheeses A and B both having 42% moisture and A with 25% fat and B with 11% fat, % wffs in A = (42x100)/(100-25) = 56; in B = (42x100)/(100-11) = 47. This reveals that A will be softer than B. This means high fat cheese will be softer because of the smaller amount of fat free solids to bind the water.

The maximum allowable wffs (water in fat free cheese) for different varieties of cheese are, hard cheese 55% semi-hard cheese 60%, semi-soft cheese 65% and soft cheese 70%.

3 Salting : Even small amount of salt may show considerable effect on the flavour of cheese. Salt may vary from 2 to 8% in the moisture of cheese. The desired salt % are 1.5, 1.7, 1.8, 1.8 and 4.0 for Rindless, Cheddar, Close textured chese. Camembert and Feta. Although salting in whey increases moisture in the curd, it limits the use of whey for feeding purposes. In cheddar all the salt is added before moulding. Rind or dry salting makes labour intensive. Brine salting using 20-22% NaCl is quite useful. It shall have 0.3% $CaCl_2$ to prevent slime formation. The pH of pbrine must be the same as that of cheese (5.1-5.2). The temperature must be

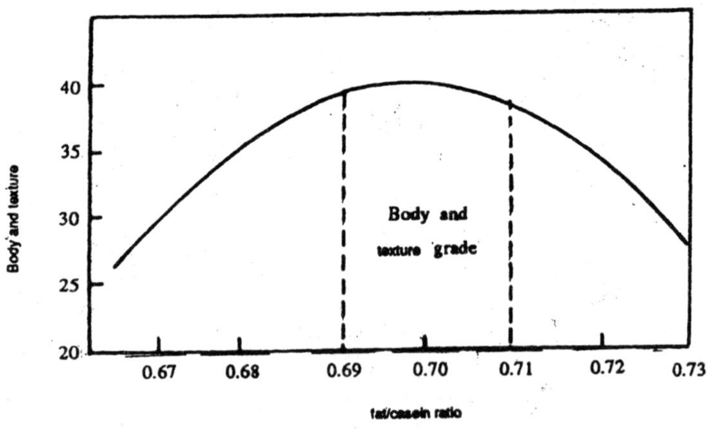

Fig 3-6 Fat/casein ratio on body and texture of cheddar cheese

controlled between 12-16°C. The nitrite content needs monitoring regularly (less than 5 mg/l). Since cheese is lighter than brine, it must be kept immersed or turned during brining. The weight loss during salting may vary (2 to 5%). Large cheeses absorb brine more slowly. High moisture cheese absorb salt faster; the reverse is true for high fat cheese.

Preparation of cheddar cheese : Consequent upon the use of pasteurized milk, it has been possible to specify a definite time for each step in the cheese making process. The time-schedule method with a dummy

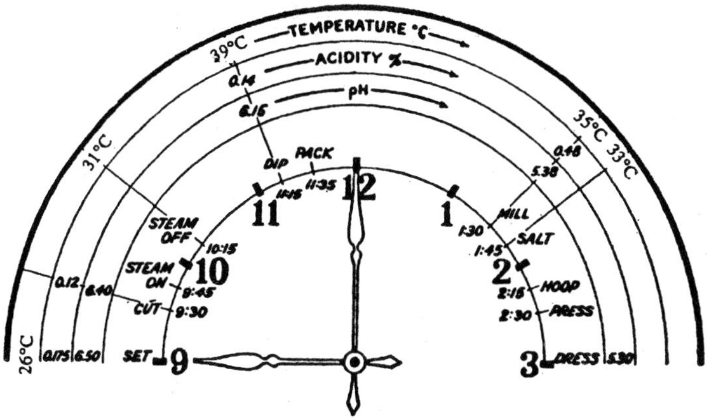

Fig 3-7 Time schedule method of making cheddar cheese

clock makes it possible to organise and simplify the work in factories having several vats. The vat clock with manual operation is shown in Fig 3-7. The operator follows time-schedule by observing the wall clock showing actual time which the cheese maker records when each step is begun. Besides, at the beginning of each step the cheese maker moves the hand of the vat clock ahead to the actual time when the next step is to begin. For example, when starter is added the actual time is recorded and the hands of the vat clock are set ahead to the actual time when the milk has to be set with rennet. Thus, when each succeeding step is begun, the time is recorded and the hands are set ahead to the time when the next step is to begin. By using this, errors can be avoided in supervising actually the work being done in each vat. It synchronises cheese making, saves time and avoids errors in following the schedule. The flow diagram of cheddar cheese making is shown in Fig.3-8.

Preparing the equipment : The cheese equipment consisting of cheese vats, cheese knives, agitator, curd strainer, curd mill and the press should be sterilized just before use by using hot water at 82°C or chlorine solution (100 mg/l available chlorine) for a minimum of 2 min. The salting and cutting operations are shown in Fig. 3-9 and 3-10.

Milk reception : High grade milk is required for cheese making. The steps followed at reception are a) odour of milk in the can or tanker, b) appearance (free from extraneous matter, c) sediment test once a week, d) titratable acidity, e) 10 min resazurin test known as rejection test for quick screening, f) examination for bacteriophage, antibiotics and inhibitory substances (as and when necessary), g) weight, h) fat and casein contents.

Preparation of milk includes filtration or clarification as deemed necessary, standardization of milk, pasteurization at 71°C/15 s and cooling

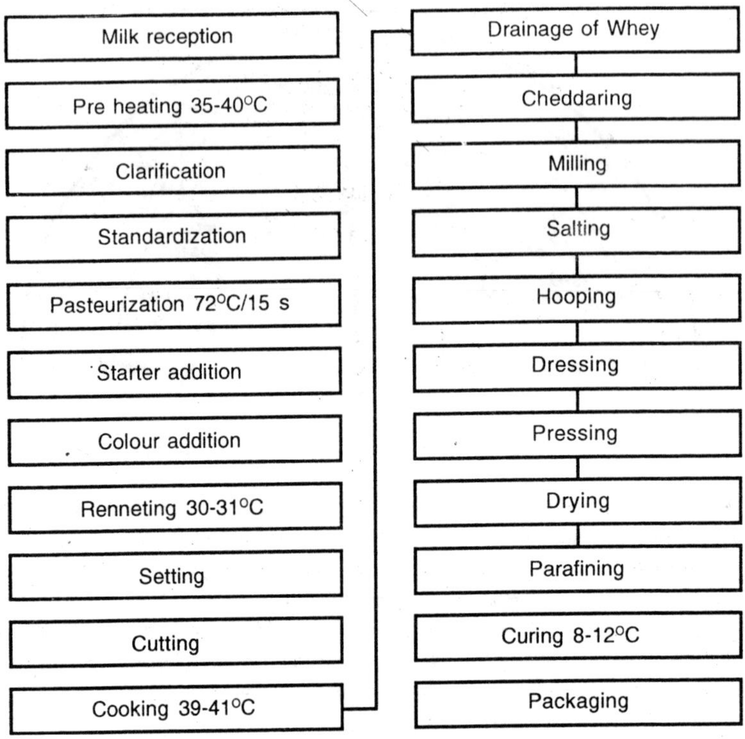

Fig 3-8 Flow diagram of cheddar cheese making

to 30-31°C to avoid reheating before setting.

Addition of starter and developing the desired amount of acidity is a prerequisite for renetting. Active starter is strained to remove lumps. Enough starter is added to produce approximately 0.5% acid in the whey drained from the vat 4 1/2 h after setting, with a ripening period of milk for one h. Nearly 0.5-1.0% starter is necessary. The starter is mixed thoroughly in the milk to produce a) desirable curd, b) check growth of unwanted organisms and c) control moisture in the curd.

Conventional method of starter handling whereby master and mother cultures are prepared at the cheese factory are steadily being replaced by the use of cell concentrate produced by starter manufacturers. They may be used for direct inoculation of the bulk starter tank or in cheese vat itself, eliminating some or all the preparation stages reducing the opportunity of phage infection. These concentrates may be available as deep frozen culture which must be maintained at low temperature throughout shipment and storage. However, freeze dried culture require no special conditions for shipment and storage. When starter is used directly to the cheese vat as

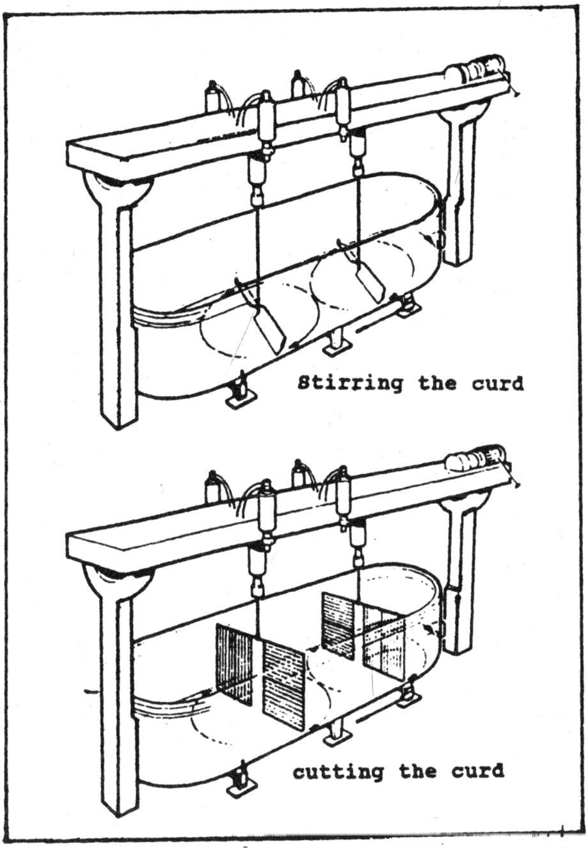

Fig 3-9 Cheese vat - cutting and stirring curd

freeze dried culture ther is no carry over of curd so that some adjustment of *make* conditions may be necessary.

Setting : Usually cheese colour is diluted 20 times with water and added with thorough mixing. The amount varies from 5 to 20 ml/100 / milk. More colour is necessary for buffalo milk.

Rennetting *:* The temperature of milk is adjusted to 30-31°C and when acidity of milk has increased by -0.02% liquid rennet 15-20 ml/100 / milk diluted with cold water (20 times) is added to the milk and distributed through the entire length of the vat with thorough stirring for 3-5 min. The milk in the gate valve is drained and added to the vat and agitator stopped.

The vat is covered to keep the surface of milk warm. First visible thickening can be noticed by lowering the back of the finger below the surface of milk. A visible depression may appear on the surface. This may take around 8 min. The time required between rennet addition and cutting can be 8 x 2.5 = 20 min.

Cutting : The curd should be firm enough to cut 30 min. after setting. This is judged by inserting a thermometer into the curd at an angle and raising it slowly. When the curd splits evenly ahead. It is ready to cut. The aim at cutting is to get uniform size of curd cubes for rapid escape of why and to control the moisture in the curd. Both horizontal and vertical knives are used (Fig 3-9) The smaller cubes drain and firm faster than larger cubes. At the time of cutting the acidity of whey should be 0.11-0.13% (pH 6.40) depending on the acidity of milk before it was pasteurized. The flow diagram is shown in Fig 3-8.

Heating the curd : The curd is stirred continuously with agitators or rakes slowly till dipping. To firm the curd, heating is started 15 min after cutting. The curd is heated slowly for the first 10-15 min and brought within the range of 39 to 41°C in 30 min with slow stirring to avoid matting and ensuring uniform heating. High temperature may retard growth of bacteria and development of acidity.

Dipping or draining whey : The curd cubes shrink to half the size at dipping. The curd is pushed back from the gate end of the vat, strainer inserted and whey is drawn 2 1/2 h after setting. The acidity of whey at this time should be 0.13-0.15% (pH 6.15).

Cheddaring refers to combined operations of packing,turning, piling and repiling of the curd cubes. A ditch is made lengthwise down the middle of the vat, the edges of the curd are trimmed and loose particles are placed on the top of the curd. The curd is packed nearly about 17 to 20 cm deep and the acidity of whey should be 0.17 to 0.22%. This takes 20 min from dipping. Cheddaring or matting the curd expels whey, develops acidity in the curd and produces a smooth silky curd that will have a meaty texture resembling the appearance of cooked white meat from chicken's breast. When cut it will be reasonably freed from mechanical openings. The piling is done slowly. Rapid piling leads to soft curd with weak and pasty body. During the entire chedaring stage the temperature of the curd should be near 38°C. The curd is cut into strips 15-20 cm wide at right angles from the sides of the vat. The blocks of curd are turned bottom side up in the vat repeatedly at 5-15 min intervals till the curd is ready to mill. If curd contains more moisture it is cut narrower and turned more frequently. Nearly 45 min after the curd is first cut into strips, the blocks are piled into 2 layers 2 deep and after 20 min 3 deep and later on in deeper layers Shallow piling gives dry curd. The temperature should be uniform throughout the mass of the curd at 35° to 38°C. If the temperature of the curd is lower than 38°C, the cheese may have openings in the rind.

Miling is done to get uniform pieces (2 cm x 4 cm) for even salting on well spread curd and stirring after each application. It permits escape of whey and gases and make it convenient to handle in the cheese hoop. Both hand and power mills can be used.

Salting is done 15 min after milling salt is added in 2 or 3 applications

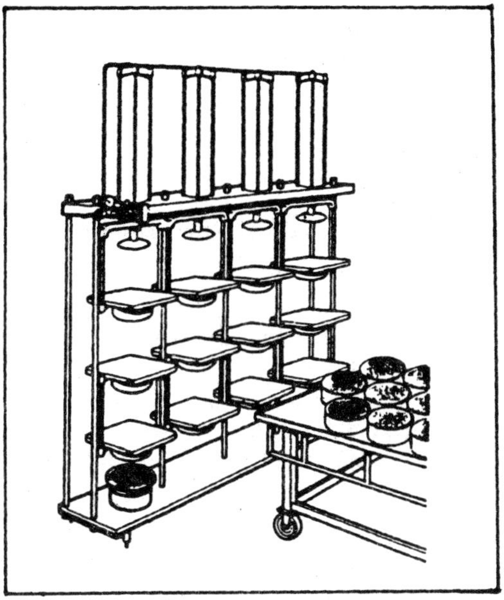

Fig 3-10 Vertical cheese press

at the rate of 2% by weight of curd kg curd. Salting improves flavour, body, texture and keeping quality of cheese, besides checking undesirable fermentation. The temperature at milling is between 35 to 37.8°C.

Hooping : Fifteen to 30 min after the salt has dissolved completely and the curd smooth and velvety the curd is ready for hooping. The curd should be stirred to avoid clumps and the temperature should be between 29° and 32°C. The cheese hoops are carefully lined with cheese cloth without wrinkles before they are filled with curd to form close rind bandage.

The cheese curd is accurately weighed to make cheeses of uniform size. For rindless cheese, the curd is placed in rectangular forms.

Pressing The curd is pressed in for 30 min at low pressure 1.5 kg/cm^2 to get a shape and removed for proper arrangement of bandage cloth and put back in the press. The cheese should not be removed from the press and taken out of the hoops till the rind is free. During pressing some whey escapes (pH 5.3) and the air prockets and why-pockets get closed up.

Pressure is applied gradually at first and full pressure 1.75 kg/cm2 in 30 min. The temperature of cheese is maintained at 22°C throughout the pressing. Various types of presses, horizontal, vertical, hydraulic, spring and screw presses are available. The pressing lasts for 24 h. The cheese is then stamped for identification with factory number, vat number and date made.

The pre ripening is eliminated by using very active starter and using a higher % of inoculum. The total time taken from setting to dipping is 2 1/2 h; from dipping to milling another 2 1/2 h; and milling to dressing 1 1/2 h making a total of 6 h. Processing can be followed by assessing acidity or pH as the case may be.

Drying : The cheese are then cleaned by scraping and washing and placed in dry shelves in a drying room at 12-16° C and turned once a day for 3-4 days to form rind. Drying is also done by blowing hot air at 60° C.

Paraffining is done to a) reduce moisture loss during curing by about 3%, b) prevent surface mould growth, c) minimise the risk of cheese mites and other pests and d) reduce fat loss by sweating. The paraffin coat of sufficient thickness gives good appearance. The cheese already at 12°C is dipped in paraffin at 130°C for 4-5s drained cooled and cured at 12°C. The composition of cheese wax in paraffin 75%, microcrystalline wax 20% and polyisobutylene 5%

Curing is done at 8-12°C with R.H. 75% in a refrigerated room automatically controlled for adequate flavour development for 2-6 mo. Yield of cheese may range from 9.25 to 11%.

According to Van Slyke formula Y=(F+C) N where Y is yield of cheese from 100 kg milk, F fat in kg/100 kg milk; C=casein in kg/100 kg milk and N is 1.63 for green cheese or 1.555 for cured cheese.

Cheddar cheese from buffalo milk : Certain modifications have been suggested based on work done at NDRI. The 3 methods given below differ mainly in the stage of addition of salt. Czulak recommended salt addition in whey at the end of cooking after 1/2 whey is drained. The presalting procedure suggests 1% salt addition initially to milk itself, increase in setting time, higher piling of cheese at cheddaring and ripening cheese in 2 stages. (15°C/ 3 weeks; 8-10°C/3 mo). The comparative steps are given below :

	Czulak	**Burde**	**Presalting**
Standardization C/F ratio	0.7	0.7	0.7
Pasteurization oC/30 min	63	63	63
Salt addition %	-	-	1
Ripening temperature °C	30	31	28-29

(Cont'd)

Rate of starter %	1.5	2.5	2.5
Ripening period min	10	10	10
Amount of rennet g/100 l	2.5	2.5	2.5
Salting time min	35	30	55
Acidity at cutting % l.a.	0.11	0.11	0.13
Final cooking temp. 0C	36.6	38	36
Cutting and 1/2 whey drainage min	50	-	-
Salt addition	1	-	-
Total cooking time	60	50	45
Acidity at drainage % l.a.	0.12	0.12	0.15
acidity at milling % l.a.	0.40	0.44	0.45
Salting rate % of curd	2	2	2
Yield of green cheese%	12.6	12.7	13.2
Moisture in cheese %	34.9	35.9	37.8

Some representative varieties of cheese

Parmesan is a very hard cheese of italian origin made from low fat milk. (2%) using thermophilic starters, giving high scalding temperature and long immersion in brine. Around 600 / of milk is used to make one cheese. Milk is set at 32-35°C using 1% S.thermophilus and L. bulgaricus culture. After short ripening, lipase rich rennet is used at 25ml/100/. Milk coagulum is cut to 3 mm size and scalded first at 40°C/15 min and at 56°C/ 15 min. After settling of curd, whey is drained in special cloth for 30 min and pressed over night. the cheese is kept in brining room for 3 days at 15°C and then immersed in 26% brine at 8-10°C before transfer for ripening (10°C/ RH 85 for 6 mo). The cheese is turned frequently washed and rubbed with vegetable oil to inhibit mould growth. It is matured for one to 2 years. Proteolytic and lipolytic changes produce strong flavours. The cheese is generally dry and used for culinary purposes after grating.

Emmental is one of the difficult type to make. Only correct combination of milk, 3 species of bacteria in an active culture and well combined conditions of production can there be hope of getting a typical Swiss cheese. Raw milk testing 2.8 to 3.1% fat is used. Clarification improves the quality of cheese. To remove Clostridial spores bactofugation is done at 60°C in big plants. Milk is set at 30-35°C. The culture consists of S. thermophilus (0.1%), L. helveticus/bulgaricus (0.20%) and small dosage of propionic bacteria. Rennet is used at 16 ml/100 / milk, the coagulum cut into stripes, then cubes and finally into particles 3 mm diameter. Temperature is raised to 45°C slowly and then to 57°C to kill non-thermodurinc bacteria. (Heating is done for 45 min). When curd is firm, it is collected in dipping cloth and lowered to mould, pressed for 24 h by gradual increase. The cheese is turned at intervals for drainage. When curd cools acidity increases causing matting to an elastic mass. After pressing, the cheese is transferred to salting room at 10°C for cooling, turned at intervals with dry salt, removed from hoop and immersed in 23% brine at 8-12°C. The cheese is turned daily and transferred to chill room (10-12°C/RH 85%) for about 10 days. The cheese is brushed, turned and dry salted. Finally the cheese is taken to warm room (20°C and RH 85%) for development of eyes. Frequent turning is necessary for 4-8 weeks with dry salt to prevent mould growth. The cheese is ripened at 13°C/RH 80-85% for 3-9 mo. The outstanding feature of this cheese is eyes which may measure o.5 to 2 cm in diameter. It has sweet hazelnut flavour, firm meaty body and close texture.

The special manufacturing details are, a) curd cut to finer particles, b) high cooling temperature, c) no cheddaring, washing or milling and d) salting by diffusion in brine plus rubbing with dry salt.

Gouda cheese : Edam and Gouda cheeses originated from Holland, edam is in the form of balls weighing around 2 kg. Gouda is in the form of small wheels weighing 2.5 to 3.5 kg. Both are sweet curd rennetted cheeses. Milk of high quality is standardised to 2.8% fat and fat/casein ratio 0.7. It is pasteurised and cooled to 30°C and inoculated with 0.5% of mesophilic starter culture. Potassium nitrate (15g/100 milk) is added to prevent growth of spore forming bacteria and cheese colour at 9-15 ml diluted with water. Single strength rennet (28 ml) diluted with 40 times with water is added and stirred. The curd is cut and stirred slowly when it is firm. The curd is heated in stages by the addition of water at 55-60°C. Water dilutes the whey and reduces the acidity of whey. With careful stirring for 30 min, the temperature is raised from 33 to 40°C with hot water. While stirring the desired texture is obtained, The whey is drained and the curd piled and matted. It is pressed in the vat, cut into blocks and transferred to cheese hoops and pressed in 3 stages, 0.5kg/cm^2 till the blocks are well formed. The cheese is removed to the drying room, turn daily till rind formation and brine salted in 20% solution at 15°C for several days, removed, dried for a few days and paraffined with red coloured wax. Sorbic acid may be used as fungicide. The cheeses are cured for 1.5 to 5 mo at 10°C with RH 85-90%). The high pH of the curd (5.3.-5.4.) and absence of lactic acid to suppress spoilage bacteria, emphasise the importance of using good quality milk. Early work under the ICAR project at Aarey milk colony reports that satisfactory quality to Gowda cheese can be made from buffalo milk which is diluted with 15% water. Due to high Ca-ions in the milk, the curd undergoes extensive syneresis with low moisture retention capacity requiring longer curing period to develop good texture.

Blue veined cheeses are internal mould ripened cheeses made from high acid semi-soft curd involving slow acid development and long drainage period. Blue green mould *Penicillin roqueforti* is used for Gorgonzola in Italy, Roquefor in France. Stilton in England and Blue in USA. Use of sheep milk is mandatory in Roquefort area of France. Clean milk is heated to 30°C for setting with 2% active starter. After one h 20 ml rennet is used for 100 milk and set for one h. the curd is cut to cubes of 12 mm size, allowed to settle for 10 min, dipped with cheese cloth for 30 min till the curd becomes firm to put in cheese forms. The curd is now ready for inoculating with mould powder by sprinkling and transferred to draining room at 18°C. The cheese is turned 4 to 5 times on first day and twice a day thereafter until they are ready for salting. The cheeses are washed each morning to free from saline for 3 to 4 days . The cheese is salted twice by rubbing with salt and left for a week. The cheese may be piled 3 high. A week after the cheese is punctured in 30-40 places and put on edge in curing room to allow oxygen which is essential for mould development at 9°C RH 90-95%. After 10 days first scraping is done. Two additional scrapings develops red slime. When there is good mould growth in the interior it is wrapped in tin foil and placed in storage at 8°C for 6 weeks for further ripening before marketing. The mould produces distinct rancid flavour. Blue cheese from pasterurized homogenized milk ripens more slowly than made from raw homogenized milk. The compounds that contribute characteristic flavour are lower fatty acids and ketones.

Camembert is a soft cheese of French origin. It is made from pasteurized milk using 1.5-2.5% active S. lactis culture and ripened for one h at 33°C before rennet (16 ml/100 milk) is added. Coagulation takes place in 25 min. The curd becomes firm in 70 min from renneting. The curd is ladled into perforated moulds and drained for 1 h. The curd shrinks to half the size and acidity increases to 0.6%. The curd is turned and left to drain overnight at 22°C. After 24 h it is dry salted and held at 20°C for 24 h. The cheese is sprayed with a culture of *Penicillium* camemberti and after 24 h transferred to a ripening room. Low pH (4.6) less lactose and rising salt prevents the growth of other oraganisms. For 2 weeks, it is held at 11-14°C R.H. 85-90%. In 2-3 days film yeasts (Mycoderma) appear on the surface. After 12 days when acidity at the surface gets reduced by yeasts red brown spots of Brevibacterium linens appear. Due to complex series of microbial changes waxy body and flavour due to proteolysis and lipolysis is formed. The luxurient growth of snow white P camemberti over the whole surface is responsible for changes in body and texture. After ripening more than 50% of the proteins in cheese is converted into water soluble compounds and NH_3.

Feta is internal bacterial ripened and brine preserved cheese. A wide range of Feta types are on the market today. Milk is pasteurized at 72°C/15 s, standarized and if using cow milk, bleached by the addition of a chlorophyll decolouriser, a starter (2%) is added and the milk ripened. Rennet, and optionally $CaCl_2$ and/or kid or lamb lipase are added and once set, the curd is cut. Curd is ladled into moulds where whey drainage takes place. These are turned and sometimes subjected to slight pressure overnight. The following day, the cheese is removed from the moulds and cut into blocks followed by dry salting and/or immersion in brine. The cheese is transferred to sealed tins containing brine, for storage for 3-4 weeks at 8-10°C and then to 5°C until despatch. It may be consumed fresh or held up to 6 mo.

Majority of cheese is now made from ultrafiltered milk and two types known as unstructured and structured are produced. Cheese yield as a result of UF manufacture is 5500 1 milk/ton of cheese compared to 7300 ton product of traditional production. This is due to incorporation of whey proteins into the cheese and also a more efficient recovery of milk fat.

Cottage cheese is a soft, lactic acid unripened variety made from pasteurized skim milk. Cream may be added to it so that the finished product may have not less than 4% milk fat. Setting can be done with acid alone or with little addition of rennet. The acid curd produces cheese with small grains and mild acid but the yield may be low, whereas the rennet curd can produce cheese with large particles with mild acid and higher yield besides meaty body.

The curd may be formed by *short* or *long* setting methods. In short setting conditions use of 4-5% lactic starter, maintaining a temperature of 29-30°C. This sets the milk in 4-5 h. For long setting with the amount of starter at 0.3 to 0.5%, maintenance of temperature at 22°C the setting period becomes 12-13 h. Short setting is preferred. To firm the curd at cutting

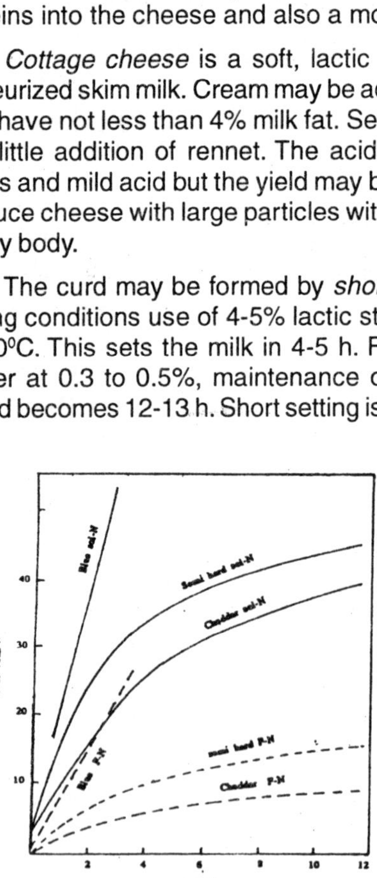

Fig 3-11 Protein breakdown during cheese ripening

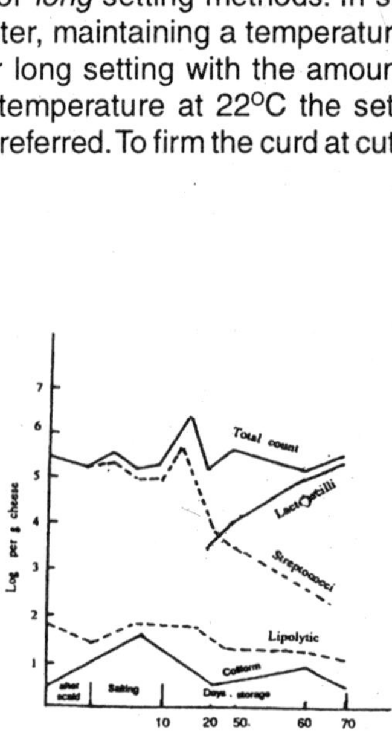

Fig 3-12 Bacterial population during ripening of cheese

and assist matting, during working a small amount of rennet is used (0.15 ml or 0.25 ml/100 milk for long and short setting respectively). When the pH attains 4.7, the coagulum is cut into cubes and cooked gradually over a period of 60 min to around 55°C. The lactic acid production ceases at 39°C. The rate of heating can be increased to 1.5°C during 5 min. After 2 h, the whey is drained off to the curd level and the curd washed 3 times approximately at 20 min interval at 22°C, 10°C and finally with chilled water at 3-4°C. The curd is then rested for one h at 2°C. Washing makes the curd firmer and removes acid-why. The curd is drained thoroughly and salted at 1% level. Packing is done in small cartons. Creaming can be done by using homogenized cream to give 4% fat in the finished product. The yield of uncreamed cheese is around 15% and that of creamed one 18%. The cheese is highly perishable. It is stored in refrigerator and consumed within a week. Buffalo skim milk can be used for making this cheese.

Extreme care is needed during manufacture to avoid microbial contamination and air borne yeast and mould. Wash water with 5 mg/l active chlorine is useful. Because of the open texture it is ideally suited for yeast and mould growth causing slimy film due to growth of psychrotrophs leading to off flavour.

Mozzarella cheese is a fresh white unripened Italian soft cheese originally made from buffalo milk with elastic structure, slightly acidic taste with pleasant aroma. Buffalo milk is standardised to around 5.5% fat and heat treated at 72°C. It is cooled to 37°C and inocculated with an active mixed culture of S. lactis, S. thermophilus and L. bulgaricus at 2%. After thorough mixing and setting for 45 min, when developed acidity increases by 0.01% microbial rennet (2g/100 ml) is added and after stirring for even distribution left for 45 min at 37°C. When desired firmness is noticed in the curd, it is cut to 10 mm cubes, allowed to stand for 5 min. The curd is then cooked gradually till temperature attains 90°C in 2 h. The whey is drained when acidity is 0.42% and the curd dray salted at 2-3% of the curd. After 5 min the curd is scalded in boiling water for 4-5 min. The curd is plasticized by using a wooden worker till it forms a uniform mass. At this stage the curd can be stretched like a long ribbon. The curd is then put in hoops, cooled by dipping in pasteurized water to 4-5°C/2 h. The cheese slabs are transferred to wire strainer for 2 h, suitably packed in sterilized plastic/ polythene bags and stored at 8°C till disposed off. Instead of starter culture, direct acidification can be done by using citric acid (1.35 g/100 l milk) and brine salted also. The cheese is used for layering pizza where good melting and fat leakage of cheese are very necessary. The stretchability is an unique property (ability to form fibres or strings when hot) which is irreplaceable by any other variety of cheese. The yield ranges from 15-19%. The proximate composition is moisture 53.4%, fat 21.7%, protein 20.4%, lactose 0.8%, ash 2.5% andsalt 1.3%. The storage life is around 2 wk at 8°C.

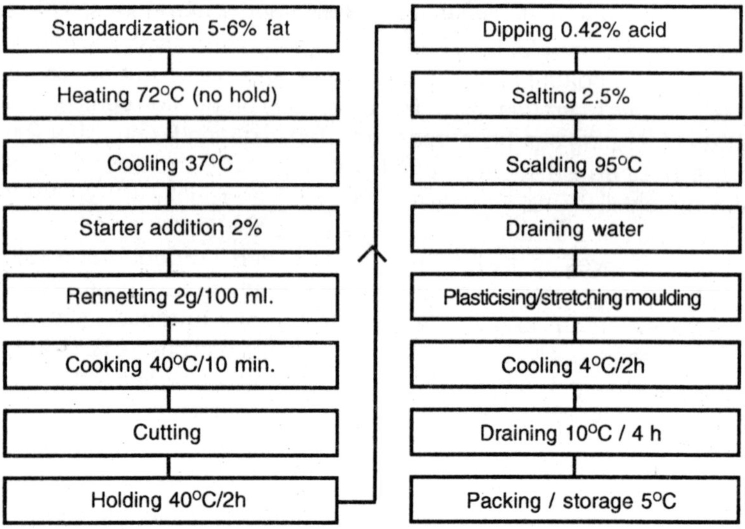

Fig 3-13 Flow diagram of making Mozzarella cheese

Surti cheese : It is an indigenous variety of soft cheese made from buffalo milk or whole milk adjusted to about 6% fat. The milk is heated to 78°C for 20 s and colled to 35°C. A good quality lactic starter is added 35 g of starter for 100 kg of milk. This is followed by enough diluted rennet to assure a firm coagulum in one h the curd is ladled in thin layers in small bamboo baskets in which it is drained. Salt at 1% of milk is sprinkled on cheese during dipping. The cheese is turned every 30 min by inverting an empty basket over the basket containing the curd and then both baskets are turned a half turn. Draining is continued until all free whey is removed. The cheeses are then removed from the baskets and immersed in whey for 12-16 h, during which time they ripen. The ripening time depends on the temperature used and the final acidity desired. The final acidity of whey may be around 0.5 to 0.6%. The relatively high fat helps in providing a fine and smooth texture. The cheese is also transported in acid whey containing salt for over 300 km distance for the market.

Bandal cheese is a soft indigenous variety of cream cheese similar to Surti but smoked.

Dacca cheese is a small medium-pressed cheese. The milk is clotted ith rennet and when set the curd is broken by hand and filled into small wicker baskets, and the whey pressed out by placing a board weighted with stones on the baskets. After 10-12 days the cheese becomes dry and develop a thin coat of hardened cheese due to evaporation. The cheese is then smoked with wood or cow dung smoke after which whey keep well for one or two months. No mellowing of curd flavour may be noticeable. The tarry and furfuraldehyde flavour is unpleasant to some. The amout of milk entering into the manufacture of indigenour cheeses is small, in fact, infinitesimal.

Whey cheese : Ricotta, Mysost and Gjetost (goat milk) are soft cheeses made from whey. They are soft and creamy, tan in colour, creamy body and caramelized flavour. Ricotta is made by heating whey to 85°C by direct steam injection. The whey proteins are precipitated by adding citric or acetic acid and the curd transferred to drainage moulds for 4-5 h and packaged. Mysost and Gjetost are made by evaporating whey to 60% total acids, in a double efect, evaporator or open pan transfered to a vacuum cooker and further concentrated to Ca 85% total solids. The brown concentrate is further heated for getting brown colour and flavour . The product is kneaded and moulded into blocks and packaged. It can be stored upto 6 mo at 5°C. It undergoes no ripening. The moisture is Ca 15-20%.

Direct acidification technique is also carried out in the manufacture of cottage, Mozzarella and Feta cheese. It decreases production time, eliminates problems associated with starter cultures, improves consistency of the product and provides greater process control. Milk is acidified cold (3-5°C) with phosphoric acid by using helical mixer coupled with acid dosing pump. The pH is set for 4.9 (for cottage cheese). The acidified milk is heated in a vat at 30°C and an acidogen (D-glucono-delta lactone) is added. Gluconic acid is produced at controlled rate (similar to lactic acid production by starters) till pH 4.7 is obtained. Some times a small amount of coagulant is also added to assist curd formation. The flavour is bland starter distillate can be added to give creamy flavour. Direct set materials are produced by some firms.

Ultrafiltration technique has been applied to the manufacture of many soft cheese, including Camembert, quarg, cottage cheese, Feta, Danish blue and Mozzarella. The advantages are, a) higher protein recovery due to incorporation of whey protein (over 20% of total protein in milk), higher fat recovery due to reduced loss in whey, reduced volume of fluid to be processed, requiring less rennet and starter and leds itself for continuous processing. Ultra filtration can be used in 4 ways; a) preconsentration of milk upto 2 times and concentrate processed in conventional method, b) production of concentrate followed by cutting of the coagulam produced after addition of rennet and starter and permitting some texurization of product, c) producing pre-cheese where milk is effectively concentrated to required solids of cheese with a concentrate or retentate being dozed after adding starter and rennets; this limits whey drainage and increases yield and d) concentration of whey proteins and subsequently returned to cheese vat as a slurry. A number of continuous systems of production are available.

Packaging of cheese

Rind formation : The rind protects soft cheese against a) attack of microorganisms, and b) drying. It acts more or less as a wrapper for the edible cheese. The rind has lower moisture content than the rest of cheese inside. To get a tough and cohesive rind, the outer surface should not ripen as much as the cheese inside. During pressing operations some rind is formed which continues when cheese is in concentrated brine. The extent of rind formation is usually determined by temperature, humidity and air circulation in the cheese store. Vigorous air circulation at regular intervals helps to form a good rind.

Monitoring the temperature and humidity is very important. The textured, kneaded and dipped cheeses must develop a smear coat together with a suitable rind. Smear coat provides a protective layer round the cheese to prevent mould growth. The cheese smear is formed by the growth of *Brevibacterium linens* (red smear bacteria). Storage of cheese in a warm room with high humidity 85-90% is conducive for smear growth. Cheese must be turned every day until hard rind is formed on both sides of the cheese. However, turning cannot be dispensed with altogether. A synthetic film and a stiff carton replaces the protective function of rind in the rindless cheese.

The purpose of packaging is to a) protect cheese from flavour contamination, external microorganisms, insects etc. b) prevent loss of moisture and c) enhance its appearance. A protective coating of wax or some kind of plastic film is given for hard cheese. Semi-hard cheeses are often wrapped in aluminium or plastic films and packed in cardboard boxes. For long term wrap waxed cellulose, nylon film, cellulosic-pliofilm, cellulose polyethylene, plio film, poly ethylene and poly ethylene polyster laminates are used. For short term wrap, plio film, poly vinylene chloride (cryovac) saran and poly vinyl chloride films are in common use.

Rindless cheese : With the advent of synthetic plastic films, the manufacture of rindless cheese have become widespread. This method was first developed in USA for cheddar cheese. Rindless cheese is a cheese where in the wrapper is a synthetic plastic film. The advantage of film wrapping is that a) it replaces the protective action of rind, b) eliminates the work involved in tending the cheese during ripening considerably since cheese need not be surface treated, turned or cleaned (labour saving), c) reduces shrinkage or moisture attack of microorganisms, d) prevents mechanical damage to cheese, e) makes full use of cheese (no rind waste) in making processed cheese, f) minimises strict humidity control during ripening and storage (although 60-70% RH is ideal) g) its transparency makes possible detection of mould growth on the surface of cheese and h) helps to make pre cut packed product to be sold in retail store.

Block cheese can be wrapped in very tight adhering film after taking from the cheese press when the surface is plastic by hot pressing or vaccumising and heat shrinking in hot water. For less strongly acidic cheeses salted completely after some weeks and stored at higher temperature during the first week more permeable films to moisture, CO_2 and O_2 may be necessary. The rate of CO_2 formation and elimination must be taken into consideration in the selection etc. for making suitable selection. The characteristics of the film wrap are a) low permeability of O_2 CO_2 and water vapour, b) stability to fats and lactic acid, c) stability under cold and warm conditions of storage, d) low shrinkage on storage unless shrinkage is needed, e) easy for application with required elasticity and stiffness, f) amenable to air tight seal around the cheese by heat or other method.

Foreign organisms should not grow underneath the film as unclean flavours may easily diffuse into the body of cheese. It is desirable to do wrapping in a special room with air inside disinfected.

Cheese ripening or maturing is the final stage in the manufacture. It promotes compositional changes due to the combined action of various microorganisms and enzymes. The maturing period varies from 2 weeks to 24 mo. according to the type of cheese.

Main changes : Initially the activity of lactic streptococci used as starter are inhibited but the lactic acid bacteria particularly lactobacilli multiplies progressively during the late stages of ripening of all cheeses especially in the hard varieties. Within a week any residual lactose present disappears having been converted to lactic acid and other organic acids. The enzymes present in the lactobacilli bring about a number of chemical reactions responsible for the development of flavour and aroma.

Proteins are rendered more digesible due to its breakdown by rennin combined with proteases. Eventually the proteins are broken down to polypeptides, peptides and amino acids which contribute to the flavour but also make the casein softer.

Some of the milkfat is also broken down by enzymes into glycerol and fatty acids. The lower water soluble fatty acids are volatile and strong smelling in nature. These also contribute to the aroma.

Both amino acids and fatty acids are broken down still further by enzymes, resulting in a variety of low molecular compounds such as amines, alcohols and ketones. These also contribute to the flavour of mature cheese. The ultimate flavour of cheese is derived from a very large number of compounds some present only in minute quantities. Apart from external inoculation of pencillin particularly in Blue cheese and surface source of organism the cheese maker can do very little to further the influence of microbial content. It may be of interest to know that the total number of lactobacilli and streptococci both living and dead is extremely large and probably accounts for 0.1% of this weight of cheeses (Fig 3-12). This amounts to about log 10 organisms/g of cheese (Fig 3-11).

Physical changes : The fresh rather bland rubbery mass of curd becomes less cohesive, pliable, sliceable and tasty mass. These changes depend on temperature, humidity, moisture content, pH, salt and microbial content of the curd.

Chemical changes taking place are a) fermentation of lactose, b) proteolysis and c) lipolysis. These changes are brought about by a) enzymes of lactic acid bacteria of the starter cultures b) non-lactic bacteria in milk, c) rennet, d) quality of the milk and e) other microorganisms growing in or on the surface of cheese.

Fermentation of lactic and citric acids: In most cases the entire content of lactose is converted by lactic acid bacteria within 3-4 days. The aroma bacteria ferments citric acid to acetic acid, diacetyl and CO_2. Propionic acid bacteria converts lactates to propionic acid, acetic acid and CO_2 and also contribute to the formation of round eye holes particularly in Swiss cheese.

Proteolysis : The para casein molecules are split into shorter polypeptides and subsequent action of bacterial enzymes form amino acids, NH_3, CO_2, water and H_2S. All these processes happen simultaneously during ripening. However, complete breakdown of amino acid does not take place to any significant degree inside the cheese. All these processes proceed more or less rapidly at higher temperature (upto 25-30°C) and also at an high moisture level in the curd. the pH is very important for protein splitting and also for the ripening of cheese. The residual rennet action is quite high at pH 5.2 and also at 3% salt concentration in cheese. The pH values during 3 and 50 days, 9 and 24 mo in cheddar cheese are 5.05, 5.13, 5.32 and 5.38 respectively. This increase in pH is due to release of alkaline amino groups and NH_3. In hard cheeses when microorganisms die, the cells release introcellular enzymes and ripening progresses evenly. In quick ripened soft cheeses, proteolysis is through extracellular poroteinases released by various microorganisms which grow on the surface of the cheese. Mold cheeses undergo extensive proteolysis during ripening particularly under high moisture and fat content and becomes soft, velvetty and spreadable. Here also increases in pH during ripening makes casein soluble. The progress of cheese ripening is assessed by the extent and depth of protein splitting action. The extent of ripening is defined as % of total N of the cheese in water soluble compounds (Ripening index). Therefore, the value of the extent of ripening is a measure of how much of the casein has been converted to soluble form. The depth of ripening is defined as how large a part of the Total Nitrogen content of the cheese is found in the form of amino acids and NH_3 as judged by Formol titratable N (mostly free amino acids and NH_3). Fig 3.12 shows that in Blue cheese proteolysis is rapid due to the action of mould and yeasts, that in cheddar less than in semi-hard cheese. Low moisture, low pH and low storage temperature generally slows down proteolysis as seen in cheddar.

Lipolysis is also not extensive in the ripening process. Only a small degree of fat splitting is found, leading to well balanced flavour. The lower fatty acids have sharp and pungent flavour which is desirable to some degree in many cheese varieties. Fat is broken down by enzyme lipase. Lactic acid bacteria do not produce lipase and there is *normally* no lipase in rennet.

Aroma : The proportion of protein and fat changed during ripening is relatively small. Nearly 2/3rds of casein in ripened cheese exist as in-tact casein. So also most of the milkfat except some used up in lipolysis, the bacterial population changes continuously both in number and species although starter used has no lactobacilli, there is a rise in number of these organisms. The aroma arises mainly from volatile compounds released in the curd as ripening proceeds these include ester, fatty acids, aldehydes, ketones and alcohol amines, H_2S and NH_3. The aldehydes ketones and alcohols are probably most important. As ripening proceeds, the earlier flavour compounds may be used up and the harsher flavour disappears, and are replaced by more acceptable mellow flavour. In mold cheeses, lactic, malic isobutyric, caproic and capryllic acids predominate and contribute to flavour. As far as taste is concerned, in the amino acid pool some like methionine, histidine and lysine, tryptophane, leucine, iso-leucine, arginine, phenyl alanine, tyrosine are bitter; serine, glycine and alanine, hydroxyproline, proline, valine and threonine are sweet in taste. the peptides are bitter.

Ripening methods : In most cases cheese is first stored for some times at a fairly *high* temperature and when ripening has reached a suitable point, storage is continued at a lower temperature as shown below :

Name	**Fermentation temp°C**	**Room time(mo)**	**Ripening temp°C**	**Room time (mo)**
Emmental	18-25	2-3	10-14	2-6
Close textured cheese	15-20	1-4	8-12	2-6
Cheddar	-	-	8-12	2-6
Blue Veined	8-10	3-6*	2	3*
Camembert	10-14	2-4*	2	3*

*Weeks. Emmental is kept in pre ripening room at 12°C for 2 weeks before transfer to fermentation room.

Common ripening periods of some cheeses are shown below :

Type	Name	months	Type	Name	months
Very hard	Parmesan	24-48	Semi-soft	Brick	1.3-5
Hard	Cheddar	4-12	Mold ripened	Roque fort	3-6
Semi hard	Edam/ Gouda	1.5-5	Soft	Commen- bert	1-6

Curing temperature

Cold curing at 2°C with 75% R.H. for 3-12 mo. leads to mild flavours with less bacterial defect.

Warm curing at 12°C with 80% R.H. for 1/2-2 mo. causes sharp flavour and pronounced bacterial defect.

Typical data on some cheese varieties are given below :

	Parmesan	Emmental	Cheddar	Blue	Camenbert
Milk pasteurised °C			72	62	72
Homogenization				++	
Culture	S.Lactis + Thermophilus		DL+	DL+	
	Thermophilus + Propionic		0	Penicillium commenbert	Penicillium Commenbert

	Parmesan	Emmental	Cheddar	Blue	Camenbert
Curd grains mm	2	2	5	12	20
Scalding °C	55	52	38	-	-
Stirring h	1	2	1.5	-	-
Moulding					
air between grains			++	++	
cheddaring			++		
Pressing hr	72	20	20	-	-
Size kg	50	100	20	3	0.2
Salting					
brine days	21	3		2	4 h
dry			+		

(Cont'd)

% Nacl	2.5	0.8	1.7	3.3	1.5
Storage					
Temperature °C	10-15	10-25	10	9	10-15
months	24	10	5-10	2-3	1
surface ripening		+			++
Appearance	no opening	larger eyes	no opening	irregular eyes+mould	no opening +
Flavour	Sweet	Sweet	Clean acid	sharp	NH_3
Consistency	Brittle/ hard	Hard/ rubbery	Hard short	Soft short	Very soft
% wffs	40	50	52	62	70
pH min 24 h	5.1	5.3	5.0	4.7	4.5
ripe	5.6	5.8	5.5	6.5	8.0
% Protein hydrolysed					
Total	30	40	40	50	40
Amino acids	10	20	10	20	15
Fat hydrolyses	Low	Average	Low	High	Medium

Accelerated cheese ripening There is increasing interest in methods which may enable cheese manufacturers to produce matured flavoured products in a short time, thus yielding savings in both of capital cost and running costs for storage facilities. Another wish is to obtain a more cheese flavour. Practical methods currently in use to achieve the objectives are a) elevated storage temperature, b) use of modified starters, c) addition of lipolytic and proteolytic enzymes and d) adding intensive Biological Culture (IBC) or any combination of the four. Two groups of components in the cheese contribute to flavour development - the milkfat and the protein.

Milkfat breakdown during cheese ripening is carried out by esterases and lipases which are either endogenous to the milk or of microbial origin (psychrotrophic microorganisms and lactose starters). The lipids are hydrolysed to free fatty acids and partial glycerides. The free fatty acids contribute to a desirable flavour but too high concentrations of free fatty acids may induce rancid off-flavours in the cheese. A flavour enhancement induced solely by the acceleration of free fatty acid (FFA) formation is a Desirable effect in several, mostly soft cheese varieties, often produced from goat's milk. Of these can be mentioned Feta, but also Italian varieties such as Provolone, Romano and Parmesan use lipases for the purpose of flavour enhancement and accelerated ripening. Crude rennet pastes produced bar macerating or grinding the stomachs and stomach contents from young ruminant animals such as the calf, kid, goat or lamb. These contain both milk-clotting enzymes and lipolytic enzymes. The primary enzymic functions of pregastric lipases is the hydrolysis of triglycerides.

Triglycerides + water ---> Diglycerides + Free fatty acids. The short chain FFA are responsible for the *piccanto* and *peccorino* flavour profiles in Italian cheese.

The most commonly used lipase products are standardized powders prepared by desiccation of pregastric tissue prepared by a) grinding, frozen pregastric tissue, b) mixing with suitable carrier like whey or non-fat dry milk, c) drying under vacuum or freeze drying, d) milling the fine free flowing powder and e) adjusting strength and packaging (available chr.Hansen's Laboratory). They are used in making Provolone, Romano, Mozzarella, Parmesan and Feta cheese.

The lipases are added to cheese milk at any time after addition of starter culture but before addition of rennet. The lipase is suspended in 20 volumes of cold water and stirred for 15 min and then added to cheese milk. Usually 10-15 g are added to 100 / of milk.

Calf pregastric lipase generates a buttery and slightly peppery flavour Kid pregastric lipase gives a sharp, peppery *piccante* flavour Lamb pregastric lipase gives very strong piquant *peccorino* flavour.

Protein breakdown in *cheese ripening :* Lipases enhance the flavour, but they do not accelerate the physical body breakdown of the cheese. To achieve this proteolytic enzymes are necessary. The breakdown of casein is carried out by proteinases and peptidases, in a balanced way an order to obtain an optimum balance between the two groups of enzymes, thereby evolving a desirable taste and flavour of cheese and avoiding bitterness. The enzyme system with peptidases has to increase the pool of amino acids and peptides, which can be further metabolized into flavour compounds like amines, aldehydes, and sulphur containing compounds.

From the cheese slurries three *Lactococcus lactis* strains (subsp. lactic named CR-I and CR-III) and a third *Lactococcus lactis* subsp.*cremoris* (CR-II) were developed each contributing its own characteristic cheddar flavour to the overall cheese flavour. From each strains lactose-negative variants are developed for the production of a frozen direct Vat starter culture for direct addition in cheese vat. The CR-I enhances overall flavour intensity of cheese and when used with a fast, temperature insensitive starter strain, the cheese develops a balanced, clean, mild flavour in 6 weeks as compared with the use of normal starter. The CR-2 provides mellow, balanced flavour, similar to cheddar cheese in 6 weeks ripening.

The CR-3 gives sharp, harsh flavour. The combination of all three strains give flavour enhancement as well as flavour intensification.

The IBT Products Ltd., London have developed a range of products to accelerate ripening of cheese by adding Accelase (enzyme systems to reduce maturation time of full fat cheese and to improve flavour and texture of cheeses) during normal cheese making. Accelase AHC contains a mixture of exo-peptidases. Accelase FIST contains a mixture of peptidases from *Aspergillus Oryzei* as well as *Lactococcus lactis.* They are applied to the curd when salting. Accelase and Savorase systems are used at high levels for very fast ripening of high flavour block cheeses for forced ripening for 6-10 weeks. The reliability of accelerated ripening systems has improved markedly over recent years. Several enzyme systems are now available which are compatible with different manufacturing procedures.

Mechanization In cheese making : The present day cheese making systems involve handling large volumes of milk ranging from 250 000 to 10000 000 l/day and the reduction in the manual work and drudgery is logical. During the last 2 decades, all operations in the cheese making process have been mechanised, permitting the use of automatic control wherever it is required. The extent of mechanization depends on the economics of production and ranges from simple mechanical handling aids to automated systems controlled manually or programmed and supervised from a control computerised control station. Some of the mechanical systems in use since 1970 in UK, Australia, New Zealand and North America for hard, semi hard and semi-soft varieties are a) Bell-Siro cheese maker (Australia), b) the cheddar master (New Zealand), c) Alf-o-matic cheese maker for de-wheying, matting the curd, cheddaring, milling, salting, mellowing and block forming (Alfa Laval Cheddar cheese systems), d) the Damrow matting conveyor and milling equipment (USA) and f) the lactomatic system (Tasmania). The development is grouped as follows: a) curd formation, b) de-wheying, texture forming and handling, c) milling, salting/brining and/or mould filling and d) pressing and packaging.

1 Curd formation: The developments are mostly in the use of enclosed cheese vats of vertical or horizontal design, and improved cutting and stirring devices. The totally enclosed vats are available with Affa-Laval OST-II (Fig 3-15), the Damrow "double 0" vat, the Pasilac CT horizontal vat, the Tabel CST-III & IV. The MKT cheese vat and the APV Swiss cheese vat. Some of them have built in cutting and stirring devices (cutting curd in one direction and stirring in reverse direction ((Fig.3-15 to 3-16).

High speed vacuum packaging mechines of form, fill and seal type with longitudinal and cross cutting units to separate cheese portions have become popular for bulk and consumer package with heat-shrink cryovac bags or waxed cellulose laminate or Pukka film.

For soft cheese like Camembert, Feta, Mozzarella and Cottage cheese, continuous curd production can be done on equipment such as Alpma and Alfa Laval Alcurd coagulators. The coagulator handles both milk or UF concentrate. The unit consists of a sectional belt of semi-circular cross section on which all different manufacturing steps involved in traditional manufacture are carried out. Milk, to which rennet, starter and mould culture (where necessary) have been metered is filled into a section of rubberised flexible belt which is formed into a semi circular cross section by stainless steel walls. Milk is compartmentalised by the lowering of a stainless steel spacing plate, and coagulation proceeds when the belt slowly moves forward. The spacing plates are removed prior to cutting of the coagulum and return via an automatic cleaning systems, to the beginning of the belt for reuse. The belt advances the curd through automatic cutting devices which gives uniform curd cubes, and these pass the end of the belt system where some whey drainage occurs. The partially drained curd is filled through a tubular devise into block moulds, which are then conveyed, automatically stacked, turned and forwarded for demoulding salting and storage.

2 The de-wheying and texture forming operations: The Alf-O-matic

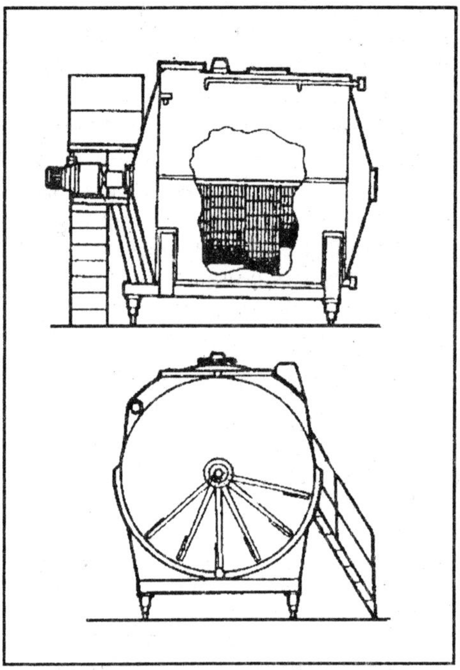

Fig 3-15 Totally enclosed horizontal cheese tank

cheese maker has enclosed design for de-wheying matting the curd, cheddaring, milling, salting, mellowing of the curd with separate tower block former for vacuum pressing. The Damrow Swiss cheese has provision for de-wheying, pressing, block cutting devices before transfer of blocks to brine tank. The MKT system is provided for de-wheying, pressing, cutting and transfer to brine tank. Pre-pressing towers are used in casiomatic-Tabel system, curd moulding by Stork and Pasilac/Silkeborg A/S prepressing towers.

3 For curd recovery system: The fine particles of curd are separated in the Russel Fines sifter, Azo fluid sifter, Damrow cheese Saver II and in AES systems (USA) using troughs with perforated linings, and vibrating separators.

4 Milling, salting, brining and mould filling: The Alf-O-matic and Damrow units have automatic milling/salting facilities. The brine tanks have salt dosing, equipment, temperature controller and provision for eccentric movement of racking unit in brine tank for keeping cheese in position.

5 Pressing and package: The use of block shaped perforated stainless steel or light plastic moulds has eliminated the use of cheese cloth. Feeding of curd is done by using vibrators and automatic weighing has helped to control weight. The pneumatic, hydraulic or mechanical spring presses have replaced lever type of presses. The demand for close textured cheese has led to the technique of vacuum pressing. The Ton press handles 1016 kg of curd in a large hoop consisting of a chamber of rectangular cross section with piston at the bottom for compression and extrusion of the pressed curd at the top. The cheese blocks are cut by mechanical cutters from variously shaped blocks and film packed (Fig 3.14)

3-25 Judging and grading of cheese: Cheese is graded by making use of human senses coupled with chemical, physical and microbiological analysis. Chemical analysis establishes whether a particular cheese satisfies current regulations with reference to moisture, fat and other additives. The grading points vary from.country to country and with types of cheeses also. For instance, Denmark follows 15 points - 11-15 good, 9-10 average, 1-8 fair and 0-6 poor. The ADSA scale for cheddar is flavour and aroma 45, body and texture 30, finish and appearance 15 and colour 10, making a total of 100.

For examination, the cheese is tempered, sampled and the colour, appearance, body, texture and flavour are examined by a group of judges. For a high grade cheese, the requirements are: Colour uniform and light amber to ivory; finish and appearance smooth, unbroken rind, clear cut and without openings; body somewhat elastic, bendable and not hard as plug; texture compact, homogenous, free from openings, fissures, cracks or holes; *flavour* pleasing, mild, salty, pleasant sensation in the mouth leaving pleasant after taste like nuts.

Some of the defects noticeable are: in *colour,* bleached, unnatural, mottled, wavy; *finish and appearance,* cracked rind, rind rot, mouldy surface, uneven on the top, scaly or cracked paraffin; body crumbly, corky, dry, rubbery, soft, wet pasty, greasy: texture yeasty holes, gassy pin holes, mechanical opening; *flavour* bitter, sour, high acid, rancid, mouldy. Grading is a complex matter as it requires the assessment of not only the extent to which the cheese satisfies the general demands of the cheese variety, but also the specific demands of the consumers (market) for whom it is intended.

Processed cheese: Cheese with the exception of soft cheese is rarely consumed in a totally fresh condition. It is enjoyed at a stage of ripening particularly appreciated by the consumer. The pleasurable ripening stages are the characteristics of particularly rennet cheeses. Every cheese undergoes a ripening process depending on its size, circumference, speed of draining etc. Above all, ripening is a function of the original moisture content and temperature of storage. The ripening process does not stop

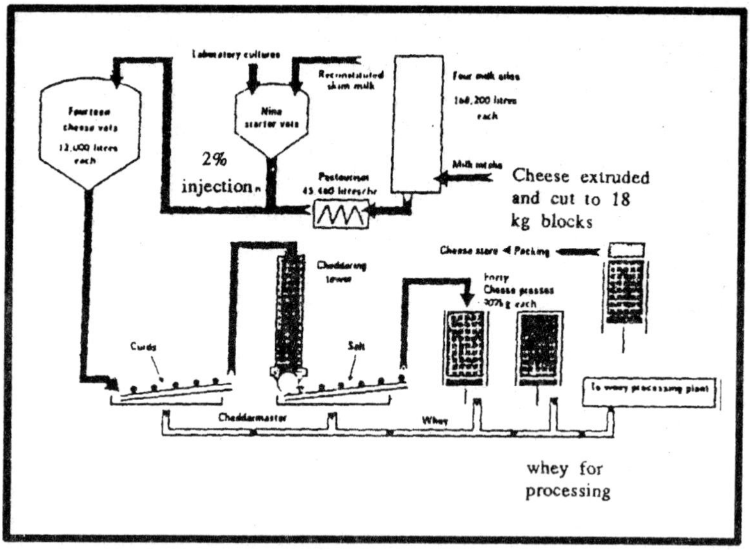

Fig 3-14 Processing line of large scale cheese production

when the desired optimum flavour is reached for the taste of consumer. It carries on further in an accelerated degree with more or less decomposition of protein and fat also (mould cheeses). A high increase in protein degradation causes naturally a) a loss in weight and b) lessening in food value due to detrimental changes in organoleptic characteristics. Finally, the cheese reaches a stage which makes it unfit for consumption. Because of this, controlled protein decomposition all types of cheese including hard variety become unsuited for long storage. To overcome this situation, soft cheese like Camembert was given in-can pasteurization which became a success. Early 1900 Dutch cheese in-cans was heat treated and nearly a million cans of 300 g content was exported overseas. this was successful for soft and semi-hard cheese. Kraft introduced processed Cheddar cheese in 2.2 kg cans for Army supply from which the basic colloidal gel-so-get conversion of ripened cheese emerged by the use of emulsifying salts. This invention in early 1900 and its advantages is a very important step forward in -the dairy field. It (a) guaranteed enhanced keeping quality, (b) made possible to pre-cook young cheese (at a time of milk glut) which cannot be stored for any length of time due to lack of cold store and use it as stable reserve, (c) permitted easy transport of hot fluid mass of processed cheese by pump and pipe lines, (d) permitted hygienic packaging and (e) effective surface pasteurization by contact of hot fluid cheese on the inside of the foil. It led to the creation of unexpected possibilities for different types of cheese as cited below: a) manufacture of block cheese in slice size portions b) mixing various types of cheese differing in pH, age, flavour and consistency. c) permits addition of milk constituents like whey, butter or curd. d) permits use of fruit juices, jam, coffee, chocolate, dietetic substances and vitamins e) enables conservation of sterilized cheese in cans f) making spreadable processed cheese from hard, semi-hard or soft cheese of similar flavour g) permits manufacture of dried processed cheese for sprinkling on soups or spread by addition of water; preparation of bakery goods (flavoured biscuits); as binding agent for sausage goods, mayonnaise and soups; h) making dried processed rennet curd for use in confectionery (as substitute for meringues, biscuit base.

The advantage of finished packaged processed cheese are: a) a long storagability, b) elimination of surface infection from microbes. c) refrigerated storage made less crucial, d) eliminates cutting and weighing of cheese in small units, e) eliminates rind waste, f) avoids unpleasant flavour retaining good digestibility specially as diet food g) attractive packaging for display and h) easy availability.

Basics: Ripened cheese can be stabilized only by creating a colloidal chemical intermediary stage of the casein sol by heat treatment. This involvement of the intermediary fluid state which is called processing is dependent on the participation of ion exchange action of the emulsifying salt. The process must change the insoluble para casein sol with the aid of suitable emulsifying salt and by the application of heat into homogenous, flowing condition where the cheese mass is effectively pasteurized, accurately filled and protected by injection into the containers. During the cooling process, the mass is changed back to gel, which differs however from the original gel by its improved homo geniety and bacteriological stability. The intermediate sol and the gel produced at the end of the process can vary in consistency, texture and other characteristics in different types of processed cheese. The consistency and texture of sol resulting from processing and that of the resultant sol are first determined by the quality of raw cheese and the chemical mechanical and thermal forces which influence the casein. The various forces which are activated in the gel-sol-gel processes are a) emulsifying salts, b) water, c)temperature, d) agitation, e) homogenisation,of duration of processing and g) added whey solids, precooked cheese, butter and other additives. Among the electrolytes, the univalent and bivalent positive ions such as sodium and calcium as well as multivalent anions like phosphates and citrates are important. The univalent Na ions and the bivalent Ca ions are antagonistic to casein. The sodiumion acts dispersively, dissolving, peptising and swelling, whereas the Ca ions condenses polymerizes peptides, causing visible coagulation. Both are in equilibrium and stabilise the protein. Sodium salts of multivalent anions (citrates and phosphates) can cause disturbance in protein complex. It acts on Ca containing colloid system and exchange bivalent anion for equivalent cation Na. It removes bivalent cation and doubles the dispersive action of univalent anion. It thus inactivates bivalent Ca which enhances the stability of the cheese gel.

Emulsifying salts Three types of emulsifying salts commonly in use are monophosphates, poly phosphates and polyphosphate citrate. The most important property of the salt is a) its ability to make casein soluble by formation of homogenous sol (varies with different salts), b) ability to peptise casein and c) stability in consistency and keeping quality of cheese (buffering and regulating action). These are evident in monophosphate, diphosphate and citrate. The bactericidal and bacteriostatic action are less evident with citrates and monophosphates, but polyphosphates exhibit better keeping quality effect on cheese.

Every kind of cheese is characterised by its protein content. The absolute in-tact casein content in finished cheese determines its structure. The amount of emulsifying salt depends on the intact casein content of cheese. When the in-tact casein content in cheese declines, the need for emulsifying salt also becomes less, say 3.6% for 30% in-tact casein and 3.0% for 24% intact casein. This will be the range for most of the hard and semi hard cheeses commonly used for processing.

Some useful combination of different cheeses ripened for different periods for processing are shown below:

Type	Young %	medium %	Ripe%
Block cheddar	40	40	20
Firm slice cheese	50	40	10
Spreadable 20-45% FDM	30	50	20

Cheese spread 50-65% FDM	60	40	-
Processed cheese slices	60	30	10

pH has the most decisive influence on consistency and structure. The pH range of processed cheese is relatively limited and lies essentially between 5.4 and 6.2. A decrease in pH causes sometimes coagulation. A good process cheese can have pH of 5.4 to 5.7 and for a spreadable cheese 5.7 to 5.9.

Water: Although the ripened cheese contains some amount of moisture, it is firmly bound up in the molecules and 'could not be sufficient in most cases to dissolve the salt added to peptise casein. Depending on the protein content of cheese, fat and emulsifying salt sufficient water must be used for getting a good homogenous processed structure. Too little water may cause fat separation. Calculated amount of water in 2 portions one towards the beginning and the rest towards the end of processing completes the creaming action more quickly.

Heating : The casein gel to a homogenous sol is best done by heat between ranges 70°C to 75°C. For block processed cheese heating between 70° to 75°C for 4-6 min is enough. Spreadable processed cheese requires higher heat treatmeht upto 90-95°C for 8-15 min.

Agitation : For perfect dispersion suitable 3 speed agitators are used. For block processed cheese slow agitation at 60-90 rpm is enough; for spreads fast agitation around 120-150 rpm.

Completing a process cheese mix with cheddar of different ages

	Cheese/age	***DM%***	***FDM%***	***Absolute fat %***
	Cheese 3 mo	*65.4*	*44.8*	*29.3*
	Cheese 4 mo	*64.3*	*50.4*	*32.4*
	Cheese 8 mo	*68.0*	*52.6*	*35.7*
	Butter	*82.0*	*82.0*	*82.0*
43	*kg 3 mo*	*28.12*		*12.60*
20	*kg 4 mo*	*12.86*		*6.48*
30	*kg 8 mo*	*20.40*		*10.71*
7	*kg Butter*	*5.74*		*5.74*
100	*kg mix*	*67.12*		*35.53*
3	*kg emulsifier*	*3.00*		*3.00*
103	*kg*	*70.12*		*38.53*

Fat in Dry Matter % (38.53/70.12)x100		54.94
Yield Dry Matter (DM) kg	70.12	
DM Finish cheese	55.0	
kg cheese yield (70.12/54.94) x 100 = 127.63		
kg Raw cheese + salt	103.00	
kg water needed	24.63	

Preparation of processed cheese consists in a) bringing different types of cheeses from curing room to the tempering room (16-20°C) and retaining for 2 days, b) sampling cheese for analysis, c) deciding quantum of blending varieties based on analysis, flavour and aroma, d) cleaning and removal of paraffin, inedible portion by scraping, e) quartering and conveying to grinder for shreading, cutting, milling, roller refining etc., f) calculated weighed addition of cheese, emulsifier salt, water (in 2 portions) and additives like essence, permitted spices etc., g) heating slowly in a kettle through jacket with slow agitators to desired temperature and time, h) observing for suitable consistency and gloss in cheese, i) stopping heating and stirring, j) transfer of hot product to automatic filler and sealer in packages of different weights and shapes, k) cooling the packs slowly at 18-20°C and transfer to cold room at 2-4°C. A good processed cheese should contain not more than 10 000 microbes yeast and mould 60 aerobic spores 200 and anaerobic spores 100/g with no coliform in 0.1 g.

The melting kettles vary in size from 25 to 75 kg for batch operations. Some kettles can be closed air tight with lid and melting can be done under vacuum wherein unclean flavour (with some agreeable flavour also) are removed. In large factories, the hot cheese can be piped to packing machines and several cooling arrangements are provided to cool cheese.

Definition of processed cheese : As per PFA, 1984 processed cheese is a product obtained by heating cheese with permitted emulsifier' and/or stabilizers, viz., citric acid/sodium citrate/sodium salts of orthophosphoric acid and polyphosphoric acids with or without condiments and acidifying agent viz., vinegar, lactic acid, acetic acid, citric acid, phosphoric acid. Processed cheese may contain not more than 4% of anhydrous permitted emulsifier and/or stabilizers provided that the anhydrous inorganic salts in no case exceed 3% of the finished product. It should not contain more than 47% moisture. The milkfat should not be less than 40% of the dry matter. It may contain 0.1% sorbic acid and/or its Na, K, Ca salts (calculated as sorbic acid) or 0.1% nisin either singly or in combination.

Specification for processed cheese foods/and spreads

Characteristics	Processed cheese	Cheese foods+	Cheese spread+
Moisture (max)	47	44	60
Fat/Dry matter (min)	40	23	20

*PFA 1984 +IS:2785, 1964

In cheese food part of its solids are added as cream, milk, skim milk, whey or albumin from cheese whey. pH need not be adjusted lower than 5 with added acids.

Cheese spread is prepared by mixing with the aid of heat one or more varieties of hard cheese with or without the following ingredients into a homogenous plastic mass which is spreadable at 21°C. Carob bean gum, gum tragacanth, gelatin and algin may be added in amounts not exceeding 0.8% of total weight of the product. The pH is lowered to 4.0. Heat treatment is not less than 66°C/30 s. Before heating the following ingredients are added - a) dairy ingredients, b) emulsifying agents, c) acidiying agents (pH not below 4.0), d) sweetening agents, e) edible common salt, f) annato or carotene, g) spices or flavours permitted (PFA 1975).

The variables for the preparation of processed spreadable cheese spread and slicing processed cheese are given below:

Variables	Processed cheese spread	Slice processed cheese
Cheese		
age	young+middle+ripe	mostly young
Relative		
casein %	60-75	75-95
Emulsifier		
Polyphosphate	low m.w. for creaming	high m.w.for struc ture/non creamy
Water		
amount %	20-45	10-25
addition	in portions	once
Temperature		
°C/min	85-90/8-15	80-85/4-8

pH	5.7-5.9	5.4-5.6
agitation	rapid	slow
filling min	15-30	5-15
cooling	rapid 15-30 min	slow 10-20 h
Treatment	Intense	light

Legal standards : As per PFA Rules (1984), hard cheese shall contain moisture not more than 43% and milkfat not less than 42% in the dry matter. It may contain 0.1 % sorbic acid or its Na, K, Ca salts or 0.1 % nisin.

It is a product obtained by draining after coagulation of milk with a harmless coagulating agent under the influence of harmless bacterial cultures. It shall not contain any ingredient not found in milk, except coagulating agent; NaCl, $CaCl_2$ (anhydrous) not exceeding 0.02% by weight, annatto or carotene; and may contain certain emulsifiers and/or stabilizers namely citric acid, sodium citrate or sodium salts of orthophosphoric acid and polyphosphoric acid not exceeding 0.2% by weight; wax used for covering the outer surtac a should not contain anything harmful to the health. In case wax is coloured only permitted food colours may be used.

Nutritive value : Cheese is a highly nutritious food; a rich source of protein with all essential amino acids for growth and replacement of tissues; a good source of fat having most of the essential unsaturated fatty acids and Ca, P and an excellent source of fat soluble vitamins and a good source of water soluble vitamins, a poor source of lactose; highly digestible and a good source of concentrated form of energy (1.68 MJ/ 100 g). For those who have poor lactose intolerance the cheese is an important food product.

Chapter 3

BUTTER

The production of creamery butter in India is estimated to be 6% of the total world production and 11% of the milk used for dairy products.

Basic principles in butter making : Butter is a product having similar constituents of milk but with different distribution. In butter making, the milk fat is concentrated roughly 20 times. In other words, milk with 4% fat and intermediate churning-cream with 40% milk-fat finally results in butter with 80-83% milk-fat. In this transformation, the constituents like protein, lactose, minerals (MSNF) and r gets reduced as shown below :

Composition	Fat	Protein	Lactose	Minerals	Citric acid	Salt	Water
Milk	4.0	3.4	4.6	0.8	0.2	-	87.0
Butter	82.0	....	1.5(MSNF)	....	....	1.0	15.5

The concentration of fat takes place in 3 steps, a) during cream separation where skim milk is removed, b) during churning of cream where the butter milk is drained off and c) during working where excess water is eliminated. Due to the difference in the densities of milkfat and skim milk, application of centrifugal force on milk causes physical separation as skim milk and cream having 10 times concentrated milkfat. Fat and other associated lipid materials are: present in milk as small individual globules predominantly in liquid state it 37°C. Nearly 3000 billion globules may be present in a liter of milk. Attached to each fat globule is a layer of protein and phospholipid material. Due to this adsorbed layer formation of larger globules are prevented. In other words, the milk is, an oil-in-water emulsion. When milk or cream is churned, the mechanical agitation causes the breaking of film covering the globules and then the fat of the individual globules continue to form a cohesive continuous mass with some dispersed fat globules as butter leaving the separated serum as buttermilk. The oil-in-water emulsion of cream is converted to the desired water-in-oil emulsion of butter, a phenomenon is known as the inversion of a colloid. (Fig 4-5).

The butter becomes ready for consumption only after it attains certain hardness which is a structural change in butter. The fat which is in a ,continuous phase has to be crystallised in a specific pattern and this is aided by storage of butter at 5°C in a cold store before it is released for sale. Factors like the composition of milkfat, temperature, treatment of cream, the working temperature, the working method and the temperature of storage help in providing the proper hardness to the finished butter.

Batch method of butter making : The main equipment used is the churn which consists of a barrel, adjustable drive and all assembled in one unit. The churn is made of stainless steel and the inside sand blasted to prevent sticking of butter. The barrel is of short length with large diameter, either cylindrical or conical in shape. Baffles are fitted internally to improve agitation. The baffles raise the cream in horizontal churn when the churn rotates and when butter is formed, continued raising and dropping gives necessary working. The churning speed can be varied from 60 to 100 rpm and working speed 25-500 rpm. The speed can be varied py special changing device fitted with drive mechanism and clutch. Provision is made for chilled water spray arrangement on the outer surface of the churn to control the temperature. In horizontal churn butter is dropped into a wheel mounted trolley placed below the opening in the barrel of the churn. In conical churns pressure is applied for expelling butter from the churn and pumping through a special pump direct to the packaging unit. The barrel is provided with air-vent, sight glass, buttermilk outlet, opening for inlet of cream, outlet for cleaning solutions. For getting close texture of butter and reducing air content provision is also available for vacuum build up during rotation. Cream can also be sucked into the churn by vacuum.

Manufactur ing steps : The usual procedure is as follows:- a) reception, testing of milk and chilling to 5°C, b) cream separation at 35-40°C, c) neutralization of cream to 0.12-15% lactic acid, d) pasteurization of cream at 87-90°C/ 15 s, e) cooling of cream to 7°C in summer or 10°C in winter and held for 4 h or preferably overnight to effect crystallization of milk-fat (cream ripening optional), f) cleaning and sanitizing the churn, g) Pumping the cream into the churn, h) adding colour, i) rotating the churn until butter granules are formed, (breaking point) and get the size of popcorn, j) draining the buttermilk, k) rinsing the buttermilk from the interior surface of churn with clean cold water, l) washing the butter with sufficient water to bring total volume to that of original cream, m) draining. the wash water, n) adding required salt, o) working the butter sufficiently to bring granules and water into compact mass, p) sampling and testing for moisture, q) adding water if insufficient (below 16%) or permitting escape from the churn if test reveals high moisture, r) working the butter until it becomes firm and waxy, s) sampling and testing for moisture, salt and curd, t) removing the butter from churn, u) packing and storage at 5°C, v) after unloading the butter, the churn can be loaded

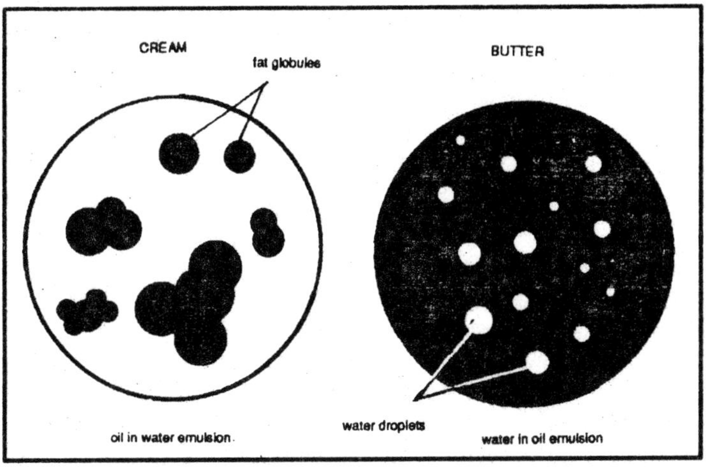

Fig 4-5 Phase inversion during churning of cream

with cream for the next batch of butter, w) At the end of the day's operation the churn is given chemical cleaning and sterilization.

Care : The door of the butter room should always be closed. Line testing is done to trace contamination of microorganisms and prevent the defect if any, the rail guard should be kept in position when the churn is in motion. The butter colour should be stored in cool place and dairy salt in air tight containers.

Operation of churn includes a) closing down door and butter milk valve, b) positioning sight glass along with cream pipe line coming from cream tank, c) opening sight glass and connecting cream pipe into the churn, d) opening cream valve of cream storage tank e) starting of cream pump and permitting 50% of load in the churn, f) adding calculated quantity of butter colour through sight glass opening, g) closing the sight glass, h) rotating the churn at 28-32 rpm a few revolutions and releasing air from churn, i) churning at 28-32 rpm till butter granules attains proper size, j) stopping the churn and draining buttermilk through strainer, k) washing butter grains twice with pasteurized chill water, i) pre-working at 4-6 rpm/15 min with partial closing of churn door, m) rotating churn at 8-12 rpm/10-15 min and stopping churn to bring down moisture to 14-14.5%, n) adding calculated salt and main working at 8-12 rpm under vacuum and with chilled water on, o) testing for moisture and adding required amount of water and continuing working at 16-18 rpm under vacuum, p) unloading the butter into the trolleys, by placing the trolley below the churn and opening the door. By careful rotation of churn (4-6 rpm) butter slides down smoothly into the trolley. q) wing trolley to package room for immediate packing and storage at 5°C for hardening.

Quality of cream : The cream may be of good bacteriological quality. Cream with antibiotics or disinfectants is not suited for making sour cream butter. In cold stored milk psychrotrophic organisms produce lipolytic enzymes which can survive pasteurization temperature and cause rancidity defects in butter. Chilling raw milk at 4°C immediately on reception and pasteurization earlier than 24 h after arrival is important.

Heat treatment : The churning cream is given intense heat treatment say 87°C/15 s or more is necessary to minimise defects in butter. High heat treatment a) destroys unwanted microorganisms, b) provides perfect growth conditions 'for the bacterial culture, c) inhibits rancidity in butter due to destruction of lipase, d) destroys bacteriophages and help in cream ripening, and e) releases hydrogen sulphide groups which reduces tallowiness in butter on storage. More severe heat treatments should be avoided, as the higher the temperature, the greater the migration of copper from the milk serum into the milkfat. Increasing the level of copper in milkfat makes it more susceptible to the development of oxidative rancidity, formation of cooked flavour and can reduce shelf life of butter.

Vacreation : If the cream has any undesirable flavouring substances of a volatile nature, entering milk from feeds, vacuum treatment may be included before pasteurization. Any flavour gets bound in the fat will be transmitted to the butter unless removed. The cream is first preheated to 78°C and then led under pressure to a vacuum chamber where the pressure corresponds to a boiling point of 62°C. The reduced pressure causes volatile

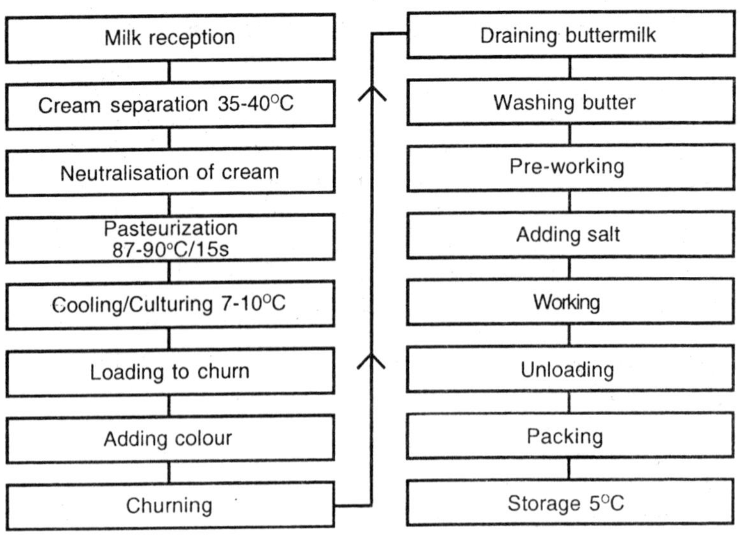

Fig 4-1 Flow diagram of traditional butter making from ripened cream

flavouring and aroma matter to escape in the form of gas as the cream is cooled by expansion. After this, the cream is returned to the pasteurizer. The vacreator was developed mainly for the treatment of cream collected from a variety of producers at the farm in New Zealand and Australia. Indiscreminate vacreation is not desirable as this treatment affects the consistency of butter and yield.

Heat treatment of cream prior to churning. Cream is given a program of heat treatment mainly to control the crystallization of milkfat and secure right consistency to the resultant butter. Consistency involves properties such as hardness, plasticity, viscosity and spreadability of butter. Some important fatty acids in milkfat triglycerides are shown below:

	Fatty acid	**% of total fatty adds**	**melting point °C**
Saturated	Lauric	2.0-5.0	+ 43.6
	Myristic	7.0-11.0	+ 53.8
	Palmitic	25.0-29.0	+ 62.6
	stearic	7.0-13.0	+ 69.3
Unsaturated	Oleic	30-40	+14.0

The four most abundant glycerides of fatty acids in butter are myristic, palmitic, stearic and oleic acid. The first 3 are solids and the last is a liquid at room temperature. The relative amounts of these can vary considerably and hardness of fat is influenced by these. Larger amounts of saturated fatty acid glycerides like palmitic and stearic acids in butter make butter hard. More of oleic acid glycefrdes lead to soft butter. Indirectly iodine value which is a measure of oleic acid content will indicate whether the butter is soft or hard. This value normally varies from 24 to 45. When cows are on pasture the butter may have high iodine value showing higher oleic acid content indicating soft butter. Animals fed more of concentrates may lead to a butterfat with more of saturated fatty glycerides. Normally the iodine value for optimum hardness in butter should be around 32 to 37. The quick-estimation of refractive index of milkfat can also be used to assess the hardness of fat.

If cream is given the same heat treatment, it will be the chemical composition of milkfat that will reflect the hardness of butter. A soft milkfat leads to soft greasy butter and hard milkfat a hard and stiff butter. If heat treatment is modified to suit iodine value, the consistency of butter can be regulated.

To reduce the fat loss in cream as much as possible, before churning, crystallization of milkfat in each and every fat globules is very important.

Hence, cream after pasteurization must be deep cooled to 5°C and held at that temperature for atleast 4 h or longer for extensive growth of crystal network to enable stable crystal modification of milk fat before commencement of churning. If churning recovery is the only factor for consideration, deep cooling after pasteurization would be preferable. For sweet cream butter, the cream is warmed to churning temperature around 10°C in summer and 13°C in winter.

If consistency of finished butter has to be regulated stepwise cooling of cream may be necessary. The butterfat in butter is present as dispersed fat globules and continuous fat phase. The size and composition of the continuous fat phase determines the consistency of butter. If continuous fat phase is large, the butter will be soft, and if it is small, the butter will be hard.

Treatment for hard winter fat : The cream after pasteurization is cooled to 8°C, held for 2 h with stirring when large number of small crystals of fat are formed. It is heated to 19°C with warm water and cultured. After incubation for about 8 h the cream thickens (pH 5.2). The cream is further cooled to 16°C. Prior to churning the cream is cooled to 12°C. By modifying the cooling programme, the size of the crystals in fat globules and the nature of the continuous fat phase are regulated. Initially rapid mass crystallization binds the fat from the liquid continuous phase to their surface. When the temperature of cream is raised to 19°C, bulk of the crystals melt leaving only hard fat crystals to grow larger.

When the temperature is lowered to 16°C the hardest fat is fixed in crystal form and the rest liquified. During holding at 16°C, fat with mp 16°C or higher are added to the crystals with little absorption of low melting liquid fat which can be pressed out in continuous phase during churning and working.

Treatment for soft summer fat : Cream after pasteurization is cooled to 19°C and inoculated. After 5-8 h when pH reaches 5.2 cream thickens. The cream is cooled to 16°C and held for 5 h till pH becomes 4.8. Further rapid crystallization of fat glycerides at 8°C binds much of the liquid fat within the globules, thereby decreasing the continuous fat phase and making it hard. The cream is then warmed to 10°C for churning.

Since the iodine value of milkfat varies in different months of the year, the programme of cooling treatment shown below may be applied.

Iodine Value	First Cooling°C	Heating souring°C	Ripening °C	Starter %
Less 28	8	21	20	1
28-29	8	21	16	2

(Cont'd)

30-31	8	19	13	5
32-34	6	19	12	5
35-37	6	17	11	6
38-39	6	15	10	7
Over 40	20	8	11	5

The consistency related programme can be modified.

Ripening of cream : Bacterial ripening influences aroma, CO_2 production and contribute flavour to butter. It also acts as bacterial preservative. The mildly cultured butter has a pH 5.2 and that of uncultured sweet cream butter pH 6.0. The ripening depends on inoculum temperature and time. Generally 3 to 6% butter starter is used. Incubation temperature ranges from 18-22°C followed by ripening temperature of 14 to 16°C. The incubation time of culturing and ripening of cream varies from 12 to 20 h. Cooling from incubation to ripening temperature depends on pH 5.2. Active DL culture consisting of S. lactis, S. cremoris, S. diacetylactis and L.cremoris is used.

S. diacetylactis may vary from 0.6 to 13.0% and L. citrovorum content from 0.3 to 6.0% of the total count. The proportional relationship between aroma producers depend on growth conditions. The aroma substances are acetic acid, CO_2 and diacetyl. The diacetyl concentration depends on availability of O_2. The active cultures must produce acid rapidly (count 1000 million/ ml). A one% of inoculum at 20°C should produce about 0.27% lactic

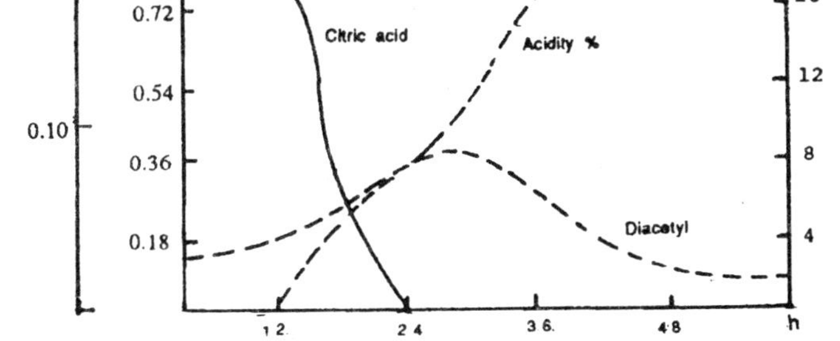

Fig 4-2 Acid and aroma development in skim milk at 20°C with DL-starter

acid in 7 h. Skim milk heat treated 90°C/15 min can be used as substrate for the starter. The range of diacetyl content of bulk starter, cultured cream, fresh and stored butter are 1-10, 2-15, 2.0- 4.0 and 0.5-2.5 mg/kg. A concentration of 1-2 mg of diacetyl/kg butter is enough for pleasant aroma. (Fig 4-2)

The ripening and heat treatment of cream to get optimal consistency in butter takes place simultaneously. The ripening tanks are normally triple shelled insulated of stainless steel. The heating and cooling media are made by circulation between the shells. These tanks have reversible scraper agitators for efficient storage. Heating and cooling are done gradually to get desired consistency in butter. The cream is suited for churning when acidity is around 0.9% of lactic acid.

Alternative process of culturing the butter : In the production of ripened butter, the ripening process, adds to production costs and migration of copper to the fat increases the susceptibility of butter to oxidative rancidity. Addition of salt to the ripened butter causes further destabilization. Acid buttermilk also presents a disposal problem, as it can rarely be converted economically into other dairy products and so most often be sold at nominal cost for animal feed. To overcome the problems with acid buttermilk, the Netherlands Institute for Dairy Research developed a process which is referred as NIZO method or modified Indirect *Biological Culturing* (IBC) method. This process used sweet cream which is churned to yield sweet buttermilk (suited for further processing) and unripened butter grains with low moisture (13.0-13.5%).

Starter culture and concentrated lactic acid preparation (80% acid in amount corresponding to 0.056% to regulate pH to 5.2) are added to the unworked butter which is then worked and packed in the normal way. The characteristic flavour and aroma develop in the butter on storage to give a similar product like traditional butter. The aroma is obtained by adding special D-culture having 20-25% S. diacetylactis at 2.0%. The addition of starter at upto 2.0% of the butter is not sufficient to reduce the pH of the butter to less than 5.3 as required by Dutch regulations. This was overcome by adding a culture concentrate together with the leuconostoc culture. The diacetyl content may range from 80-100 mg/l. To convert acetaldehyde and get mild flavour L. cremoris bulk starter is also added to get mild flavour. The storage life of this butter is as good as that made from cultured cream.

Preparation of D-bulk starter : It is made by a) using skim milk enriched to 16% MSNF, b) inoculating with deep frozen freeze dried special D-culture with 20-25°!0 of S. diacstylactis, c) incubating at 22°C, d) stabilizing diacetyl formed by cooling to 5°C, e) adding 80% lactic acid solution corresponding to 3.7% of starter, which reduces the pH to 3.3 and stabilising the diacetyl and f) aerating the starter for a while. The starter can be stored for 2-3 days at 5°C.

The use of starter organisms for flavour development can also be avoided by using a flavour based on diacetyl, preferably a distillate from a specially cultured skim milk (Hansen's 15 x.starter distillate). Acidity can be increased by the addition of lactic acid. Salt which normally inhibits the starter organisms may be added to the mixture of distillates and lactic acid to help flavour to butter.

The churning process Churning of butter into larger grains helps the draining off of the buttermilk. To avoid over churning particularly in summer when the butter is soft, the churning speed is reduced by half after the grains have formed. If butter is to be washed, the grains should be smaller, about the size of the pea. This will provide a larger grain surfrace area for removal of more buttermilk during washing. The churning time is around 45-60 min in summer and about 30 min in winter. In summer temperature of churning is around 6-10°C and in winter 10-16°C.

Buttermilk When fat is concentrated in butter grains,most of the remaining constituents are separated as buttermilk. Small sized fat globules finds way into the buttermilk. The composition of buttermilk depends on a) amount of water added during churning, b) composition of milk solids not fat (MSNF) and c) the churning recovery. SNF in buttermilk depends on the quality of milk used. It contains no citric acid as this has been fermented into aroma compounds and CO_2 by aroma producing bacteria. Butter churning recovery leads to a lower fat content in the buttermilk. The average composition of buttermilk is:

Protein	3.4%	Fat (triglycerides)	0.4%
Lactose/lactic acid	4.6%	Phospholipids (lecithin)	0.1%
Mineral salts	0.7%	Water	90.8%

Buttermilk when fresh has a clean aromatic smell and taste. It has special nutritional value since precipitated casein particles are small and easy to digest. The phospholipids contain choline and Polyun-saturated fatty acids. However, it is prone to oxidation. It is no longer widely used for direct consumption and finds its way for feeding calves.

Churning recovery : The fat content of the buttermilk must be as low as possible ,to maximise fat outturns in butter. Various methods have been in use to assess the loss. The fat content in buttermilk is influenced by the water used to rinse tanks and. pipes and by the original fat content of the cream. However, it cannot give a correct evaluation of the churning recovery. The fat loss can be reasonably accurately assessed by making use of churning recovery value (CRV). This reflects the % of fat in cream lost in buttermilk.

$$CRV = \frac{(100-1.2x\%\ \text{fat in cream}) \times \%\ \text{fat in buttermilk}}{\%\ \text{fat in cream}}$$

For example, if the % fat in cream is 38 and that of buttermilk 0.5, the CRV is (100-1.2x38) x 0.5/38= 0.75. Both cream and buttermilk should be sampled properly. The buttermilk is sampled only after 15 kg of buttermilk have passed through the buttermilk valve. The sample should be taken immediately after the churn has been stopped. Normally CRV of 0.8 is considered satisfactory. High fat cream leads to a better CRV than low fat cream. High churning temperatures in summer and low churnipg temperatures in winter should be avoided for maximum CRV.

Just as it happens in cream separation, it is mainly the small sized fat globules are lost in churning. This may be due to the difficulty in pressing out the liquid fat during churning to enable them to stick to the walls of froth bubbles and take part in forming butter grains as reported by Rahn. The figures given below makes it clear

dia.fat globules	μm	0-1	23	4-5	6-8
fat globules in butler	0	68	93	99	

Washing in butter : Washing removes buttermilk residue on the surface of the butter grains. This is done after the buttermilk has been drained off by either loading water or to 2 degrees lower than churning temperature into the churn or by spraying the grains with water and then rotating the churn briefly before draining water. Fe and Mn contents of wash water must be low to prevent catalytic oxidation of butter. Butter is most vulnerable to spoilage by water borne bacteria. The most dangerous are those that are strongly lipolytic, proteolytic and grow at low temperatures. Many spoilage organisms are more resistant to chlorine than are pathogens. Dairy water can be chlorinated to high levels, even upto 20 mg/l, with safety and very high levels of chlorine (upto 100 mg/l) in wash water have little or no effect on butter flavour. In good commercial practice, washing of butter grains should only be done if a) the cream had for some reason inadequately cooled or b) cream having off-flavours was being churned. In the later case, washing can only reduce the level of off-flavour, if the causative agent is water soluble.

The *advantages* of washing are a) since buttermilk solids are removed, it assures better bacteriological keeping quality, b) regulating working temperature and thereby hardness of butter and c) reduces problems in reducing the moisture content during washing to below 16% by washing prior to working (because the protein in buttermilk residue has greater binding capacity than fat).

The *disadvantages* : The average MSNF of non-washed butter and washed butter are 1.6% and 0.7%. The MSNF must be replaced with fat and hence washing yields less outturn of butter. Besides intensive washing eliminates 30-40% of the diacetyl with the buttermilk residue and consequently the aroma of butter gets reduced,

Salting : The purpose of salting is to influence flavour, keeping quality and over-run. The quality of salt should be good, pure white in colour and if it dissolves completely, it must give clear solution with no sediment, coarse grained and free from lumps, pass through IS-sieve-85 with bacterial counts less than10/g. The salt must be stored in closed container in a clean dry room to prevent contamination and lumping (IS:1845, 1961). Usually, common salt is added at the rate of 2% of butterfat. The amount of salt to be added to butter in a churn is calculated as follows: Fat in churn 500 kg, and butter to have 2.0% salt. Assuming no loss during working and butter to have 80% fat, the salt needed per 100 kg fat = (2.0x100)/80 = 2.5 kg: Since churn contains 500 kg fat, salt needed = (500x2.5)/100=12.5 kg.

There are several methods of salting butter: Dry salting, wet salting, slurry salting and brine salting. In dry salting, salt is sprinkled over the surface of the butter during working. In wet salting, the salt is thoroughly pre moistened in enough potable water to allow a thick salt paste to form before adding to butter. In brine salting, the predetermined amount of salt is completely dissolved in water (26% NaCl). Dry salting adds no water to the butter. In wet salting, the crystals dissolve and only small amounts of water are added. Brine salting has the advantage that the salt crystals are completely dissolved, but on the other hand, so much water is added that the moisture content in the butter must be worked down to 12-13% before the brine is added. Care is necessary to ensure that the salt is completely dissolved before the butter is worked to a dry body; otherwise the undissolved salt crystals will attract the moisture droplets in the butter making it leaky after packing. In normal churning, salt dissolves into butter over a period of 20-30 min at a low working intensity that the'butter remains moist, and only then the butter is worked to a dry body.

In evaluating the preserving effect of salt, the amount dissolved in the aqueous phase is important, because microorganisms are found in the aqueous phase. The relation between salt in butter and in aqueous phase is shown below:

Salt in butter %	Salt in aqueous phase %
0.8	4.8
1.0	6.0
1.2	7.1
2.0	11.3

An average salt of 0.8% provides no preserving effect to butter. When the salt content in butter is 1.0%, aqueous phase will have 6.0% salt, it begins to have preserving effect particularly for certain groups of spore forming anaerobes which are also inhibited by low pH of cultured butter.

Yeast and moulds are salt resistant and hence not inhibited even at high salt concentration. High salt concentration in cultured butter increases the tendency to become oily. On the other hand, non-cultured as well as mildly cultured butter may be salted more liberally. The preserving effect of salt is due to their high pH values.

Working refers to the kneading of butter. The purpose is to a) expel buttermilk and to control the moisture and composition of butter, b) completely dissolve, uniformly distribute and incorporate the added salt, c) incorporate added make-up water and d) compact butter grains for satisfactory consistency, appearance and keeping quality. During working, the content of water and salt is adjusted by direct action. However, the MSNF is influenced only indirectly because part of it is drained off with the excess water. After the content of water, salt and MSNF are adjusted the remainder of the butter is fat. This means that the butterfat content is influenced indirectly during working. From the profit point of view, the composition is obtained by adjusting the moisture, salt and MSNF to as high values as legally possible while making sure that fat is with the legal minimum (making fat content as low as possible).

During working the moisture in butter is reduced to droplets which should be mostly sterile. There should be no free moisture on the trier plug drawn from the butter. Throughout the working the temperarure should be controlled. Working and unloading temperatures should not exceed 15°C. over working and under working are harmful, the former damages the body and texture, while the latter produces leaky butter. Working increases the air content of butter (1 to 10 ml/100 g butter). The air content affects microbial and oxidative spoilages. Butter can be worked under partial vacuum of 68 cm of Hg in vacuum churns. Vacuum worked butter will be having close texture with glossy appearance. The air bubbles remaining in the butter themselves contain a vacuum. This enables air bubbles to absorb liquid fat. Too high a vacuum will lead to too much low melting liquid fat collecting in the air bubbles, resulting in fat separation. This is the reason why summer butter cannot be subjected to high vacuum.

The mechanical working of the butter progresses as it is pressed, rolled and turned in the churn. As the butter is worked, part of the liquid fat is pressed out of the fat globules, thereby increasing the continuous phase. Moisture droplets and air bubbles are reduced in size and butter constituents are thoroughly mixed. It is important to apply optimum working intensity. Therefore, the working speed of the churn is increased during the main and final stages of working. The moisture in the dispersed phase must be in fine droplets without any free moisture when working is completed. In the initial stages of working the moisture content drops markedly as free moisture and the large droplets are easily pressed out of butter. When working continues moisture content drops and at a certain point, it stops. Continued working causes division of droplets and makes them so small that they cannot be pressed out of the grains. The moisture depends on the hardness of butter, working intensity and mixing. The dispersion takes place when the butter is soft and working intensive it is, therefore, necessary that butter must have appropriate hardness and gentle working to reduce moisture content. Otherwise moisture dispersion will make the removal of more moisture impossible. Moisture dispersion is sufficient when the largest droplets are around 10 μm diameter. After intensive working the largest droplets will only be around 5 μm. If the butter is not sufficiently worked it will have many large droplets and its consistency will be loose and leaky. Such a butter is conducive to the growth of microorganisms. Therefore, the working must bring a dry body to the butter. When scraping a layer of butter visible moisture droplets should not be seen. An indicator paper is also used for this purpose.

Moisture control : The legal limit for moisture content in butter in many countries is 16%. In India, it is 80% fat. After working a representative sample of butter is taken for 1st moisture test. From this, the amount of make-up water to be added is calculated and added to the churn. The working is continued until the make-up water is thoroughly incorporated in butter. The moisture % in the finished butter is then checked. An useful simple formula for the amount of make-up water in kg (W) is W = F x 1.5 x (M-m)/ 100 where F is fat in the churn in kg; M = moisture desired, and m = 1st moisture test %.

Continuous butter making : This process is economical in labour and working space. It produces butter of uniform hygienic quality, texture, moisture and salt contents. It requires a) no foundation, b) causes no dynamic impact loads requiring heavy duty components normally required in conventional butter churns, and c) eliminates butter holding or transfer trolley since direct pumping of butter to chilling room for package/storage is possible. There are 3 main systems, a) churning chilled cream of normal composition (40% milkfat) with high speed dashers to break the emulsion in a few seconds draining the buttermilk, working and extrusion under controlled temperature conditions using Fritz, Westphalia (buttermatic), Silkeborg (HCT type ,butter maker) Contimab (Simon-Freas) and Paasch machines; b) Phase reversal of high fat cream (80-82% fat) emulsion and chilling in a special cooler and agitation and extrusion of butter as in New Way, Maleshin (Russian) and Alfa-Laval machines; c) separation of partially oiled-off low fat cream and using rich oiled off milkfat cream mixtures (80-82% fat) for standardization, cooling, reemulsification and extrusion of butter as in Cherry Burrell and Creamery Package machines. Processes using normal cream are popular in European countries and also in India due to the simplicity of the process and compactness of the machine and process involving partial oiling off of cream is common in USA. The through put of butter made in continuous butter making equipment may be upto 10 t/ h which is much higher over the throughput from traditional butter churn methods of manufacture. The Alfa and New Way processes utilize a two unit operation. Normal cream is reseparated in an air-tight separator to about 80% fat before introducing to a transmutor where it is chilled and agitated. The oil-in-water emulsion in high fat cream is not stable. On chilling, the cream becomes viscous and agitation of the chilled cream gets destabilised and breaks. The agglomeration occurs within the cream phase than at air/plasma interface. The extrusion temperature is around 10°C for the Alfa process and 2°C for New Way process. The liquid fat remains in super cooled state and crystallization continues some time after manufacture. A high curd content and a finely dispersed aqueous phase is characteristic of these butters. The globular fat is more (11-31%) in Alfa butter than in New Way butter (6%).

In Cherry-Burrell and Creamery Package processes the cream is broken prior to chilling and working. In Cherry Burrell method the cream is reheated and destabilized by agitation and complete destabilization occurs in reseparation step. The Creamery Package process uses homogenization to destabilize the reseparated cream. In both processes, the fat and aqueous phases are separated. The standardized mixture is fed to chill workers and later worked to required consistency. These processes resemble margarine/ anhydrous butterfat preparation. Some of the comparative figures about the structure of butters are given below:-

Characteristic	Conventional	Fritz	Alfa	New Way	Cherry Burrell
1. Structure in free fat	FG + WD	FG+ WD	FG+ WD	FG+ WD	WD
2. Free fat %	54-98	83-88	69-89	94	100
3. Globular fat %	2-48	12-17	11-31	6	few
4. Diameter WD	1-30	1-15	1-7	1-7	1-30

FG = Fat globules WD = Water droplets

Fritz process (Fig 4-6)

Cream is fed into the continuous butter maker at the top of the first churning cylinder via a balance tank through a positive displacement pump. This cylinder is cooled by chilled water jacket. The mechanical dasher driven through a variable speed gearbox operating at 1000 rpm breaks the cream emulsion. It aerates the cream and damages the fat globules within 2 s. The speed of the dasher blades are adjustable to get desired butter grains. Higher speed gives larger butter grains and excessive speed increases fat loss in buttermilk. The mixture of butter grains and buttermilk drops into the 2nd chamber where butter grains are consolidated. The second chamber has perforated rotating drum, larger than the 1st cylinder and can be rotated slowly (35 rpm) so that butter grains pass along the inclined rotary screen. The gentle tumbling action causes further aggregation of butter grains. Most of the buttermilk drains away through the rotating drum. The buttermilk is

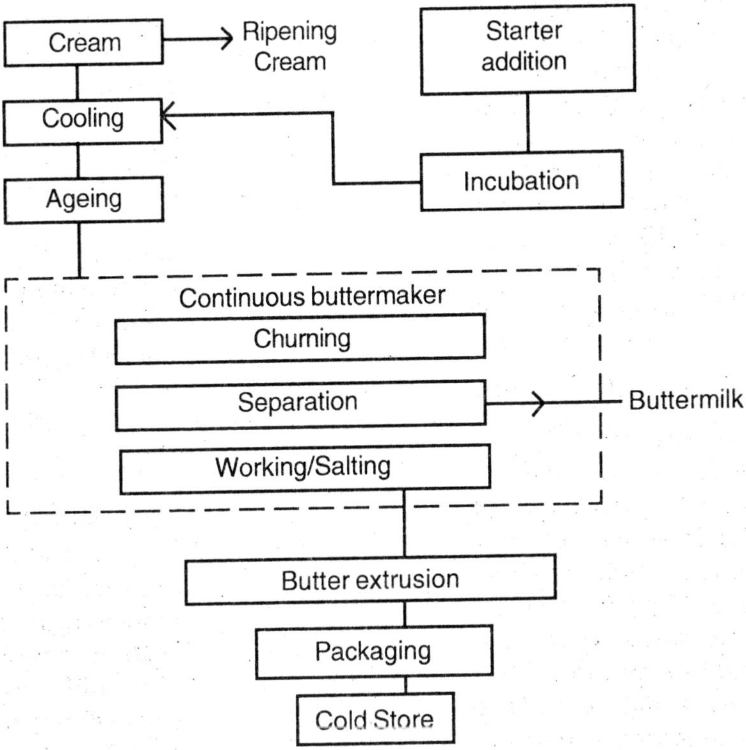

Fig 4-6 Flow chart of continuous butter making

pumped away but some may be cooled and then recycled into the 2nd cylinder to cool the butter grains. From the 2nd cylinder the moist grains of butter fall into the working section where contra rotating augers consolidates the butter grains into a heterogenous mass expelling the buttermilk as they are squeezed together and carried upto a series of perforated plates and mixing vanes. The expelled buttermilk collects at the base of the working section. The level of this pool is kept constant as it will affect the moisture content of the butter. Fat globules in buttermilk floats and are reincorporated into the butter. Butter grins may also be, recovered by running it over sieve before pumping away for further treatment. Better recovery can be achieved by using vibrating sieve which will not block so easily and will agglomerate the butter fines. However, recovery of fat will never be complete. Compacted butter grains are fed from the auger through a series of alternating perforated plates and impeller blades. The shear forces consolidate the butter grains and also break up the droplets of buttermilk remaining in the matrix of fat to form a dispersed aqueous phase of the now water-in-oil emulsion. The droplets of aqueous phase should have a dia meter less than 10 μm. Partially worked butter may have more than 5% entrained air. This is reduced by passing the butter through a vacuum section to get denser fine textured product with less than 1% air. A second set of augers removes the butter from the vacuum section and forces it through a further set of orifice plates to complete emulsification before discharge from the butter maker. Finally milled salt of high quality with grain size less than 50 μm is dozed as a continuous stream into the butter maker preferably in the first working section. Allowance is made in running the butter maker to produce butter grains with a lower moisture content to compensate for the water in the brine, if saturated brine is used. If salt level of 2% is needed brine slurry is metered to the butter maker by positive displacement pumps. A dozing system is also used for adding good quality water to unsalted/slightly salted butter to maximise yields.

The modern machines may be cleaned without dismantling. The butter contact surfaces are sand blasted which helps to retain a fine film of water which reduces sticking. Before churning a sanitizer having silicate is circulated. This is followed by a cold water rinse.

Controls : The important parameters to be controlled are moisture and salt levels. Traditional chemical analysis of butter is slow when production rate of butter is high (around 80 kg/min). Micro-computers are necessary to aid the optimization of the processes. Dielectric constant of the butter is useful to sense the level of moisture. Continuous butter making equipment can be controlled by means of a videomaster system (having screen, microprocessor and key board). It enables the operator to communicate with the machine. Pictures of what is going on in the machine can be displayed on a screen as well as a digital indication of the functioning of the individual

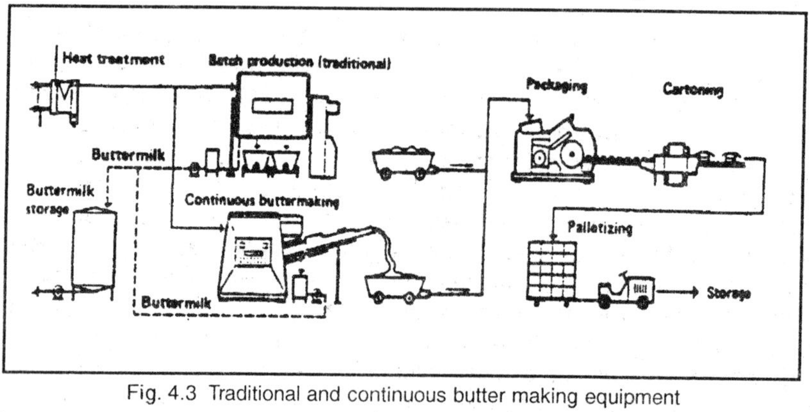

Fig. 4.3 Traditional and continuous butter making equipment

sections. The operator can supervise and control the equipment as necessary.

Comparison between traditional and continuous butter making: (Fig 4-3)

Traditional process:

a) Cream is churned to separate butter and buttermilk for about one h at 45-60 rpm.

b) *Preworking* is done for the removal of excess water with low speed for about 15 min.

c) In first main working salt and water are worked in with removal of air at a low speed for about 40 min. Vacuum treatment is given at 15-30 cm Hg depending on the season.

d) In final working additional water is distributed and air removed at low vacuum 10-20 cm Hg. Between preworking and main working

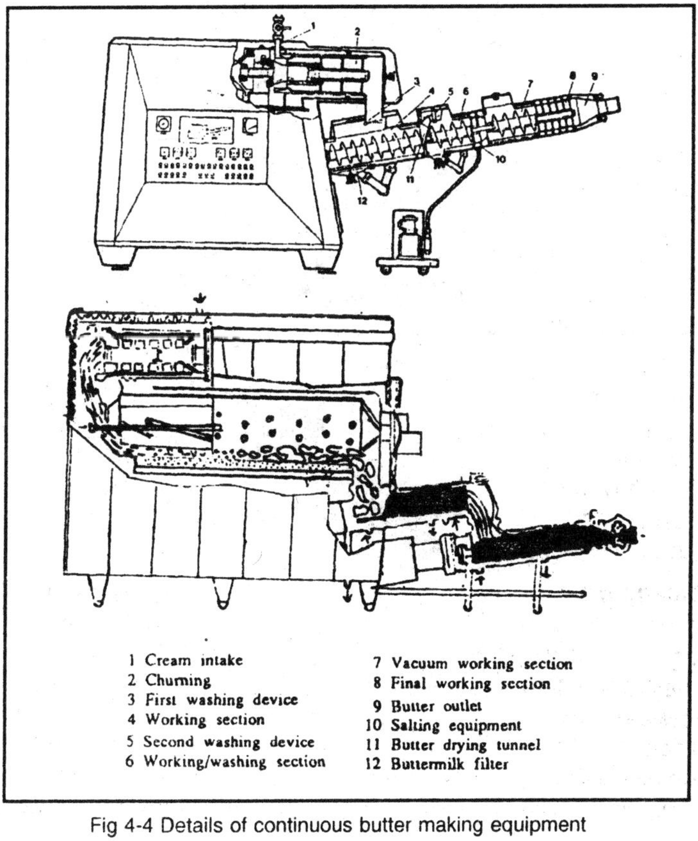

Fig 4-4 Details of continuous butter making equipment

salt and special culture concentrate are added for flavour and moisture is brought to correct level. After final working moisture and salt contents are determined.

Continuous butter making (Fig 4-4)

a) *In churning section* I cream is churned to separate butter and buttermilk at high speed of 1000-1400 rpm.

b) In separating section post churning of butter grains, control of fat loss and separation of butter milk and butter are effected with the help of rotating cylinder with baffle plates and rotating strainer drum at low speed of 15 rpm.

c) *First working* is done for removal of excess water and distribution of salt and water in Section I at low auger speed (15-20 rpm) and regulating valve. Butter is mixed with 2 mixing vanes with dozing of water and salt and "special starter concentrate."

d) *Second working* is carried out for removal of air under vacuum between working sections I and II at 10 cm Hg. The final working and distribution of salt and water is carried out at working section II at high auger speed 50 rpm with 2 mixing vanes. Final moisture and salt content are determined.

Butter handling : Butter from the batch churn is dropped onto the butter trolleys, wheeled to the packaging room and then either tipped off or shovelled into the feed hopper. This handling is unhygienic and labour oriented. Continuous butter making equipment may be set up to discharge into the silo or feed hopper of a bulk packer through a butter pump silo system to minimise the risk of contamination. In the automatic bulk package system, erect and weighed empty cartons lined with polyethylene films fills about 100 g short weight. The carton is then reweighed and filled within allowance tolerance, sealed, labelled and palletised. Repacking of bulk butter into consumer packets is done by tempering the frozen butter at 6-8°C in a clean dry mould free room reblending to break the matrix of fat crystals, increase salt or moisture levels as necessary through continuous butter, mixer/blender and pumped to packaging machines as is done for freshly made butter.

Packaging of butter : Butter may be packed and distributed bulk or as packets. The packed butter may vary in size from 10 g to 5 kg. The packaging material may be Alu. foil, tins, tubes or Al foil lined with parchment paper. They are packed in cartons of 10/25 kg net weight. Protecting the butter between production and consumption or other use and attractive presentation of the product to the consumer are the main aims of packaging. The machines used are fully automatic and can be set for different sizes (10, 15,250 or 500 g). Due to evaporation of moisture from butter packs during storage, there is some loss in weight which is referred as shrinkage. Moisture proof/grease proof wrappers reduce shrinkage. The greater the quantity of free moisture or the longer the storage period, the more the shrinkage. Shrinkage is less at low temperature. All butter packs in a lot must have an average net weight which is atleast as high as that marked on the packet but for individual packet, a specific negative deviation from the stated net weight is accepted in some countries. Depending on the packet the negative tolerance may be 1.5 to 6%. Generally, a certain weight allowance must be made to inaccuracies that may occur during packaging, cartoning, weighing or that may develop during storage. An allowance should cover such possible inaccuracies. The packaging material must be grease proof, water proof and impervious to flavouring and aroma substances. If parchment paper is used as packaging material mould contamination of the product is possible. To prevent this, dry parchment is immersed in concentrated brine having 0.5% sorbic acid. Parchment paper is being replaced by 0.001 gauge food grade, low density, virtually sterile polyethylene film in several countries. Aluminium foil and other laminates are widely accepted because they provide light barrier in super market display cabinets. After wrapping the packets are put in card board boxes, loaded on pallets and trucked to the cold store.

Storage life of butter Butter should be placed in cold store after wrapping and chilled to 5°C for 1 or 2 days. The initial freshly churned somewhat ointment like consistency is transformed to the consistency typical for, butter. Butter cannot be considered finished until it has been chilled. Low temperature reduces the risk of the packs becoming deformed during distribution. The maximum time of storage depends on the temperature of storage as indicated below:

Temperature of storage °C	Poor keeping quality	Good keeping quality	Excellent keeping quality
20	3 days	10 days	3 weeks
15	3 days	20 days	5 weeks
10	1 week	4 weeks	2 mo
0	4 weeks	6 weeks	3 mo
-12	3 mo	6 mo	9 mo
-25	6 mo	9 mo	12 mo

The shelf life depends on the initial quality of the butter also. Ripened cream butter as well as salted butter have shorter storage life than sweet cream butter. From the data given below it can be noticed that experts are able to detect defects much earlier than the consumer when the butter is stored at -25°C.

Storage life (days)	Expert evaluation	Consumer acceptance
Cultured salted butter	160	400
Cultured, unsalted butter	250	600
Non-cultured salted butter	350	710
Sweet cream butter	400	780

Sweet cream unsalted butter has maximum storage life. However, both salt and cultured butter improve keeping quality in fresh consumption butter by preventing bacteriological deterioration. The factors affecting the shelf life of butter are, a) temperature of storage, b) copper and iron content of butter, c) salt, acidity and curd contents d) oxygen content and c) exposure to light.

Spoilage of butter Post-pasteurisation contamination may occur from improperly sterilised equipment and from the water used in the butter washing process. The most dangerous are those that grow at refrigeration temperature (5 to 10°C) These include species of *Pseudomonas, Alcaligenes, Achromobacterand Flavo bacterium..* These species, in addition to coliforms are associated with defects in butter and can grow in water and outbreaks of spoilage especially surface taint, are often associated with contaminated water supplies. The faults caused are a) hydrolysis of milkfat, liberating short chain fatty acids leading to a rancid flavour (*Pseudomonas fragi* and *Pseudomonas flourescens*), b) putrid flavour caused by the break down of casein (*Pseudomonas pufrifaciens*), c) stinking odour (*Pseudomonas mephitica*), d) black discolouration on surface (*Pseudomonas nigrifaciens*), and e) discolouration due to moulds and yeasts. Coliform organisms die fn butter held below 0°C.

Dairy water can be chlorinated to high levels even upto 20 mg// safety and very high levels (upto 200 mg/l in wash water have no effect on butter flavour. With improved methods of manufacture and hygiene, it is perhaps, unnecessary to wash butter grains. Water with less than 50 mg/l of $CaC0_3$ and total colony count less than 10/ml at 37°C is good. Aerial contamination or unsterile processing equipment may be revealed by yeast and mould colony count. Less than 10 colonies/g is desirable.

Legal standard : According to PFA Rules, table (creamery) butter is a product obtained from cow or buffalo milk or a combination thereof or from cream or curd obtained from cow or buffalo milk or a combination thereof, with or without the addition of common salt, annatto or carotene as colouring matter. It should be free from other animal fats, wax or mineral oils, vegetable oil and fats. It must contain not less than 80% by weight of milkfat not more than 1.5% by weight of curd and not more than 3.0% by weight of common salt. Diacetyl may be added as a flavouring agent, but if so used the total diacetyl content must not exceed 4 mg/kg. Calcium hydroxide, sodium bicarbonate, sodium carbonate (and sodium polyphosphate may be added, but not exceed the weight of butter as a whole by more than 0.2%.

The Agmark standard include quality characteristics also viz., flavour, clean, pleasant and free from objectionable taint or rancidity; body and texture, firm at 15.5°C, not greasy or oily, compact and uniform fine granular surface on breaking; colour, uniform yvith no stickiness, mottling, stains or curd with only added annatto colour.

Desi (cooking butter) butter means the product obtained from cow or buffalo milk or a combination thereof without the addition of any preservative including common salt, any added colouring matter or any added flavouring agent. It shall be free from other animal fats, wax and mineral oils, vegetable oils and fats. It shall contain not less than 76.0% of milkfat by weight.

The types of butter available in different countries are: a) creamery butter, b) pasteurised cream butter (from sweet cream with mild flavours pH 5.0-5.4), c) ripened cream butter delicate aroma developed before a churning cream pH 4.5- 4.7), d) sweet cream butter (made from cream with less than 0.20% acid pH > 6.0, e) fresh butter stored less than 3 wk at 5°C and f) cold store butter (stored at -18°C for periods ranging from 1 to 6 mo. before made available for sale, g) unsalted light salted 0.5%, standard salted 1.0% and extra salted 2%.

Judging and grading of table butter: Apart from PFA Act and Agmark standards, Indian Standards Institution (IS:3507:1966) have recommended sanitary grades on the basis of yeast and mould content of butter. The sanitary index is classified as good, fair, poor and very poor if the yeast and mould counts in butter/g are below 20, 21 to 50, 51-100 and over 100 respectively. Besides this, the following score card has also been recommended for creamery butter.

Characteristics	Maximum points	Minimum points
1. *Flavour* (clean/free from taint and rancidity	50	40
2. *Body* and texture at 15-16°C (firm/neither greasy nor oily and showing granular texture on breaking	20	15
3. *Colour,* appearance and *finish* colour even/free from streakiness/mottling/ stains or signs of curd *appearance* and *finish bright* and clean	20	15
4. *Moisture* (on pressing should not exude beads of free moisture	10	5
Total	100	75

For classification in the above grade, the points scored for a particular characteristic should not be less than the minimum. Butter scored 95 and above *is classified as excellent*, 90-74; very good and 85-89 *good.*

Examination procedure : Judging in a well ventilated clean room at 15°C, tempering the butter in advance at 15°C. taking a sample plug by using a butter trier, with drawing a plug of butter slowly, inhaling for odour and aroma, observing the colour, examining the body and texture by pressing with the thumb against the sides of the plug, observing presence/absence of free moisture beads of water, breaking the plug, chewing until it melts, rolling in the mouth, examining undissolved salt and observing taste and smell as well as after taste. After judging rinsing the mouth with saline is desirable.

Requirement of high grade butter: The package should be neat,clean and tidy in appearance with a good finish. The salt should have dissolved properly with uniform colour throughout. The body should be firm, waxy, compact with a close-knit texture. The flavour should be mildly sweet, clean and pleasant.

Butter is classified *No* grade when the following flavour defects are observed: a) chlorine smell due to chlorine left inadvertently in butter or churn, b) absorbed foreign smell due to petrol, kerosene, fly spray, paint or varnish while handling/storage of butter due to absorption by fat and c) surface taint caused by proteolytic organisms when acidity and salt content is low in fat.

Defects in butter may be due to use of poor quality milk; incorrect treatment of milk/cream at the dairy, ineffective cleaning of dairy utensils, using improper butter making technique and inappropriate storage.

1 Appearance:

Free moisture : as seen as moisture droplets in trier plug. Large droplets are due to incorrect working and incomplete salt distribution and prone to microbial attack.

Mottled : seen as discoloured spots on indicator paper and due to inefficient salt distribution.

Wavy : cut layers show varying colour due to short working and commonly seen in continuous butter.

Oily : cut surface exhibit droplets or butteroil due to use of low vacuum during working.

Mouldy : visible mould growth due to faulty packaging

2 Body and texture

Crumbly : due to underworking/low iodine value/sudden chilling of butter after production.

Greasy : due to intensive over working or use of high temperature wash water.

Leaky : due to under working.

3 Flavour and aroma are indefinable defects but often due to chemical or bacteriological action.

Acid / sour	:	Use of sour/under neutralized cream or high culturing.
Alkaline	:	Over neutralisation of cream
Bitter	:	Animals consuming bitter weeds, lipase or proteolytic activity in raw cream.
Cheesey	:	Growth of proteolytic bacteria causing casein breakdown.
Cooked	:	Over heating of cream
Feeds/weeds	:	Cows consuming tainted feeds within 3h before milking.
Fishy	:	High acid salted butter in presence of high Cu, Fe
Flat	:	low diacetyl or salt or excessive washing of butter
Green	:	Less acid development in butter, poor starter growth, less of citric acid formation leading to acetaldehyde build up.
Salty	:	Strong salt flavour with after taste, high uneven salt distribution
Stale	:	Low storage of poor quality cream, storage at high temperature for long periods.
Tallowy	:	Fat oxidation of milk, cream, butter exposure at sunlight, presence of Cu, Fe
Yeasty	:	Use of old yeasty cream (rare)

Butter having chlorine, petrol, kerosene, fly spray, paint, varnish smell are defective and generally not classified for grade. Tallowiness is prevented by intense heat treatment of cream. Butter from sweet cream, unsalted has maximum keeping quality under commercial storage. For fresh consumption both acidity and salt improve the keeping quality by preventing bacterial spoilage.

(Cont'd)

The composition of butter is as follows:

	From sweet Unsalted	cream Salted	From sour Unsalted	cream Salted
Moisture %	15.8	15.8	15.8	15.8
Fat %	82.5	82.0	82.5	82.2
Protein %	0.6	0.6	0.6	0.6
Lactose %	0.7	0.7	0.5	0.5
Lactic acid %	-	-	0.2	0.2
Saft %	0.1	0.1	0.1	0.1
NaCl %	-	0.2-2.0	-	0.2-2.0
pH value	6.5	6.5	4.4-5.6	4.4-5.6
Cholesterol %	0.25	0.25	0.25	0.25
Diacetyl mg/kg	-	-	1.0-3.0	2.0-3.0

Compared with sweet cream butter, the sour cream butter has lower pH besides aroma contributed by diacetyl.

Chapter 4

YOGHURT

For Yoghurt and other similar fermented milks, production is generally achieved by the action of thermophilic starter organisms and not by spontaneous fermentation processes.

Many countries have their own name for yoghurt. The consistency, taste and aroma vary from one district to the next. In certain areas, yoghurt is produced in the form of a highly viscous liquid, whereas in other countries it is in the form of a soft gel. Yoghurt is also produced in frozen form as a dessert or as a drink. Yoghurt is characterised by its viscous consistency, a strong aciduous taste due to high acidity (pH around 4.0) and a distinct aroma caused by acetaldehyde which should be present in a concentration of about 15-25 mg/kg. Yoghurt is usually classified into two types; a) Set yoghurt which is packed immediately after inoculation with bulk starter and is incubated in retail packages. The coagulum is a continous semi-solid mass and b) Stirred yoghurt which is inoculated and incubated in a tank. After incubation, the coagulum is broken down prior to final cooling and packaging (Fig 6-1).

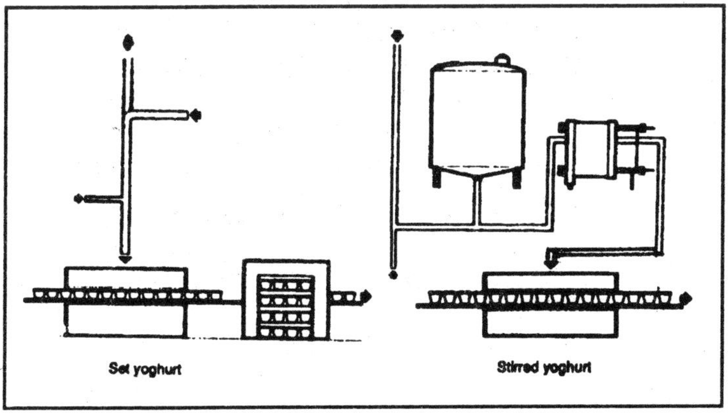

Fig 6-1 Difference in set and stirred yoghurt process

Factors affecting the quality of yoghurt : Numerous variables are to be controlled during the manufacturing process if a high quality yoghurt is to be produced, with the necessary taste, viscosity, aroma, consistency, appearance, freedom from whey sepration and long shelf life. Most of these factors are closely related to the choice and pre-treatment of the milk and to the preparation of the culture. The factors include :

a) Standardization of milk, b) Additives to improve viscosity and texture c) Homogenization d) Heat treatment and e) Culture preparation and addition.

Pre-treatment of milk : Legal standards for yoghurt are mainly based on the chemical composition of the product, i.e., fat% and SNF%. As minimum specification for SNF or total solids is included by some countries, but the main differences are based on the basis of fat content. Yoghurt may have a fat content ranging from 0.1 to 4.0% and can be classified as a) high fat yoghurt (fat 3%), b) low fat yoghurt (fat 1.5%) and c) Fat-free yoghurt (fat less than 0.1%). A flow scheme of the main steps in making set and stirred yoghurt is shown in Fig 6-2.

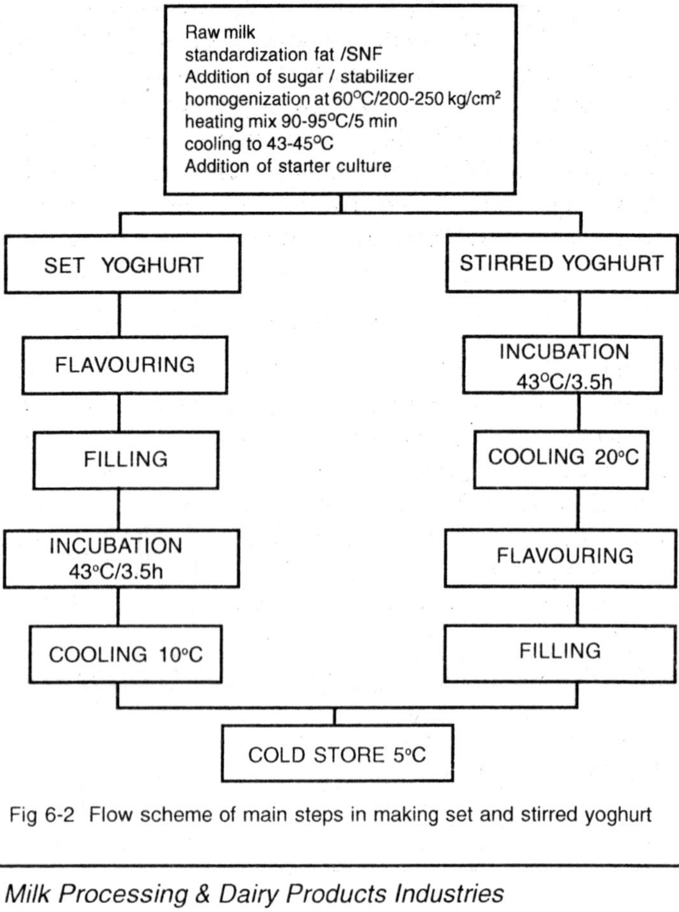

Fig 6-2 Flow scheme of main steps in making set and stirred yoghurt

Choice of milk : The milk used for yoghurt must be of the highest bacteriological quality i.e., it must have a low count of bacteria and substances which may arrest the development of the yoghurt culture. The milk must not contain penicillin, bacteriophages, residues of CIP solution or sterilizing agents. It is desirable that the dairy obtain the milk for yoghurt production from selected, approved milk producers.

Clarification refers to the treatment which takes place in a special separator. The purpose is to remove visible dirt and somatic cells from the milk. Clarification can be done either in a specially designed clarifier or in a standard milk separator. The latter is designed to clarify and separate the milk. Foreign particles and somatic cells can also be removed by filtering through a specially woven cloth. These filters of the cloth type are used in duplicate so that when one filter is being used, the other can be opened for renewal of used cloths.

Standardization of fat content can be done by adding skim milk to whole milk, by mixing determined amounts of the whole milk with skim milk or by adding cream to skim milk. Simple rearson square method can be used.

Additives to be added: The addition of dried milk is carried out with the purpose of increasing the total solids, which in turn improves the consistency of fermented milk. Generally, 1-3% of mostly skim milk powder is added. In some countries, however, the addition of skim milk powder is prohibited. The level of MSNF has to be raised, for without this additional protein the gel produced during fermentation will be unacceptable to the consumer, i.e., thin and watery and prone to syneresis. Excessive use of stabilisers could mask this deficiency but as most countries ban the use of stabilizers in natural yoghurt, the tendency is to minimise their use across the entire range of retail products. Since nutritional vale of yoghurt is enhanced by raising the SNF, most manufacturers resort to adjustment by one or two alternative approaches.

The powder widely used is antibiotic-free skim milk powder which is readily available. The description, antibiotic free is called CYP - powder suitable for cheese and yoghurt. Total freedom from antibiotics is, in normal farming practice - almost impossible to get. The powder should have not more than 0-62 IU/g of inhibitory substances. Residues above 0.02 IU/ml of reconstituted milk can inhibit the activity of starter cultures. The powder should be a) easily dispersed, b) fully soluble with no gritty particles and c) free from scorch particles to avoid specks in natural yoghurt. Semi-instantised powders are desirable. Rapid mixing of the powder with minimum lump formation is necessary. If powder contains numerous heat-damaged or insoluble particles, the resultant milk may a) damage the orifices of homogenicer or b) lead to gritty mouth feel. That the addition of skim milk powder increases the protein content and nutritive value of yoghurt is made clear from the data presented below:

Added skim milk powder %	Increase in milk		Increase in yoghurt	
	Protein %	MSNF %	Protein %	MSNF %
0	-	-	3.30	8.50
1	0.3	0.92	3.60	9.42
2	0.6	1.84	3.90	10.34
3	0.9	2.76	4.20	11.26
4	1.2	3.68	4.50	12.18

If solid content of initial milk is known, it is possible to calculate the amount of skim milk powder to be added to reach a desired total solids content in the fermemed milk. The added skim milk powder raises the whey protein content which contributes to good gel formation in the finished product. The extent of increase in whey protein in the mix is indicated as follows:

Added skim milk powder %	Increase in		Total whey protein in milk %
	Protein %	Whey Protein %	
0	-	-	0.700
1	0.33	0.066	0.766
2	0.66	0.132	0.832
3	0.99	0.198	0.898
4	1.32	0.264	0.964

Co-precipitated whey protein, whey protein concentrate, whey powder or concentrated whey can also be used as an optional addition of yoghurt to raise the protein level in milk.

Cane sugar is added in the manufacture of flavoured yoghurt and occasionally in the production of fermented milks. If sweetened fruit concentrates are used, no sugar may be added. The amount of added sugar should be less than 12%. It is usually added to the milk in a granular form. Sugar addition is followed by rather intensive stirring of the milk. Sugar is added to the milk prior to heat treatment to destroy osmophilic yeasts and moulds that may be present in the sugar. The effect of added sugar in the inhibition of lactic acid development in 4 h incubation's at 42°C is shown below:

°/ added sugar	% lactic acid produced
0	1.60
6	1.25
9	0.75
12	0.40

This explains the reason for the addition of 5% sugar to this base mix and desired amount made up through sweetened fruit preparation or otherwise later.

Stabilizers which are binding, swelling and thickening agents may be used where legislation permits in. the manufacture of yoghurt to prevent whey separation and improve the consistency and viscosity of the yoghurt. They may be incorporated into the milk by a) uniform premixing with other dry ingredients with stirring, b) converting into a paste with small quantity of water and then added with stirring or c) dissolved in a small quantity of water or milk and then added under optimal stirring. Some soluble stabilisers like Gelatin, agar agar, Na-alginate, Carageenans and soluble starch are added to warm milk prior to pasteurization. Some hydro colloids like locust bean gum, Gum guar and Pectins precipitate casein in milk and hence they can be added only to acid milk after fermentation. The concentration of stabilizers recommended for fermented milks are a) special starch 1.0-2.0%, gelatin 0.2-0.4%, Agar Agar 0.8-1.2%; Locust bean gum 0.3-0.5% Guar gum 0.3-0.5%; Pectin 0.05-0.2% for yoghurt beverages.

Evaporation of milk : The increase in SNF of milk can be achieved by evaporation under vacuum or in open pan. Commonly the solids content is increased by 1-3% (corresponding to evaporation by 10-25%). The data on degree of evaporation and equivalence to added milk powder are given below:

	Total milk solids			Equivalence to added
Evaporation %	Initial %	Increased by evaporation	Final %	milk powder %
5	12.0	0.60	12.60	0.65
10	12.0	1.20	13.20	1.30
15	12.0	1.80	13.80	1.95
20	12.0	3.00	15.00	3.26

Another method of fortification of base mix is by concentration of whole or skim milk by ultra filtration or reverse osmosis. Reverse osmosis concentrates all constituents of milk whereas ultra filtered retentate provides concentration of proteins and fat only. Membrane processing is not a cheap alternative. Economic considerations will limit the extent to which yoghurt milk is modified by this system in commercial practice.

Homogenization of milk a) decreases the size of the fat globules and prevent creaming during incubation of milk and maintain uniform distribution of fat b) improves the consistency and viscosity of the yoghurt, c) causes little or no whey separation, d) gives whiter appearance and creamy taste. Lipolysis may happen if homogenization is not immediately followed by heat treatment of milk. A pressure 150-200 kg/cm^2 in optimal for the viscosity of the fermented milks. Homogenisation is usually performed between 60 and 80°C.

***Heat treatment of milk* a)** destroys the pathogenic organisms which may be present b) reduce the number of other microorganisms in order to increase the keeping quality, c) inactivates certain enzymes (lipases) d) improves the consistency of the fermented milk, e) denatures the whey proteins thereby improving the consistency and viscosity of the finished product besides preventing whey separation. Production of plain yoghurt with minimum total solids (9.5- 12.0%) requires a more extensive denaturation of whey proteins. On the other hand, production of plain fermented product with a higher total solids content (above 14%) or fruit yoghurt, requires less denaturation of whey proteins. Hence, temperature-time ratios for the heat treatment of milk should be adjusted according to the solids content. The recommended heat treatment results in whey protein denaturation between 70-95%. The denaturation of UHT treated milk is lower than in other heat treated milks. Denaturation of serum proteins of 80-85% should be considered good from technological and nutritional points of view. This corresponds to heat treatment of 95°C/5 min or 80-85°C/20-30 min. When making yoghurt with higher total solids content (14% or more) a lower denaturation of 70-75% may be enough. This corresponds to heat treatment of 85°C/5 min, 90°C/2 min, 95°C/1-2 min or 130-135°C/2 s.

The heat induced changes in milk can be grouped as nutritional and microbiological. Nutritionally, the denatured proteins are easily digestible by enzymes of the intestinal tract causing soft-curdling of the casein in the stomach and destroys some heat-labile vitamins. Microbiologically, the pathogens are destroyed, other organisms are reduced in numbers, by reduction of microbial numbers and destruction of phages and inactivation of lipases, enhances the keeping quality of yoghurt, causes better growth of starter organisms due to production of formic acid, reducing redox potential and inactivation of antimicrobial substances, expulsion of oxygen from the mix and providing microaerophilic conditions needed by the starter organisms, improvement in consistency and viscosity of yoghurt and preventing whey separation, and any inhibition of fat oxidation particularly at longer storage by the formation of antioxidative substances.

Cooling the heated milk: The milk is cooled after heat treatment, first in regeneration section and then by means of water to the inoculation temperature of 40-45°C, the preferential range 42-43°C, which is a compromise between and optimum growth conditions for Streptococcus salyarius subsp. thermophilus and Lactobacillus delbruckeii subsp. bulgaricus. The milk is then ready for inoculation.

Preparation o! the culture in the production of yoghurt and incubation time requires maximum accuracy and hygiene. The aseptic process described under starter cultures are generally used in production. The ratio of cocci to bacilli in the cultures is usually about 1:1 or 2:1. However, the balance can be easily disturbed unless all variables such as inoculation quantities, time and temperatures are kept under close control. The cultures may have to be replaced at regular intervals since repeated transfer will after the ratio. The Lactobacillus delbruckeii subsp bulgaricus will dominate and this may cause sharp taste by excessive acid and acetaldehyde production. The desired fermentation is achieved within a short time of 2.5 to 3 h depending on the inoculation rate e.g., 2-3%.

Packaging : Rigid or semi-rigid unit containers or flexible form-fill-seal single service containers for UHT product are commonly used. The packaging material must be resistant to low pH. The unit container may consist of glass, plastic or laminate. The packaging line may have a) insulated buffer tank to hold cold yoghurt for a short period, b) fruit mixing c) blending equipment and d) filling machine.

Plant hygiene : The cleaning and sanitization of the processing equipment is very essential for handling fermented milk products. As usual, the CIP system consists of prerinse detergent wash water rinse, sanitization treatment and final water rinse to remove the stcrilant residues from the processing equipment.

Storage and keeping quality: The product is stored in refrigerated cabinets at 2°C and transported in refrigerated vehicles. The product is commonly coded for a three-week shelf life, after which the bacterial growth, although restricted, will increase the level of acidity to such an extent as to impair flavour eventually rendering it unpalatable. Ultimately the microorganisms are destroyed and the yoghurt becomes separated into curds and whey. Yoghurt is particularly susceptible to attack by yeasts and moulds. Spoiled yoghurts are referred to as blown. This condition is due to yeast where fruit and sucrose are present. Fermentation of the sugars takes place producing $C0_2$ which builds up a pressure under the foil cap of the carton, although this may not tie obvious for about a month at 5°C. Although no official standards exist for microbiol ical condition of yoghurt, a satisfactory yoghurt at the time of sale may have counts of Streptococcus salvarius subsp. thermophilus 10^8/g and Lactobacillus delbruckeii subsp. bulgaricus also 10^8/g.

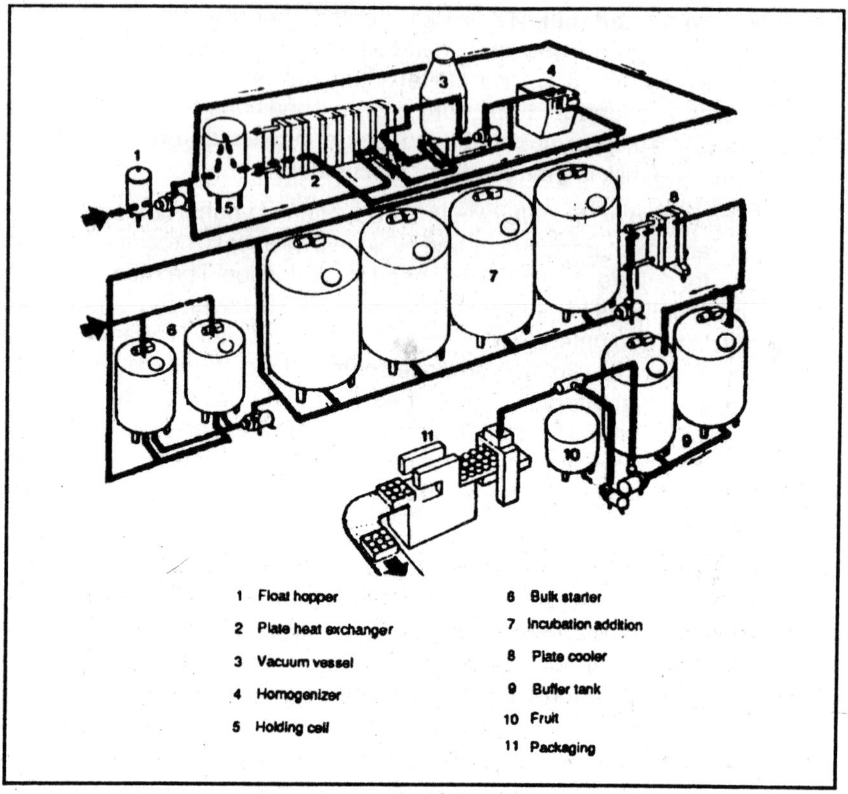

Fig 6-5 A typical process line for stirred yoghurt

Long life yoghurt : The shelf life of cultured milk products can be extended by a) heat treatment of the finished product, either in the pack or immediately before packaging. A stabilizer is used before treatment and b) producing and packaging under aseptic conditions.

In the production of stirred yoghurt, the gel from the incubation tank is heated to 72-75°C in a plate heat exchanger and is held for a few *s* at this temperature before being cooled. Packaging is then done aseptically to prevent reinfection. Set yoghurt can be heat treated at 72-75°C/5-10 min., in the packs and then cooled. Heating kills all virulent organisms in the yoghurt. In some countries yoghurt is defined as a product in which microorganism is kept alive right upto time of consumption and hence heating yoghurt cannot be done. Stabilizers are also forbidden by law or permissible only to a limited extent. Application of freezing and drying can extend the shelf life of yoghurt to three months or more. These treatments do alter the nature of the end product.

Frozen yoghurt : The cold stirred yoghurt with fruit syrup, emulsifier, stabilizer and sugar are frozen in conventional ice cream freezer. The average composition is fat 2.6%, MSNF 5 -10%, sugar 8-20%, stabilizer 0.21.0%. The overrun is about 60%. The hard frozen product may have 80% overrun. The flow chart is shown below:

Natural stirred yoghurt

HARD FROZEN	*SOFT FROZEN*
65% Yoghurt base	80% yoghurt base
35°io fruit syrup	20% fruit syrup
with emulsifier/stabilizer	with emulsifier/stabiliser
batch freeze	batch freeze
package	package
harden at -20°C	harden at -5°C
Cold store	Cold store

Drinking yoghurt is stirred yoghurt of low viscosity and this product is consumed as a refreshing drink. The stages of production and handling coagulum are similar to stirred yoghurt. Fruit syrup is used and the coagulum is homogenised after fermentation. Three different types could be produced; firstly, the coagulum is not heated and the product has a shelf life of 3 s at 10°C; secondly, pasteurization of yoghurt at 75°C for few *s*, followed by cooling and packing given a product a few weeks shelf life at 10°C and thirdly, UHT drinking, -yoghurt is heated to 110°C for 4s, under aseptic condition. The latter type has the shelf life of several months at ambient temperature. The composition may be fat 1-2%, MENF 9.25%, stabilizer 0.27%, sugar 5.5%, fruit yoghurt (14% TS) 5.5 %.

Other yoghurt-related products are a) lactose hydrolysed yoghurt b) condensed/concentrated yoghurt (Lab-neb) consumed with bread which is popular in the Middle East. A low cost nourishing food - the soy-ghurt makes an excellent source of vegetable protein, the essential amino acids pattern makes it an useful product. The process consists in soaking the soybean in 0.5% sodium bicarbonate for 12 h, boiling for 30 min, cooling and dehulling in water, disintegration of the cotyledons, addition of skim milk, heating the slurry to 65°C, addition of sugar and 5-10% yoghurt, two stage homogenization, pasteurization 90°C/5 min, cooling to 40°C, addition of 3% yoghurt starter, incubation at 40°C/4 h, cooling and storage at 10°C or freezing and hardening at - 15°C for frozen yoghurt. The composition of yoghurt is fat 2.5%, protein 3.4%, carbohydrates 14.0% and moisture 79.0%.

Chapter 5

EVAPORATED AND CONDENSED MILKS

Introduction: Condensed milk is the product obtained by evaporating part of the water of whole milk or fully or partially skimmed milk, with or without the addition of sugar. The product may be supplied in bulk as a raw material for the food industry. It is mainly prepared for direct consumption, in which case it is packed in relatively small quantities in sealed tins.

In areas or in countries where enough milk is available, the consumption of condensed milk packed in sealed tins is as a rule relatively small arid mainly confined to some applications for which the concentrated form has special advantages, such as use in beverages. Condensed milk is of far more greater importance for the milk supply in remote areas with a shortage of milk because the concentrated form gives a considerable saving in cost of packing, transport and storage. As the bacterial contamination of milk cannot be prevented by evaporation alone, separate measures are taken for the preservation of concentrated milk. This preservation is done by two methods, a) Sterilized condensed milk otherwise known as evaporated milk which is a sterile product obtained by heating the tinned concentrated product at high temperatures and b) Sweetened condensed milk otherwise known as condensed milk, which is a concentrate, the watery phase of which, due to the addition of sugar, provides a high osmotic pressure in which no microorganisms can develop.

Standards : Though condensed milk is made with different milkfat and milk solids contents, the standards given below is :

	Milk fat %		Total solids %	
Type of milk	**UK**	**USA**	**UK**	**USA**
Full cream evaporated	9.0	7.9	31.0	25.9
Full cream sweetened	9.0	8.5	31.0	28.0
Skim evaporated	-	-	20.0	20.0
Skim sweetened	-	-	26.0	24.0

According to PFA Rules (1984), evaporated milk is a product obtained from cow or buffalo milk or a combination thereof, or from standardised milk by the partial removal of water. It may contain added calcium chloride, citric acid and sodium citrate, sodium salts of orthophosphoric acid and polyphosphoric acid not exceeding 0.3°/a by weight of the finished product. Such additions need not be declared on the label. Unsweetened condensed milk should not contain less than 8% milkfat and not less than 26% milk solids.

Unsweetened condensed skim milk (evaporated skimmed milk) is the product from cow or buffalo skimmed milk or a combination thereof by the partial removal of water. The additives are similar to that of whole milk product. It should not contain less than 20% of total solids. The fat content should not exceed 0.5% by weight.

The composition of evaporated milk (%) is:

Water	Total solids	Fat	MSNF	Proteins	Lactose	ash	TS
31	69	9.0	22.0	8.3	12.2	1.5	31.0

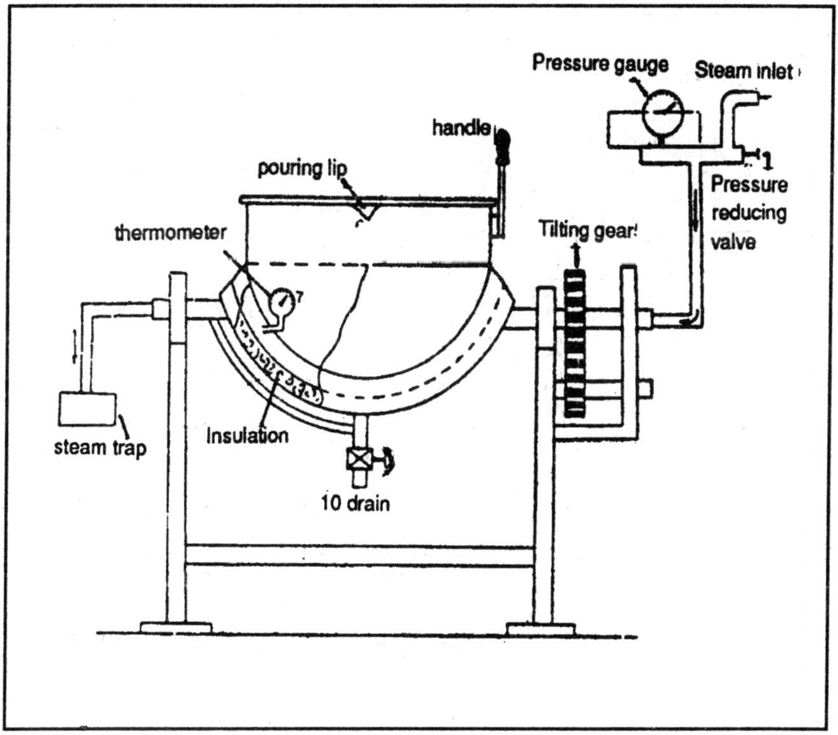

Fig 7-1 Jacketed steam tilting kettle

Condensing of milk : Evaporation is a process by which a volatile liquid is separated from a solution or suspension by vapourizing the volatiles by the application of heat. An evaporator is a heat transfer device. Evaporation is done to obtain such products as evaporated or sweetened condensed milk which have long life time and are convenient for certain use. It is also preferred to save costs of heat energy in making powdered products.

The stationary or tilting type of kettle with internal stainless steel construction and provided with steam jacket, steam trap, steam pressure gauge, thermometer and other ancillaries finds its use in open pan concentration of milk in the process of making desiccated milk (khoa) or removal of water from butter in the process of making ghee as well as melting cheese in the preparation of processed chesse (Fig 7-1). The limitations of this type are high working temperature and the heat energy from the vapour is not recoverable. A prolonged temperature and slow evaporation of moisture adversely affect the quality of the product. To meet this disadvantage and accelerate evaporation, the milk is condensed under low pressure, so that it boils at a lower temperature. Heat energy requirements of evaporating 1 kg of water from milk at atmospheric pressure and at reduced pressure at 56°C is shown below:

Heat energy required kJ	Evaporation	
	Atmospheric pressure	Vacuum
Sensible heat	186	84
latent heat	2 261	2 370
thermal heat equivalent of work done by vacuum pump	-	121
Total	2 447	2 575

This shows that there is no specific saving,in thermal energy in condensing milk in vacuum. But, the data given below reveals that a) evaporation is rapid under vacuum, b) the higher the(vacuum the faster the speed of evaporation and c) doubling steam pressure causes very little increase in the rate of evaporation. On the other hand, at atmospheric pressure the rate of evaporation is directly proportional to steam pressure. This suggests that low temperature saturated steam is sufficient for vacuum evaporation. Besides under vacuum milk is protected against heat damage.

Temperature of milk °C		kg water evaporation/m² heating surface/h	
		0.35 kg/cm²	0.70 kg/cm²
Atmospheric pressure	100	28	50
	61	145	165
	39	210	230

Evaporation under vacuum avoids excessive denaturation of proteins and destruction of vitamins. When the total solid concentration is low, only the whey proteins are denatured at high temperatures, but when the total solid concentration is high; casein will also precipitate and the risk of precipitation taking place in the evaporator will be greatly increased. Under vacuum, the boiling point of milk is low since water evaporates more readily as the vapour pressure over a liquid falls. The relationship between pressure and boiling 'point is shown below:

Atm.absolute pressure	Vacuum (m head)	Boiling point °C
1.0	0	99.1
0.8	2.1	93.0
0.6	4.1	85.5
0.4	6.2	75.4
0.2	8.2	59.7
0.1	9.3	45.5

Parts of milk evaporation plants :

Milk evaporation plants comprise mainly the following parts: a) the milk heater, b) the vapour separator, c) the condenser and d) the milk discharge pump and the vacuum pump.

The milk heater In the milk heater the-heat required for evaporation is transmitted to the milk so that part of the water can evaporate. The oldest forms consisted of a pan with steam jacket and later, steam coils were introduced. Subsequently the developed heaters use stainless pipes fitted in a steam heated body. Today heaters with plates are also in use. The condensate formed in the steam space is constantly drawn off by means of a special condensate pump.

The vapour separator: The heat applied to the milk evaporates the water in the milk. The vapour formed is separated from the milk in the vapour separator, where owing to the large space, the vapour has a small velocity so that small milk droplets carried along with it are not lost. The milk flows back to the heater to be heated again.

The condenser: The vapour released in the separator must be discharged as fast as it is produced. This purpose is served by the condenser, which is connected with the vapour separator by means of a wide pipe where the vapour is condensed by passing, through sprays of cold water (spray condenser) or by being brought in with contact with cold metal surfaces by means of a wide pipe where the vapour is condensed by passing through sprays of cold water (spray condenser) or by being brought into contact with cold metal surfaces (surface condenser), In the case of a spray condenser the cooling water and vapour condensate are discharged by means of a barometric drain (barometric condenser) or a wet vacuum pump. Besides, the non condensable gases such as air, which get into the evaporator through leaks are introduced with the milk, must be removed, as otherwise the vacuum would gradually run off.

Vapour preheater Part of the vapours from the last effect of an evaporator can be used in a low temperature preheater. Fresh milk can be preheated from 10°C to 43°C. All the vapours liberated at the evaporation chamber cannot be used for this purpose since major quantity of vapour is required at the condenser creating necessary vacuum for low boiling point of the end.

Entrainment separator. The concentrated milk and vapour mixture flow down the evaporator tubes into the entrainment separator where milk and entrained droplets of milk in vapour are separated from vapour. The most commonly employed types of separator is centrifugal or cyclone separator which is very effective for the purpose. The liquid-vapour mixture enters the cylindrical separator tangentially. Under the influence of centrifugal force the heavier liquid droplets are thrown to the wall from where the liquid spirals down. The vapour escapes through the stock at the top of the separator.

From the early vacuum pan, evaporators of different designs such as long tube vertical evaporators, climbing film evaporators, falling film evaporators, plate evaporators have been developed. Each type has its own advantage and disadvantage, eventhough most of the evaporators developed were not originally meant for condensing of milk but were extended for its use.

The criteria for the acceptance of any of these types of evaporators in the dairy industry has bee, the time- temperature relationship of milk processed in the equipment. Exposure of milk to higher temperature for longer time causes certain undesirable effects. Earlier emphasis in the selection of evaporator was placed upon the reduction in temperature for protecting the heat sensitive milk constituents. This, of course, resulted in developing equipment with improved product characteristics but at considerable increase in cost. The present trend is on the control of retention time of milk in the evaporator. This is based on the stress that time is more important of the time temperature variables. Based on this fact the vapour induced evaporator systems are being replaced by improved short retention time vacuum evaporators. Improvement in these techniques have extended the conventional falling film type cvaporator as a high velocity single pass unit. Very long tubes upto 10-12 m with very high film velocity and low retention time are in use. Evaporators using plate type heat exchangers provide similar advantage. There are also single pass except that they are plate heat exchangers rather than tubular surfaces.

Selection of equipment: As explained earlier, the first and foremost function of an evaporator is to transfer a great deal of heat energy. This point more than anything else determines the type, size and cost of the evaporator selection. Two types are available for condensing milk: a) the batch type and b) the continuous type. The batch type evaporator generally consists of a vessel heated by means of external jacketed or internal steam coils or by calandria with liquid inside and outside the tubes. Continuous evaporator generally consists of tubular calandria or plate packs. Continuous type has almost superseeded batch type in dairy industry as this affords a much shorter holding time. The continuous evaporators are divided into three main types; a) natural circulation, b) forced circulation and c) single pass.

An important point to consider in selection of an evaporator is the number of effects in economising consumption of steam. Double and triple effects are preferred in the dairy industry. The main advantages of a multiple effect evaporator is that they reduce the steam consumption roughly in the inverse proportions to the number of effects. Incrase in the number of effects does not after the total amount of evaporation and the capacity of the plant remains unchanged. Increasing the number of effects on the other hand causes increase in the heating surface required, which in turn increases the capital cost. However, the load on the condenser system for cooling the vapour is considerably reduced with greater saving in water requirements. The vapour from the evaporator contains heat energy and the reuse of this by either thermal vapour compression or mechanical vapour compression some economy in steam consumption can be achieved. However, the capital cost of the equipment will increase.

The economy by use of thermo compression in multiple effect evaporator at the temperatures of evaporation 50-60°C; totalsolids 48-50% is given below:

Kg steam/ ***Type***	***Kg water/*** ***kg evaporation***	***kg evaporation***
Single effect	1.06	20.0
thermo compression	0.45	8.0
Double effect	0.65	6.0
Thermo compression	0.45	6.0
Triple effect	0.40	5.0
thermo compression	0.25	4.0

Selection of evaporator. Milk properties greatly influence the selection of evaporator and its operation. Some of these' are viscosity, temperature sensitivity, fouling, foaming and corrosion. Milk increase in viscosity under evaporation which may cause a decrease in heat transfer rate and hence capacity. Milk is sensitive to heat. To reduce risk of heat damage, low boiling temperatures and shorter residence times should be used. Evaporation may have to be worked at low pressures more specifically under more vacuum. Satisfactory temperature differences can then be achieved under heating medium (steam) at correspondingly lower temperatures. During evaporation, milk solids tend to adhere on the heat transfer surfaces. This fouling may be due to adhesion of suspended solids present in milk. More usually scale gets deposited from milk which may interfere with heat transfer surfaces and lower overall heat transfer coefficient and evaporation capacity. Fouling creates cleaning problems. To reduce labour costs, milk is processed by evaporators affording easy access for cleaning and CIP. Milk tends to foam during boiling,more so under vacuum. A stable foam accompanies the vapour out of the evaporator causing heavy entrainment. Milk partially dissolves copper and its alloys, tin and aluminium. All parts of evaporator have to be made of stainless steel.

Falling film evaporator is the type most often found in the dairy industry (Fig 7-2). The tubes are vertical and the product forms Ahick film on the inside of the tubes while the steam surrounds them. The product is preheated at a slight pressure somewhat above the temperature of generation in the evaporator. From the preheater the product is led to the top section of the evaporator. By creating a vacuum, the temperature in the evaporator will be below 100°C. By means of a nozzle shaped device (1) the product is distributed over the spreader plate (2). Since the milk is somewhat superheated, it expands as soon as it leaves the nozzle, where part of the water is immediately vapourized. The steam thus formed presses the milk outwards against the inside of the tubes in a thick film which runs down

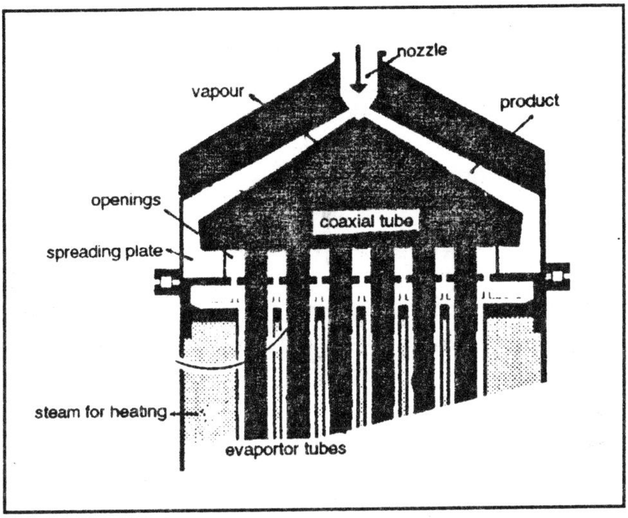

Fig 7-3 Upper Section of falling film evaporator

along the walls of the tubes. The water in the film evaporates rapidly as the milk passes through the tubes. A steam separator is fitted under the evaporator to separate the steam from the concentrated milk (Fig 7-3). The holding time in the falling evaporator is very short, about one minute as only a small amount of the product is treated at the same time.

To improve the thermal efficiency of evaporation, the secondary vapour

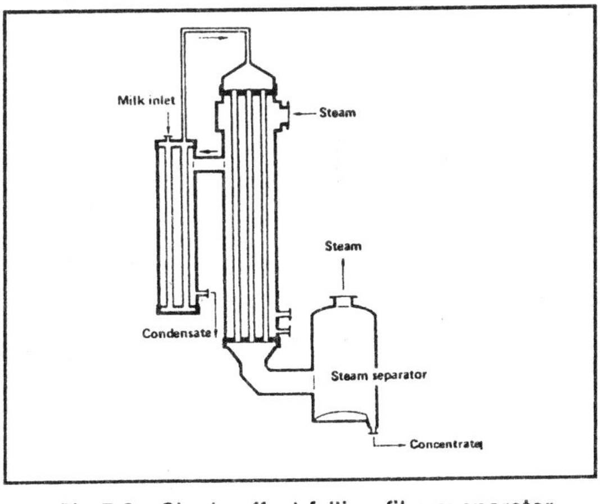

Fig 7-2 Single effect falling film evaporator

generated from the milk can be compressed and used as a heating medium in the evaporator by using thermocompressor. From Fig 7-2 it can be seen that part of the vapour from steam separator of single effect evaporator is fed to the thermocompressor to which high pressure steam is connected. The compressor converts the high steam pressure to kinetic energy and steam gets ejected at high pressure through the nozzle. The ejector effect causes the vapour from the product to be entrained and compressed to a higher pressure. A single effect evaporator with thermocompressure is almost as economical as a double effect unit. Thus, the use of thermocompressor together with multiple effect units reduce energy costs.

Double effect milk evaporators : In this system (Fig 7-4) milk is fed from a float hopper to the first separator (1) to be heated to 40°C and subsequently in the second preheater (2) to 75°C. The milk then passes to the first falling film evaporator (3), which is at a vacuum corresponding to a temperature of 85°C. As the film of milk passes through the tubes, the

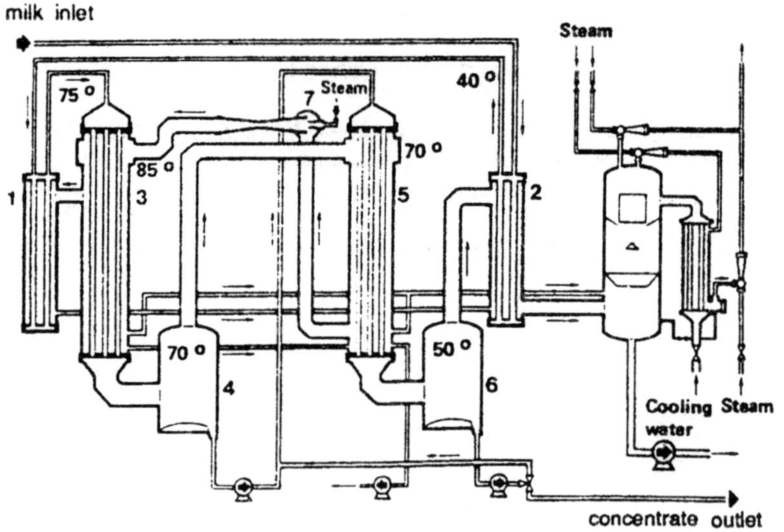

1 preheater -1
2 preheater - 2
3 evaportor 1.st effect
4 steam separator 1.st effect
5 evaporator 2nd effect
6 steam separator 2nd effect
7 Thermocompressor

Fig 7-4 Double effect falling film evaporator for condensed milk

water evaporates-and the milk gets concentrated. The milk concentrate is separated from the secondary vapour in the steam separator first effect (4) and pumped to the top of the second evaporator (5) where the temperature is lower (70°C). After evaporation in the second effect the concentrate is separated from the vapour in the steam separator (6) and pumped out from the system. Part of the concentrate is returned to the inlet of the second effect to increase the volume of liquid through this effect, as lack of moisture on the heating surfaces may lead to deposits.

The thermo-compressor (7) by injecting high pressure steam, raises the pressure of the vapour generated from the concentrate in the second effect (5). The mixture is then used as the heating medium in the first effect (8).

The factor limiting the number of effects is the temperature range applied. The temperature should not exceed 70°C in order to limit protein denaturation, vitamin destruction and Maillard reaction. The evaporating temperatures applied in the various effects are shown below:

No.of effects	**boiling point -°C in plants with number of effects**				
	3	**4**	**5**	**6**	**7**
1	65	68	68	69	70
2	58	63	63	65	67
3	47	56	57	61	64
4		48	53	57	60
5			46	52	55
6				45	50
7					45

An alternative to concentration by evaporation is concentration by membrane filtration.

Vacuum producing equipment: Mechanical pumps or steam jet ejectors are used to produce vacuum in the evaporator initially and to remove air from the system which may have accumulated through leaks during operations. Mechanical pumps of reciprocating or rotary type can be used to remove the condensing vapours simultaneously. Steam jet ejectors are more commonly used as they are economical in operation at a vacuum greater than about 65 cm Hg. They are simple and need little maintenance. In principle, a high pressure steam 7 kg/cm^2 is fed through a nozzle into a chamber where it entrains surrounding gases, and the mixture pass at high velocity through a venturi producing vacuum in the suction line. A single stage ejector may produce vacuum upto 63 cm Hg and a two stage unit about 73 cm Hg.

Tightness test is essential for proper operation of the evaporator that is completely air tight. Even small air leakage can raise milk boiling temperature. Before start a test is conducted by closing inlet valve, building up vacuum of 61 cm Hg; stopping the vacuum pump and in 10 min subsequent period vacuum must not decrease more than 3.8 cm Hg. The defect if noticed must be rectified.

Method of making Evaporated milk

Milk reception : The quality of milk required for condensing is basically the same as that required for the manufacture of ordinary milk products. When milk is received at the plant, its temperature should be 10°C or below. The milk should be clean, sweet, free from off flavours and odour and reasonably free from extraneouos material. Contamination of antibiotics and other chemical residues is highly undesirable. Acid development is objectionable, for not only does this indicate an excessive bacterial count, but it also reduces the heat-stability of milk. Among the platform tests at milk in take are alcohol test to weed out abnormal milk, mastitis milk causing sweet curdling and clot on boiling test. Two important considerations are a) the level of spores and heat-resistant bacteria in the milk and b) the ability of the milk to tolerate intensive heat treatment without coagulation in the sterilizer. Evaporation takes place under vacuum at a temperature not exceeding 65-70°C. However, at temperatures below 65°C spores and heat resistant bacteria will find ideal growth conditions which could lead to the entire batch being spoiled. Thus, a precise control of bacteria in the process is necessary. The ability of the milk to withstand heat treatment depends to a great extent on its acidity, which should be low and on the salt balance in the milk. The salt balance is subjected to seasonal variation, nature of the feed and stage of lactation of cows, although it is possible to improve the ability of the milk to withstand the level of heat treatment by suitable additions of stabilizers.

Forewarming: The standardised milk must undergo intensive heat treatment. It destroys yeast and moulds, eliminates pathogens, inactivates undesirable enzymes particularly lipase, helps in rapid evaporation in the evaporator, permits withstanding of intense heat during sterilization and controls viscosity of evaporated milk. The time/temperature of forewarming extends over a wide range such as 85 to 93°C for 15 to 5 min or 116° to 140°C for 5.0 to 0.5 min. The modern trend is towards high temperatures short time heating. The exact heating conditions is controlled to provide optimum viscosity of the finished product, without inducing excessive thickening or thinning during storage. Tubular heat exchangers are commonly used for forewarming either double- tube or shell-and-tube heat exchanger.

Evaporation : The heated milk is passed to the evaporator which may be double or triple effect falling film type. The milk passes through steam heated tubes under vacuum. Boiling takes place between 50 and 60°C. The formation of steam bubbles are separated from the milk in a steam trap. The total solids) content of the milk increases as the water is boiled off. Regular check is made on the density and the concentration of dry solids is correct when density has reached 1.07. At this stage, 1 kg of evaporated product with 8% fat 18% SNF may result from the standardized milk. It is customary to slightly overcondense the milk to facilitate standardization later by the addition of enough water.

Homogenization: The concentrated milk is pumped from the evaporator to the homogenizer which is set for 2 stages, the first stage at 100 kg/cm^2 and the second stage at 50 kg/cm^2. These pressures also vary from plant to plant. The milk received from suppliers always contain small dirt particles apd hence to be removed either by centrifugation or by filtration at 35-40°c.

Standardization: Evaporated milk is marketed with a prescribed amount of fat and milk solids not fat. The prescribed standards for fat is 8% and MSNF 18%. Thus the ratio of fat to solids not fat is 8:18 or 1:2.25. The prescribed percentages are minimum values which must be maintained.

Neither they should exceed by more than reasonable margin for economic reasons. Operating levels may be set, for example at 8.05% fat and 18.10% SNF. The standardization of fat content is done by the addition of skimmilk or cream to the whole milk depending on whether there is a requirement to reduce or increase the fat content of the whole milk. The SNF is adjusted by the addition of skim milk. The standardization should be accurate for any error in the levels present in the raw milk will be magnified many times in the course of the evaporation process.

Available data

Cream testing	40% fat	5.4% SNF
Skim milk	0.2% fat	9.0% SNF
Milk 6500 kg	3.5% fat	8.8% SNF

Desired

Condensed milk 7.9% fat 18.2% SNF
Amount of cream/skim milk to be used
Amount of finished product
Water removed by evaporation

Solution

1 Ratio in condensed milk SNF/fat = 18.2/7.9 = 2.3

2 Desired % fat in whole milk = 8.8/2.3 = 3.826

3 Difference in fat% of whole milk and final product 3.826 - 3.50 = 0.326

4 Wt of fat needed for 6500 kg milk = 6500 x 0.326 = 21.19 kg

5 Fat for cream for standardization = 5.4% SNF/2.3 = 2.348

6 Available fat in cream = 40-2.348 =37.652%

7 Crear needed for standardization = 21.19 kg milk fat/37.652% = 56.28 kgs.

		kg fat	**kg SNF**
Original milk	6500	227.500	572.00
added cream	56.28	22.520	3.039*
Total	6556.38	250.012	575.039

Wt. finished product 250.012/7.9% = 3164.7 kg

water to be removed 6556.38-3164.7 = 3391.58 kg

Proof kg SNF / kg fat = 575.039 / 250.012 = 2.3

It is to be noted that in earlier years a soft curd in the sterilizer was necessary to give evaporated milk some viscosity to prevent fat separation. This was done by superheating after condensing and adjusting the rotary sterilizer by stopping occasionally to develop viscosity. All these are now avoided. Homogenisation improves control of heat coagulation, shortens sterilization process, removes the need for shaking the evaporated milk cans after sterilization and preventing cooked flavour or discolouration in the product. Homogenization should not be too intensive to avoid the stability of the protein with the consequent risk of milk coagulating during sterilization.

Cooling storage and final standardization : The milk is cooled to 5-8°C to await sample sterilization. In some plants milk is standardized before condensing, purposely over condensed and then calcylated amount of water is, added to reduce the concentration of total solids to the percentage required. In some other plants all standardizing is done after condensing after estimating fat and-SNF% in the condensed product. If milkfat should be needed, it must be added before the product is homogenized. It is preferable to prestandardize and manage the operation so that the standardization after concentration can be done by the addition of SNF or water if needed and not- milkfat.

Sample sterilization : The stability of the condensed milk can be improved by the addition of certain salts like sodium citrat or disodium phosphate. The quantity to be added is determined by pilot sterilization. Where the sample sterilization has been done, the manufacturer, on the basis of previous day's result is certain that the milk will withstand sterilization, then the milk is cooled to 12-14°C and the required quantity of stabilizer is thoroughly mixed with the milk before the milk is packaged. In uncertain cases, on this point, a fresh pilot sterilization is necessary.

Pilot sterilization: A 10% solution of the stabilizer is prepared for use so that 0.1 ml of this solution is equivalent to the addition of ml/g of dry salt for every 16 kg of evaporated milk. The amount of stabilizer to be added to any batch is determined by trial using 8-10 sample cans. They are filled with different measured amounts of the stabilizer solution and then with 170g (6 oz) of evaporated milk to be tested as follows:

170 g unsterilized milk plus		*CANS*						
		1	2	3	4	5	6	
	ml 10% stabilizer solution	0.0	0.0	0.2	0.4	0.6	0.8	1.0
	ml.distilled water	0.0	1.0	0.8	0.6	0.4	0.2	0.0
Rate of stabili-zer/in g/16 kg product	0	0	2	4	6	8	10	

These cans are sealed and put under pilot sterilization at 117°C/15 min and cooled rapidly to 24°C. These cans are then opened and examined for smoothness, colour and viscosity. The viscosity is measured as degree of retardation of a pendulum immersed in the sample. For example, the retardation degree R for fresh milk before condensing may be 15, after condensing 20, and after sterilization 150. Suppose can 2 which is smooth with R 150 and can 3 gives rough texture with R 250°, it can be concluded that (can 2) 2 g of dry disodium phosphate would be sufficient for 16 kg of evaporated milk. Based on this the salt is added to the batch, filled in containers, sealed, tested for leaks by submerging them in hot water and leaky cans are resealed. The cans are sterilized in batch or continuous sterilizers to preserve the product for long period.

The bath sterilizer consists of a large horizontal drum opening at both ends. Inside the drum there is a revolving frame working between 6-12 rpm into which the cantorking between 6-12 rpm into which the cans are loaded. At the bottom of the drum there is a steam distributing pipe, a drain and water distribution pipe. The sterilizer is provided with safety valve, water, steam and vacuum gauges and a high temperature thermometer. With the revolving frame containing cans running, water is introduced so that the cans are all submerged in one position. In this way each can is completely covered by water once with every revolution of the frame. Steam is introduced to bring the temperature to 118°C in 20 min. This coming up period is followed very closely and the rise of temperature during the last 10 min should be at the rate of 2°C for every min. When 118°C is reached the frame is kept revolving for 3 min and then stopped during the holding period of 20 min. At this stage viscosity increases. The holding time is regulated by steam. The reel is then started, steam supply stopped and cold water is turned into'the sterilizer till the temperature comes to 30°C in about 15 min slowly to avoid bulging of cans. Continuous sterilizers operate by movement of cans for various operations.

The continuous sterilizer generally consists of three sections preheater, sterilizer and cooler, each .with appropriate pressure - holding valves. In each section in a rotating reel the cans move spirally from entrance to discharge end, each can in its own compartment, the rolling of cans accelerates the rate of heat exchange and encourages uniformity of heating. Each tin has its own compartment so that the period of treatment is equal for all tins. After sterilization all cans may be automatically examined for leaks and underweight. In some cases the cans are put in a mechanical shaker for about one min. The cans are inverted to minimise fat separation at storage temperatures of 16°, 21° and 27°C at intervals of 3-6 mo, 2-3 mo and 1-2 mo respectively.

Salt balance : In a colloidal suspension, ion concentration is of considerable importance in the stability of the suspension. In milk the positive ions are H, Na, K, Ca, Mg and the negative ions OH, Cl, HCO_3, H_2PO_4, HPO_4 and citrate. Of these, Ca, Mg, phosphates and citrates are mainly concerned in maintaining salt balance of milk. Casein has maximum stability to heat when it in combination with a definite amount of Ca. When Ca is above or ba this optimum concentration, the casein is less stable to heat. The Ca 's further distributed to casein, phosphates and citrates. Further, Mg reacts by replacing Ca in the phosphates and citrates. The effect of Ca and Mg is opposed to the effect of phosphates and citrates. The Ca casein combination is stable to heat, when the two groups of mineral salts are in balance. An excess of either group increases heat coagulation.

The unstable milk could be classed into two groups - one would increase the coagulation by the addition of citrates and phosphates and behave normally to the addition of Ca and Mg. The second group would respond to the addition of citrates and phosphates while addition of Ca and Mg would cause heat coagulation. In either case where a salt addition improves the heat stability of milk, an excess of the same will make it less stable. This shows that there is a balance between Ca and Mg on the one hand and phosphates and citrates on the other. In the case of evaporated milk, lack of stability because of ion excess of Ca is far more common. The flow diagram of evaporated milk manufacture is shown in Fig.7-5.

Judging and grading : High grade evaporated milk should have a mild pleasant flavour, a relatively viscous body and uniform smooth texture and uniform colour. The American Dairy Science Association standard is furnished below as a guide for judging and grading of evaporated milk.

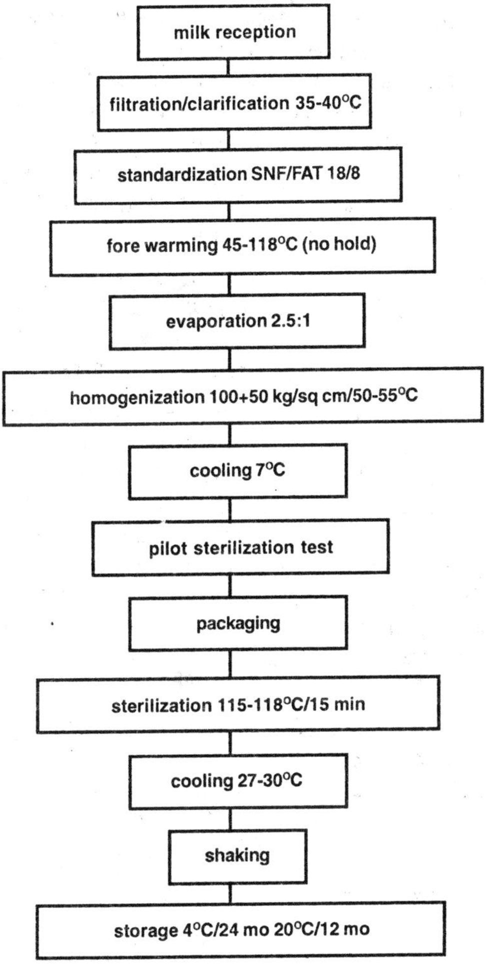

Fig 7-5 Flow Diagram of evaporated milk manufacture

Item	*Perfect grade %*
Flavour and odour	40
Body and texture	35
Colour	5
Fat content	10
Total solids	10

Adulte ants/preservatives must be absent

The n ethod of examination and evaluation of the product is cooked flavour may be due to high heat treatment during sterilization by the conventional method. The perfect score for the body are also more here than sweetened condensed milk. Excessive low heat stability of milk cause coagulation in sterilization. Age thickening is another common body, defect. Viscosity gradually increases till a stiff pudding like consistency takes place. This may happen in some weeks or may take after long time. Fat separation on the top may result due to inadequate homogenization pressure or storage at higher temperature. Gassiness or bloats may result due to low temperature and time of heating during sterilization.

Browning and discolouration is caused by excessive high heat treatment during sterilization. High temperature storage also causes this defect. Excessive high viscosity leads to feathering in coffee. Mineral deposit may occur in high temperature storge/long storage.

Sweetened Condensed Milk (SCM) : According to PFA rules (1984) sweetened condensed milk is a product obtained from cow or buffalo milk or a combination thereof; or from standardized milk by the partial removal of water and after addition of sugar. It may contain refined lactose, calcium chloride, citric acid and sodium citrate, sodium salts of ortho phosphoric acid and polyphosphoric acid not exceeding 0.3% by weight of the finished product. Such additions need not be declared on the label. Sweetened condensed skim milk should contain not less than 26% total milk solids and not less than 40.0% cane sugar. The milk fat content should not exceed 0.5% by weight.

The Indian Standard Specification for sweetened condensed milk is as follows (IS:1166, 1973)

Characteristics	*Sweetened condensed milk*	*Skim sweetened condensed milk*
Total milk solids (% wt) min	31.0	26.0
milk fat (°/ wt)	NLT 9.O	NMT 0.5
Sucrose (% wt) min	40	40.0
Acidity (% lactic) max	0.35	0.35
Bacterial count (g)	500	500
Coliform count (g)	negative	negative
Yeast and mould (per g) max	10	10

NLT = Not less than *NMT = Not more than*

Method of making SCM

1 Milk reception, filtration/clarification procedures are the same as for evaporated milk.

2 *Standardization* is done to conform legal requirements in the finished product. The fat/SNF ratio in raw milk is adjusted by adding cream/ skim milk depending on whether there is a fat shortage or fat surplus.

Forewarming or preheating: The standardized milk is preheated to destroy lipase, yeast, moulds and microorganisms. This treatment is very important as the milk after condensing is not heat sterilized unlike evaporated milk but preserved by high concentration of sugar. The time-temperature of heating extends over a wide range like 116 to 149°C for 5 to 0.5 min (flash) or as in earlier days at 82-93°C for 15 to 5 min in a hot well before the milk is drawn to the vacuum pan.

Condensing : When the concentration required is reached in the vacuum evaporator the batch is struck. To judge the level of concentration, various instruments are available. Generally, the density is estimated by using a refractometer or taking a Baume hydrometer reading and applying suitable temperature correction to get correct density.

Addition of sugar : Cane sugar is added generally. The sugar used should be bacteriologically and chemically pure. It is used to preserve the final product. Other sweeteners like glucose or corn syrups can be used to replace sugar by 5 to 25%. It is important that right proportion is added for safe keeping of the final product. The amount should be sufficient as it depends on its osmotic effect being sufficiently high. A sugar content in the aqueous phase of atleast 62.5% is required to produce osmotic pressure high enough to inhibit the growth of microorganisms. Two methods are used for addition of sugar a) the addition of dry sugar before heat treatment to milk so that it can dissolve properly or b) the addition of 65% syrup of sugar in the evaporator (Fig. 7.4). The stage at which sugar is added affects the viscosity of the final product. Early addition of sugar can cause the product to become too viscous during storage.

If sugar is added, it should fulfil its intended purpose. It must be present in the condensed milk in such sugar-in-water concentration as will prevent bacterial spoilage. The sugar- in-water concentration in SCM is referred as sugar ratio. It is expressed as %. A 62.5% of sugar ratio means that the water present in SCM contains 62.5% of added sugar. A range of 62.5 to 64.5% is generally considered a reasonably safe range. However, the milk should be of high bacteriologial quality and sanitary precautions are to be taken into account during manufacture. Sugar ratios above 64.5% should be avoided because such a concentration approaches the point of sucrose saturation. This is more noticeable when the product is stored at 2-3°C when sugar will be in super-saturated condition and may tend to crystallize out causing objectionable coarse texture (sandiness). The desired amount of sugar to add may be calculated on the basis of either fat-sugar ratio or total milk solids-sugar ratio in the final product.

Problem

A — Available standardized milk testing 3.75% fat and cane sugar

Desired — a) SCM testing 8.55% fat-and 45% sugar
b) Amount of sugar to be added

Solution % sugar to be added = (3.75/8.55)x45 = 19.74 kg
Ratio of concentration (8.55/3.75) - 2.20 : 1
Sugar in SCM = (19.74 x 2.28) = 45%

B — Available skim milk with 9.09% MS

Desired — a) Sweetened Condensed milk with 24% MS and 47.5% sugar
b) Amount of sugar to be added

Solution Ratio of concentration = (24/9.09)=2.64

Amount of sugar to be added = (9.09x24)/47.5 =18 kg

The batch is struck when the Baume hydrometer reading is at 120°F (48.9°C). The reading is around 32°B. For other temperatures a correction factor used is 0.03°B for each °F of deviation from the standard 120°F. The evaporated milk may have 7°B at 120°F.

Homogenization is invariably done before the product is cooled for crystallization. This procedure is not generally mentioned in text books. The object is to obtain a uniform fat emulsion and reduce fat separation to a minimum degree during storage. The pressure is 100 kg/cm^2 first stage and 50 kg/cm^2 in second stage.

Cooling sweetened condensed milk : This process is very important for SCM. This is necessary because a) it delays the tendency of age-thickening b) it delays the tendency of discolouration during storage and c) it provides thedesired smoothness of texture in the finished product. The smoothness of the product is controlled by the number and size of lactose crystals it contains. The solubility of lactose at room temperature is about 18%, but in SCM (having about 62% cane sugar in water) the solubility is only about 15%. The condensed milk as it comes from the evaporator is a saturated solution of lactose. At ordinary room temperature it is super saturated solution of lactose. Therefore, as the temperature falls from the evaporator there is a tendency for some lactose to crystallize out. Getting a permanently smooth texture in condensed milk is not a problem of preventing lactose crystal formation during cooling since lactose will crystallize out. The main problem is to prevent the crystals from growing larger after cooling. The cooling must therefore be completed in such a manner as to produce numerous small crystals conditions necessary for the formation of small crystals are a) rapid crystallization b) agitation nd c) inoculation of the product with numerous crystal centres. To get mass crystallization, there should be forced crystallization. This is done by retarding and increasing the cooling time with vigorous agitation at the optimum temperature of 30°C. Therefore the condensed milk is seeded at 30°C with powdered lactose and held for an hour at this temperature with vigorous agitation. Milk contains two forms of lactose - alpha and Beta. At temperatures below 90°C, only alpha lactose will crystallize out. Crystallization is slow because to maintain super-saturation of alpha lactose, the highly soluble beta has to change over to alpha to maintain equilibrium. Besides the high viscosity of SCM reduces the rate of crystallization. The seed material used is powdered lactose or the SCM produced the previous day. The seed must be in the form of fine powder to give more crystal centres. It must be sterile to avoid contamination. Only alpha lactose can be used. The amount used is generally 375-500 g/1000 kg of condensed milk or around 0.30 of previous days' SCM. Uniform distribution is essential. Therefore, the powder is added with agitation to a small amount of condensed milk and then mixed to the day's run. After the crystallization is over the condensed milk is cooled to 15-20°C. Various types of batch or vacuum cooling systems are available. The room in which the product is packaged must be kept in hygienic condition. Pre sterilized cans are used with automatic filling machine.

A number of defects which have been encountered in earlier days are discolouration, tallowy/rancid flavour, bloats in cans, button shaped red brown firm mass of growth on the internal sides of can, age thickening, sugar down and sandiness. The relation between number of lactose crystals and degree of sandiness is illustrated as follows in a product with 9% fat, 22.5% SNF and 42.5% cane sugar, and 12.2% lactose.,

No.of crystals mm^3	*length of longest edge of crystal in micron*	*Scale of sandiness*
4 00 000	9	Excellent
3 00 000	10	Good
2 00 000	11	Slightly pasty
1 50 000	13	Pasty
1 00 000	15	Fine, mealy
75 000	16	Fine mealy
50 000	19	mealy
25 000	23	Fine sandy
12 500	29	sandy
7 500	35	Very sandy

(Condensed milk and milk powder, Hunzlker)

The flow diagram of Sweetened Condensed milk manufacture is illustrated in Fig 7-6.

Condensed milk containers: The evaporated milk containers must withstand the pressure changes in the process of sterilization. There are two types of cans a) the sanitary type (the can with solder seal) and b) the vent hole cans. The vent hole cans are used for evaporated milk. These cans have a small orifice for filling the product and are sealed by tipping the

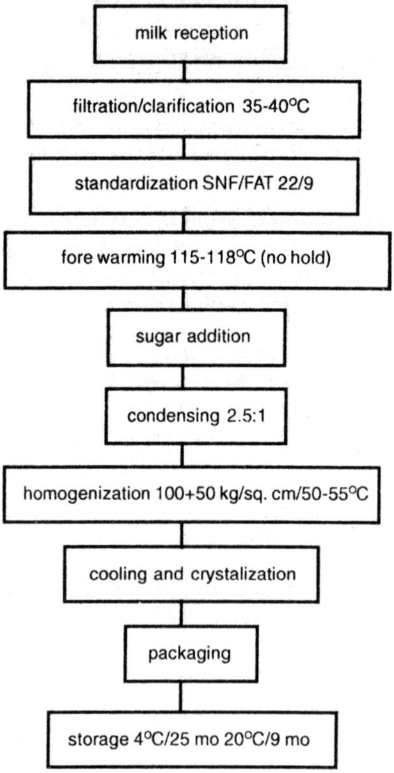

Fig 7-6 Flow diagram of SCM manufacture

vent hole with a drop of solder. The cans should be filled as nearby full as possible without fouling the surfaces of the tin or around the vent hole causing interference with the solder. If cans are filled too full it may cause flipping because of limited air space to allow for unavoidable expansion. When filling vent hole cans there is a tendency for the milk to wet the surface around the orifice. This may interfere with proper functioning of the solder. Hence, the top of the can should be clean and dry. The filling machines have automatic multiple piston pumps.

Leak detection: The cans are passed through a hot water bath. In case of leaking can, the pressure inside expels some of the excess air causing visibility of air bubbles. Such cans are picked off and returned to the can inspection for repair.

Sweetened condensed milk : The sanitary cans are open at the top and provided with separate lid. After filling SCM as full as possible, the lid is placed and the edges seamed by machine. A gasket cement in the peripheral rim of the lid assists in providing dependable hermetic seal. The contamination between storage tank and sealing machine must be avoided.

The sealing room must be kept in sanitary condition, clean and free from accumulation of orubbish. It should be closed to the outside and visitors. Filtered air should be used in the filling and sealing rooms.

The filling machines should be emptied after day's run; all detachable parts to be dismantled washed, scalded, steam dried and replaced in the machine. The filling machines should be hooded when not in use to protect them from dust, chance insects and other agencies of contamination.

Judging and grading of sweetened condensed milk A score card prepared by American Dairy Science Association is furnished below

Items	*Perfect score*
Flavour and odour	30
Body and texture	25
Colour	5
Fat content	10
Milk solids	10
Bacteria	10
Sugar	10
Total	100

High grade condensed milk should have clean, pleasant aroma, a pronounced sweet taste, smooth and uniform body and texture, uniform light colour.

Uses : Sweetened condensed milk is useful in remote areas where milk is not readily available, for reconstitution as sweet milk beverage, tea and coffee whitener, in ice cream preparation, in candy and confectionery and in prepared foods. Bulk condensed milk is used as a source of milk solids for candy, bakery products in considerable quantities.

Evaporated milk is used for reconstitution into milk for feeding infants and persons with weak stomachs. The consumer must be aware of the perishability of evaporated milk once the can is opened. Opening the can under kitchen conditions is almost certain to lead to some bacterial contamination. The product will keep for several days under refrigeration if contamination is avoided.

Chapter 6

DRIED MILK / MILK POWDER

Introduction : Dehydration or drying is one of the simplest methods of preserving extremely perishable food and conversion of surplus milk into dried powder with a moisture content low enough as not to promote bacterial growth and deterioration of quality during long storage. The dried milk/milk products can be reconstituted to supplement the short supplies of milk during the lean season of the year and in places where fluid milk is in short supply.

Drying of milk started in the beginning of this century on a modest scale and it took some years before equipment were developed on a commercial scale. From 1930 onwards there was growing development in spray drying. This was greatly accelerated during the second World War to meet the needs of the armed forces in many countries. Subsequently, World production further expanded by the introduction of spray drying in still more countries where milk production had increased or seasonal surpluses presented a problem. The emergence of spray drying as a major drying process is perhaps the most striking development in recent years.

Skim Milk Powder (SMP)

The Roller drying process is the oldest successful method and has changed very little since its introduction at the beginning of this century. Basically it is a simple process and comprises heating a thin film of milk for 2-3 s at atmospheric pressure on a metal surface heated by steam about 163°C. A common design consists of two steam heated hollow cylinders mounted horizontally and parallel to one another with a very small gap of about 0.50 to 0.75mm between them. Dam plates are fitted across the ends of the rollers to form a trough between them into which milk is fed. The rollers are made of special steels alloys accurately ground to a smooth surface. The rollers rotate towards each other at 16-24 rpm and are mounted in a heavy iron frame work. Steam is admitted to the rollers and maintained at 163°C. Milk fed into trough between the rotating rollers spreads as a thin film over the hot surfaces and after about three quarter of a revolution is completely dried. The scraper knives across the upper surface of each roller removes the dried film of milk as a continuous sheet which is collected at the bottom in a tray and removed by a screw conveyor for sifting and grinding (Fig.8.1). The scraper knives should be sharp and aligned properly. The condensate from the rollers are removed by siphon arrangement as rapidly as it is formed from steam. The vapourised moisture is removed through the hood. The entrainment of fine milk flake into the vapour can be considerable. The exhaust from the driers presents a pollution problem. The milk supply is usually preheated to 71°C. Control of steam pressure, alingment of rollers shapr scraper knives are essential. Slight preconcentration of the milk (18-25% TS) increases the output.

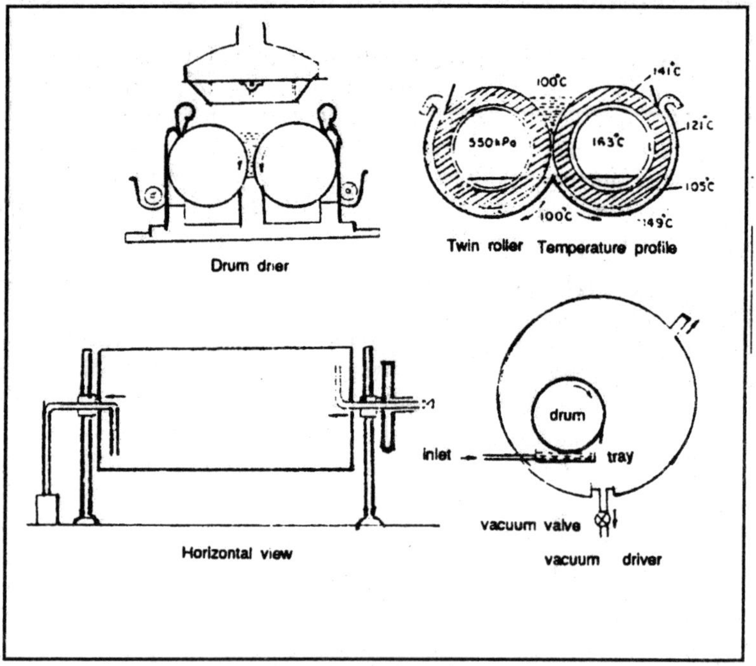

Fig 8-1 Roller drier

The particles of roller dried powder are solid, flat with irregular edges and no entraped air. The absence of occluded air retards oxidation. The keeping quality is good. Excessive high heat treatment causes protein denaturation, cooked flavour and low solubility (only 80%). However, it has some advantages.

Vacuum Drier : A single drum enclosed in a vacuum drum operates in vacuum chamber of 65-75 cm Hg. The inside of the drum is heated with low pressure steam and the vapour released from the product is continually withdrawn to maintain vacuum. The milk film is picked up by the roller from a shallow pan. The thickness of milk film is controlled by a spreader. The dried film is scrapped by knife. The solubility of the powder is comparable to spray dried production. Vacuum drier provides a) lower moisture content in the powder, b) lower drying temperature, leading to better solubility of the product, c) shorter drying period, d) greater temperature difference and hence attainment of higher rate of evaporation and e) safeguards atmospheric pollution in the product. It had limited use because of high equipment cost and became less popular (Fig 8-1).

In contrast to the roller process, spray drying involves large and complicated plant requiring a tall building to house it. The capital cost is high and the process is economical for handling large quantities of milk. The ideal is a daily run of 20 h with 4 h period for cleaning. The spray dried powder is superior to the roller dried product in flavour, appearance and solubility. It attained considerable international importance in both old established and newly developed dairy industries of the world. It meets the vital need in supplementing inadequate diets in various countries where malnutrition is prevalent.

Manufacturers of milk powder within European Economic Community (EEC) have the advantage of guaranteed outlay with minimum price for the so called Intervention Board, but this arrangement only applies to spray powder. The fact that roller powder is not covered by the intervention system has been a further set back for powder manufacturers within the EEC to shift from roller drying to spray drying.

Preheating of milk is essential to destroy bacteria and inactivate enzymes present in milk. The spray drying process kills many bacteria but its effect varies considerably between different species - bacterial spores, thermoduric streptococci and micrococci which are generally resistant. Nevertheless 100% destruction is rarely attained in any species. The process (unlike roller drying) cannot be relied upon to kill pathogens with certainty, for which purpose a definite pre-heating process is needed. Therefore, the preheated milk must satisfy phosphatase or other standard control tests. Preheating is performed at 73-74°C/1-3 min. This treatment yields a low heat powder product. For full cream milk high-heat treatment is necessary for which preheating at about 80-82°C is often used.

Extensive use of heat in vapour for pre-heating the feed to the evaporator is necessary to obtain high thermal efficiency. For this purpose, external straight tube preheater is the best. The milk is generally drawn from milk silos at 4°C and heated in spiral heaters placed in the condenser and in the calandrias. These are not accessible for mechanical cleaning and inspection but costs less than external straight tube preheaters. Special preheaters are used for making heat classified powders.

Preconcentration of milk is necessary for two reasons: a) If the milk is not pre-condensed, a very light, fluffy powder results. This would be too bulky from the stand point of packaging and actually the powder would be more difficult to use, not going into suspension in water or other liquids as readily as a somewhat coarser powder. b) The cost of evaporation by spray drying is appreciably greater than in customary condensing operations. For this reason as much of the evaporation as is practicable is done by pre-condensing.

Therefore, most of the water to be removed from milk in the manufacture of milk powder is removed in an evaporator. Under the conditions shown below in the preparation of 100 kg of skim milk powder 871 kg of water (89.6%) is removed in the vacuum evaporator and 101 kg of water (10.4%) is removed in th spray drier. The efficiency of the evaporator is thus of major importance in minimizing energy use in the overall process.

Raw skim milk 1072 kg 9% TS

EVAPORATOR ---------------> water 871 kg

Skim milk concentrate 201 kg 48% TS

SPRAY POWDER ----------------> water 101 kg

Skim milk powder 100 kg 3.5% moisture

The means by which improved economy has been sought has been to increase the amount of water removed in the evaporator. It is apt to mention here that the energy required per kg water evaporated in the spray drier is 16-20 times the energy required per kg water removed in the evaporator.

Principle of spray drying : Spray drying has been found most suitable for removing the last part of the water (the most difficult water) from the milk. This is because spray drying can convert a liquid milk product into a powder while still keeping the valuable properties of the milk and because this can be done fairly inexpensively.

The principle of all spray driers is to transform a liquid feed into many small droplets which are then exposed to a fast current of hot air. Because of the very large surface area of the droplets, the water evaporates almost instantaneously and transforms the droplets into powder particles which are then separated from the air. Spray drying is thus a combination of unit operations, like a) atomisation of the feed, b) evaporation and separation of moisture from each droplet, c) separation of the powder from the drying medium and heated air and d) collection of the powder at the discharge end of the dryer.

Advantages of spray drying are:

1 Suitability for feed in the form of solution or dilute suspension that can be atomised

2 Short holding or retention of the product in the drying chamber (less than 3 s) and rapid drying.

3 Relatively small amounts of water to be removed from large amounts of solids and therefore use of large capacity units (20 000 to 40 000 l milk/h)

4 Uniformity of production with regard to particle sizes, moisture content, colour and solubility due to uniform distribution of particles and their free moving state during dehydration.

5 Amenability of drying a variety of milk products in the same, unit.

6 Elimination of thermal deterioration since the wettest material remains in contact with hottest gases (air) for very short period permitting use of higher temperatures of air at the inlet to the drying chamber.

7 Amenable for final packaging of the product as it leaves the drier.

8 Fully automatic in operation and can be controlled from a control panel.

9 Low hold-up in the system helping quick commissioning and shut down of plant and easy adjustment of operating conditions.

Characteristics of spray drying process: It is amenable for large capacities and continuous operation (20 h/day) making it economical in-capital cost, labour, utilities and maintenance cost. There is practically no contact of the product with drier surfaces until the product is dried since moisture is removed by the hot air with freely floating droplets of the product. Exposure of large product surface area provides quick removal of moisture from the product. Quick and efficient separation of hot air and product after drying maintains product quality. Spherical shaped particles often hollow is advantageous for dispersion during reconstitution. The equipment is easily cleanable. The air has a function of supplying heat for evaporation and it also acts as a carrier for the vapour and powder.

Air inlet temperatures upto 210°C are used for drying of milk. Due to evaporation.in the drying chamber the temperature drops immediately. The temperature in the drying chamber is equal to air outlet temperature of around 95°C with single stage drying and lower with multistage drying. In co-current drier the product temperature will be 20-30°C below the air outlet temperature. The powder is cooled immediately as it comes out of the drier either in a pneumatic powder cooling system or in a fluid bed. The powder may be removed in cyclones and other dust recovery systems.

The components of a spray drier are:

1 An atomizer for transforming the liquid feed into a spray of droplets

2 An air disperser with air supply systems to give the hot drying air at the right direction and velocity.

3 A drying chamber which by the mutual positions of the atomizer and the air disperser which determines the air flow pattern and the way in which the product and the air are removed.

4 Auxiliary equipment for heating and transport of air, for pumping the feed, for removal of the product from the chamber, for separation of product and drying air for transport and cooling of the product.

5 Measuring and control equipment for indication, registration of control of some or all important process parameters.

Atomiser: The speed with which water evaporates from the droplets when exposed to the hot air is proportional to the surface area of the droplets. Thus, the purpose of an atomizing device is to produce large number of reasonably uniform droplets of optimum size. Two types of atomizing devices (Fig 8-7) are at present used in the dairy industry, the rotating atomizer or stationary pressure nozzles. Pressure nozzles originates from USA where they are still used and the centrifugal atomizers developed in Europe is the preferred system. The concentrate is converted to tiny droplets varying in size between 10 and 200 μm with greatest portion in the range of 40-8 μm. The atomizer wheel is a partially closed bowl. The concentrate feed enters the bowl close to the centre and by centrifugal force, is thrown out to the discharge orifice on the periphery. It leaves the atomizer as a,thin film with a velocity of 100 to 200 m/s. Very soon the film is broken to droplets. The diameter of the disc may range from 22 to 40 cm. For low velocities, a V-belt drive or a high frequency motor may be used. The speed of the disc ranges from 10 000 - 12 000 rpm. the atomizer is very expensive. It can handle viscous products than a nozzle atomizer. The tiny droplets in the drying chamber have a large surface area from which evaporation may readily take place. A litre of concentrate may provide around 15 billion droplets with a total surface area of around 100 m^2. The droplets leave the atomizer wheel or nozzle at a speed of Ca 150 m/s and come into contact with the flow of hot air whose velocity is approximately 20-30m/s. Droplets with dia within the normal range of 10-100 μm will be slowed down by the drying air within 0.1-1.0 m of the atomizer wheel or nozzle. In this area, therefore, heat transmission to the droplets and evaporation from the droplets will be considerable. The moisture content will drop to 10-12% and the temperature of the drying air will fall from approximately 180 to 100°C. At this point the outer layers of the droplets will have dried but water will still be there in the centre. The remaining water will diffuse through the dry outer surface via cavities in the droplets. The residence time in the drying chamber is about 25 s. As the droplets release water during the whole drying period , their surface is constantly cooled and thus, their temperature is always lower than the temperature of the drying air. This means the powder temperature

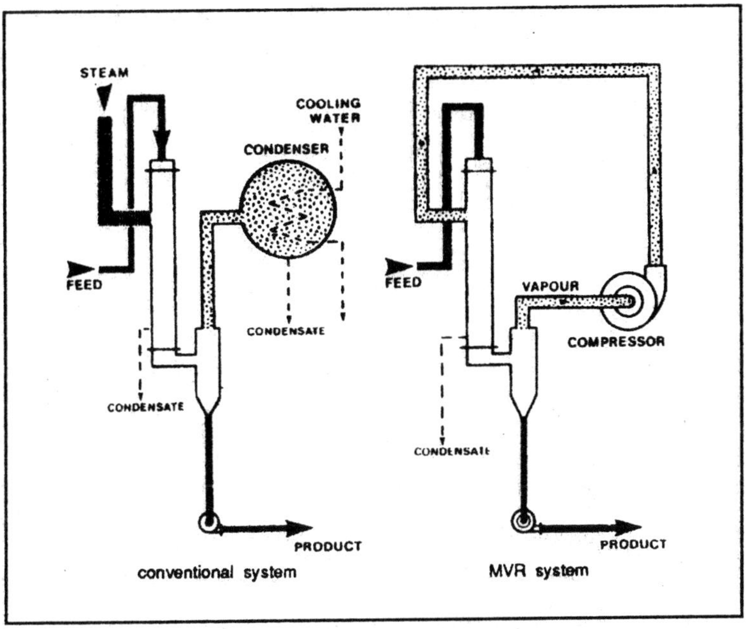

Fig 8-6 Comparison of conventional and mechanical vapour recompression system

may never be 75°C in one-stage drying and even lower in 2 stage drying.

The feed pump to the atomizer must be sanitary with variable speed drive. The temperature sensor controls the speed of the feed pump. To control variations in the total solids of the feed to the atomizer, it is necessary to vary feed rate to the atomizer to maintain a constant temperature of the outlet air from the dryer and have constant moisture content of the powder.

The pressure nozzle is a simple and inexpensive item, but it requires high pressure 3 piston pump giving 300-400 kg/cm^2 which is costly. The pump must have a variable speed drive. The nozzle is exposed considerable wear and hence the orifice must be of a hard metal.

Air heating system : Steam has been used for heating the crying air. But in modern drier, the air inlet temperature may be as high as 220°C. For this along with steam boosting by another heating systems is usually done. because saturated steam of 10-12 kg/cm^2 may give air temperature of 170-180°C only. Stainless steel tubes with aluminium fins provide good heat transfer characteristics. Apart from this, thermic fluid is widely used to heat the drying air either singly or as booster. In this, an oil or gas fired heater heats the transfer fluid which is then pumped to the air heater battery. It is a simple system operating in closed circuit and the efficiency is around 90%.

Desired inlet air temperature could easily be obtained. In another system, the oil or gas is burnt in a cylindrical chamber and inlet air is drawn over the external surface of a stainless steel heat exchanger. Electrical air heaters are costly but sometimes they are used as booster system.

Direct gas fired air heaters have been in use for many years in milk driers in North America as natural gas was available. No heat exchanger is required for this. The mixture of combustion gases from the burner and ambient filtered air are led to the drying chamber as the drying medium. The efficiency is almost 100%. This provides a saving of fuel consumption of 15-20% as compared with indirect heating. Lower capital and maintenance costs are added advantages. One main drawback is that the oxides of nitrogen contained in the combustion gases contaminate the milk powder. The nitrogen oxides reacts with milk proteins to produce nitrosamines which constitute cancer promoting health hazard. Conventional gas burners produce an NO_x level ex-burner of between 50 ppm and 150 ppm special burners are designed to produce the minimum amount of not more than 1 ppm NO from the burner mouth. The content of nitrosamines must be below one ppm and WHO has sued standards for the maximum amount of nitrite allowed in food products. Primarily only skimmilk and whey are spray dried in USA whereat the production of whole milk powder and fat filled powder is significant. Problems are perhaps more pronounced when powder contains fat. Water is another product of direct combustion of gas but one m^3 gas produce 1-7 kg water. This is equivalent to about 20% of additional water to be evaporated in the drier.

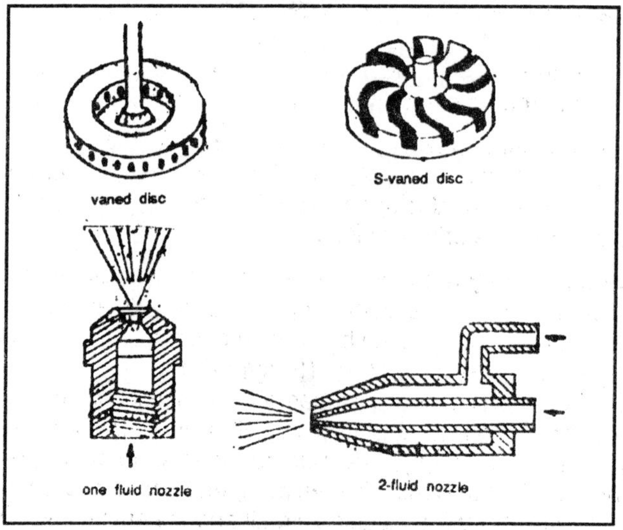

Fig 8-7 Types of atomizing nozzles

Drying chamber: The drying chamber may be cylindrical with a flat bottom from which the powder is sucked from the chamber by means of rotating powder collector or the chamber may be cylindrical with a conical bottom from which greater portion of the powder is removed by gravity. Flat bottom drier require low building height, controlled residence time and easy access for cleaning. Vibrators or hammers on the chamber are not necessary.

Fig 8-8 shows that the concentate from 1 is pumped by 2 to atomizer device 3 operated by drive 4. Air is drawn through filters, 5 heated at 6 and enters the drying chamber 8 through spiral inlet 7. The powder is separated at 9 and air together wither powder leaves at 10 to cyclone separator 11. The powder is discharged at 12 (powder extraction device) to powder drum 13. The main air fan draws air from the systems at 14. This is a cocurrent drier with a scraper.

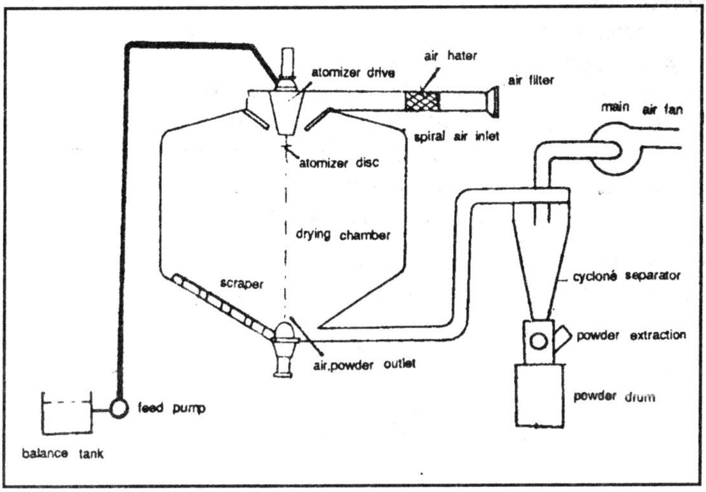

Fig 8-8 Flat bottom milk drier - LUWA

The conical bottom drying chamber is a) adaptable for two or 3 stage drying, b) separation of the powder into coarse fraction from the chamber and fine fraction from the cyclone with recycling of finest atomization zone to get dust free, partly agglomerated powder and c) suited for drying high fat powder (35-40%) which has a tendency to stick to the interior surface of ducts and cyclones and permitting greater portion of the powder to be discharged direct from chamber and leaving only a small quantity to pass through ducts and cyclones. Still to avoid a build up of powder on conical bottom it may be necessary to use external hammers or vibrators on the cone. Hammers may cause cracks in stainle steel sheet lining of chamber causing bacterial contamination some times. The air distributor to chamber must direct the floating particles downward to prevent moist powder sticking on the walls of the chamber nearer atomizer disc. To avoid charring of milk solids at hot air entrance, an annular cooling ring around the milk distributor is provided at the ceiling. The drying chamber can be installed in the open without building to save building costs. Normally insulation is provided by cladding plastic coated mild steel sheets. The insulation may be around 100 mm inside building and nearly double if drying chamber is located in the open.

The NIRO spray drier is an example of counter current conical bottom drier (Fig 8-9). The feed is led to an adjustable pump unit 1 which feeds concentrate to atomizer 2. A fan 4 draws air from open through filter 3, then to a steam heated battery 5 where the temperature of air is controlled.

The hot air is carried through an insulated duct ending in air disperser 6 below atomizer. The dry powder slides down the conical bottom from where it is taken out through a rotary valve. The air is exhausted from the system by fan 10 through exhaust hood. The powder from the drying chamber is discharged through pneumatic conveyor duct to a smaller cone 14 from which it is collected into a bag or from direct rotary valve. The transport air is sucked by fan 12 from the small cyclone. The transport air mixes with the main, air systems at a point between drying chamber and main cyclone collector 9. A cocurrent *horizontal* drying chamber is illustrated in Fig 8-10. It has pressure nozzle atomizer and cloth filters bag dust collector also.

Powder recovery system: Although there are several types of dust recovery systems, the commonly used are cyclone collector or bag filter. Cyclone

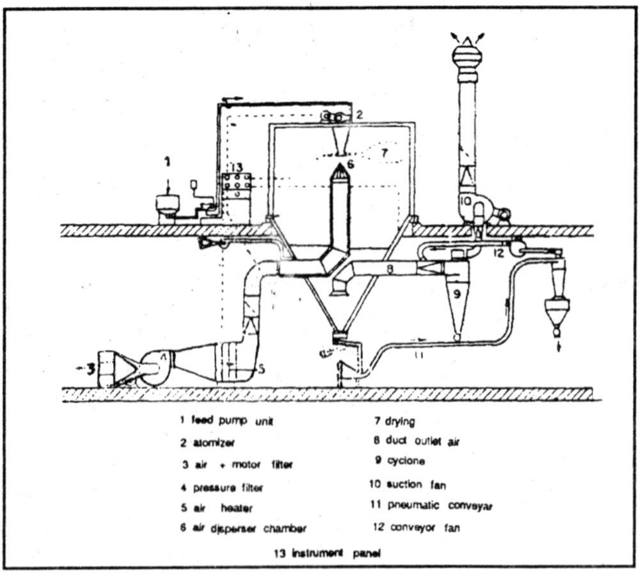

Fig 8-9 NIRO spray drier

separator is most widely used for removal of dust dairy product from air discharged from drying chamber. It works on the principle of centrifugal force. The mixture of air and dust enter a cylindrical conical chamber tangentially at one or more points at high velocity (about 30 m). Since mixture enters the chamber of large cross section, the velocity inside the chamber decreases. The direction of air flow changes from horizontal at inlet to vertical at the exit. The particles in the mixture thrown outwards against the cylindrical wall of the chamber due to centrifugal force settles down by gravity or particles of 10 to 200 μm this separator is efficient. The efficiency depends on dia of cyclones, mass of the particle and the air velocity. Particles below 5-10 μm constitute the loss to the atmosphere. The loss is expressed as mg solids per standard m^3 of air. In most countries legislation has been introduced in recent years to limit the emission levels by specifying maximum permitted amount of solids contained in the discharge medium. In Europe the permitted temission level from milk driers varies from 50 to 100 mg/St m^3 air discharged. The cyclone loss varies widely as detailed below:

	Loss	
Product	*% total production*	*mg/St m^3*
Skim milk	0.5	200
Wholemilk	0.35	150
Whey	1.00	400

The figures indicate that the loss exceeds permitted emission level. The wet scrubbers used in USA long ago was abandoned due to bacteriological hazard. A textile fabric bag filter can be used in addition to cyclone as secondary collector. It can protect environment and also increase the recovery of the powder. The loss of powder from filters very small. Less than 10 mg/St m^3 recovery is possible from the loss of 200 mg/St m^3 through cyclone collector. In this system air is introduced into the bottom part of the filter from where it enters the inside of the bags. The solids are collected inside the bags. The air goes through filter bags into the filter housing and then to the atmosphere. Stainless/steel, rings provided prevent bags from collapsing when there is negative pressure. The powder recovered from the filter is discharged from the cyclone of the pneumatic bag cleaning system into the powder from the drier. The textile filter a) protects environment, b) increases yield of powder and c) provides clean air for heat recovery from the outgoing air contributing to a 20-25% fuel saving.

The temperature and chemical tolerance of bag filter fabric for use in spray drying plants are:-

Fabric	Temperature tolerance °C	Chemical resistance	
		Acid	Alkali
Dynel	71	good	good
Polyethylene	74	good	good
Cotton	82	poor	good
Wool	93	good	poor
Polypropylene	93	excellent	excellent
Nylon	93	poor	good
Orlon	127	good	fair
Dacron	135	good	fair
Teplon	204	excellent	excellent

Efficiency of drying depends on a) moisture content of the feed at inlet to drying chamber, b) temperature and velocity of drying air and c) ratio of hot air to feed.

High thermal efficiency is achieved by high air inlet temperature, low outlet temperature, recycling of exhaust heat to preheat inlet air or feed, insulated and airtight chamber to reduce heat leakage to atmosphere and ambient air temperature. That is thermal efficiency % $E = (t_1 - t_0)/(t_1 - t)$ where t_1, is inlet air temperature, t_0 outlet air temperature, and t the ambient temperature. Assuming inlet air temperature is 200°C, outlet air temperature 95°C and ambient temperature 25°C, E = (200-95)/(200-25) x 100 = 60%. If inlet air temperature is 156°C and outlet temperature 90°C, the efficiency would be only 50.4%.

One stage drying is a process that is completed in one step. In this, the product is dried solely by the heat of the drying air which is led to the drying chamber around the atomizer device. The moisture content of the powder must be reduced to 2-4% before it leaves the drying chamber. This needs higher air outlet temperature than that used in 2 stage drying. The powder leaves the plant through the bottom of the drying chamber and through cyclones. Cooling of powder may take place in a pneumatic system in which the powder is transported in a high velocity air flow (4-6 times the volume of the powder) to a transport cyclone and bagged. The t powder has low volume and high density, relatively dusty and lumpy (fat products) and a tendency to form lumps when reconstituted. The powder may also be cooled in a vibrating fluid bed instead of a pneumatic transport.) Fluid bed cooling is used for the manufacture of fatty powders which cannot be transported in the pneumatic system and also to get powders with reduced dustiness (Fig 8-8).

Two stage drying : In this final drying takes place in a fluid bed after the powder has left the drying chamber. The fluid bed can either be stationary and integrated in the drying chamber or vibrating and placed after the drying chamber. In the fluid bed, the powder is thoroughly aired at moderate temperatures using a relatively small amount of air. The advantage is that the final temperature of moisture is more gentle at low temperatures. The temperature of the outlet air from the drying chamber is lowered by 10-20°C. This means that the moisture content of the resulting powder is 5-7% when it is transferred to the fluid bed. As the temperature of the outlet air and thus of the product is lower, heat damage to the powder particles (shell formation) is avoided during the critical period when their moisture content is 10-25%. As a result, the powder has a) less dustiness, b) less air content and high density and c) good solubility. These advantages coupled with lower energy costs incurred when water is removed in a fluid bed, make 2-stage drying the most wide spread drying method today.

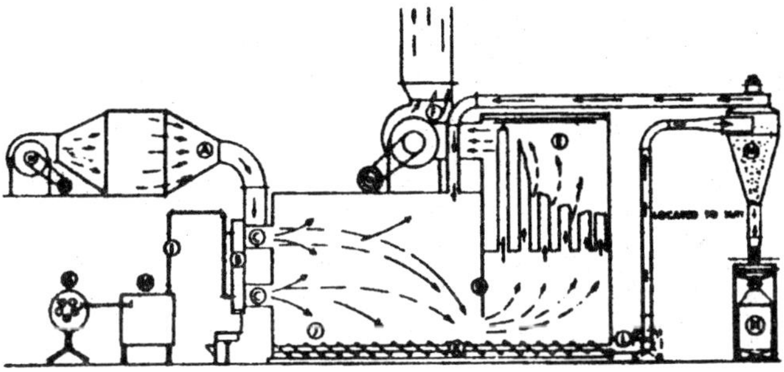

A air supply
B cone distributor
C air inlet and spray nozzle
D baffle
E cloth filterbag
F air exhaust
G Cone preheater
H high pressure pump
I high pressure line
J reciprocating conveyor
K screw conveyor
L outlet chamber
M cooling cycle
N Sifter - bagger

Fig 8-10 Horizontal spray drier

Three-stage drying: By including a combination of the 2 types of fluid bed available, i.e., an integrated and an external fluid bed, after the drying chamber, a 3 stage drying plant is obtained in which spray drying in the drying chamber is the first stage, drying in the integrated fluid bed is the 2nd stage, and external fluid bed is the 3rd stage. At the same external fluidiser can be used for effective and gentle cooling of the powder. These characteristics may be desired in different combinations depending upon the powder type having good solubility, little entrapped air high density, minimal dustiness, good solubility, low moisture (2-4%) and rapid reconstitutability. Factors like total solids concentate, rpm of atomizer, inlet spray angle in relation to air flow, air currents, drying temperature, and drying method can be effectively used to make powder with desired characteristics.

The following are the steps in the manufacture of whole milk powder or skim milk powder by the spray process.

Reception of milk. Only high grade raw milk should be accepted. Milk should be fresh with no sign of lipolysis and with an acidity of less than 0.15% lactic acid and free from copper contamination.

Standardization: to required fat/SNF ratio is necessary for whole milk powder.

Clarification improves the keeping quality of the powder.

Homogenization Milk is preheated to 71° C and homogenized at 150 and 50 kg/cm^2 in a 2 stages wherever whole milk is used.

Preheating is done to destroy microbes and inactivate enzymes. Skim milk is preheated at 85°C/20 min and Whole milk at 93°C/3 min.

Condensing to 40-50% TS is done at 70, 60 and 45°C in a vacuum triple effect evaporator.

Drying The whole milk concentrate is spray dried at air inlet of 180°C (200°C for skim milk) and at outlet temperature of 90-92°C for whole milk or 95-96°C for skim milk and cooled at 32°C.

Powder Whole milk dried to 2.3% moisture and skim milk to 3-5%° moisture.

The flow diagram for manufacture of whole milk powder, skim milk powder are shown in brackets wherever applicable. The second and third stage method of making spray dried powder is shown in Fig. 8-12.

Packaging is done in a dry atmosphere between the drier and sealed package and promptly in hermetical moisture proof package. Since powder is hygroscopic, it should not be exposed to humid atmosphere to prevent sticking and cake' formation in storage. Fat decomposition resulting in a tallowy flavour is a major storage defect in whole milk powder.

Packaging by hand is undesirable and it is difficult to avoid dust, wastage, manual contact and general discomfort. Different types of filling machines for skim milk powder and whole milk powder are available. Skim

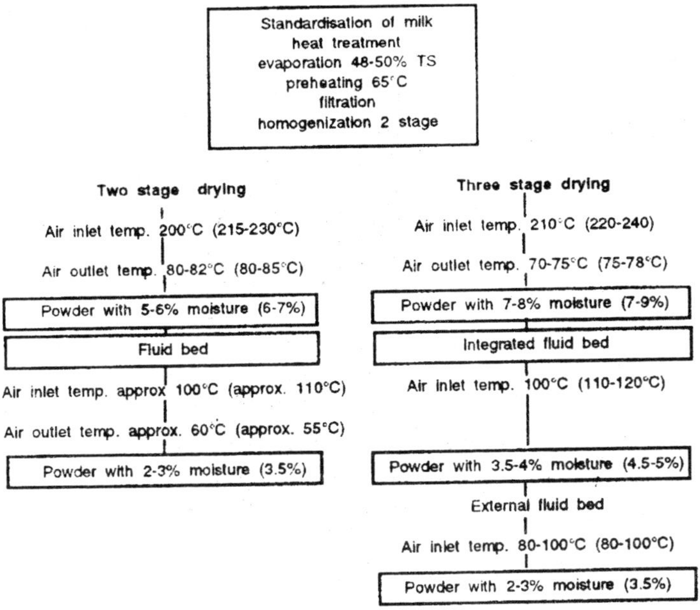

Fig 8-12 Flow diagram for the manufacture of WMP and SMP in 2 and 3 stage drying, SMP is shown in brackets.

milk powder is usually packed in bulk either in bags or in barrels. Skim milk powder is packaged in multiwall kraft paper sacks with loose inner liners of plastic which is heat sealed. Whole milk powder is generally nitrogen gas

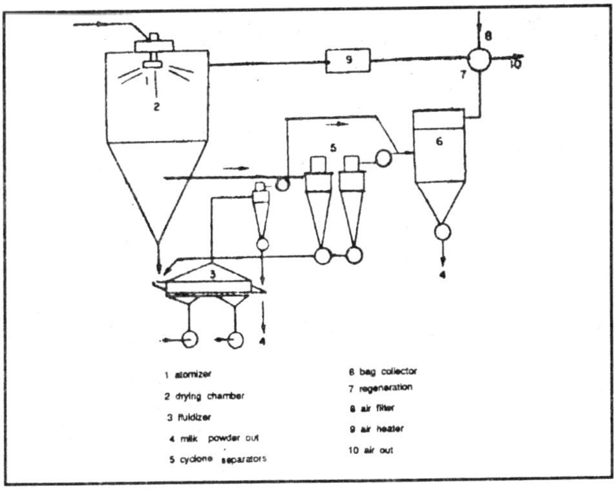

Fig 8-11 Two stage drying system

packed in the containers. Milk powders are stored in vapour proof moisture proof rooms in cool, dry place.

Powder is normally sifted before transfer to containers. Powder is stored in silos to facilitate packing in one shift. The silo may hold 16 h production so that in one shift 22 h production can be packed. Dry fat rich products are filled in tin containers, evacuated at 72 cm Hg and nitrogen gas is introduced to occupy the head space above powder level through 1 or 2 mm dia hole on container lid. The hole is soldered after releasing the gas valve. Gas packing reduces oxygen content in the powder. The gas packing system is shown in Fig 8-13. Gas packing is the most effective method of extending shelf life in tropical climate. A 2 mil polythene bag inside 4 ply kraft paper bag is a common package for skimmilk powder for domestic commercial trade. Storage at 24°C is desirable in a vapour proof moisture proof in a dark cool dry place.

Quality of milk powder Standards for dry milk products based on specific analytical procedures were many years ago defined by American Dry Milk Institute (now called American Dairy Products Institute). The specification for the extra grade powder is shown below :-

	Skim milk powder	***Whole milk powder***
Butterfat	max 1.25%	min. 26%
Moisture	4%	2.5%
Titratable acidity	0.15%	0.15%
Bacterial count/g	max. 30 000	max. 30 000
Solubility index	max. 0.5 ml	max. 0.5 ml.
Scorched particles	A	A

This specification is widely accepted for edible milk powder offered for sale to the intervention Board of the European Economic Community.

Instant milk powder: Normal milk powder has poor flow characteristics, does not easily reconstitute in cold water and has tendency to form dust.: The wettability, dispersability and sinkability are important characteristics which makes the powder to dissolve in cold water instantaneously.

Characteristics of instant milk powder: The term instant refers to the ability of the milk powder to redissolve (reconstitute) rapidly in water. This characteristic is advantagenous in milk powder used for household purposes and is dependent on the following factors:

a) *Wettability* referring to powder's ability to become wet when transferred to a water surface of appropriate size.

b) *Sinkability* referring to powder's ability to sink in appropriate amount of water after becoming wet.

c) *Dispersability* referring to powder's ability to disperse (spread out) in an appropriate amount of water to prevent lumping.

d) *Solubility* referring to the properties of the powder in connection with the formation of a solution or a stable emulsion.

The regular milk powder is deficient in these properties. To find better domestic use, these deficiencies are overcome by subjecting the powder to an instantising process. The instant quality of milk powder is obtained by changing the structure of the powder particles from individual particles to large, irregular, agglomerates. Agglomerates create a more coarsely grained powder with lower density. The coarsely grained structure is a great advantage when the powder is reconstituted as water can more readily enter the cavities (interstices) between the .agglomerates and wet them. Typical sieve analysis comparisons are as follows:-

Size in microns	*Whole milk powder*	
	Standard %	*Instant %*
>50	0	2
250-500	4	43
125-500	22	41
<125	74	14

The figures indicate that 125-500 micron sizes in instant powder is much higher than standard powder and emphasises agglomeration of particles in instant powders.

Powder with individual particles will also be wetted, but owing to the close structure of the powder, the water will enter the powder slowly. The particles dissolve and from the shell of highly viscous concentrate which prevents the water from penetrating further into the powder. Further, the powder will float on the surface of the water and stirring will only result in formation of lumps with center consisting of completely dry powder. Instant powder can be manufactured by returning the fine powder dust (the fines) from the cyclones to the atomizer zone in the drying chamber, the small individual particles can be made to adhere to the still moist concentrate droplets thereby forming agglomerates. The agglomerates with their coarsely grained structure and considerable capillary, are retained in the fluid drying process in the fluid bed. As a result the volume of powder will be increased.

In the straight through method : The spray drying conditions are adjusted to give a coarse powder (primary agglomeration) with a high moisture content 5-7%. The drying of the powder is finished in a gentle slow treatment of the agglomerates in a vibro fluidizer to required moisture. The powder is cooled in the last section of the bed and sieved for packing. The fine particles

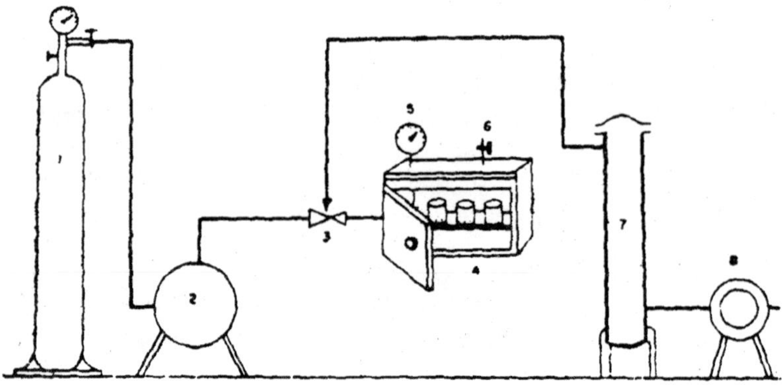

Fig 8-13 Nitrogen gas packing system

blown off are separated in a cyclone. These fines together with powder collected from the main cyclone are returned to the atomising moist zone where they adhere to the same moist particles to give secondary agglomeration recycled for agglomeration. The satisfactory conditions of instantizing to get of around 300 μm are a) high solids in the feed; b) low feed temperatures, c) low outlet air temperature, d) low nozzle pressure or atomizer speed and e) efficient recirculation of fines.

The characteristics of the powder are:

	ordinary skim milk powder	*instant skim milk powder*
Particle size (μm)	20-80	300-500
Specific volume (ml/100 g powder)	120-140	200-300 o73
Specific surface (cm^2/g powder)	5 600-9 000	2 400- 5 500
Wettability s(+)	> 10,000	< 100
Dispersability %(++)	60-70	80 -90
Solubility index (+++)	< 8.2	0.2-0.5

\+ 2.5 g powder is transferred to the surface of 25 ml water (24°C) in a 50 ml beaker. The time it takes for all the powder to become wetted is stated in s.

++ 52 g powder is transferred to 400 ml water (24-C) and stirred under controlled conditions. The reconstituted milk is poured through a 210 μm mesh sieve. The total solids content of milk that has passed through .the sieve is estimated and the result calculated as % dispersability.

+++ 3 g of powder is dissolved in 100 ml water at 24°C.Atter 5 min, it is centrifuged for 2x5 min. After first centrifugation 2/3 of the contents of the glass is poured out and replaced with fresh water. The amount of sediment centrifuged out indicates solubility index.

The lecithination method: The straight through method is not suited for whole milk powder where the free fat on the surface of the particles make them hydrophobic. The moistening effect is improved by adding lecithin which provides desired reconstitution abilities. The well agglomerated, high density, low solubility index whole milk powder, with very little fines is made by straight through method. The powder is conveyed through a vibrofluidizer 2 where it is heated to 50°C. Lecithin is dissolved in hot butter oil (1:1) from 5 and sprayed hot in the powder in the fluidizer to give lecithin content of 0.2% in the powder. The agglomerate formed is conveyed to another fluidizeer to hold in the lecithinated powder for about 5 min at around 45°C to keep the fat in fluid condition and to provide effective coating. The powder is then gas packed (Fig 8-14).

The re-wet method This is a popular method based on the work of Peebles where skim milk is used for agglomeration. Basically the centrigual atomizer in the drying chamber is replaced by an agglomerating tube. Powder with low fat content as well as low heat powder, (WPN 600 mg/g) is preferable to avoid cooked flavour and have a good physical strength to thc agglomerate. The skim milk powder (particle size 25-50 μm) is wetted in the agglomerating tube with warm water mist or steam. The wetted stricky powder is retained in a small drying chamber to give a residence in 2 small drying chamber to give a residence time enough to settle the moist clusters to the base of the chamber. The secondary drying and cooling are carried out in a vibrofluidizer. The large particles (size 200 μm) are separated by sieving. The fines from the sieve and from the main cyclone separator are recycled for agglomeration. The mechanical strength of the agglomerate results in lower instant property. Damage to the agglomerates should be avoided during nitrogen packing (Fig 8-15).

Standards : *PFA (Legal) : Whole milk powder (WMP)* According to PFA rules (1984) WMP is a product obtained from cow or buffalo milk or a combination thereof or from standardized milk by the removal of water. It may contain calcium chloride, citric acid and sodium citrate, sodium salts of orthophosphoric acid and poly phosphoric acids, not exceeding 0.3% by

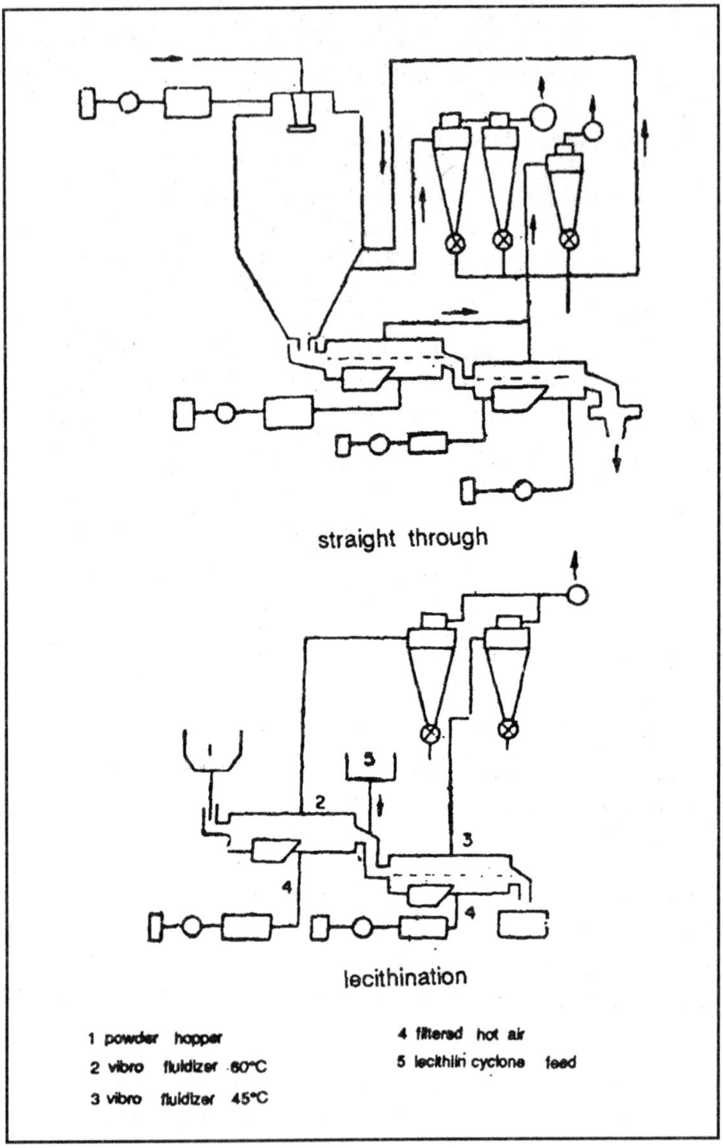

Fig 8-14 Instant milk powder system

weight of the finished product and 0.01% butylated hydroxy anizole (BHA) weight of the finished product and 0.01 % butylated hydroxy anizole (BHA)ft by weight of the finished product. Such additions need not be declared on I/ '° the label. Milk powder should not contain not more than 5.0 % moisture and not less than 26% milkfat. The total acidity expressed as lactic acid

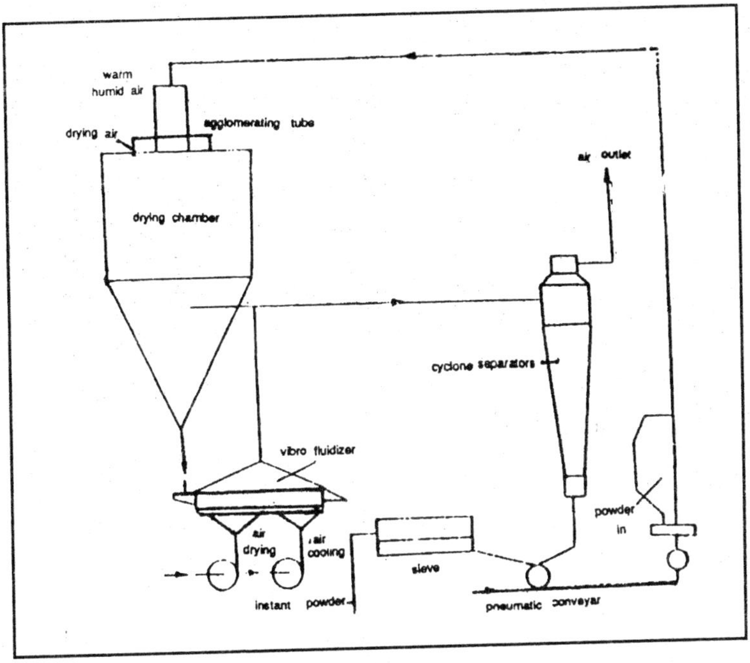

Fig 8-15 Re-wet instantantizer

should not exceed 1.2%. The standard plate count may not exceed 50 000/ g and the coli count~may not exceed 90/g. It is permitted to add 0.5% lecithin to improve dispersability. The maximum solubility index should be 15.0 for a roller dried and 2.0 for a spray dried product.

Note The process d drying must be mentioned on the label. The spray dried product must be packed in hermetically sealed containers when net quantity exceeds 510 g.

Skim milk powder- (SMP) According to PFA Rules (1984) skimmilk powder is a product obtained from skim milk of cow or buffalo milk or a combination thereof, by the removal of water. It may contain added calcium chloride, citric acid and sodium citrhte, sodium salts of orthophosphoric acid and poly phosphoric acid, not exceeding 0.3% by weight of the finished product. Such additions need not be declared on the label. Skim milk powder may not contain more than 1.5% milkfat and moisture may not exceed 5.0%. The total acidity expressed as lactic acid should not exceed 1.5%. The standard plate count should not exceed 50 000/g and the coli count must not exceed 90/g. The maximum solubility index should be 15 for spray dried product and 2.0 for roller dried product.

Note The process of drying must be mentioned on the label. The spray dried product must be packed in hermetically sealed containers when net quantity exceeds 510 g.

The Indian Standards (ISI) for dried milk are given below:

Characteristics	***Whole milk powder***		***Skim milk powder***	
Flavour and odour	good		good	
Moisture (% wt max)	4.0		5.0	
Total milk solids (% wt)	96.0		95.0	
Solubility index (max) ml	15.0		15.00	
roller dried	2.0		2.0	
Solubility (% wt min)				
roller dried	85.0		85.0	
spray dried	98.5		98.5	
Total ash (% wt max)	7.3		9.3	
dry basis				
Fat (% wt)	26	(NLT)	1.5	(NMT)
Titratable acidity	1.2		1.5	
(% lactic max)	50 000		50 000	
Bacterial count max/g	90		90	
Coliform count max/g				

NMT = Not more than NLT = Not less than

Defects in powder

Scorched particles caused by the product being burnt during preheating, evaporation or drying (atomizer disc or drums). Scorching may be the result of too high temperatures (inlet temperature), but is mainly caused by deposits in atomizer wheel, the air distributor and the drying chamber.

Reduced solubility of protein to form colloidal solution. It may be caused by too high acid content or incorrect salt balance in the milk, excessive evaporation temperature or inlet and outlet temperature in the drier, too high TS content in concentrate, drying method, structure of powder particles, Incorrect powder storage (non air tight packing or excessive humidity or temperature.

Density should be normally as high as possible (about 0.6). Deviation may be the result of too low or too high TS content in the concentrate, the air inlet temperature, drying method or structure of powder particles.

During storage several defects appear in flavour, colour and solubility of the powder.

Stale musty flavour occurs in powder during extended storage. This is promoted by high moisture content and high storage temperature. These

The American Dry Milk Institute (ADMI) standards

	Instant	Spray		Roller	
Characteristics	**US extra**	**US extra**	**US standard**	**US extra**	**US standard**
SKIM MILK POWDER					
Moisture (NMT)	4.25	4.0	5.0	4.0	5.0
Milk fat % NMT	1.25	1.25	1.50	1.25	1.50
Titratable acidity % NMT	0.15	0.15	0.17	0.15	0.17
Scorched particles mg/g NMT	15.0	15.0	22.5	32.5	
Solubility index ml NMT	1.0	1.2	2.0	15.0	15.0
Standard Plate count/g NMT	35 000	50 000	100 000	50 000	100 000
Colitorm count/g NMT	90	-	-	- -	
WHOLE MILK POWDER					
Moisture (NMT)	2.25	2.26	3.0	3.0	4.0
Milk fat % NMT	26.0	26.0	26.0	26.0	26.0.
Titratable acidity % NMT	0.5	0.5	1.0	15.0	15.0
Scorched particles mg/g NMT	15.0	15.0	22.5	22.5	32.5
Solubility index ml NMT	0.15	0.15	0.17	0.15	0.17
'Standard Plate count/g NMT	30 000	50 000	100 000	50 000	100 000
Coliform count/g NMT	90	-	-	- -	
Copper ppm NMT	1.5	1.6	-	1.5	-
Iron ppm NMT	10	10	-	10	-
Oxygen % vol NMT (If gas packed)		2	3	- 3	-

NMT = Not more than NLT= Not less than

are caused by lactose-protein changes. Lactose-protein reaction causes browning (Maillard reaction).

Insolubility assessed by the solubility index indicates protein denaturation. Low moisture content and low storage temperature minimises this defect.

Fat decomposition in whole milk powder during storage is due to oxidative or hydrolytic action on milkfat. Tallowiness is inhibited by intensive heat treatment prior to evaporation, homogenization of concentrate and gas packing of powder in tins to an oxygen content of less than 2% in the head space. This defect is more common in spray dried powder than in roller dried powder, a fact which may be due to more intensive heat treatment connected wit roller drying. Higher acidity of initial milk is also a contributory factor Addition of antioxidant BHA at 0.01% by weight of finished powder may reduce oxidative changes in milk fat. Inadequate preheating of\he milk resulting in reduced inactivation of lipase may cause rancid flavour in the powder.

The ADSA has a score card for dry milk with perfect score of 45, 20, 5 and 30 for flavour, appearance, package and laboratory tests respectivel

Uses of milk powder

Skim milk powder is used a) for preparing toned, double toned and recombined milk, b) for ice cream mix, c) for making cultured milk products, d) for use in tea and coffee in times of short supply of milk, e) in candy, chocolate making, f) enrichment of bread, biscuits etc. g) in making Indian sweets.

Whole milk powder is used a) for reconstitution, b) in tea and coffee, c) baby food preparation, d) in candy and confectionery. A spray dried powder is preferred as complete reconstitution is easy.

Chapter 7

ICE-CREAM

Introduction: Ice cream is a very popular dairy product throughout the World. Its production and consumption is rapidly increasing and substantial part of milk produced is being utilised for the manufacture of this frozen dessert.

The essential ingredients of a normal icecream mix are, cream and skim milk powder to provide desirable body, texture and richness, sugar for palatability, stabilizers like gelatin, polysaccharides and gums to retard the formation of large ice crystals during freezing and hardening, emulsifiers to improve whipping ability and pleasing flavours like vanilla or chocolate. The base of these ingredients are either dissolved in emulsion or in colloidal suspension.

Composition and quality of ingredients : The approximate composition of various types of commercial ice cream is given below.

Type	Milk fat %	SNF %	Sugar %	Stabilizer/ emulsifier %	Total solids %
Economy	10	10-11	13-15	0.3-0.5	36-37
12	9-10	13-15	0.25-0.5	-	
Average	12	11	15	0.3	37.5-39
14	8-9	13-16	0.2-0.4		
Delux	16	7-8	13-16	0.2-0.4	
18	6-7	13-16	0.25	40-41	
20	5-6	14-17		0.25	

The advantages and limitations of ice cream ingredients are:

Milkfat

advantages: enhances richness of flavour, gives characteristic texture & provides good body.

limitations: Cost, hinders whipping quality, high fat limits consumption and high calorific value.

Solids-not-fat

advantages: Improves texture, provides good body, increases overrun without flaky texture & cheap source of milk solids.

limitations: higher % causes sandiness & may cause salty or cooked flavour.

Sugar

advantages: cheap source of solid improves texture enhances flavour. limitations: excessive sweetness lowers whipping ability & needs longer freezing and hardening time.

Stabilisers

advantages: provides smooth texture and effective in providing body *limitations* leads to excess body and melting resistance.

Emulsifiers

advantages: improves whipping quality, provides smooth body and texture and reduces whipping time.

limitations: needs homogenization, favours shrinkage, leads to excess body and melting resistance.

Total solids

advantages: provides smooth texture, gives better body and enhances nutritive value.

limitations: leads to heavy, soggy, pasty body

Flavour

advantages: increases consumer acceptance

limitations - intense flavour quickly satisfy desire

Colour

advantages: improves appearance and helps in identifying flavour

limitations : unnatural colour reduces acceptability

Common ingredients used Ice cream ingredients may be grouped into dairy and non-dairy products. Some dairy products supply major source of fat, others solids-not-fat and still others both fat and SNF. The non-dairy products include sweetening agents, stabilizers, emulsifiers, flavours and colours, fruits/nuts etc.

Ingredients of ice cream:

Fat: This makes up about 11% of the volume of the dairy ice cream may be either milkfat or vegetable fat. In the former case it may take the form of whole milk, sweet cream, unsalted butter, plastic cream or anhydrous milkfat. Some or all of the milkfat in ice cream may be replaced by vegetable fat in the form of rape seed oil,cotton seed oil, coconut oil, or palm kernal oil. The use of vegetable fat results in a slight difference in flavour and colour as compared with milkfat, but the difference is small. If colouring or flavouring additives are also used the difference may be hardly noticeable. Use of vegetable fat in ice cream is however prohibited in some countries.

Milk solids not fat: MSNF consists of proteins, lactose and mineral salts. They are added in the form of skim milk powder, condensed skimmilk (plain/ sweetened, sweet cream butter milk/whey powder. MSNF contains proteins, lactose and mineral salts. For best results the quantity of MSNF should be in a certain proportion to the quantity of fat. (say 12.0% fat and 11-11.5 % MSNF).

Source of both fat and MSNF are whole milk, whole milk powder and condensed whole milk (plain/sweetened).

Sweetening agents used mostly is cane sugar besides corn sugar, corn syrup, corn syrup solids (dextrose + maltose) and invert sugar (glucose + fructose)

Stabilizers in use are gelatin (animal source), sodium alignate, locust bean gum, guar gum and sodium carboxy methyl cellulose.

Emulsifiers in use are glyceryl mono stearate, poly oxylene sorbitol mono stearate or mono oleate.

Flavours: Vanilla is the most popular flavour all over the world; next comes chocolate. Strawberry, pine apple, lemon, banana, mango and orange flavours are also used to some extent.

Colour: Permitted Food Grade synthetic colours of red, green, blue or yellow tints are also used.

Functions of the constituents

Butterfat gives smoothness-and richness to ice cream and also contributes to the texture.

Milk solids-not-fat (MSNF) improves the body and texture of ice cream when used in proper amounts. SNF binds and replaces water. It also affects the correct distribution of air in the ice cream during the freezing process. It provides better standing up quality. It inhibits the formation of large ice crystals. Milk proteins contribute to stabilization of air bubbles whipped into the ice cream mix during freezing. MSNF lowers the freezing point of the mix, thereby contribute to a softer product. Excess MSNF may cause soggy, heavy body mix leading to danger of sandiness. MSNF have high nutritional value also.

Sugar increases palatability, flavour, sweetness and smoothness to ice cream. Excess sugar depresses the freezing point of mix leading to an increase in freezing time and requiring more refrigeration.

Emulsifiers are substances which assist emulsification by reducing the surface tension of liquid products. They also help to stabilize the emulsion once formed and improves the whipping quality of the mix. They contribute to smoothness of body and texture of the ice cream and reduction in the melting rate of ice cream. The yolk of the egg is a well known emulsifier but it is expensive and less effective than the most commonly used types which are non-ionic derivatives of natural fats which have been esterified to give them one or more water soluble (hydrophilic) radicals bonded to one or more fat soluble (lipophilic) radicals. The emulsifiers used in ice cream manufacture can be divided into 4 groups; glycerine esters, sorbitol esters, sugar esters and esters of other origin. The amount added is of the order of 0.3 to 0.5% of the volume of the mix.

Emulsifiers stabilize the mixtures of both fat-in-water and air-in-water in ice cream products. This means that fat and air can be more evenly distributed in the mix, partly by homogenization, partly by whipping in air during freezing resulting in a more full, smooth and rich texture and increasing melting time (standing up quality). When ice cream is produced at home, the addition of egg yolks (1-2 egg yolks) serves as stabilizer and emulsifier, because egg yolk have a high content of both phospholipids (emulsifier) and proteins (stabilizer). Since milk and milk products contain natural stabilizing and emulsifying substances (protein, fat, lecithin and citrates), excellent ice cream, can be made without added emulsifier/stabilizer.

Stabilizers are agents which because of their water binding capacity a), prevent formation of large ice crystals during freezing and storage, and b) increase the viscosity of the mix, which also helps to stabilize the distribution of air whipped into the product. They can also bind water during melting, whereby the melting resistance is increased. The stabilizer added amounts to 0.2-0.4% volume of the icecream mix. Tha stabilizers used are partly proteins and partly polysaccharides. Milk protein in the milk and cream of the mix and gelatin (animal source) are good stabilizers. Gelatin requires long aging time and may create a joyyg texture. Some of the commonly used polysaccharides are, alignates (extracted from brown algae), Car rageenan (extracted from red algae), (locust bean gum and guar gum,, gum arabic, cellulose derivates of carboxy methyl cellulose). They have characteristic advantages and disadvantages. Ice cream factories prefer to buy ready made and tested combinations from manufacturers. Normally stabilizers are commonly combined with emulsifying agents because they promote dispersion in water or milk/cream.

Flavouring matter is very important to customer's choice of ice cream. These can be added at the mixing stage. If the flavouring takes the form of larger pieces like nuts and fruits, they are added after the mix has been frozen. Cocoa is widely used to give ice cream bars, cones and bricks a coating of chocolate. For this purpose cocoa is mixed with cocoa fat to give chocolate coating the correct viscosity, consistency and elasticity.

Colouring matter is added to the mix to give the ice cream appearance and enhance the colour of the fruit flavouring additives. The colouring matter is added in the form of powder or paste which is mixed with water and boiled. Sodium berizoate (if permitted by Act, is added as a sterilant. The dosage varies from 10-20 ml / 100 / mix. Only approved dyes and sterilants may be used.

Classification: Some of the important frozen desserts can be classified as follows:

Plain: An ice cream in which the colour and the flavouring ingredients together amounts to less than 5% of the volume of unfrozen ice cream Vanilla ice cream).

Chocolate: Ice cream flavoured with cocoa/chocolate.

Fruit: Ice cream containing fruits with or without additional fruit flavouring or colour. Fruits may be fresh, frozen packed, canned or preserved.

Nut Ice cream containing nuts like almonds, pistachio, walnut, cashew nut etc. with or without addition of flavouring or colour.

Softy Sold as drawn from the freezer without hardening

Milk ices or milk lollies: .According to PFA Rules (1976) these refer to frozen product obtained from milk, skim milk or milk product with or without the addition of cane sugar, eggs, fruits, fruit juices; nuts, chocolates, edible flavours and permitted food colours. It may contain permitted stabilizers not exceeding 0.5% of the product. The mixture should be suitably heat treated before freezing. The product should contain not more than 3.0% milkfat, not less than 3.5% proteins and not less than 20.0% total solids./

Ices: Made of fruit juice, sugar and stabilizers with or without additional fruit acid, colour, flavouring or water and frozen to the consistency of ice cream. They usually contain 20-30% sugar, 20-25% over run and no dairy product.

Sherbet: vary in, composition, taste, colour and eating characteristics. Generally, they contain fruit or fruit juice, some added acid for greater tartness, about twice as much sugar as ice cream, 1-2% mikfat, from 25%,by weight total milk solids and from 0.2-0.5% stabilizer, depending on type and strength.

Water ices are similar to sherbets except they do not contain any milk solids.

Novelties are frozen confection in an especially shaped and usually a low priced package containing an individual serving whose main appeal consists in its shape, size colour or convenience of eating. They are usually stick or stickless lollies or bars, extruded bars, small cups and ice cream cakes or pies. Many have chocolate or other coatings and some are elaborately / decorated.

Categories: There are two broad categories; hardened products and soft serve products. Hardened products are packaged in the semi-frozen state as extruded from an ice cream freezer, then frozen in hardening room, tunnel or other device and stored. prior to distribution. Soft serve products are those which are served directly to the consumer in the semi-frozen state as extruded from ice cream freezer.

Standards: According to PFA Rules ice cream is the frozen product obtained from cow or buffalo milk or a combination thereof or from cream and or other milk products, with or without the addition of cane sugar, eggs, fruits, fruit juices, preserved fruits, nuts, chocolate, edible flavours and permitted food colours. It may contain permitted stabilizers and emulsifiers not exceeding 0.5% by weight. The mixture must be suitably heated before freezing. The product should contain not less than 10% milkfat, 3.5% protein and 36.0% total solids. However, when any of the aforesaid preparation contain fruits or nuts or both the content of milkfat may be proportionately reduced but may not be less than 8% by weight. Starch may be added to a maximum amounts of 5%, with a declaration to that effect on the label.

The ISI specifications for ice cream as per IS:2802 (1964) second print, August 1981 are as follows:

	Requirements Ice cream	
Characteristics	**Normal**	**fruit/nut/ chocolate**
Weight in g/l (min)	525	540
Total solids (% wt) min	36	36
milk fat (% wt) min	10	8
acidity (% lactic) max	0.25	-
sucrose (% wt) max	15	15
stabilizer/emulsifier (% wt) max	0.5	0.5
Standard Plate Count/g	not more than 2 50 000	not more than 2 50 000
Coliform count/g	not more than 100	not more than 100
Phosphatase test of mix	negative	negative

The post war shortages, particularly milkfat led to almost all the ice cream in the UK being made from fats other than milkfat resulting in Food Standards (Ice cream) Regulations 1959 which had the following requirements

Type	*milkfat* %	*other fats* %	*SNF* %	*fat+SNF* %
Ice cream (min)	-	5.0	7.5	
Ice cream + fruit pulp (min)	-	7.5	2.0	12.5
Dairy ice cream (min)	5.0	-	7.5	-
Dairy ice cream + fruit pulp (min)	7.5	-	2.0	12.5
Milk ice (min)	2.5	-	7.0	-

Artificial sweeteners forbidden in all the products.

Preparation of gelatin, vanilla and chocolate

A brief account of the common stabilizer and flavouring agents is given below.

Gelatin is derived from the proteins collagen and ossein by hydrolysis. It is prepared from calf skin trimmings, pork skin or bones. The material after washing is heated in water when collagen undergo hydrolysis and become water soluble. The broth so obtained is filtered, concentrated and dried. The bones are first treated with dilute acid to dissolve mineral matter and then proteins are extracted in hot water several times. The extract is concentrated in vacuum pan to 20-25% solids and flown over rubber belt to form a layer and passed through refrigerated tunnel to solidify as thin pliable sheet and later hot air dried. The final product is ground to fineness. The concentrate is also drum dried. The grading is expressed as Bloom gel strength. A simpler test is that prescribed by Dahlberg using test tubes and skimmilk. Bloom of 150, 200 and 250 strength are available.

Vanilla is extracted with alcohol from fermented vanilla beans of a perennial orchid climbing plant *Vanilla plantifolia*. Good beans are available in Mexico, Africa, Java and Malay Peninsula. The beans are exposed to the Sun then covered in blankets in boxes to sweat and cured for nearly 4 mo; to develop aroma. Single-fold vanilla beans contains the extractive matter from 10 g vanilla beans/100 ml of 35%a alcohol. By distilling off alcohol, concentrate is made. Vanilla are also synthesized and sold in crystalline form.

Chocolate and Cocoa are made from the bean of cocoa tree known as

Theobroma cacao. The trees are grown in tropics, northern and south America, Central America, West Indies, Africa, Ceylon and India too. The pod contains 20-40 almond shaped seeds. Sweating is done to ferment and removal of pulp. The seeds are sorted and roasted at 125-140 248°C till acetic acid flavour is lost. Nibs are separated from crushed beans by sieves and air currents. Grinding the nibs frees fat, which amounts to about 50%, and the heat of grinding makes it liquid. The combined liquid fat and flavouring material are known as chocolate liquor, or when solidified, as bitter cooking chocolate. Sweet milk chocolatE is prepared,solidified, adding sugar, milk and coca butter to chocolate liquor. Hydraulic pressing of cocoa beans removes the practically flavourless cocoa butter (fat) leaving cocoa cake which contains about 22% fat and nearly all the flavouring of the bean. Cocoa is produced by grinding and sifting cocoa cake. Darker and less bitter cocoa is produced by the Dutch processwhich involves treatment of cocoa beans with alkalies at the tires of roasting. About 3% cocoa and about 5% chocolate liquor are required to flavour mix for chocolate frozen desserts. Imitation chocolate flavours are also available. Cocoa products meant for flavouring purposes are given below:

Cocoa type ,	flavouring use	fat %
High quality	ice cream, icings, beverage chocolate syrups	25-35
Breakfast cocoa	Chocolate bisbuits, crackers, cakes and fudge	22-25
Semi dry cocoa	Chocolate milk drinks, chocolate flavoured desserts, chocolate pies, syrups	15-18 33
Dry cocoa	Chocolate milk beverage	10-12
Very dry cocoa	Imitation chocolate coatings	6-8
Defatted cocoa	Imitation chocolate, adjusting powder	0.5-3

Method of manufacture: The method briefly includes a) calculation and blending of several ingredients as per requirement, b) preheating of the mix, c) homogenization, d) pasteurization, e) cooling, f) ageing, g) freezing and h) packaging, i) hardening and j) storage.

Calculation of the Ingredients:

Problem 1

Desired: 900 kg mix, 12% fat, 10% SNF, 14% sugar and 0.4% gelatin

Available: Cream 40% fat 5.4% SNF

milk 4.0% fat- 8.6% SNF

Sweetened condensed milk 0.2% fat, 26% SNF and sugar 42%.

Solution:

a) Wt of sugar + gelatin = 112 + 3.2 = 115.2 kg

Wt of milk products 800-115.2 = 684.8 kg

b) Wt of cream = x kg

Wt of condensed milk = y kg

Wt of milk = (684-76 - 0.58y) kg

c) $0.40\ x + 0.002\ y + 0.04\ (684-x-0.58\ y) = 96$ kg

$0.054x + 0.26\ y + 0.086\ (684-x-0.58y) = 80$ kg

d) $0.40x + 0.002\ y + 27.36 - 0.04\ x - 0.0232y = 96$ kg

$0.054\ x + 0.26\ y + 58.824 - 0.086\ x - 0.04988 = 80$ kg

e) $0.36\ x - 0.0212y = 68.14$

$-0.0032\ x + 0.21012y = 21.176$

f) $0.01152 - 0.000\ 6784Y = 2.19648$

$-\ 0.01152\ x + 0.0756432\ Y = -\ 7.62336$

$+\ 0.074\ 9468\ y = 9.81\ 584$

$y = \underline{130.99267\ \text{kg}}$

g) $0.36\ x - (0.0212 \times 130.99267) = 68.64$

$0.36x = 71.4170$

$x = 98.380\ 67$

h) milk = 684 -(130.99267 + 98.38067) = 409.64358

i) sugar in condensed milk = 130.99267/0.42 = 55.0169214

j) sugar to add = 112-55.0169 = 56 983

Proof

Ingredients (kg)		*Fat*	*SNF*	*Sugar*	*Gelatin*
Cream	198.38	79.35	10.71	-	-
milk -	409.64	16.30	35.22	-	-
SCM	130.99	0.26	34.05	55.02	-
sugar	56.98	-	-	56.98	-
gelatin	4.00	-	-	-	4.00
Total	799.99	95.99	79.98	112.00	4.00

Problem 2

Desired : 100 kg mix with fat 10% SNF 11.0% sugar 14.5% and stabilizer 0.3%

Available : Whole milk 6.8% fat 9.6% SNF Cream 40% fat 54% SNF; Skim milk powder 0.5°/a fat 97.0% SNF Sugar and stabilizer

Solution : Wt. of cream = x kg Wt of powder = y kg Wt of milk =

(85.2 - x - y) kg

Fat equation : 4/100 x +0.5/100y + 6.8/100 (85.2-x-y) = 10.0 kg

SNF equation

5.4/100 x + 97/100 + 0.6/100 (85.2-x-y) = 11.0 kg

a   0.40x+0.005y+5.79-0.068x-0.068y = 100

     0.332x-0.063y = (50.0-5.79)= 4.21 kg

b   0.054x+0.97y+8.179-0.096 x - 0.096y = 11

     -0.42y + 0.874y = (11-8.179) = 2.82

c   0.332x-0.063y = 4.21

     -0.042x-0.874y = 2.82

d   multiply

     0.01394x -0.002 646 y = 0.1764

     -0.01394x + 0.290 168 y, = 0.9362

     +0.2875 y = 1.1126

     y = 3.87 kg

e   add

     0.332x - 0.063y = 4.21

     0.332x - (0.063 x 3.87) = 4.21

     0.332x = 4.21 +0.2438 = 4.4538

     x = 4.45 38/0.332 = 13.35 kg

f   milk = 85.2-(13.35 + 3.87) = 67.98 kg

Proof

Ingredients (kg)		*Fat*	*SNF*	*Sugar*	*Stabilizer*
Milk	67.98	4.622	6.536	-	-
cream	13.35	5.340	0.721	-	-
SMP	3.87	0.019-	3.715	-	-
Sugar	14.50	-	-	14.5	-
Stabilizer	0.30	-	-	-	0.30
Total	100.00	9.981	10.962	14.5	0.30

Making the mix. All liquid ingredients (cream, milk, condensed milk, etc.) are placed in a vat and the agitation and heating started at once. The dry ingredients including skim milk powder, sugar, stabilizer, are added while the liquid material is agitated and before temperature reaches 49°C. Proper suspension to avoid lumpiness of dry ingredients may be obtained by either mixing thoroughly with part of sugar before slowly adding it to the liquid. Gelatin is mixed ,with equal weight of sugar and added. Sodium alignate in cold water)is aced when the temperature of the mix reaches 66°C. When frozen cream, plastic cream or butter are used, they should be cut into fairly small pieces to allow complete melting before pasteurization temperature is reached.

Pasteurization : Proper pasteurization of all ice cream mixes is compulsory to destroy pathogens and safeguarding public health. The mix is rapidly heated to definite temperature, holding it at that temperature for definite time. The heating and holding conditions are 70°C/30 min or 80-90°C/ 15 s.

Homogenization is indispensible for commercial ice cream. It a) prevents churning of fat during freezing, b) reduces ageing time, c) aids in obtaining good over run, d) makes possible the use of butter, frozen cream etc. in the mix, e) improves whipping ability and f) produces more uniform quality ice cream with a smoother texture. The mix is homogenized at 70°C in two stages 170-210 kg/cm2 and 40 kg/cm2 and 40 kg/cmz in the second stage.

Cooling and ageing of mix. The mix is cooled to 5°C and aged for a period depending upon the type of stabilizer used. Mix having gelatin requires longer ageing period (6 h) and for others for 4 h. Ageing gives time for the fat to crystallize and proteins and stabilizers to bind water. Ageing contributes to the consistency of ice cream and whipping capacity of the mix. Ageing involves two basic processes; partly a crystallization of the fat in the fat globules, partly a binding of water molecule to protein molecules and stabilizer molecules. The crystallization of the fat is necessary to avoid a buttery texture development during freezing nd whipping. The binding of water to proteins and stabilizers in hibits the formation of large ice crystals and creates a more smooth texture and uniform melting. The ageing tanks are insulated and equipped with agitators for gentle stirring and double jackets for ice-water cooling to 2-3°C during ageing.

Addition of flavouring and colouring matter: At the end of the ageing the mix is pumped to the freezer. The flavouring and colours are to be added. This can be done in a surge tank or by direct injection into the line ahead of the freezers.

Freezing the mix: Fast freezing is very essential for getting a smooth product because ice crystals that are formed quickly are smaller than those formed slowly. Therefore, it is desirable to freeze and draw from the freezer in as short a time as possible. A continuous freezer accomplishes this in a few s while batch freezers take 7 to 10 min depending on various factors. The freezing continues after the ice cream is placed in the hardening room. The ice crystals formed during the hardening period are larger because they form more slowly than in the freezer. For this reason, it is good to freeze the ice cream as stiff as possible and yet have it liquid enough to draw out of the freezer.

The functions of the freezer is to freeze a portion of the water of the mix and to incorporate air into the mix. This involves the lowering of the temperature of the mix from ageing temperature to the freezing point, freezing a portion of the water of the mix, incorporating air into the mix and cooling the ice cream from the temperature it is drawn to hardening room temperature. The rapid agitation reduces the viscosity by destroying the gel structure and hastens incorporation of air into the mix. When freezing point is reached, the liquid water changes to crystals which appear in the mix. Increasing the concentration of these solutes causes the freezing point of the liquid portion to be slightly lower so that the temperature must be lowered before more crystals will form. When temperature drops, more ice crystals are formed increasing the concentration of sugar and other solutes in the remaining liquid water until the concentration is so great that freezing will not occur. Thus, all of the water is not frozen even after long periods in the hardening room. The percentage of water frozen in ice cream at different temperatures are shown below:

Temperature °C	***% Water frozen***
-3.9	33
-5.0	47
-6.1	56
-7.2	62
-8.3	67
-26.3	90

The first phase of the freezing process accounts for 33 to 67% of the water depending on the drawing temperature. The hardening room process then may account for 23 to 53% depending on the drawing temperature. Thus, the texture of the ice cream is dependent on the presence of ice crystals, air cells and unfrozen material of the mix. Such a material consisting of liquid, air and solid is a three-phase system.

Thus in the first stage mix is frozen to get 80-100% overrun. i.e., admixture of 0.8-1.0 /of air// of ice cream mix. The quickly frozen mix leaves the freezer at a temperature of -3 to -4°C. Its texture will be similar to that of soft ice cream and some 40-45% of the water content of the mix will be in frozen condition. After the freezing fruits' and nuts can be added before the mix is filled into moulds or other packaging materials.

Hardening: The partly frozen mix is filled into moulds in an ice cream bar freezer or into other types of packaging material (cups, cartons, cones) and then the temperature is lowered to - 15°C to -18°C as quickly as possible, which is done by means of brine bath in ice cream bar freezer or in a hardening tunnel in which air is circulated at high velocity at a temperature of - 40 to -45°C. At the end of his stage nearly 80% of the water in the mix is in frozen condition.

Storage: After hardening, the ice cream is cold stored at a temperature of -25°C. At this temperature, 90% of the water is frozen. It is very necessary to maintain this temperature and slow subsequent decreases in temperature, the result may be that of large ice crystals form (sandy) mixing Fig 9-1 steps in manufacturing of ice cream.

Overrun in ice cream: When the ice cream mix is frozen, its volume increases due to incorporation of air. This excess of volume over the volume of the mix is expressed as %. The overrun is influenced by a) the composition of the mix, b) method of processing and c) method of freezing. Sugar and serum solids delays over run. Egg yolk promotes overrun. High fat, high serum solids and chocolate mixtures delays overrun. In order to secure uniform overrun, overrun testers are used for control of freezing. The desirable overrun % for packaged ice cream varies from 70-80; bulk ice cream 90 to 100; and soft ice cream (softy) 30-50.

Freezing equipment: There are two types of ice cream freezers: the batch type and the continuous flow type. Batch freezers are used in very small ice cream factories. Batch freezers are generally of the horizontal cylinder type with the freezing cylinder refrigerated with freon mostly. R 22 or R 507. A mix supply tank is located above the freezing cylinder so that the mix will flow by gravity into the cylinder when the valve is opened. The usual procedure is to charge the freezer, turn on the dasher and allow the refrigerant. The functions of the dasher are a) to scrape the frozen film of the mix from the cylinder wall, mix it and carry it to the centre to effect uniform freezing, b) to beat the mix and incorporate air to get the required overrun and swell, c) to mix flavour colour, fruits etc. uniformly and d) to assist in ejecting the product from the freezer at the end of the freezing operation.

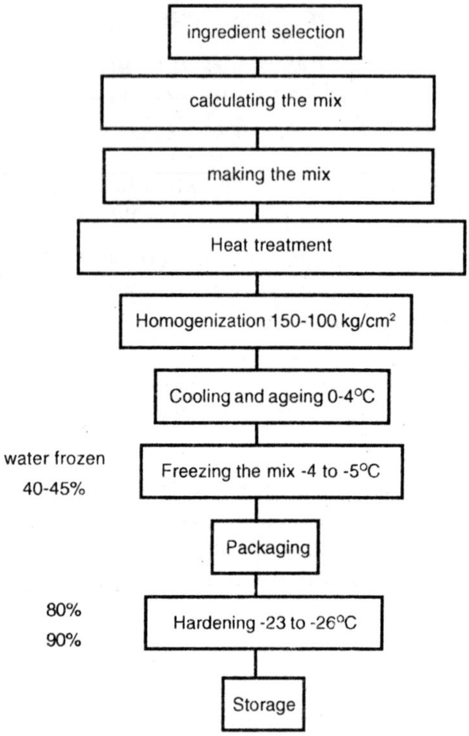

Fig 9-1 Flow diagram for making ice cream

When the freezing has increased the power required to turn the dasher to a value which indicates sufficient freezing, the refrigeration is cut off, and air is whipped in until the desired overrun is obtained. This is judged by drawing samples for overrun determination. At this point, fruits, flavours etc. may be added directly into the open part of the front door and mixed into the ice cream. A slide or pivot valve at the bottom portion of the front door allows the ice cream to be drawn into the containers. The dasher is designed to propel the product towards the discharge port. A new charge is put into the mix supply tank as soon as the previous charge is drawn out. A batch of ice cream can be made every 6-7 min. The temperature of the frozen ice cream may be around -5°C. The capacity of the freezers may range from 40 to 100.Since the freezer works at atmospheric pressure, the ice cream has both larger ice crystals and bigger air cells than the ice cream made with continuous freezers. Over run control is also difficult. It may vary to some extent from the beginning of the drawing the batch to completely empty the freezer. This occurs because the whipping continues all during the drawing time. The dasher and scraper assembly is shown in Fig 9-2.

Continuous freezers: The continuous freezer has two functions, a) to whip and control the amount of air in the mix and b) to freeze the water content of the mix in the form of large number of small ice crystals. Theca freezers are manufactured in Europe, Japan and USA by nearly 10 manufacturers and cater the needs of 60-70% of the world requirements and 80% in terms of production capacity. The capacity of the unit may range from 300 to 3000 μm/cylinder. They have rotary type pumps to pump against pressure 7-10 kg/cm^2 with good volumetric efficiency. All equipment have horizontal freezing cylinder and mix getting frozen within the pressurized cylinder. They can have programme controller or micro processor to operate and control most of the functions of ice cream freezer. Some have one freezing cylinder and others with 3 independent cylinders. The size of ice crystals could be as low as 22 mμ and air cell wall thickness around 50 mμ. Those who handle 25 000 l mix/day use mechanical or automated mix blending systems and HTST pasteurizers.

The *advantages* of the continuous method are : a) less stabilizer is needed, b) shorter ageing time, c) requiring less flavouring material, d) smoother ice cream because the ice crystals are small and uniform, e) less tendency towards sandiness due to rapid freezing, f) leads to uniform yield and less shrinkage. However, the initial cost of the equipment is high.

The operation : A constant supply of mix is metered by a positive type pump to a second pump Which displaces about twice the volume of the first. Then, sufficient suction is produced tol incorporate air into the mix

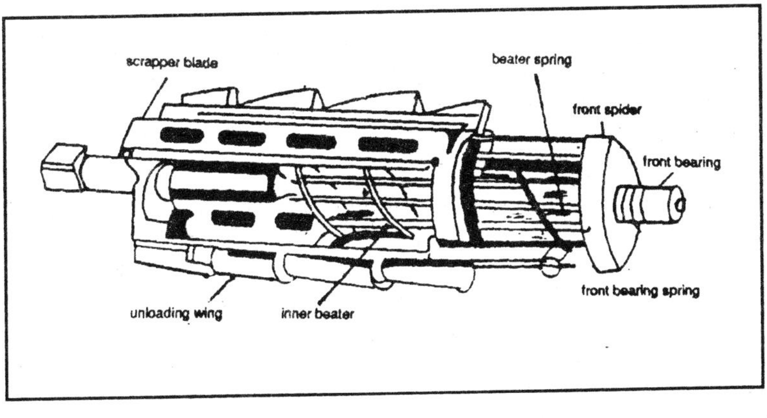

Fig 9-2 Dasher / scrapper assembly

from a filtered air inlet. Air and mix move into the cylindrical refrigeration chambers where whipping is accomplished by an agitator dasher(mutator); Sharp blades scrape frozen mix from walls on which it freezes. As liquid mix, enters one end of the chamber, it displaces frozen mix through the oher. Liquid refrigerant (ammonia) is pumped to an insulated space surrounding the freezing chamber where it takes on heat and become gaseous. Ice cream mix serves as the contributor of heat and is cooled. The diagram showing the freezer with mutator and dasher and chabers for refrigerant and frozen dessert mix is shown in Fig 9-3. With properly run

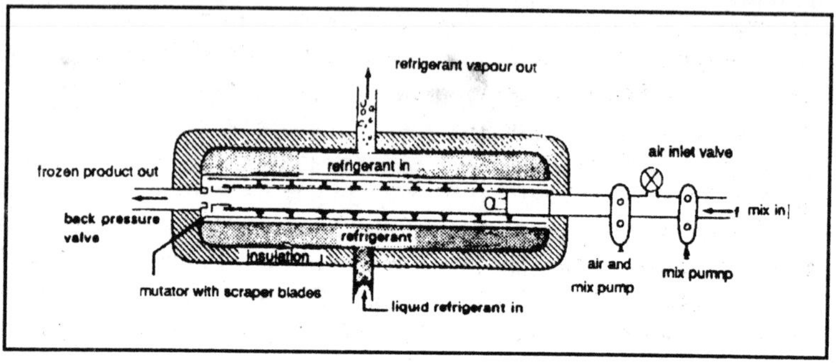

Fig 9-3 Diagram of continuous ice-cream freezer with mutator / chambers for refrigerant and frozen mix.

freezer overrun should vary no more than 3%. Refrigeration control is the most important step in overrun control. Drawing temperature should be as low as practicable commensurate with capacity. The lower the temperature of the freezer outlet the smaller the volume that can be produced by a freezer, because of the additional refrigerant load. Rate of freezing largely determines the size of the ice crystals foi any given mix. The faster and more completely freezing can be done in the freezer the better, because completion of the freezing process in the hardening room is certain to progress more slowly. About 54% of the water in the ice cream mix is frozen at -5°C, but more than 60% is frozen at -8°C. Therefore, drawing at the latter temperature produces smoother product. The scraper blades must be sharp and the interior wall smooth and round.

Packaging equipment is available for all types of containers. Packaging, filling machines designed to handle paper board cartons may store the flat folded carton in a feed cartridge, set it up for filling, fill it and close it. Filling may be done on weight / volume basis. Closure depends on carton design. Carton fillers are available for various sizes from 250 ml through 4 l. There are also bulk containers 2,4 and 6 l size used in Europe. After filling the cartons may be bundled in larger units by using shrink-wrap machine before being hardened. House-hold packs are filled in special automatic mass production machines which perform all necessary operations, assembly, fill, seal, pack or fill and cap the card board or plastic boxes.

Cones and cups are filled in special machines. The cones are located into magazines from which they are moved on conveyors through the machine, passing successive stations for filling decoration and sealing. The machines can be equipped with accessories for making different types of ice cream, e.g., fillers for 2-3 flavours, for ripple flavouring, for insertion of cylindrical plugs of flavouring ingredients and for adding drying ingredients. Cone and cup filling machines with capacity 1000-14000 units/h are available.

Hardening rooms: Ice cream as drawn from the freezer and pack is only partially frozen (-5°C) and the amount of ice formed is 45-55% of the water in the mix. It is fairly soft. If the product is to be rigid enough to store properly, to transport, and to maintain the overrun, body and texture it must have additional freezing quickly to around -18°C core temperature. The faster this is done, the better the quality of ice cream. It may take about 12 h. The hardening room is equipped with shelves or racks on which the product is placed in bundles or baskets. For rapid hardening air at -25°C must pass on all sides. The air should be circulated with enough velocity.

Larger factories use hardening tunnels where air at -30°C to - 35°C is circulated at a velocity of 180 m/min. Hardening is done in about 2 h for package upto 2 *l*. Spiral/straight through tunnels with suitable conveyors are also in use. In other cases rapid contact plate freezers serve as excellent hardening device. Hardening is possible in about 2 h and it requires no fans.

Manufacture of Ice cream bars : These are made in special machines with freezing pockets in which ice cream is moulded. The pockets are surrounded by a brine solution at a temperature of -40 to - 42°C. When the ice cream from the freezers are introduced into the pockets, final crystallization takes place and the ice cream solidifies. When it is hard enough, a wooden stick is inserted into each pocket. To remove the moulded bards, the pockets are dipped in a bath to melt the surface layer of the ice cream, after which the bars can be lifted out of the pocket. The bars, then dipped in chocolate or other coating and surplus chocolate is then allowed to run off and harden before the bars are finally wrapped in paper.

The chocolate coating is prepared by melting a kg of unsalted butter with vanilla extract. Into this, a kg of mixture (cocoa+SMP+powdered sugar in the ratio of 1:2:3) is added, stirred and dipping is done at 40°C.

Cleaning of the freezer : Same in-place cleaning procedures used for pasteurising plants can be used. Before starting the operation chlorine at 100-200mg/l can be run through the entire system or rinsing with warm water, dismantling the plant washing with detergents and physical methods of cleaning, reassembling, rinshing with clean water, sanitizing, final rinsing, draining, allowing they equipment to dry and santitizing before start of the: next day's run.

Distribution : When the frozen product is marketed, the material should be transported at the same temperature as it is maintained in the cold store. Dry ice can be used and transported in card board box reinforced with corrugated card board. However, this is costly. Refrigerated truck is commonly used for transport. The truck is refrigerated over night and loaded with hardened ice cream in the following morning jacketed metal containers called Eutectic pads which contain calcium chloride of specific gravity 1.1 are refrigerated in brine tank whose specific gravity is 1.6 (temperature -32°C). The pads attain a temperature of : -21°C. These are placed around packaged ice cream. The whole package is kept in insulated box. This is used some times for air lifting ice cream.

Judging, grading and testing of ice cream:

The score card as per ADSA:

Item	*Perfect score*
Flavour	45
Body & texture	30
Bacteria	15
Colour/package	5
Melting quality	5

Flavour defects can be subdivided into 4 categories flavouring, sweetener, dairy products, and processing. Flavouring may be too intensive, lacking or unnatural. the latter is usually most undesirable and is associated with artificial flavours. Sweetener may be excessive, lacking or like syrup. The latter is associated with use of excessive or low quality corn syrup solids. Flavour associated with quality of dairy products are acid, lacking freshness, metallic old ingredient, oxidised, rancid and unclean. The major flavour caused By processing is cooked. It should not be excessive.

Body and texture defects: The coarse defect is most common of all body and texture defects. Large ice crystals and air cells are responsible. Smoothness is associated with crystal sizes of 35 to 55 µm. Below 35 µm, extreme smoothness is encourrtered and above 55 µm coarseness is observed. Sandiness though similar in mouth feel is observed when lactose crytallises sufficiently to be detected. This is a serious defect which renders product unsalable. A weak bodied product lacks resistance and is associated with high overrun and insufficient total solids or stabilizer. Soggy heavy body results from low overrun and high total solids (especially sugar) and .from too much or improper stabilization. Improper emulsification produces crumbly ice cream.

Colour defects: Wide variations cJccur with some colours being unnatural. Variation in distribution may occur.

Melting quality: known as melt down is affected by stabilizers, emulsifiers, salt balance in dairy ingredients and processing or storage conditions that might destabilize proteins. A desirable product melts at a moderate rate, leaving liquid with the appearance of original mix. Common defects are foaminess, curdiness and slow melt.

Bacteria & examined quality is as per IS:2802 (1964)

Food value: Ice cream is an excellent source of food energy contributing 880 kJ/100 gm. It is a good source of valuable proteins and fat, rich source of Ca and P and other minerals and rich source of most of the vitamins. With high nutritive value, it is a good food for growing children and persons who need to put on weight. With its sweet flavour; smooth and velvety texture, glistening coolness and high palatability with attractive and appealing form and variety it stimulates the flow of digestive juices. It is an ideal food for one snd all. The fact that it is a quite concentrated food, easily digestible, makes it an ideal dessert for many invalids suffering from throat infection and stomach ailments when other foods do not appeal or cannot be tolerated. Perhaps low temperature of the ice cream provides temporary anesthesia. There is also less tendency to vomit ice cream in whooping cough than other food.

Mellorine and Imitation frozen desserts: Mellorine contains the same ingredients as ice cream except that the milk fat is replaced with vegetable fat and the minimal fat content of 6% (USA). It contains not less than 2.7% proteins.

Persons with cardiac and circulatory ailments may require a diet low in Na. A frozen dessert is made from spraydried milk low in Na. This would not contain more than 3 to 10 mg Na/100 g. Sugar free ice cream is a product in which sorbitol is used instead of sucrose. As sorbitol is not having the same sweetening; power of sucrose, a non-nutritive sweetening agent saccharine is also used within legal limits. Cyclamates were used as nonsweetening agent. The finding that large,doses of cyclamates caused cancer in rats resulted in the prohibition of this in ice cream in 1970 in USA and later in Canada too. Commercially, a mixture of sorbitol and mannitol is used. These compounds are assimilated slowly in the body and have low calorific value (11 kJ/g compared with 16.8 kJ/g of sugar). Glycerine also often added to lower the freezing point to a desirable level.

Consumption: In USA, the consumption of ice cream remained virtually unchanged for 30 years with a growth rate today of between 0.5-2.0% per year. Nevertheless, the consumptiort exceed 20 l/head/year. In Europe, on the other hand ice cream consumption is on the increase and amounts of 5 l/head/year. The consumption exceeds 10 l in the Scandinavian countries but does not exceed 3 l in Spain and Portugal. In countries with insufficient milk production, consumption is still very low, but has a fantastic potential in the years to come. After quick frozen yoghurt, yoghurt ice cream is currently enjoining a surge in the popularity, either the just aroma is mixed in or the actual yoghurt itself, including its microbes, sometimes supplemented by *Lactobacillus acidophilus*. The yoghurt is added in liquid form or in powder form, which facilitates its transportation.

Chapter 8

SOME DRIED DAIRY PRODUCTS

Manufacture of whey powder: When drying whey by methods of spray drying or drum drying that are commonly used in the drying of milk products, the lactose contained in the freshly dried whey is present in the anhydrous form consisting of syrup or an amorphous glass. With the lactose in this form, the whey powder because of its very high lactose content (70%) is intensely hygroscopic. It absorbs moisture rapidly from the air and even at ordinary relative humidities, becomes unmanagably sticky. The lactose then crystallizes and this causes humid whey powder to cake and harden progressively during storage. This physical instability in dried whey is further increased in the case of sour cheese whey. To make the powder moisture stable and permanently free flowing at ordinary relative humidities, the method'of manufacture must be modified as to cause lactose crystallization before the dried whey is ground preparatory to packaging.

Drum drying : In early days, a non hygroscopic, non- caking drum dried whey powder was made by using a 2-stage double drum drier (Fig 10-1). The upper set of drums rotate outward and the knives are located on the underneath of the drum. The lower set of drums rotate inward towards each other and the knives are located on the underneath of the drum. Upper drum is provided with pendulum feed. Pre condensed whey is fed to the trough between the upper drums working at 4 kg/cm^2 The knives scraps partially dried whey(87-85% TS) into the trough between the lower drums working at 2 kg/cm^2 The knives remove the whey films and seeded crystals that adhere to the drum surface and the dried whey with beta lactose type (97.8% TS) comes off in flake form which can be pulverised. The lactose is present largely in the form of beta lactose crystals. Due to high cost in production it gave way to spray drying process. In some cases filler such as wheat or rye bran was mixed into the whey before drying to make the dried product easier to scrape off. Spray drying is currently the most widely practised method of drying whey.

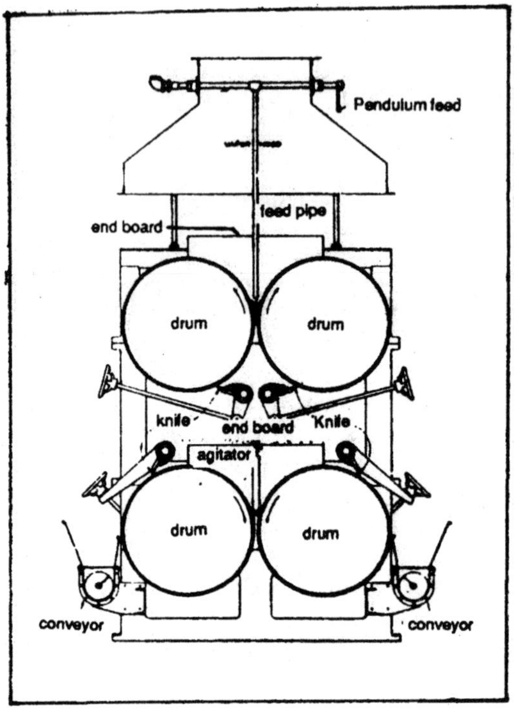

Fig 10-1 Two stage double drum drier

Spray drying

Fat separation: Casein fines are always present in the whey and as they have adverse effect on fat separation and hence they are removed first. For this, various kinds of filters are available. Milk fat is normally recovered by separation from sweet whey for manufacture into whey cream or butter, which is preferred to sweet butter in a number of processing applications. The most important of the remaining ingredients is undoubtedly the protein. The presence of high levels of Ca, P and amino acids is of nutritional benefit and this is best utilised by including of the total whey into other food products. Consequently, whey process aims at total recovery of whey solids or fractionation to produce products high in either protein or lactose.

Chilling and pasteurization : Whey that has to be stored before processing must be either chilled or pasteurized directly after the fat has been removed. For short period of storage say 10-15 h, chilling is usually sufficient to reduce bacterial activity. Longer period of storage may require pasteurization and cooling as well. If legally permissible whey can be preserved by adding such chemical as H_2O_2. If whey is not cooled, it results in a very high content of lactic acid which makes the whey very difficult to dry and makes the powder highly sticky and hygroscopic. When whey is collected from small cheese factories to be dried at a central factory, it is often in a very poor condition, after having travelled long distances, at high temperature.

Following pasteurization, the seven basic operations that can be continued in various ways and sequences to give the desired finished product are :

a) Preheating
b) Concentration
c) Pre crystallization
d) Spray drying
e) After crystallization
f) Fluid-bed drying
g) Fluid-bed/pneumatic cooling

Pre-heating: A preheating temperature of 80°C for 20s ensures fast and rich crystallization, good quality of the product and avoids excessive viscosity to the concentrate.

Concentration: Whey is concentrated in a falling film vacuum evaporator with 2 or more effects. Evaporation using MVR and Reverse Osmosis are closely compatible. For many applications, the most economic mix appears to be the use of RO to concentrate whey to about 25% TS with further concentration by conventional methods. Two of the main properties of whey concentrate to be dried are viscosity and degree of lactose crystallization. The viscosity is highly influenced by heat treablient before concentration. The viscosity increases very quickly when concentrating whey and at 65% TS the viscosity is so high that the product when cooled, becomes - solid.

Whey concentrates with solid content of 55% at a temperature of 38°C or more represent super saturated lactose solution. To avoid spontaneous crystallization in the evaporator, the flow pattern for the last evaporator stage has to be adjusted in such a way that sufficient high temperature is maintained.

Pre crystallization: In order to create optimum conditions for lactose crystallization, the concentrate is subjected to a flash cooling by passing through a flash cooler. The flash cooler is in principle working as evaporator stage without heating. The concentrate is pumped to a flash cooler where a vacuum brings it to boil. During crystallization, the concentrate is kept under controlled temperature in a jacketed and insulated tank equiped with a very efficient agitator (Fig 10-2). When agitator is well covered, agitation is started. Immediately after, the finely ground alpha lactose monohydrate is added at one kg/ton of concentrate. The crystal size should be 20-30 /μm. The holding time is around 3-4 h. Cooling of the concentrate should then start, the rate being 3°C/h until 10°C is reached. The agitator ould break the concentrate and effect thorough mixing. The agitator speed may be 10 rpm and direction of rotating should be reversed every 30 s. The degree of lactose crystallization

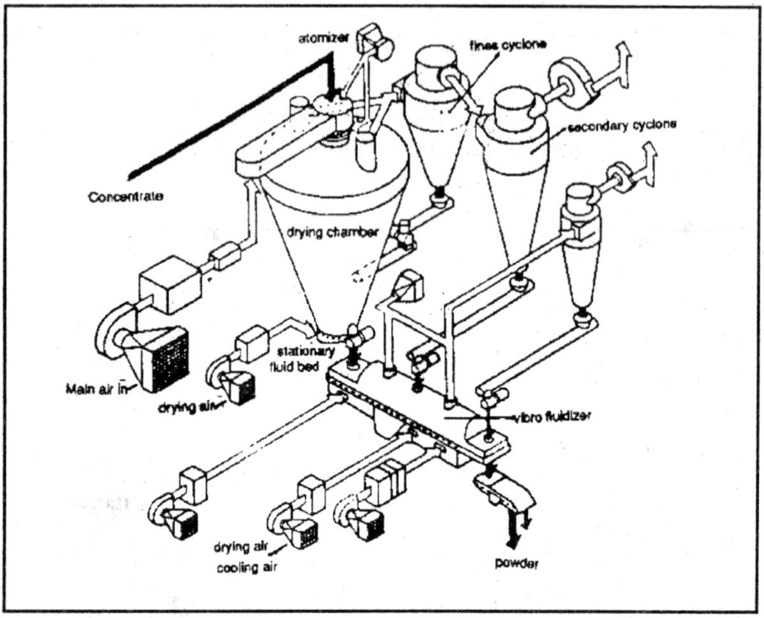

Fig 10-3 Three stage spray drier

should be checked and when it has reached about 85% the concentrate is ready for drying.

Non *crystalline* whey powder is produced by concentrating the whey to about 42-45% TS followed by spray drying immediately by single stage drier. The inlet air temperature is 180°C and the outlet, temperature is fairly high to prevent deposits from the very hygroscopic powder. This whey powder is very fine grained, dusty, sticky and hygroscopic due to lactose being in the glossy, amorphous state, which is the most hygroscopic form of lactose. During storage moisture gets absorbed very easily. This results in caking, browning, Maillard type reactions and deterioration of the powder solubility.

Crystallized whey powder: Whey powder with much better properties and storage stability is obtained by crystallization of the lactose. By precrystallization in the whey concentrate and post crystallization in the powder, the final product possesses optimum non-hygroscopic properties. With preheating at 80°C before concentrating, it is possible to feed the dryer with 55-60% TS at air inlet temperature around 200°C. Besides, if final drying is done in vibro fluidizer, lumping is avoided and there is hot in stream for final drying and using cold air in the last stage of the fluid bed the powder is cooled to the desired temperature. The operation of multistage drying system allow consistently high dry air intake, temperature of 220-230°C with integrated fluid bed. In the 3-stage belt drying process (Fig 10-3) the preheating of

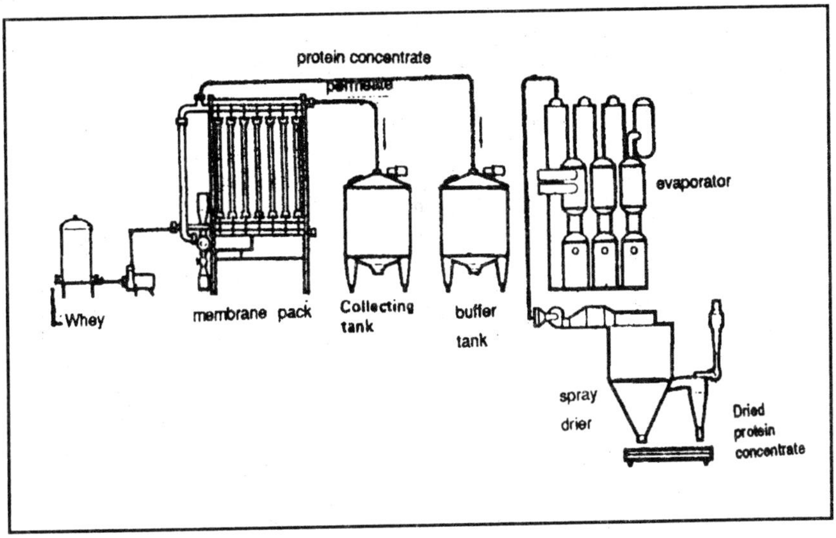

Fig 10-10 Dried whey protein making process

whey is 80°C, concentration is around 50% TS, spray drying with inlet temperature 150°C and outlet temperature gives a moisture content from the chamber 12-15% which is maintained for about 15 min on filtermat belt conveyor (Fig 10-4) mounted between the chamber outlet and the fluid bed where the final drying takes place. The important properties of the whey powders are given below :

Properties	Ordinary whey powder	Pre crysta llised whey powder	Non caking powder 2 stage	Non caking powder 3 stage
Moisture %	3-4	3-5	5-6	4-5
Cakiness %	100	40-100	0-5	0-9
Crystallization %	0-10	50-75	75-85	85-95

It is possible to prepare best whey powder with low moisture, non-caking and with high degree of crystallization as in 3 stage drying.

Lactose : The most important source of lactose is cheese whey, although in some countries hydrochloric acid - casein whey is being used. The batch process has given way to continuous process by the introduction of decanting centrifuge for the separation of lactose crystals and using falling film evaporator for high concentration of whey. The introduction of a membrane for ultra filtration accelerated the change to the newer process. In the earlier method the whey is boiled to coagulate the proteins and the filter cakes are separated. Subsequently the deproteinised whey is concentrated in vacuo, the lactose crystallized the mother liquor separated by centrifugation after which the lactose crystals, are dried and packed. In the later method the whey protein is not denatured the whey concentrated to a high degree 50-62% TS. In multiple falling film evaporator, the product crystallized and separated through decanter centrifuge. The lactose crystals are then dried, classified and bagged. (Fig 10-11). This gives edible lactose with UF permeate First concentration is done in falling film evaporator to around 65% TS and then transferred to crystallization tanks where seed crystals are added. The crystal slurry then is passed through decanter centrifuge for, separation of crystals, which are dried to powder and packed. The lactose crystals formed should exceed 100 μm in size. The bigger the better is the separation. The degree of crystallization should be carefully controlled. The horizontal decanter centrifuge operates continuously and it is equipped with screw conveyor for unloading lactose (Fig 10-12). Two machines are installed in series, the lactose from the first is being reprocessed in the second for efficient separation. During the separation impurities are washed from the lactose to get a product of high quality. The residual moisture content of the lactose may be around 10% and the pure lactose accounts for about 99% of the dry solids. After the second stage separation the lactose is dried in a fluidized bed dryer. The crystals are ground to powder immediately after drying and packed. Although the lactose is edible, for some pharmaceutical applications, it has to undergo further refining treatment. The process in short comprise, high concentration, crystallization decanter centrifugation, fluidized bed drying and packaging.

The specification of different grades of lactose is given below :-

Characteristics	*Requirement %*		
	Crude	*Edible*	*USP*
Lactose	98.4	99.0	98.85
Moisture-monohydrate	0.3	0.5	0.1
Protein (Nx6.38)	0.8	0.1	0.01
Ash	0.4	0.2	0.03
Liquids	0.1	0.1	0.01
Acidity lactic	0.4	0.06	0.01
Standard Plate Count/g	-	<30	<30
Coliforms, yeast, moulds	-	-ve	-ve

The requirement of the commercial lactose (IS:1000:1959) is total ash% max 1.5; fat % max 2.5%; Nitrogen % wt max 0.05; lactose % wt min

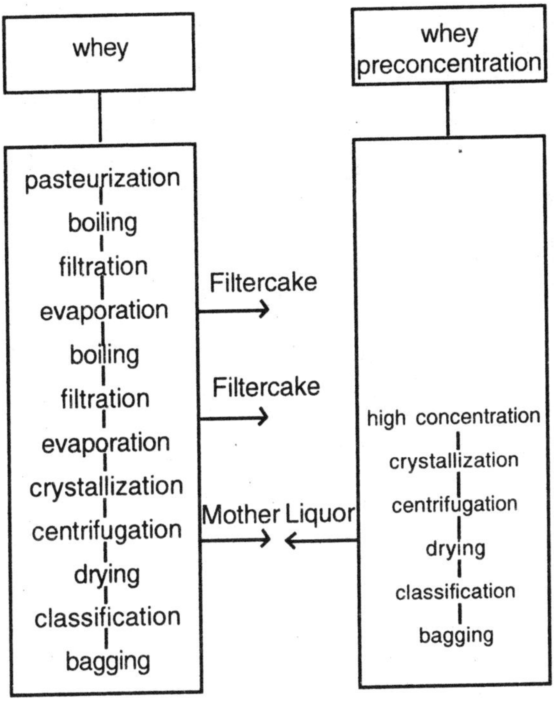

Fig 10-11 Production of edible lactose

90.0; specific rotation 52.0-52.6; lead max. ppm 2.5; arsenic max ppm 1.0.

The major use is for production of simulated human milk. It is a flavoru enhancer without causing excessive sweetness and hence used as dusting powders to flavour potato chips and pudding. It is used as anticaking agent; in flavour enhance. Lactose excels in absorbing flavours, aromas and colouring materials and hence used as carrier for flavourings for many years by pharmaceutical industry as filler or inert carrier for capsules and tablets.

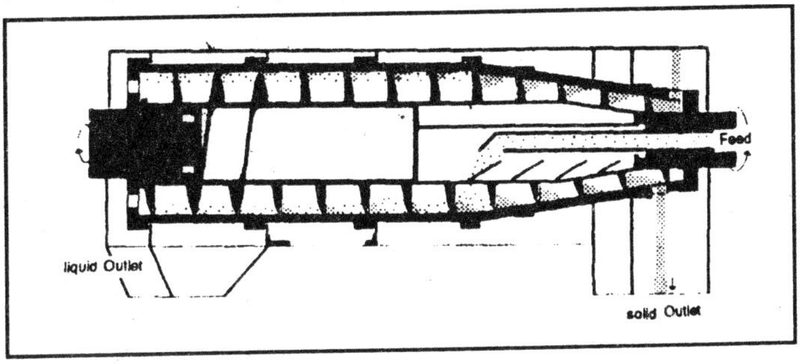

Fig 10-12 Section of decanter centrifuge used for lactose recovery

Dried ice cream mix

There is considerable demand for ice cream in summer season when milk production is low. The average composition of dried ice cream mix is given below.

moisture%	fat%	Serum solids%	sugar%	stabilisers%
1.0-2.5	25-29	25-30	37-42	0.5-1.2

Method of preparation: The ingredients used are milk/skim milk/cream/ skim milk powder/pre gelatinized potato starch as stabilizer and between 80 as emulsifier. The composition of the mix is adjusted so that it contains only 25% of the total sugar before drying. All the ingredients are weighed so that the mix contains 17.1% fat, 14.2% SNF, 5.3% sugar, 6.7% pre gelatinized starch and 0.07% tween 80. The starch is mixed with a little amount of sugar and added to milk or skim milk and heated with agitation. The required amount of cream is now added and temperature raised to 50°C. Skim milk powder mixed with the remaining sugar is added to the mixture. The content is filtered and tween 80 added to the mixture. The temperature is raised to 70°C and homogenized at 175 kg/cm^2 and 35 kg/cm^2 in two stages. The mix is then pasteurized at 68°C/30 min, cooled to 5°C and aged for 16 h. The mixture is preheated and spray dried with inlet temperature 73°C and atomizer speed 16 500 rpm. The powder obtained is dry blended with refined sugar in the ratio of 100:41. The composition of the final product will be moisture 17-20%, SNF 21.5-26%, fat 31-32%, sugar 40-41%, starch 1.3% and tween 0.13%. The product is packed in laminated polythene bags can have shelf life of 9 mo at 30°C. Ideally the powder should be rapidly cooled,blended with required powdered sugar (if not added While drying) and dry flavouring materials and gas packed in an inert atmosphere.

For preparation of ice cream, one part of the powder should be mixed with 1.6 parts of potable water at 45°C, cooled and frozen in a freezer to about 100% overrun. A kg of the powder reconstituted in 1.6 kg water may give 36 cups (125 ml) of ice cream. Wherever pasteurizer, homogenizer and other accessories are not available, only with a freezer ice cream having desired body, texture and melting quality can be prepared.

Malted milk powder is a product made by combining whole milk with the liquor separated from a mash of ground barley malt and wheat flour with or without the addition of sodium chloride, sodium bicarbonate in such a manner as to secure the full enzymic action of the malt extract and by removing water. The resulting product should have not less than 7.5% of milk fat and not more than 3.5% moisture. Malted milk was developed by William Horlick of Wisconsin in 1883 and marketed in 1887. As the popularity of the product grew, other manufacturers entered the field.

The finished malted milk consists of 25% milk solids, 25% barley malt and malt syrup and 50% wheat flour. The details will follow. After this mixture has been prepared it is reduced to a powder. The original method was to concentrate the mixture in vacuum pan, finishing in a pan that is equiped with powerful agitator. In this pan the boiling was continued until only 3% moisture remained and the highly viscous mass would be expanded as a porous foamy mass, in which form it would solidify with the agitation and heating continued until just before the point of solidification. After this gets fully solidified and some what cooled, it was removed from the vacuum pan by chopping it out in pieces, which were ground to the desired fineness. The grinding and packaging must be done in a dry atmosphere because the product is hygroscopic. This method has largely been superseded by vacuum drum drying, tray drying and currently by spray drying also.

The barley malt is to provide the enzyme to digest the starch and also proteins in wheat flour and barley malt. The malt flavour is derived from barley malt, supplemented by malt syrup added as such. These 3 ingredients are prepared as mash working for a few h.

The average composition of the malted milk powder is:

moisture %	fat%	protein %	lactose %	Ash %
3.29	7.55	13.19	72.40	3.66

The sugars include maltose and dextrin also. According to PFA Rules (1976) malted milk product is obtained by mixing whole milk or partially skimmed milk or milk powder with malt extract and cereal grain flour in such a manner as to secure complete hydrolysis of starchy material. It should not contain added sugars, foreign fat, added colours and preservatives. It may contain cocoa powder. Maltcd milk food should be in the form of powder. The PFA standard is given below:

Characteristics		***Requirements***	
moisture	max	5.0%	
total ash	max	5.0%	(dry basis)
ash insoluble in dil HCl	max	0.1%	-do
milldat	min	7.0%	-do
nitrogen	min	2.0%	-do
solubility	min	80.0%	-do
starch test		negative	
bacterial count/g	max	50 000	
coliform count/g	max	10	

The IS:1806:1975 requirements are given below:

Characteristics	Type I	Type II*
moisture % max	4	4
total protein (N x 6.25) min dry	13	11.5
fat % min dry	7.5	7.6
total ash % max dry	5	5
acid insoluble ash% min dry	0.1	0.1
solubility % min	85	8.0
cocoa powder % min dry	-	5
test for starch	-ve	-ve
bacterial count/g	50 000	50 000
coliform count/g	10	10

*with cocoa powder

Method of making : Barley malt is crushed (through roller milk) and steeped in a kettle in about 6-7 times its weight of water at 38°C for 30 min for diastase action. Simultaneously, wheat flour rich in starch and protein is cooked at 93°C for 2 h to make a paste. The ratio of barley malt to wheat flour is 25:1. The barley malt and its steeping water and the cooled wheat flour paste are transferred to a mashing kettle where they are mixed. The mixture is held at 45°C for 30 min. The temperature is then raised to 70°C in 30 min and held at that temperature for 2 h to complete the action of conversion of starch to maltose and dextrin. The enzymic action ensures breakdown of wheat proteins into simpler digestible compounds. The characteristic pleasant flavour of barley malt is conveyed to the liquid extract from the barley husk. The husks are allowed to settle and the liquid portion of the mash is discharged to a hot well. The residue in the enzymic kettle is washed with 2 rinsings of water which are added to the wort in the hot well To this wort which contains about 11% cereal solids, calculated amount of wholemilk is added to meet the statutory requirements of 7.5% fat. The mixture is then forewarmed at 70°C and condensed to 65-70% TS and dried in a special vacuum pan/drum dryer/spray drier.

The finished product is ground and packed in an atmosphere of low humidity. For packaging glass bottles with screw type metal lids or containers impervious to moisture are used. The product is stored at room temperature. Nitrogen packing is not generally done. The cereal products perhaps exert an anti oxidant and protective effect.

Food value : It is high in protein and sugar in digestible form. It has pleasant flavour and used for feeding children, invalids and convalescents.

Baby food (Dried Infant Milk Food) : Human milk is universally regarded as an ideal food for the feeding of infants, or children below one year of age. Yet, owing to various causes, an infant may not derive adequate nutrition from the mother and it may become necessary to feed the infant either wholly or partly with milk from other soures. Unless a substitute is found from other sources, malnutrition may set in, damage to child's health with consequences which may prove fatal. The average composition of milk used for infant feedings is given below in %.

Species	*water*	*fat*	*protein*	*lactose*	*SNF*	*casein*
human	86.4	4.6	1.2	6.9	9.0	0.03
cow	66.7	4.5	3.4	4.9	8.8	0.13
buffalo	83.7	6.5	3.8	5.1	9.8	0.20
goat	86.8	4.5	3.3	4.4	8.7	0.13
sheep	81.6	7.5	5.6	6.4	10.0	0.20

The figures reveal that human milk is characterized by a lower protein and calcium content both of which contribute towards the formation of soft curd, which is easily digestible. The sugar content is also high. Other milks are generally modified for infant feeding by dilution with water and addition of sugar. For the past few decades, modified cow milk has been successfully dried in developed dairying countries for infant feeding.

According to PFA Rules infant Milk Food (baby food) means the product obtained by drying cow or buffalo milk or a combination thereof or by drying standardized milk, with the specific addition of carbohydrates cane sugar, dextrose, dextrin, maltose or lactose, iron salts and vitamins. It should contain no starch or antioxidants. The moisture content should not exceed 5.0% and milkfat content should not be less than 18.70%; total carbohydrates, should not be less than 35.0%; milk proteins not less than 20.0 %; total ash not more than 8.5%; ash insoluble in hydrochloric acid not more than 0.05%, Fe not less than 4.0 mg/100 g ; vitamin A not less than 15.IU/g. The drying process used should be indicated on the label. The infant milk food must not have a standard plate count of more than 50 000/ g. The solubilty index of a roller dried powder may be a maximum of 15.0 ml, and that for spray dried product, 2.0 ml. The product should be packed in hermetically sealed containers and the label shouldbear the date by which the product is to be consumed. The Indian Standards Specification for infant milk foods IS:1547, 1968 are given below:

Characteristics		Requirernents
Moisture (% wt)max		4.5
Total milk protein (% wt) min		20.0
Milk fat (% wt) 18.0-28.0		
Total carbohydrates		including
	dextrose, sucrose, dextrins,	
	maltose (% wt) min	35.0
Total ash (% wt) max,		8.5
Acid insoluble ash (% wt) max		0.01
Solubility	a) solubility index (ml) max	15.0 (if roller dried)
		2.0 (if spray dried)
	or b) solubility (% wt)min	85.0 (if roller dried)
		98.5 (if spray dried)
Vitamin -A IU/100 g min		1500
Added vitamin-D IU/100 g		400-800
Iron mg/100g (min)		4.0
Bacterial count/g (max)		50 000
Coliform count/g (max)		10

The addition of vitamin C is necessary. The normal vitamin C requirement of an infant is 30 mg/day.

The % chemical composition of some Indian brands of infant milk foods as printed on the label is given below:

Brand	% Moisture	Fat	Protein	Carbohydrate	Ash
Amul	3.0	18.0	22.0	52.0	3.0
Glaxo	2.9	26.5	24.9	38.5	5.6
Lactogen	3.0	19.0	21.6	50.8	4.8
Nestogen	3.3	12.0	20.2	60.0	4.7
Vijayspray	-	19.0	22.0	50.0	-
Parag	-	18.0	24.0	49.0	-

Carbohydrates include sucrose, dextrose or dextrins, maltose or lactose

Method of manufacture : The successive steps are :

Milk reception and pretreatment: Only high grade raw milk should be accepted. The milk is preheated to 35-40°C for filtration/clarification and cooled to 5°C for temporary storage.

Standardization is done to conform to legal standards. The fat:SNF ratio is adjusted to 1:3.227. The standardized milk may contain 2.9-3.05% fat and 9.6% SNF. Phosphate buffer solution is added to react with Ca and reduce the curd tension of milk. Ferrous sulphate is added to provide Fe and sugar to increase the palatability.

Preheating: The milk is preheated to 80°C/no hold for destruction of pathogens, other harmful microorganisms and to inactivate enzymes.

Concentration: The milk is concentrated in a multiple effect vacuum evaporator to around 25-30% TS for roller drying or 43- 48% for spray drying.

Homogenization : To reduce size of fat globules and to get uniform dispersion the milk is homogenized in two stages 50 kg/cm2 and 25 kg/cm^2.

Chilling and temporary storage : The concentrate is chilled to 5°C and held at this temperature. The pH is adjusted to 7.0 with bicarbonate or disodium phosphate if needed.

Preheating is done to 70°C before feeding to rollers or in the spray drier.

Grinding and sifting is necessary for roller dried powder.

Fortification: Amino acids, minerals and vitamins are dry mixed properly for even distribution.

Packing: The final product is tested for quality, nitrogen gas' packed and labelled in presterilized tin cans under hygienic conditions and sealed with pre sterilized lids.

Storage is normally done at room temperature. The keeping quality is reasonably good. Reconstitution is done as per manufacturers instructions for infant feeding.

Dry sodium caseinate : High grade edible casein is first prepared by selecting proper raw material. The casein curd is dispersed in alkali solution at 65°C and pH adjusted to 7.0. The solid content of the. slurry is controlled to 15-20% for spray drying. The casein should be in complete solution before spray drying at 90°C to reduce moisture to around 3.0%. The % composition of the caseinates is given below:

caseinate	Sodium caseinate	Calcium Caseinate	Potassium
Protein (N x 6.30) min	95.0	94.5	95.0
Fat max	1.0	1.0	1.0
Lactose max	0.2	0.2	0.2
Ash	3.3	3.5	3.3
moisture	5.0	5.0	5.0
Na mg/g	12.0	1.0	0.6
K mg/g	0.2	1.0	16.5
Ca mg/g	1.0	10.6	3.0
Cu mg/kg max	5	5	5
Fe mglkg max.	20	20	20
Pb mg/kg.max	5.0	5.0	5.0

These are recommended norms for various uses. The product is screened and packed in in kraft paper bags with plastic liner. The recommended microbiological norms are total plate count/g max 5 000; coliform/g max one; yeast and mould 50; and salmonellae nie in 25 g. The product is stored at room temperature.

Uses : Caseinates' increase the protein content of food stuffs, dietetic products and feeds. They have good watertbinding capacity and act as emulsifier. They also have good overrun and stabilizing properties and enhance the flavour of the product.They increase overrun in ice cream. They are used as coffee whitener and in sausages. Some of the proprietary pharmaceutical products for special foods using sodium caseinate are Meritene (Doyce), Nutrament (Drackett), Portagar and Sustacal (Mead Johnson); using calcium caseinate are Casilam, Complan (glaxo), Metrecal, Sustagen, Casec (Mead Johnson).

Anhydrous milkfat: Milkfat concentrates are classified as follows:

Product	Source	Composition	
		>milkfat%	<moisture%
anhydrous milk fat (AMF)	fresh milk or butter with no neutralizer	99,8	0.1
Anhydrous butterfat	butter fresh or stored or cream of variable age	99.5	0.1
Butteroil	butter or cream all of which variable age	99.3	0.5

All the concentrated products, are similar to ghee (except flavour). The process involves a) simple decantation, b) centrifugal separation or c) direct production from cream. Simple decantation consists in melting butter and allowing it to settle for a few h until milkfat clears. The fat is drawn off from the top. This is not economical. The centrifugal separation method involves a) melting butter b) neutralization, c) decantation, d) centrifugal separation, e) vacuum drying, f) cooling and package. Melting of butter blocks is done on s/s pipes through which hot water at 65-71 °C is circulated. Butter passes through successive layers of pipes melts and falls to the bottom. Direct steam is also used in some cases on a perforated false bottom plate over a vat. The butter is also cut to small pieces to hasten melting. The melted butter may be neutralized if necessary. The scum is removed before passing to desludging separators. Moisture is removed by flashing the hot butteroil in one or two vacuum dehydrators maintained at 75 cm Hg. To get fine crystals cooling is done in stages. Lacquered metal containers are used for filling. Exclusion of 0, and gas packaging provides maximum storage quality.

The basic difference between using direct cream or using butter is connected with phase inversion. For butter making inversion is not required as this has already been done during churning of cream. The fat emulsion in cream is oil-in-water and this has to be inverted during processing to a waterin-oil emulsion. This change is needed for subsequent effective dehydration.

Creamery package, Cherry Burrell Package systems and Affa Laval continuous butterfmaking involve a partial breaking of cream inversion. Cream heated to 54 to 65°C is reconcentrated to about 80% cream by centrifugal separation prior to phase inversion by using phase inversor pump and applying pressure of 0.1 kg/cm^2. The crude butteroil is concentrated in a separator to give 96-98% oil, heated to 87°C and spray injected in a vacuum chamber at 73 cm Hg for final removal of moisture. The final product is pumped to a cooler at about 28°C and packed airtight in containers. The advantages of AMF are a) long keeping quality, b) needs no refrigerated storage, c) flexible for various uses and d) the flavour of butterfat is not altered. It can be used for producing a) recombined milk, b) sterilized milk, c) evaporated and sweetened condensed milk, d) ice cream, e) toffee, milk chocolate, cakes and f) baked foods. The keeping quality of AMF depends on the quality of raw material used copper or iron contamination, amount of air present and temperature of storage of the product.

Butter powder is a rich source of butterfat. The average composition is fat 82.0%, SNF 6.7%, emulsifier 3.5%, caseinate/citrate 6.7%, antioxidant 0.02%, and free flowing agent 0.5%. The production consists in mixing pasteurized cream and reconstituted skim milk powder to have 80% fat and 16.5% SNF (on dry basis). Sodium citrate is dissolved in the cream and homogenized at 140 + 35 kg/cm^2 at 65°C and pasteurized at 75°C/ 1 min, cooled and ripened to 0.16% lactic acid by using starter culture. Glyceryl mono stearete and BHA are blended and spray dried at 175°C inlet and 80°C outlet temperature. The product is cooled and dry blended with sodium aluminium silicate and 20% calcium phosphate as free flowing agent. The anticaking agent is also dispersed in water and applied to the walls of the dryer. The product is quickly cooled and removed from the drier and packed in tin cans. The shelf life is around 6 mo at 10-15°C. It is used fort ice oream making, bakery products, dry mixes icings and fillings.

Cream powder is fairly high in protein lactose and also milkfat. The average composition is fat 65%, proteins 13.4%, lactose 10.0%, ash 2.9% with moisture 1.0%. The method of preparation consists in standardising good quality cream to a ratio of fat:SNF of 1-:1, pasteurizing at 74°C/15 s, homogenizing at 200 kg/cm^2, concentrating to 40-50% TS in vacuum, reheated to 70°C and spray dried to 1-2% moisture. The outlet temperature in the drier should be low. since the product has tendency to stick to the sides of drying chamber, the product is packed in fibre drums with or without polythene liner. It is stored at 15°C with or without gas packing. The storage life is about 2 mo. It is used in confectionery, baking industries and for making chocolate ice cream.

Dried cheese : Moisture is removed from ordinary cheese to produce product suitable for grating and reducing bulk for transport. Tray drying, spray or freeze drying are done, Grated cheese is used for enhancing flavour of macaroni and other foods. Low moisture natural cheese with 34-45% moisture are reduced into strips or granules and exposed at 30°C in circulating warm air in bed driers at 15-20% RH. The particles are then pulverized, screened, grated and packed under nitrogen. The keeping quality is 18 mo at 4°C. 6 mo at 21 °C and 3 mo at 32°C. The main problem is flavour retention during drying. To maintain flavour in BIRS proceess dehydration is done in a long (50 m) drying tower maintained at around 30°C. The cheese is pulverized and dispersed through atomizer to give small droplet size. As droplets move downwards against rising hot air of low velocity and within a minute moisture of the powder is reduced to 10% and dried in a secondary drier. The instant spray powder has long keeping quality with retention of natural flavour.

Chhana powder : The composition is fat 41.6%, protein 46.3%, iactose 4.2%, ash 4.4% and moisture 3.5%. The product is rich in fat and protein contents. The fresh Chhana is broken into small particles by mechanical device (micropulverizer) and calculated amount of water is added to give 19-21% TS in slurry, preheated to 195°C and spray dried with inlet temperature 195°C and outlet temperature 102°C. The powder is quickly removed from drying chamber, cooled, packaged and stored at room temperature. It has storage life of 2 and 4 mo at 20°C under air and nitrogen gas packing respectively. It can be reconstituted into chhana for making sweets like Sandesh.

Khoa powder : Khoa made in small villages travels long distance for a good market. Exposure to atmospheric contamination and high atmospheric temperatures cause rapid spoilage. By reducing moisture content it is possible to make khoa powder by adopting tray, roller and spray drying processes and packing in tin containers for enhanced storage even upto 6 or 7 mon. Khoa prepared under conventional process can be ground and uniformly distributed in small layers and dried using hot air at 70°C or under vacuum of 62 cm Hg. It is also possible to dehydrate finely ground khoa with 20% moisture in fluidized bed with inlet air at 92°C and outlet air at 80°C. The product can be cooled, ground, sieved before packaging. The powder can also be made by using buffalo milk, concentrating to 35% under vacuum, preheated to slightly over 100°C to develop flavour and spray -dried with inlet temperature 190°C and exit temperature at 88°C. The dried khoa may analyse moisture 2.5%, fat 33.2%, protein 25.5%, lactose 33.9% and ash 4.9%. However, the solubility and wetting time will be higher than normal whole milk powder. It is used for making Indian sweets.

Gulabjamun mix powder (GMP) Khoa is used as a base for making Gulabjamun. This causes wide variations in flavour, texture and composition of the sweet made of the base khoa. To overcome these problems a readyto-form Gulabjamun mix powder using skimmilk powder (SMP) with keeping quality of over 6 mo can be made. Roller dried whole milk (WMP) is also suitable to replace SMP. The formulation consists of roller SMP 43.4%, 1.5% and powdered cardamom 0.1 %. All these are mixed uniformly using power driven mixer. Fat is melted to ensure proper mixing. The mix is packaged in polyethylene bags or laminated pouches and stored in a dry place. The shelf life is around 6 mo at room temperature. In whole milk powder (WMP) formulation 58.4% replaces SMP plus butterfat: The product is useful for making instant gulabjamun.

Srikhand powder : Dried Srikhand is made from Srikhand base (chakka) to which finely ground sugar (18% of base) is added, properly mixed and kneaded. Water is added at 25% of the mix to get smooth slurry. The slurry is homogenized at 100 kg/cm^2 and spray dried with inlet air at 19°C and outlet air set at 100°C. The product is removed quickly from drying chamber, cooled and packaged at room temperature. It can be gas packed also. The keeping quality is around 3 mo. under gas packed tin containers. The average % composition of powder from cow milk is moisture 3.5 (2.8), fat 22.9(32.8), lactic acid 0.25 (0.26) and total solids 96.5(97.2). the results with buffalo milk are indicated in brackets. Srikhand desiccated under open pan is also made and sold as Srikhand Wadi sweet.

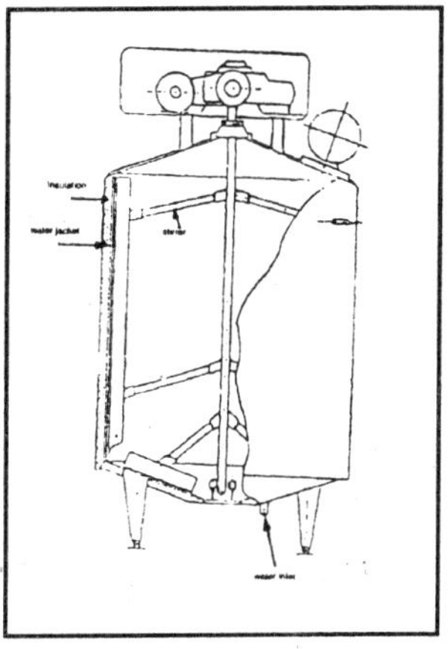

Fig 10.2 Lactose Crystallization tank

Chapter 9

MARKET DAHI AND PURE CULTURE DAHI

Dahi, a fermented milk product is being used since ancient days as an article of diet, refreshing beverage and as an intermediary in the manufacture of shrikhand, butter and ghee. The dahi making process involves inoculation with previous batch culture to milk at body temperature, followed by undisturbed fermentation and setting in a warm place overnight. Dahi is widely consumed in India. Its preparation is mostly confined to individual households and halwai shops without paying much attention in the physico-chemical or microbiological quality of milk or starter culture. Humphyreys and Plunkett also reported tha the quality of yoghurt and dahi was governed by selection of milk, standardization, heat treatment, homogenization, fermentation and storage.

In the present investigation an attempt has been made to study the physico-chemical, sensory and microbiological quality of the market dahi collected from different commercial shops of Parbhani town, Maharashtra and compare with pure culture dahi made at laboratory.

Materials and Methods

Market dahi samples : Twenty sample of dahi 500 ml each were collected aseptically from different commercial shops (halwai) of Parbhani town randomly and were used for the study. Fresh cow milk obtained from the university dairy farm standardized to 4.5% fat had 8.5% solid-non-fats (SNF) was used for the preparation of dahi at laboratory. The pure cultures namely, Lactococcus lactis, L. cremoris Streptococcus lactis and S. Cremoris obtained from the National Dairy Research Institute, Karnal, India, were used in equal proportions (1:1) for the preparation of bulk culture in sterilized skim milk by incubating at 30°C for 16 h and followed by three successive tranfer prior to use.

Preparation of laboratory dahi samples : Four liters of milk were boiled for 3 to 5 min and cooled to 40°C. The milk was divided into four parts in sterilized containers. Appropriate starter cultures were inoculated at 2% (v/v) level in combination (1:1) and incubated at 30°C for 12 h. The data presented here are the average of four replicates.

Physico-chemical analysis : Dahi samples were analysed for proximate composition, titratable acidity (TA) as % of lactic acid and pH using standard procedures (AOAC) 1965, 1975: AACC 1976). Specific gravity was determined as per BIS method (1960). Free fatty acids (FFA) content was estimated by the method of Deeth and Fitz Gerald (1976), while proteolytic activity and diacetyl content were determined as per method described by Hull (1947) and King (1948), respectively of dahi samples at room temperature. The viscosity measurements of dahi sample were carried out using Rotoviscometer RV20 (Haake, Germany). 100 ml of dahi sample was put to the sensor cylinder of the instrument and measured at a shear rate of 11.70 at room temperature using MV-1 spindle. The shear stress and sher rate values were converted to viscosity according to the viscometer manual.

Physico-Chemical characteristics of Market Dahi and Pure Culture Dahi

Characteristics	Dahi		
	Market	Pure Culture	SEM
Moisture (%)	90	86.3	1.85
Total solids (%)	10	13.7	1.85
Fat (%)	2.9	4.7	0.9
SNF (%)	7.1	9.0	0.95
Lactose (%)	2.95	3.6	0.32
Casein (%)	2.24	2.4	0.08
Total protein (%)	2.86	2.8	0.03
pH	3.93	4.64	0.35
Titratable acidity, % lactic acid	1.82	0.69	0.57
Specific gravity	1.02	1.03	0.01
Viscosity (mpa.s)	765.55	1365.89	300
Free Fatty Acids, micro equiv/g. dahi	1.86	1.17	0.34
proteolytic activity, mg tyrosine/g, dahi	0.18	0.09	0.04
Diacetyl value, mg/100g, dahi	1.88	3.02	0.57

Microbiological analysis : The total viable count (Bis 1962), total acid producing bacteria count, lactic acid count, coli forms (BIS 1981), spore forms yeasts and molds in potato dextrose agar medium were carried out for dahi samples at room temperature.

Sensory evaluation : Dahi samples were presented to a panel of 10 membered semi-trained judges selected from the staff and students of the department for sensory evaluation for appearance, taste, flavour, consistency, body and overall acceptability using a 9-point Hedonic scale. The samples stored at room temperature were served to panelists randomly for three replications of the study.

Statistical analysis : GPIS software was used for statistical analysis of data obtained for physico-chemical and sensory analysis of dahi samples.

Results and Discussions

The average proximate composition of dahi collected from different commercial shops of Parbhani town as well as dahi prepared at laboratory using pure culture is shown in the Table. Moisture content of the market sample was higher while the total solids (TS), fat, SNF, lactose and casein were lower than the dahi prepared from pure culture. These values revealed that market dahi were made from inferior quality of milk. The high acidity and low pH value of market dahi clearly indicated that the dahi were not made from fresh milk. However, excess acid production could suggest that market dahi were made from stale milk. The initial acidity and quality of milk have considerable effect on the physical and organoleptic quality of dahi. The presence of more water content resulted low specific gravity of the market sample as compared to laboratory sample.

Viscosity is an important physical property related to the quality of dahi. The viscosity data for market dahi and dahi prepared at laboratory showed a significant difference. The market dahi had no characteristic body and consistency while the laboratory dahi possessed both of these qualities. Dahi viscosity depends on the total solids contents (protein, lactose and salts) of milk which subsequently develop the firm coagulum of the product in association with bound water present in the milk. Moreover, the gel produced during fermentation stage from the low level of SNF will be thin and watery and prone to synerisis. As far as market dahi was concerned, the presence of low level of SNF and TS content produced weak body and low viscous product.

The FFA value presented in the table indicated that the market dahi had a higher lipolytic activity than the pure culture dahi. The FFA value indicates that there was fat metabolism during fermentation though it was a weak activity in fermented milk products. The tyrosine value was also higher for market dahi which indicated that those starter cultures had a pronounced proteolytic activity than those of pure culture dahi. An increase in proteolytic activity in each sample of acidophilus milk was noted irrespective of their level of inoculum. The pure culture dahi produced a fair amount of diacetyl

(3.02) while the market dahi produced marginally low. The diacetyl production is a function of fat content of the product. The market sample had a lower fat content as a result it produced less amount of diacetyl. Moreover the low production of diacetyl in dahi could be attributed to the lack of leuconostoc in the market culture. The present investigation for pure culture sample is in accordance with the finding of Pantange. Analysis of variance (ANOVA) indicate that the difference among the group means as well as the effect of treatments are extremely significant ($P<0.0001$).

The different microbial counts during dahi formation are shown. The number of total viable count, total acid producer and lactic acid bacteria counts were higher in the pure culture dahi as compared to market dahi. The viable count had a greater significance in the bacteriological production and evaluation of dahi as these viable micro-organisms initiate the fermentation process. The qualities of dahi are determined by the number of microorganisms present and substances formed as a result of biochemical process accompanying milk souring. The present results confirm the findings of Mohanan et al. (1984) for the market dahi. There were also significant differences exist in case of acid producing and lactic acid producing bacteria between market and laboratory dahi. Among acid producing bacteria the most importants were 70% Lactobacillus bulgaricus, 20% L. casei and 10% L. brevis. Several authors reported that the acid producer and lactic acid organism count were in the range of $2x10^8$ cfu/ml to $4x10^8$ cfu/ml and $52x10^6$ cfu/ml of market dahi. The observed total acid producer count was similar to those reported value while the lactic acid count was lower. Coli forms, spore forms or yeast and mold were not detected in pure culture dahi while the market sample contained a huge number of these hazardous microorganisms. Market dahi fails to meet the criteria laid down by BIS and were not fit for human consumption. The present data are in accordance with the observations of Jayaraman and Gandhi and Ray and Srinivas respectively for market dahi. The presence of these pathogenic microorganisms indicate that there is no practice of hygiene as well as no proper maintenance of microbial culture during dahi preparation.

The sensory scores of market and laboratory dahi are shown. The sensory data revealed that the above two products considerably different from each other with respect to appearance, taste, flavour, consistency, body and overall acceptability. Statistically, the difference among group as well as treatment do not significantly affect the measured variables.

Conclusion

From the results of the present study, it is obvious that the overall quality attributes of market dahi were inferior. The product was more prone to proteolysis. Moreover, the presence of higher load of pathogenic microorganisms may lead to severe public health hazards. The consumption of coli forms spore forms yeast and molds contaminated dahi could be fatal for human health. Therefore, proper hygienic measures and strict regulation should be implemented during dahi manufacturing commercially.

Chapter 10

PACKAGING OF MILK

To treat the subject of milk packaging, it would be better to look at the history which is relatively short. Milk only really became a readily safe product at the turn of the century, so we will look at the period from 1900 to the present to see the trends which have taken place to bring this product to the marketplace and to the consumer.

At the end of the 19th century, milk was almost exclusively packed in glass bottles. The reason for this was most milk was distributed by breweries, and hence the bottle being chosen as the packaging vehicle for beer, became that for milk as well. The glass bottle was a good choice. It was sanitary. It was capable of being cleaned, sanitized and reused. It presented the product well. The white milk showed up very well in the glass bottle and the cream present in the milk would rise to the top and form a different colored cream line allowing the customer to assess the quality of the milk based upon butter fat content.

It wasn't until much later, that it began to be recognized that glass bottle had shortcomings. The weight of the bottle relative to the product was great; thus its transportation costs were high. The effect of light on milk damaging the nutritive components was great. The cost of rewashing the bottle was high in terms of energy, and chemicals used in washing the bottle were to become an environmental hazard.

It wasn't until 1937 that a paper single use container became available. The package was mostly paper, and the bottom was glued together, then dipped in wax to seal it. It was then filled with milk, and the top stapled closed. There was no opening for pouring. The stapled top had to be opened with a knife still. Consumer liked the new disposable package when they were able to buy it. And, of course, the dairy received a package which was already clean, did not have to worry about returned milk bottles, and did not have to worry about breakage or recontaminating the product's stream by returning dirty bottles to a plant. However, the wax process did leave a lot to be desired since it did impart a flavour to the milk. Secondly, little bits of wax would break away from the surface of the carton and cause an unpleasant mouth feel when drinking the product. In the late 1950's and early 1960's, it was discovered the polyethylene coating of the paper would allow a paper carton to be formed and sealed on a machine without damage to the product. The benefits of the carton were then becoming very obvious.

1. The dairy received a clean sanitary package in which to package the milk.
2. The carton was opaque; thus light damage to the nutrients was much slower.
3. The weight of the carton compared to the product was small, thus making distribution costs very reasonable. As time progressed, the shelf life of milk was able to be increased by use of this carton allowing it to be purveyed through super markets with great ease.
4. Much information could be added to the carton in terms of printing, making it a source of information, (not only about the product, but how to utilize the product in cooking and various drinks). Of course, since much of the milk was fed to children, as a fiine nutritive source, the cleanliness of the product was of paramount importance.

The next step forward was the use of asepsis to process and package milk. This was based again on a single use-paper package which utilized polyethylene combined with an aluminum foil membrane, to stop the ingress of oxygen into the package. Certainly milk was a product which was available not only from refrigerated sources but from non-refrigerated sources and particularly in the countries which had a very hot climate, it was the ideal mode to package and transport milk to the customer.

In the late 1970's, it became apparent that the poly ethylene membrane in the paper carton really did all the work, and the paper was just there to support it. The blow moulded milk bottle became.a reality. This particular container was utilized on sizes from quarter liter through to a gallon size (3.74 liters). It could be fitted with a screw top and a handle could be molded onto the package. It became a very convenient package to us , particularly for the growing elderly population in some countries. However. along with improvements, there were some negative factors with the plastic bottle which are still being argued today. It is not readily biodegradable, it takes a huge amount of space because it is difficult to collapse the bottle easily so its volume in terms of disposal is a factor. Also, it is transparent, so the nutritive value of the milk is degraded in a very short period of time. This can be overcome by coloring the bottles and making them opaque. Recycling of plastic bottles becomes a cost factor since the bottle is still a single use con tainer. Thus if it has to be recycled, it has to be washed and sterilized, and rebroken down into size which can be fed into an extruder. Even then, regula tory authorities in many countries will not accept the reuse of plastic material to handle a food product.

All things being considered, the paper carton with polyethylene coating is undoubtedly the best method of purveying milk there is. It is a single use, the carton can be incinerated, and power can be generated from the heat from the incineration. Polyethylene breaks down readily into non-toxic gases, and the ash from paper)s just returning to the earth what was taken from it.

The aseptic package, though it is from the same components, does have the extra component aluminium foil which makes disposal difficult and recycling nearly impossible. Incineration, of course, would reduce aluminium to aluminium oxide which can be returned to the earth.

Other products which are conveniently handled in paper polyethylene lined containers are a full range of dairy products - cottage cheese, sour cream, yogurt. Of course, a plastic container with a slip lid is utilized for packing these foods also.

The paper polyethylene type container is a wonderful conveyance to pass on information. Recipes for use of the product can be printed on the carton. Nutrition, its suitability of feeding infants, and information on disposal of the container.

Since economics are a factor, polyethylene film has been utilized in the form of a pouch where the milk forms the stuffing for a pillow. This pouch, though suffers from the same shortcomings as any plastic material which isn't coloured-light will affect the nutritional value of the product. Since milk is consumed for its nutritional value, this should be of paramount importance when we consider a package for milk.

Milk, being a perfect food is rarely sold unpacked. (Any bacteria in the atmosphere could find home in the product and grow to an alarming rate since the nutrients are present, the water activity is right and it could become a lethal product). Hence, the packaging of milk is designed to maintain whatever quality of milk is supplied to the filling machine and package. The machine cannot improve the microbial quality of the product supplied to it. Raw milk or unprocessed milk is a product which is not recommended to be consumed by humans since it contains potentially dangerous microorganisms. Therefore, we could sum up the above statements by saying fresh or pasteurized milk should always be packaged to maintain its microbial quality and it should always be stored at a temperature of less than 45°- F. Some processing, which is commonly called UHT or aseptic, is capable of being packaged under aseptic conditions and sold at ambient temperature. The contrast between pasteurized milk and aseptic milk is sometimes difficult for the populous to understand fully. Pasteurized milk, generally speaking has a shelf life of up to 14 days, though it can be processed and packaged and held at refrigerated temperatures to maintain a shelf life of 21 days. Much work has been carried out over the last few years to increase the shelf life of pasteurized products by ultra-clean packaging, the use of modified atmospheres to restrict the growth of bacteria, and the use of packages with barrier properties which inhibit the transfer of oxygen, which is essential for most bacteria to propagate. Aseptic milk is processed and packaged so that it requires no refrigeration and has a non - refrigerated shelf life of up to 180 days.

Chapter 11

PACKAGING OF MILK AND MILK PRODUCTS IN INDIA

In a pre-dominantly vegetarian population like India, milk and milk products form an essential component of the human diet and no other single natural food meets the nutritional requirements better than milk. In India, people take milk as a part of their daily diet and hence the consumption of fluid milk is high. The country's production in 1997 is expected to exceed 200 million litres a day (74.3 million tonnes per year). Further, India is all set to continue to be the world's top milk producer in 1998 with its output projected at 78 million tonnes and an increase is also observed in the market size for milk products (Table-1). Recognizing the importance of nutrients in milk, Indians instinctively converted he liquid product into more stable products under the prevailing tropical climatic conditions. Hence, an unending array of dairy sweets and delicacies are prepared in different regions and during different seasons in the country. In the process of this conversion, the basic limitation of milk - its perishable nature - has been tastefully overcome because processing aims to extend its shelf life.

TABLE - 1

ESTIMATED MARKET SIZE FOR VARIOUS MILK PRODUCTS IN THE ORGANIZED SECTOR

Products	Market size (tonnes)
Baby food	65,000
Dairy whitener	40,000
Whole milk powder	18,000
Skim milk powder	70,000
Ghee (branded)	90,000
Table butter	33,000
Cheese	3,100
Malted foods	43,500
Condensed milk	8,150

Milk, apart from being an almost complete food for human beings, has also been shown to be an excellent culture and protective medium for the growth of microorganisms due to its water, protein, carbohydrate, mineral and vitamin content, all of which are important for the growth and multiplication of microorganisms. Milk, thus serves as a potential vehicle for transmission of disease producing microorganisms and renders itself an extremely vulnerable commodity from public health point of view. This is true for milk products, too.

It is but obvious that for microbiologically susceptible and perishable commodity like milk and its products, processing and packaging go hand-in-hand in the preservation of the product. Packaging of milk and its products is not a substitute for good processing practices; processing. If not followed by proper packaging serves no purpose.

LIQUID MILK

Fresh milk drawn from apparently healthy animals is free of pathogenic bacteria. Bacteria are single-celled organisms that multiply by dividing to form two cells. Under optimum conditions, many bacteria can double in number just in 20 minutes. That means, one bacterium can result ,in upto 16,000,000 bactelria in just eight hours. They are microscopic in size ; so small that a single drop of milk might contain upto 30 billion (30 with nine zeros!) bacteria. Many bacteria are beneficial and necessary. Others are pathogenic, i.e. disease causing and if they are present in sufficient numbers, they can cause illnesses and milk-borne diseases. Pathogenic bacteria are commonly present on the skin, in the udders of cows suffering from mastitis and in cuts, wounds, scratches, etc

In addition to the potential health risks, raw milk cannot be held for long, especially if stored at above refrigeration temperatures. The presence of various organisms bring about spoilage. This is of particular significance in our country. With the establishment of cooperative dairies in cities, milk for processing is supplied from adjoining villages and district areas. This is done in tinned steel or aluminium cans of capacities from 10-50 litres. There are few chilling facilities available at the rural collection centres and milks of different quality are mixed together, chilled and transported to large dairies in insulated tankers of varying capacities (1000 to 10,000 litres). The specifications to facilitate bulk transport of milk are outlined in IS:1373, IS:4937 and IS:1825.

Once milk leaves the animal, the retention or preservation of milk quality requires cleanliness, sanitation and careful handling. Maximum benefits are derived only when the following traits are applied to all aspects of the milk production system:

- animals and their environment

- milking system, practices
- milk storage or cooling system

The growth of many kinds of bacteria can be reduced or stopped by refrigeration and freezing - two important practices in the preservation of food, including milk. However, refrigeration alone will not kill bacteria. .

Pasteurization of milk is a standard practice to eliminate pathogens in the products purchased and used by the consumers. Pasteurization process involves application of heat below the boiling point of milk and this process has been devised to eliminate important pathogens and at the same time, to kill the majority of other microorganisms in milk. Milk may be treated either at a relatively low temperature for an extended period of time or at a higher temperature for a brief period.

The slow, or holding treatment, is a process of heating every particle of milk or milk products, to at least 62.8°C (145°F) and holding at such temperature continuously for at least 30 minutes. The high temperature, short time or flash method (HTST) requires that the product be heated to at least 71.7°C (161 °F) and held at that temperature for at least 15 seconds. The trend now is to use even higher temperatures and longer holding times, such as 7900 (174°F) for 20-25 seconds. After heating, the milk is promptly and efficiently cooled to 7.2°C (45°F) or lower and packed on form-fill-seal (FFS) machines.

The common methods prevailing for milk sterilization are: (i) in-bottle sterilization and (ii) UHT-process. In the in-bottle sterilization process, the milk is heat treated in the temperature range of 410°C to 120°C under pressure with suitable time-temperature combination. In ultrapasteurization or ultra-high-temperature processing (UHT), the product is exposed to at least 137.8°C (280°F) for-2 seconds or more. Heating is usually done by injection of steam.

It is important to understand what is being achieved by the application of a heat process. The primary objective may be to destroy microorganisms capable of growing in the product at the intended distribution temperature or of endangering the health of the consumer. Moreover, the heat process may achieve only a reduction in numbers of microorganisms such that spoilage does not occur within the expected shelf life period of the product. Heat treatment reduces the probability of survival of microorganisms.

With the heat treatment given to milk to preserve its quality, it is most important to pack the product suitably immediately after processing. The packaging operation follows closely in line to processing so that the treated product is neither exposed to atmosphere nor stored in unhygienic conditions. These undesirable practices lead to post-processing contamination with microorganisms, whereby, the heat treatment has no value if the product is not protected after processing.

The modern milk supply system to urban consumers dates back to late 1940's when Aarey Milk Colony of Mumbai Milk Supply Schem~ launched the supply of pasteurized milk in bottles for the first time in India on large scale.(From 1950 to 1970, the mode of fluid milk supply system used to be bulk vending and cans with small share for bottles. The retail sale of pasteurized milk by organized dairies was mainly through two methods: either distributed to consumers from the cans to individual containers or bottled. The different types of pasteurized milk like, standardized, single-toned, double-toned, cow's, buffalo's and skim milk, were distinguished by the adoption of aluminium caps of different colours/ designs on the bottles.

There are two types of automatic bottle fillers. The first is the gravity type filler in which the milk flows by gravity into the bottles as they are pressed against the valves. The second type is the vacuum filler in which the milk is pulled into the bottle by vacuum exerted inside the bottle. The gravity type filler is slower in operation; it also necessitates more number of filler valves around the outer periphery of the bowl. The vacuum filler has overcome these disadvantages.

Bulk vending involves the distribution of pasteurized milk to customers as per their needs. Milk is stored in a chilled condition. The customers cant' their own containers to the vending machine outlets and collect the desired quantity of milk. This practice is still continued in many places.

The 1980's saw a technological change from bottles to sachets which were more convenient to handle. Glass, though an ideal packaging material, known for its inertness, also has inherent disadvantages of heavy weight and fragility. To overcome these disadvantages, till today, packaging of pasteurized milk takes place in plastic pouches generally made of low density polyethylene (LDPE). Co-extruded LDPE-LLDPE film is also used for the same purpose, with the advantage that, pinhole defects, if any, in the pouch are eliminated. These pouches are filled on form-fill-seal (FFS) machines. Milk so packed is available in 500ml and 1000ml quantities. However, in comparison to glass bottles, pilferage, adulteration and malpractices are found to be higher with pouches.

Returnable glass bottles are still used in our country for UHT processed milk. While pasteurized milk needs to be stored under refrigeration till further use, UHT treated milk can be stored under ambient temperatures for more than 2 months. This milk is available in glass bottles with metal crown caps. Aluminium caps of 0.05mm thickness is also used for sealing.

Another technological breakthrough in processing and packaging of milk is the aseptic packaging, commonly known as tetrapak milk. An aseptic filling and packaging system refers to any piece of equipment that fills a sterile package or container with sterile product and hermetically seals it under aseptic (sterile) conditions. These systems form and sterilize the package. Hydrogen peroxide is the commonly used sterilant. Milk is homogenized, pasteurized and cooled to ambient temperature under sterile conditions ; simultaneously the cartons are formed under sterile conditions and the product is filled in the pack. A tetrapak carton has 5-7 layers of materials, including paperboard, aluminium foil, and polythylene. These products are intended for storage at room temperature for extended periods, upto 15 days to 1 month. This pack is ideally suited for Indian market since cold chain distribution and cold storage are not present at all places.

CONCENTRATED MILKS

Concentrated milks are those with reduced moisture content. They are the products manufactured by partial evaporation of water from whole milk or fully or partly skimmed milk, with or without the addition of sugar under vacuum and are being manufactured to

- improve the keeping quality of milk
- reduce the cost of transportation
- save storage and package space
- serve as milk substitute under scarcity conditions
- use as an additive for manufacture of products like, ice-cream, candies, etc.

Prevention of Food Adulteration Act (PFA) rules of 1955 specify the types of concentrated milks as follows: Sweetened condensed milk, Unsweetened condensed milk (evaporated milk), Sweetened condensed skim milk and Unsweetened condensed skim milk. In India, sweetened condensed milk is the most popular one of all other concentrated milks and the product is available in tinplate containers.

MILK POWDER

The dairy plants in our country began to face the problem of utilizing surplus milk during flush season due to seasonal fluctuations in milk production. Spray drying and drum drying are used for drying of milk to powder form, which can be reconstituted when necessary. Spray drying of milk is more suitable than foller-dried milk for reconstitution and beverage purposes. The dried milks are hygroscopic and, therefore, must be protected from moisture. Traditional packaging of 25 kgs. milk powder irrespective of type has been in polyethylene lined multiwall paper sacks. Tinplate cans are the most common materials used for retailing of milk powders, though plastic (HDPE) bottles are also used. Flexible packaging have evolved through polyethylene bags to sophisticated multiply laminates. In most cases, the sachet of milk powder is enclosed inside paperboard cartons as refill packs for the purpose of reduction in costs. In recent times, stand alone metallized polyester/LLDPE laminates have emerged, but have not replaced earlier mentioned system. It has also been shown that nitrogen flushing in Al-foil laminates prove as effective as canning to prolong the shelf-life of dried milk.

ICE CREAMS

Ice cream, as a modern frozen dairy product, is a relatively new addition in India. However, its Indian counterpart, Kulfi, dates back to many centuries. The manufacture of ice cream was exclusively confined to small scale sector and recently, with the entry of cooperative sector in this area, the production and sale is expected to go up and constitute a sizeable part of Indian dairy industry. At freezing temperatures, bacteria normally do not survive ; packaging needs of frozen foods should be designed in such a way that the pack performs efficiently to contain the product at freezing temperatures. The evolution of ice cream packaging has gone from wax coated fibre board cartons through plastic containers and now back to wax coated cartons once again. Presently, wax-coated paper board made from virgin chemical wood pulp is used to make the pack eco-friendly. Duplex board cartons, which are polylaminated, thermoformed or injection moulded plastic containers are used for the retail packs of ice cream. Laminates of BOPP/Polyester are used for dollies, candies etc. Vegetable parchment paper is used to wrap bars Crops formed of high impact polystyrene (HIPS) are used for retail packs of ice creams

BUTTER

Conversion of milk fat to butter is an age old practice in India. Many organizations especially in the private sector, collect milk, separate it into butter and convert it to ghee by heat clarification. Salted butter is common in India. Parchment paper (of 45 gsm) has been and still is used for butter packaging. The use of a laminate of parchment or grease proof paper and aluminium foil is also specified for this purpose in IS:7161. The parchment paper is susceptible to contamination with molds and use of dry parchment and/or treatment with hot brine or antifungal chemicals like, sorbic acid, potassium sorbate, propionic acid and its salts, benzoic acid and its salts help to prevent mold contamination. The wrapped butter is placed in plastic laminated paper board cartons to ease handling, distribution and storage at retail outlets under refrigeration. In recent times, embossed aluminium foil backed parchment paper has emerged for UV light protection and eye appeal. Plastic tubs with lids or plastic tubs with paper lids are also used to pack butter.

GHEE

Nearly 35% of the total milk produced in our country is converted to ghee. This product is mainly packed in lacquered or unlacquered tinplate cans of various capacities (250 gms to 15 kgs). Packaging of ghee in polyethylene bags is besieged with the problem of leakage. Since it is a product with very low moisture content (<0.5%), it needs to be protected more from chemical spoilage activated by oxygen, light, humid climates and high temperatures. Improperly packaged ghee absorbs foreign odours with which it may come in contact. The packaging material should have good water vapour and oxygen barrier properties. The use of metallized polyester laminate is adopted by some organizations. HDPE, PP laminates, polymer coated cellophane, nylon-6-polymer or food-grade PVC and their laminates need to be effectively tapped for packing of ghee.

CHEESE

In India's rapidly expanding dairy industry, cheese is gaining importance. In a few year's time, packed cheese slices and spreads, varieties of cheese such as, Gouda, Camembert, Edam and Cheddar are expected to gain~a place in Indian market. Cheeses are delicately flavoured products, with high fat and moisture contents. Ripened/cured cheeses need to be protected from moisture loss and ingress of oxygen, in order to maintain the desired quality characteristics. The most popular packing for cheese in India at present is 25 grams aluminium foil and 400 g/ 500 g tinplate containers for processed cheese. Cheese spreads are available in plastic tubs. Small quantities of spreads are also available in collapsible tubes. Processed cheese slices (slices separated by greaseproof paper or individually packed in plastic films) and chiplets packed in foil laminate are also available now. Vacuum packaging and packing in an inert gas atmosphere are popularly employed in developed countries. Indian cheese industry adopts these shelf life extension mechanisms, to very limited extent at present, but the situation-is likely to change soon.

INDIGENOUS MILK PRODUCTS

Indian dairy products provide a profitable outlet for milk. About 46% of the total milk production in India is utilized for making indigenous milk products like, ghee (28%), khoa (7%), butter (6%), milk powder (4%) and other products such as curd, paneer, shrikhand, yoghurt and similar indigenous products (2%), etc. A variety of dairy, products are made in our country (Table-2). Some products are popular throughout the country, whereas, others are region-specific. These products conserve and preserve milk solids for relatively longer periods. However, lack of proper infrastructural facilities, coupled with inadequate technological support has impeded the growth of this sector. Traditionally, Indian dairy products have been manufactured by individual sweet makers - "halwais" and small enterpreneurs. Most of the preparations are labour intensive and rely on local inputs. Very little attention is paid to sanitary handling practices and packaging. A number of surveys conducted on the market quality of indigenous milk products have revealed alarmingly high incidence of microbial contamination, large variations in chemical composition, flavour and texture. Most of the products have high water activity, leading rapid deterioration at ambient temperatures.

These products form a good substrate for the growth and multiplication of bacteria. Bacteria have the ability to utilize various milk constituents to grow and multiply in an exponential pattern. While growing at the expense of milk constituents, like, lactose, proteins and fat, these organisms release certain metabolites, like, lactic and organic acids, gases, enzymes, flavouring compounds, pigments, toxins, etc. This directly affects the quality of the products and also render the products unsafe for consumption.

TABLE-2.

INDIGENOUS DAIRY PRODUCTS

CATEGORY	PRODUCTS
Heat desiccated products	Khoa : used as the base for preparation of kalakand, gulab jamun, pedha, and a variety of burfis. Rabri Khurchan Pyodhi
Heat or acid coagulated products	Chhana or Paneer
Fermented products	Dahi Misti Dahi (sweet Dahi) Lassi/Chhaas/Mattha Chakka : base for Srikhand Srikhand
Fat rich products	Makkhan made from Dahi Ghee obtained from heat clarification of Makkhan or Butter
Concentrated products	Kheer Payasam or Palpayasam Basundi Milk sweets/Delicacies-Burfi Kalakand Gulab Jamun Pedha Rasgolla Sandesh Rasmalai

Traditionally, indigenous products have been packed in leaves, paper cartons or duplex board boxes. These materials do not provide sufficient proteection to the product from atmospheric contamination and manual handling. Consequently, the sweets soon lose their typical body and texture, absorb foreign odours, lose their aroma characteristics and show mold growth. Moreover, the products are stored in open metal trays. According to customer's demands, the item is weighed and placed in paper bags or dhak leves or earthen pots (for fermented products like dahi), glassine or grease-proof papers and/or sold in duplex boxes. What is necessary is immediate packing of products after their preparation to protect the product from atmosphere and contamination by handling. Use of saran coated films, laminates of aluminium foil with various substrates, metallied films and combinations of various packaging materials need to be tested for suitability for these products.

TABLE - 3

AN OVERVIEW OF PACKAGING MATERIAL USED IN DAIRY INDUSTRIES

Liquid milk	•Glass bottles (obsolete) •LDPE film in combination with LLDPE of octane/butane-based films •Paper laminate for tetra packs
Milk powder	•Tin plate containers, nitrogen packed and lacquered from outside. •Flexible laminates such as metallizzed PET/BOPP/Aluminium foil/Poly laminates •Refill packs: Lined cartons laminated with BOPP/PET, varnished on the outside. Paper laminated film also used. •Bag-in-box: Powder filled in laminate and packed in cartons.
Butter	•Duplex board with vegetable parchment paper •Tinplate containers •Aluminium foil
Cheese/Cheese spread	•Tin plate containers lacquered from inside •Packed in Al foil and then in duplex board carton •Injection moulded PP/HDPE container
Ghee	•Tinplate container (lacquered inside) •Glass bottles •HDPE film pouches
Ice Cream	•Thermoformed/ injection moulded plastic containers •Duplex board cartons which are polylaminated •Laminates of BOPP or PET
Indigenous products (shrikhand, gulab jamun)	•Injection moulded/thermoformed containers •Stand-up laminated pouches

For instance, products like, gulab jamun and rasogolla need protection from light, oxygen, ingress or egress of moisture and microorganisms; lacquered tinplate can is the most suitable packaging material, but this is very expensive. Hence, there is a need to develop plastic can similar to the ones used in European countries. The pack is extruded and laminated with PP-Al foil material. The foil provides the necessary water vapour barrier properties, smooth curved corners and good printing surface for multicolour designs. The ends are injection-moulded and lined with the same type of laminate as used for the body.

The size and dimensions can be adopted to suit the distribution systems and consumer's needs. The material is heat resistant and suitable for good contact. Similarly, expansions and suitable applications of retort pouches, stand-up pouches, tetra pak cartons and bricks need to be explored in the Indian dairy industry.

Recently, organized dairies have taken up the production of indigenous products like, gulab jamun, shrikhand, lassi, mishti doi, khoa and by the ball set rolling by these process, innovation is expected to gain momentum. The three-fold challenge before the Indian dairy industry is to focus on : quality, product development and global marketing. It calls for upgrading, on a sustained basis, of managerial and professional skills and updated knowledge of markets. Conscious R&D efforts are needed to expand the indigenous capacity for the manufature of dairy equipment and also bring in innovations in the fields of packaging, transportation and distribution.

Chapter 12

PACKAGING TRENDS FOR CHEESE AND OTHER DAIRY PRODUCTS

An evolution is taking place with package concepts and materials for certain dairy products.

Some marketing experts would say It's a Revolution rather than an Evolution as companies vie for market led innovations in the highly competitive segment of food retailing. These evotutions will be covered in more detail later.

As producers and retailers alike demand fresher and longer shelf-life products, the packaging industry is being required to develop more sophisticated materials and packaging systems to meet these demands.

It's not only the Producer and Retailer, but also the powerful body of people known to us all as the Consumer who is demanding healthier longer shelf-life fresher products packaged in convenient user-friendly packages.

Gone are the days when the consumer would select a piece of cheese at the delicatessen department of the supermarket and take it home wrapped in parchment paper. They (Consumer) require their cheese to be packaged in a medium that will maintain it's (cheese) freshness and individual characteristics until the last piece has been used or consumed.

Today's consumer is spending less time making decisions when Supermarket shopping. A product, at the point of sale must attract the consumer's attention either by Brand Name, Graphics, or Convenience Factors.

By Brand Name the consumer identifies a particular manufacturer or Product.

Graphics can entice a consumer to make snap decisions.

Convenience Factors are attributes such as shredded cheese, sliced natural cheese, reclosable packages. Let us now look more closely at the evolution and in some instances revolution of packaging for Specific Dairy Products.

MILK POWDER - BULK

Traditional Packaging of 25 kg milk powder irrespective of type has been in polyethylene lined multiwall paper sacks.

In recent years there has been an increase in the demand for Whole Milk Powder (WMP) to be gas flushed (Nitrogen) particularly in the S.E.A. region where heat and humidity can rapidly increase the oxidative reaction.

When gas flushed packs are called for then a coextruded LLDPE - Nylon- LDPE film is required to maintain the modified atmosphere within the package. Some markets require the milk powder to be delivered in 300 kg bulk bins gas flushed: These systems require specialised filling/gassing/ sealing equipment.

MILK POWDER - RETAIL

Tinplate Cans and laminated flexible films are the two packaging styles used for retailing of milk powder.

Tinplate cans have not changed much over the years except for the graphics.

Flexible packaging has evolved through polyethylene bags through to sophisticated multiply laminates. In most cases the sachet of milk powder is enclosed for distribution and sale inside paperboard boxes. In more recent times stand-up metallised polyester/Linear low density polyethylene laminates. The degree of sophistication built into laminates and the material types used is restrictive

Synthetic materials i.e., Nylon, Polyester, tend to generate static electricity during the packing operation. Static electricity causes powder particles to contaminate vital seal areas.

BUTTER

Parchment paper has been and still is used for butter packaging. In recent times embossed aluminium foil backed parchment paper has emerged for UV light protection and eye appeal.

These days the most popular packaging style preTerred is "Plastic" tubs and lids. There are many different shapes and sizes. .

Polypropylene and ABS(acrylic - butadience styrene) appears to be the most widely used resin for this application.

YOGURT

Yogurt packaging has had many transformations over the years particularly the design concepts rather than packing material type.

First came the single serve formed tub with a lacquer coated foil lid. Next came the multi-pack concept of four and six items jointed together. The consumer snap the required pack off the cluster. The next evolution in the mufti-pack concept was different varieties and flavours within the cluster. Then came the mini-cluster these being small serves for school lunch boxes.

Additional concepts evolved, we can now have crunchy nuts and fresh dried fruits in a separate compartment to the yogurt. When the foil lid is removed the "dry" mix can be tipped into the "wet" segment. 500 g and now one 1 litre containers are available.

Stabilised yogurts still dominate the market, however, a fast growth sector is the live yogurts with Lactobacillus acidophilus and Bitidene L-casen.

Drinking yogurt in one litre down to 250 ml plastic botttes have recently emerged in the market.

ICE CREAM

The evolution of ice cream packaging has gone from wax coated fibre board cartons again through to plastic containers and now back to wax coated cartons once again.

The latter has only evolved with boutique ice creams and isipriced at about double that of standard ice creams.

CHEESE

Rinded wax coated cheese set aside for maturation has always been subject to high levels of mould contamination and weight loss.

The invention of plastic bags with barrier properties revotutionised the bulk cheese industry.

Vacuum packaging with Barrier Bags saved the Dairy Industry thousands of dollars in Wastage and yield losses. Today there are a number of coextruded materials used for vacuum packaging bulk cheese.

Coextruded LLDPE-NYLON-LLDPE, and LLDPE - EVOH - LLDPE have good barrier properties when their oxygen permeability is measured in a dry state.For co-extruded pouches oxygen permeability readings of 5 cc (EVOH) to 35 cc (Nylon) are common. However, during storage (cheese maturation) the properties of EVOH and Nylon change as moisture uptake occurs.

Those coextruded materiais which use PVdC as the core layer for barrier properties are not affected by moisture uptake. In other words their oxygen permeability characteristics do not change. In fact they improve as the crystallisation of PVdC occurs.

Oxygen permeability properties of a packaging material plays an important part in the shelf life extension of cheese. It is obvious then that coextruded Barrier Bags with PVdC as the oxygen barrier medium is the most commonty used material for bulk cheese packaging in most western countries.

Barrier Bags can be tailor designed for a specific cheese type.

Swiss style cheese or cheese that generates carbon dioxide require Barrier Bags that allows the carbon dioxide to escape without allowing oxygen to permeate back into the package. One well known packaging company developed a shrink bag specifically for Swiss style cheese.

Hard cheese like Parmesan and Romano require Barrier Bags that have built in high abuse properties.

In-Bag-Curing under vacuum using Barrier Bag technology is now possible for Emmental and parmesan cheese without the loss of vital flavour and texture characteristics.

Cheese, vacuum packed in Barrier Bags then dipped in hot water to shrink the bag onto the surface of the cheese at the same time taking up all the excess material will have a longer shelf life than cheese packaged in conventional coextruded materials.

CHEESE - RETAIL

Retailing of cheese is very competitive, therefore the producers must market their products to the consumer to purchase not just the first purchase but repeat purchases.

Price was generally the emotion behind a purchase. This appears not to be the case these days. Convenience is becoming a greater emotion to purchase.

As mentioned earlier, today's consumer spends less time in a supermarket compared to 15 years ago. The same applies to meal preparation. Today's busy life styles along with double income households means that convenience in meal preparation is vital. Convenient meals are a major growth sector of the food industry.

Fifty percent of cheese sold in a supermarket is classified as convenient food as it is sold either pre-sliced or shredded in convenient sized packages.

Reclosable features built into the package of shredded cheese is another example of covenience.

Laminates dominate the packaging style for cheese sold out of the supermarket Dairy case.

Packaging cheese across a HFFS (horizontal form - fill - seal) machine or vacuum pack thermoform system using laminate and gas flushing with 100 percent carbon dioxide are the most common methods used by the major cheese marketing companies.

Those companies wishing to emphasise the natural shape of their product choose vacuum packaging with Barrier bags and hot water shrinking.

Laminate structures best suited for natural cheese would be PVdC coated biaxially oriented nylon/EVA and for processed cheese PVdC coated, biaxially oriented Nylon/ LLDPE blends.These structures would depend on equipment type and productivity.

New hybrid resins are emerging that will (hopefully) allow for increased packaging machine speeds.

Melt Flow Index (MFI), Hot Tack and the ability to seal through contamination (cheese fats) are three critical attributes necessary when selecting a new resin for cheese packaging laminates.

The concept of centralised cheese packaging of speciality cheese has evolved over the last 5 years and has proved very popular throughout US, Europe, UK and Australia.

Blocks of speciality cheese are cut into small random weight sizes, vacuum packed in Barrier bags, hot water shrunk then check weighed, labelled and reassembled as a large block, put back into the original carton ready for distribution.

Case-ready-cheese as it is known has been targeted at the Delicatessen section of the supermarket not the Dairy case. The Case-ready-cheese concept frees labour within the supermarket and also allows for a wider variety of cheese styles to be stocked.

Special shrink films for mould ripened cheese such as Camembert, Brie and Blue Vein are available. These cheese styles cannot, be vacuum packed as they require a level of oxygen to maintain their specific mould growth.

This is a " Thumb Nail " sketch of some trends in packaging of dairy products.

Chapter 13

MILK -BASED SOFT DRINK WITH LONGER SHELF-LIFE

The development and growth of soft drinks and beverage industry is very fast with significant increase in newer brands /varieties in the market, mainly due to : i) the change in life-style and food habits of people and ii) more profit to the producers. However, with the growing awareness of balanced diet and nutrition among the health conscious consumers, milk based beverages could find its due place as a refreshing and nourishing drink and therefore, they are becoming more popular day-by-day. Especially, the acidic or lactic drinks would find favor with many consumers all over the world. Hence, acidified milk drink has great potential even in developing countries where consumption of soft drinks is limited.

However, direct acidification of dairy products may offer some advantages over traditional culture methods during its manufacture by batch or continuous process. The advantages may include the elimination of expensive maintenance and propagation of starter cultures, greater uniformity in the final product and better keeping qualities. Thus, direct acidification is yet another better approach to make the product similar to that of cultured type dairy products. Theacceptability of such products is entirely depend on the proper balance of tartness and sweetness as well as flavour desired by the consumer. In the process of direct acidificatio of milk, the destabilisation of milk proteins due to low pH condition, is the major problem. Therefore, a special efforts has been made in our laboratory for developing a process for the manufacture of directly acidified milk based soft drink with longer shelf-life.

Product Attributes :

The unique type of soft drink developed at National Dairy Research Institute, Karnal, has the following attributes :

1) It is a new type of sterilized milk beverage.

2) It has very pleasant sweet-sour taste and is acceptable to all types

of consumers.

3) It is more nutritious and energy-giving as compared to carbonated soft drinks.

4) No bacterial culture is required for its production.

5) It can be manufactured in different colours and flavours as per choice.

6) It can be stored at ambient conditions for atleast three months.

7) It is good for health. It does not contain any harmful material.

Salient Features of Technology :

1) The technology is very simple and can be easily adopted by any dairy factory or private entrepreneur for commercial production.

2) Due to direct acidification by edible acids, it elimates the additional expenses which are required for maintenance and propagation of starter cultures in traditionally cultured dairy products.

3) Quality and uniformity in the product can be easily controlled.

4) It gives more profit margins as compared to other dairy products.

5) Products can be made available round the year.

6) The product may offer great potentiality throughout the world due to its multi-features.

7) Hence, it may become very popular and would bring a great revolution especially in the Beverage World, once it is introduced by the beverage or food industry for commercial production.

Chapter 14

FERMENTED MILK PRODUCTS - FLAVOUR AND BIOTECHNOLOGY

Introduction

Flavour, a very complex and important attribute of fermented milk products is primarily composed of aroma and taste. Flavour compounds may be produced in foods by means of biotechnological processes. In the simplest way, biotechnology may be defined as the technological process involving the application of iological systems. Biotechnological process include fermentation technology, enzyme immobilization technology, genetic engineering etc.

A variety of fermented dairy products are available namely, cheeses and fermented milks such as cultured butter milk, yoghurt, acidophilus milk, kefir, kumiss etc. The fermentation process is used to describe enzyme catalysed reactions in which compounds such as the carbohydrate/sugars are broken down anaerobically by bacterial or yeast enzymes leading to production of important food flavouring compounds such as lactic acid, acetic acid, alcohol, diacetyl, acetaldehyde etc.

The fermentation of milk by lactic acid bacteria to produce cheese is one of the oldest food fermentations known. Approximately 9000 different cheese varieties, with a variety of flavour and texture characteristics are produced worldwide. The development of cheese flavour is primarily an enzymatic process. The enzymes involved come from the coagulant (chymosin) the starter culture, added enzymes such as Propionibacterium or various molds, indigenous milk enzymes and non-starter bacteria, lactic acid bacteria, either added as starter culture or present as non-starter culture, lactic acid bacteria are known to be essential for cheese flavour development.

The bacteria found in starters used to manufacture of cultured products can be grouped as :

a) The lactic acid producing streptococci :

S. Lactis and S. Cremoris

b) The associative citrate fermenting aroma culture :

Leuconostoc citrovorum and Leuconostoc dextranicum

c) The dual purpose lactic acid and aroma producing strains of Streptococcus diacetylactis.

Diacetyl, is a key flavour component of most of the fermented dairy products. The diacetyl is produced through the citric acid fermentation.

The acid taste of naturally cultured products is largely due to presence of lactic acid. The volatile acids produced by culture organisms are considered to contribute to the mildly acid aroma of cultured products.

Acetic acid comprises the major portion of the volatile acid fraction of cultured products and is produced during citrate fermentation. Cultured buttermilk contains small quantities of formic, propionic butyric and valeric acids as flavour contributors.

A small amount of acetaldehyde is desirable for the full flavour of mixed strain butter cultures. The flavour balance of butter cultures was found to be closely related to the diacetyl : acetaldehyde ratio. Desirable full-flavoured cultures exhibit ratios from 3:1 to about 5:1.

A wide variety of compounds including aldehydes, methyl ketones, alcohols, methyl and ethyl esters of aliphatic acids have been found responsible for the flavour development in fermented dairy products.

Cheese Flavour

The unripened cheeses exhibit a mild delicate flavour that is derived from three sources, namely, the milk, heat degradation products of milk and metabolic products of micro-organisms used as cultures the manufacturing process.

The flavour development in ripened cheeses is through fermentation pathways of the micro-organisms, through enzymes from lysed microbial cells and through enzymes native to milk. In the course of these reactions, the protein, fat and carbohydrate are degraded to varying degrees to yield a very complex mixture of compounds, some of which give rise to varietal cheese flavours.

Milk fat is essential for typical flavour of most cheese varieties. The fat acts as a solvent for many of the flavour components and the fat is known to modify the flavour properties of many compounds. Fat serves as a precursor for a variety of compounds. Lactones, methyl ketones, esters alcohols and fatty acids are derived from milk lipids during cheese ripening. Lactose of milk is fermented by microbes to produce lactic acid which contributes to flavour. The amino acids are converted to flavour components via microbial action to yield aıcohols, aldehydes and other important compounds.

Blue cheese flavour is mainly attributed to presence of carbonyls, namely, methyl ketones, especially 2-heptanone and 2-nonanche. The micro-organism used is Penicillium Roqueforti. The same is found in case of Roqueforti cheese. Also substantial quantities of acetaldehyde, 2-methyl butanol and furfural are found in blue cheese along with primary alcohols such as ethanol and methanol.

Cheddar cheese flavour can be attributed to free fatty acids of intermediate chain length, acetic acid, methyl ketones.

Table 1 : Lipases and proteinases from filamentous fungi used to accelerate flavour development in cheeses.

Product	Source	Cheese Variety
Lipase	Rhizomucor miehei	Italian Cheeses
	Penicillum Candidum	Italian Cheeses
	Penicillium roquefortii	Italian and Blue Cheese
	Aspergillus oryzae	Blue Cheese
Proteinase	Aspergillus oryzae	Various cheeses

Table 2: Flavour compounds produced by filamentous fungi found in various cheeses

Compounds	Cheese Variety	Source
Methyl ketones	Blue	Penicillium requefortii
2-Pentanol, 1-octen-3-01	Blue	Penicillium roquefortii
H_2S, methyl mercapton, dimethyl sulphide	Camembert	Aspergillus oryzae
Acid soluble	White mold cheese	Penicillum caseicolium

aldehydes such as methanal, ethanal, propanal, alcohols such as ethanol and 2-butanol, esters, etc.

The primary metabolic activity of the microflors in the cheese occurs during the early stages of cheese making and ripening. During ripening, lipolysis and proteolysis occur due to decreased microbial activity and increased concentration of enzymes due to cell lysis.

Enzyme Modified Cheeses (EMC)

Enzyme modified cheese (EMC) production is another flavour enzyme application important in the dairy industry. Higher amounts of added enzymes are required to accelerate flavour development in cheese. This rapid transformation of cheese milk into cheese with characteristics flavour is significantly shorter than traditional methods which may take 3 to 12 months. The EMC process is applied to manufacture accelerated ripened processed cheese. The enzymes obtained from the species of Rhizomucor, Pencillium or Aspergillus are used to manufacture Enzyme Modified Cheese.

Enzymes that Remove off Flavours

Many filamentous fungal enzymes, can be used to remove compounds that are associated with undesirable flavours or off flavours in processed foods.

Sulphydryl oxidase from Aspergillus niger, which oxidises sulphydryl or thiol groups to disulphides can successfully remove off-flavours that appear in ultra-high temperature milk (UHT).

Table 3 : Cultures used in major fermented dairy products

Culture	Culture function	Product use
Propionibacterium freudenreichii	Flavour and eye formation	Swiss cheese
Lactobacillus delbrueckii subspp. bulgaricus	Acid and Flavour	Bulgarican buttermilk, Yoghurt, Kumiss, Swiss and Italian cheese
Streptococcus lactis subspp. diacatyl actis	Acid and flavour	Sour cream, Cheese, cultured buttermilk, cottage cheese.
Leuconostoc cremoris	Flavour	Cultured buttermilk, Sour Cream, Cottage Cheese, ripened cream butter.
Lactobacillus acidophilus	Flavour and acid therapeutic activity	Acidophilus milk.
Kefir grains or mixed inoculum from among : S. lactis subspp. diacetylactis, Candida kefir, L. acidophilus, L.casei, Kluyueromyces fragilis	Lactic acid and alcohol, refreshing drink	Kefir
L. bulgaricus,	Clean lactic flavour,	Kumiss

L. acidophilus, Kluyueromyces lactis	alcohol	
S. cremoris, S. lactis subspp. diacetylactis, L. cremoris	Acid	cottage cheese, quarg, cream cheese, cheddar cheese

Genetic Engineering

Genetic engineering is a part of biotechnological process applied to alter hereditary material, the deoxyribonucleric acid (DNA) of a living cell so that the cells can produce more or different chemicals or perform completely new functions. A major technology used in genetic engineering is Recombinant DNA technology.

Genetic engineering, commonly referred to as gene splicing has added unprecented scope and precision to the efforts to modify micro-oranisms and their utility. The fermentation milk to produce cheese and other dairy products and the use of enzymes for milk coagulation and flavour development is a constantly changing technology.

In the field of dairy, genetic engineering technology has been applied to lactic streptococci and lactobacilli for producing fermented product with desired characteristics.

The various steps involved in preparation of recombinant DNA could be briefly summarized:

1. Selection of DNA of interest (commonly referred to as passenger DNA).
2. A cloning vector or vehicle to carry the inserted piece of target DNA.
3. Restriction endonucleases which makes specific cuts at specific sites on DNA.
4. DNA ligase-the enzymes that join pieces of nucleotides/DNA together.
5. A host to replicate the vector containing foreign DNA.
6. Screening tests for recombinants produced by insertion of DNA.

Use of Genetic Engineering for Production and Improvement of Enzymes and Micro-organisms

At the heart of biotechnology is the ability to custom-design protein molecules which are composed of amino-acids linked together. The various kinds of amino-acids and the order in which they are linked determines each protein's three dimensional structure and hence its function.

The enzymes are the proteins that catalyze virtually all chemical reactions in nature. Recombinant DNA methods have a significant impact on enzymes. Improvement of properties and activity of enzymes may be brought about by genetic engineering the activity of renin (chymosin) may be improved by genetic engineering to give better results while coagulation of cheeses. Similarly genetically engineered lipases are useful in flavour generation of cheese.

Genetic engineering is an effective method to bring about improvement in fermentation technology by carrying out gene splicing of desirable strains of bacterial involved in proudction of cultured dairy products so as to improve activity of cultures while fermentation and hence resulting in quick and better flavour production. For example, it was found that gene coding for lactose metabolism in S. Lactis is carried on a plasmid. Bacteria that lose this plasmid also lose the ability to ferment lactose and hence causes reduced flavour production in cultured milk products. therefore, lactose utilization was stabilized by moving the gene from the plasmid to permanent residence on the S. Lactis chromosome.

In most streptococci, in addition to lactose metabolism, the genes for the utilization of citrate, sucrose, galactose during fermentation is carried on plasmids. Some of these genes have been cloned into other bacterial genera to retain the fermenting capability and hence production of flavours ie.e diacetyl in fermented milk products.

In planning approach to improve starter culture by genetic recombinations the considerations are :

1. Transferring genetic elements only from other food approved organisms.
2. Avoid use of antibiotic resistant strains.
3. Toxicology tests of engineered starter is done to demonstrate safety.

Bacteria as Potential Sources of Flavour Metabolites

Bacterial cultures have long been known to produce flavour and aroma metabolites. Biotechnology/genetic engineering is used to develop and improve process for baterial production of flavour and aroma chemicals.

The industrial production of diacetyl provides an example of application of biotechnological approaches to bacterial flavour production. The microbial formation of diacetyl is a function of citrate fermentation by lactic acid bacteria, primarily Lactococcus lactis var. diacetylactis. In this organism, both citrate fermentation and diacetyl formation were observed to be unstable traits that are lost. Biochemical analysis showed that mutants unable to ferment citrate and from diacetyl lacked enzymes citrate permease. This is because the plasmid coding for the trait is lost and hence caused the genetic instability.

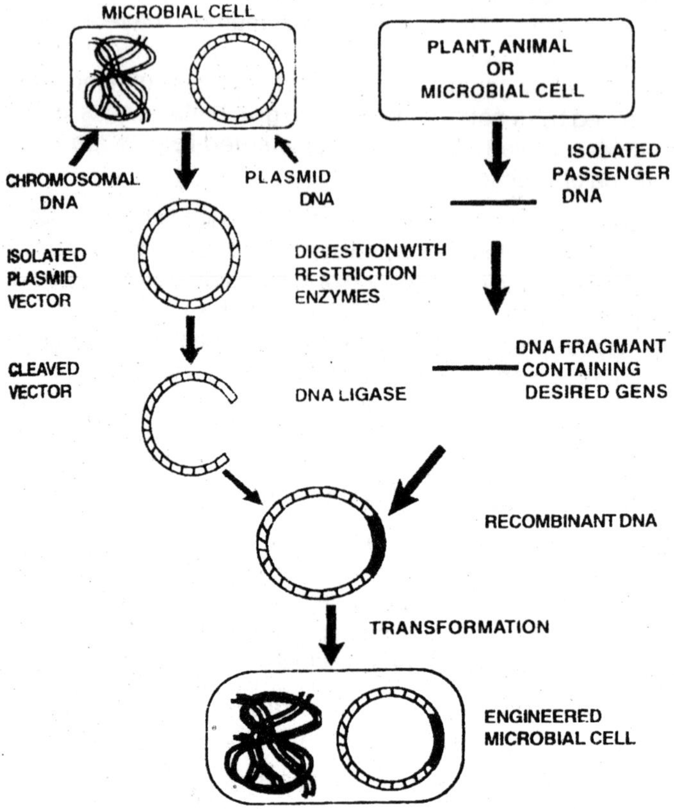

Fig.1 Gene Cloning In a Simple Bacterial Systems

A recombinant DNA (r DNA) approach provided a potential source for poor diacetyl production resulting from plasmid enclosed citrate permease activity in starter cultures. Incorporation of the citrate permease, genetic determinant into the chromosome is used to stabilize this trait.

Hence genetic engineering provides an alternative to classical mutation and selection for improving micobial starter cultures with improved metabollic properties.

Hence it is observed that flavour biotechnology plays and important role in the flavour of dairy products. The biotechnological process help to produce desirable flavour and remove undesirable off flavours by careful selective processes yileding better quality diary products and hence increasing their acceptability.

Chapter 15

LOSSES AND THEIR POSSIBLE MANAGEMENT IN DAIRY INDUSTRY

Introduction

Indian dairy industry has made tremendous progress in the past three decades. Evidently with increasing volume and cost of production, it has become essential to maximize utilization of milk, a major raw material of dairy industry. However, the present level of financial losses in Indian dairy industry is much higher than that prevailing in organized dairy sector of the developed countries. From various surveys it is found that most of our dairy organizations suffer heavily due to losses in one or the other way. Although some of the losses are uncontrollable, there is an excellent potential to bring down the avoidable losses significantly by maximizing recovery minimizing wastage and recognizing the problem. One of the reasons for losses are insufficiently trained, insufficiently supervised and badly motivated staff. Considerbale reduction of losses can be achieved only by analyzing the reasons for losses and developing a foolproof system through implementing loss management techniques, though not something which an individual alone can achieve.

Losses and their reduction

Transportation : This is a major expense in the dairying business. Adopting the following measures can minimize transportation charges.

- Maximize milk procurement per day on each route.
- Formulate compact milk routes to avoid overlapping.
- Formulate milk routes with regard to minimizing distance from factory.

Adulteration of Milk : Lack of proper testing facilities or certain other limitations encourages the milk vendors to cheat the organizations by supplying adulterated milk. Rationalizing milk purchase policy on the basis of FAT/SNF system and imposing severe penalties for adulterated milk can help in controlling such losses.

Spoilage : Spoilage of milk and milk products due to souring/curdling and return of unsold products can be responsible for heavy losses.

Recommendations :

- Secreening of milk for quality at reception.
- Reduction of time gap between milking and chilling.
- Adequate process control.
- Proper scheduling.

Spillage and Leakage : The spillage and leakage of fluid milk products like raw milk, cream, skim milk etc. are mainly due to the foaming of milk through excessive agitation, leaking valve on a tank, air eliminator, pump gland, piping unions and milk sachets. Inadequate drainage of weigh bowl, dump tank or storage tanks can be responsible for product losses.

Recommendations :

- Timing agitation.
- Proper and adequate drainage of equipment.
- Preventative maintenance programme.

Analytical Variations : Inaccuracy in sampling, weighing, testing and inaccurate glassware may sometimes cause sizeable losses.

Recommendations :

- Adoption of modern analyzers and electronic weights.
- Sampling by proper procedure.
- Employing trained analysts.

Losses during Milk Processing

Milk reception : In this process, spillage and inadequate drainage of cans or tankers are two main reasons of losses. Subsequently cooling and storage of milk, losses can occur due to leaks and drips in pipes and pumps.

Recommendations :

- Proper connection of tanker to the transfer pump.
- Avoidance of delay for unloading from tankers.
- Allow adequate time for drainage of milk from tanker.
- Sufficient time provided for drainage from cans (at least 30 sec.).
- Use drip pan saver for complete drainage of milk from cans.

Separation, homogenization and pasteurization : Insufficient fat separation of milk results in loss of fat. Losses of milk solids during homogenization occur mainly as a result of leakage and the cleaning process. Start-up and shutdown as well as product changeovers during pasteurization are important sources of wastage in the dairy.

Recommendations :

- Proper design and control.
- Proper temperature control.
- Use of airtight separators.
- Minimize the number of startups and shutdowns.
- Sufficient supply of raw material for the process.
- Avoid unnecessary cleanup between proudcts.

Losses during Product Making

During butter making inadequate cream ageing, incomplete churning, faulty processing, lack of temperature control, lack of overrun, lack of moisture control, overweight in packing etc. result in fat loss. In ghee making, fat losses resulted mainly from spillage and overcooking. Disposal of by-products like buttermilk, ghee residue and whey is one of the major sources of waste in dairy industry. Any significant escape of whey, washings of curd and curd fines during the manufacture of cheese, paneer or casein, to the sewers, is also costly. In condensing of milk, losses may occur due to heavy scale formation, entrainment in evaporator, spillage of milk and condensed milk, milk left over in pumps and calendria evaporators. While the main sources of wastage in milk powder production is from spillage of milk and milk powder occuring in most steps of the process. In iececream manufacture the considerable losses are due to spillage during agitation, adhering of the ice cream mix and product on the equipment surfaces, breaking of packages etc.

Recommendations :

- Proper process control.
- Intelligent utilization of by-products.
- Efficient recovery of milk solids during various processes.

Losses during Packaging : Variation in filling temperature causes loss to dairy plant by affeting the weight of fluid products. Besides this, overfilling, foaming, leaky valves and leakages due to mahine fault can cause extensive losses.

Recommendations :

- Adoption of modern packaging machine.
- Regular monitoring of operations.

Storage Losses : Storage of product for long period, product stored under inappropriate conditions or insufficient packaging materials and containers may cause spoilage of product.

Recommendations:

- Effective use of product within short period.
- Ensuring suitable storage conditions.
- Proper packaging of product.

Loss of Packaging materials : Loss of packaging materials are mainly due to sealing problem in packaging machine, insufficient width of packaging rolls and storage of packaging materials for long time.

Recommendations :

- Delicate handling and optimum utilization.
- Regular checking of packing materials.
- Controlling machine speed and effective cooling of electrodes.
- Maximizing film usage.

Loss of chemicals and cleaning agents: Purchase and use of low-grade chemicals or cleaning agents can cause appreciable loss. Similarly free availability of chemicals or cleaning agents to attendants who are not aware of norms of consumption for cleaning operations result in financial losses.

Recommendations :

- Purchase of chemicals on competitive rate through tenders.
- Exercising effective control on use of chemicals.
- Regular checking of quantity and quality of chemicals.

Wastage of Water : Water is now recognized as a second expensive item in dairy industry. Water leakage is so familiar that it becomes like an old friend.

Recommendations :

- Judicious use of water.
- Conservation of water to save energy, distribution and disposal costs.
- By reducing product wastage, water use is reduced automatically.
- Control of leakage and spillage of water.

Measurement of Losses

Before an effective step can be taken to prevent losses, management should know the extent of the losses (Table) and the economic consequences.

Effective losses monitoring technique requires a complete inventory of the factory, processes and accurate plans of the drainage system for waste. Measurement of losses by balance method is not appropriate to provide the necessary data on a daily basis, while monitoring wastewater best done daily , gives direct measurement of losses. This also gives Management a more accurate estimate and identifies the source of the losses so that corrective action can be taken. The BOD_5 can be used for rough estimate of the product losses from a dairy plant. For instance, suppose a waste water has a volume of $50m^2$ and a BOD_5 of 1000 mg/l, then the BOD_5 load is equal to (weight of wastage *BOD_5 in mg/l)/10^6, i.e., 50 kg. If the losses

Table : Milk Wastage arising from various dairying operations

Operation	Kg milk lost / 1000 kg of milk processed		
Milk reception, churn washing & clean up	1.0	-	6.0
Cooling raw milk, storage, washing tanks and pipelines	0.6	-	2.8
Washing tankers	0.9	-	3.6
Separating, Storage of skim milk and cream	0.8	-	2.3
Churning and washing butter	2.3	-	7.3
Concentrating & spray drying of skim milk	1.3	-	13.6
Milk pasteurizing and storage	0.9	-	4.9
Bottle washing	0.5	-	3.4
Cheese making (Hard)	2.0	-	18.2
Manufacture of sweetened condensed milk	10.9	-	15.5
Manufacture of evaporated milk	4.5	-	9.1

are known to be due to skim milk mainly, the total loss can be expressed in kg of wasted skim milk by dividing the BOD_5 load with 0.0675. Similarly, the loss of whole milk can be calculated by dividing the BOD_5 load with 0.11. On the other hand the COD gives more constant values than BOD for individual milk produts and is therefore better suited for estimation of losses, producing results within 2 hrs. of sampling. For example 400 m^3 effluent with COD 900 mg/l gives 360 kg COD load. As 1 kg of milk equals to 0.21 kg COD, the effuent represents the loss of an average 360/0.21=1700 kg of milk. For loss monitoring, COD analyses are appropriate for powder, while total nitrogen and milk fat analyses for butter and suspended solid content for casein and cheese fines are used for estimation of losses.

Methods of Monitoring losses:

Once losses are known and quantified, Management decisions can be taken for appropriate action to reduce loss economically. Conducting and maintaining a campaign for good housekeeping and minimizing water use, raw material and product loss can make substantial saving. Further an effective waste elimination programme requires a complete commitment of the plant management. Some of the steps that should be considered for loss management have been discussed under the previous headlings and some additional points are given hereunder:

Proper utilization of manpower

- Efficient handling of manpower.
- Daily and monthly balance sheet for man-hours utilization.
- Proper distribution of manpower.
- Control of manpower through monitoring results of balance sheet.

Effective quality control

- Controlling spoilage of milk products at different stages of processing.
- Controlling loss due to production of sub-standard milk products.

Efficient maintenance of machinery

- Simple and practical system of lubrication.
- Maintenance of machinery according to present schedules.

Marketing

- Marketing at right time, right place and right price.
- Proper distribution network.
- Price changes quickly as per market trends.
- Monitoring market feedback and prompt attention to complaints.

Administration

- Minimum staff purely on merit as per requirements.
- Create harmonious and disciplined working environment.
- Inoculating team spirit.

Effective purchase and inventory control

- Standardize and prescribe for clear specifications of all store-items.
- Reject sub-standard or inferior quality goods.
- Purchase at competitive rates.
- Maintenance of stock of inventory at desired levels.

Efficient financial management

- Strict budgetary control.
- Review of daily handling of statutory dues and professional monitoring of financial performance.

Chapter 16

CULTURED MILK PRODUCTS IN HUMAN NUTRITION

Milk is an inseparable part of human diet. Besides being consumed in fluid form, there are other facets to milk. The development of fermented cultured milk products is an important aspect of dairying. Cultured milk plays a vital rile in human nutrition. During the ancient days of civilization, the role of these products in humand diet was known. the initial purpose of development of cultured milk products seems to be the preservation of milk, but their health benefits are listed in the old Indian treatise " Sushruta Samhita" which describes dahi as food promoting appetite and strength. In modern times, the initial documentation of virtues of cultured milk products was triggered by Elile Metchnikoff in 1907, who attributed the longevity of Bulgarians to ingestion of large quantities of Bulgarian milk, prepared with the help of a lactic acid bacteria, Lactobacillus bulgaricus. This revelation led to development of newer fermented products of modification of the existing ones.

Definition and Composition

The International Dairy Federation (IDF) has defined the fermented milk products as products prepared from milks - whole, partially or fully skimmed, concentrated milk or milk substituted from partially or fully skimmed dried milk, homogenized or not, pasteurized or sterilized, fermented by means of specific organisms. The scope of this definition is widened by the incorporation of specific microbial cultures into product. The basic requirement of any cultured milk product is that at the tie of consumption, it should have the cultures in the living state. Though the exact number of organisms required to exert effect on health is still a matter of debate, broadly it is considered that the product should have at least 10^9 - 10^{11} cells per millilitre of the product.

The composition of any cultured milk product depends upon a number of factors like the initial type of milk, these type of culture used for fermentation and process parameters. The IDF has given the following composition as a standard composition of cultured milks.

Constituent	Level Percent
Dry matter	14-18
Protein	4-6
Fat	0.1-10.0
Lactose	2-3
Lactic acid	0.6-1.1
Carbohydrates	5-25

The pH range is 3.8 to 4.6

Types of cultured milks

The number of fermented milks are diverse and more than 400 products are available the world over. Most of these products with different generic names are similar in nature. The organisms carrying out fermentation are generally of similar type. The cultured products have been classified into different categories on the basis of acid content as well as on the type of organism carrying out the fermentation. On the basis of acid content, these are categorized as :

- Acid alcohol, e.g., Kefir and Kumiss
- High acid, e.g., Bulgarian sour milk
- Medium acid, e.g., Acidophilus milk, dahi and yoghurt
- Low acid, e.g., Cultured buttermilk and cultured cream

  Recently, these products have been classified on the basis of culture carrying out the fermentation.
- Yeast lactic fermentation, e.g., Kefir, Kumiss Acidophilus - yeast milk.
- Lactic fermentation - contains mesophilic as well as thermophilic fermentation and all major fermented milk product around the globe belong to this category.
- Mould lactic fermentation, e.g., villi.

Beneficial Effects of Cultured Products

The worldwide research on the therapeutic aspect of cultured milk products has revealed that these products impart a number of beneficial effects on human health. The cultures used in these cultured milk products with aim of fermentation also offer a number of health benefits to the consumers, and are commonly known as probiotics. The probiotics are defined as living microorganisms which upon ingestion in certain number exert health nenefits beyond inherent basic nutrition. An effective probiotic has to operate under variety of hostile environmental conditions and has to survive in different forms. Hence, it should possess the following characteristics before being incorporated in any milk product:

- Should be normal inhabitant of intestinal tract
- Should survice in upper digestive tract conditions like low pH, bile secretion.
- It should maintain viability and activity in the carrier food for long periods under storage and field conditions before consumption.
- It must be capable of being prepared as viable product on an industrial scale.

Effect on Intestinal Metabolism

Control of intestinal pathogens

Cultured milk products show inhibitory effect towards many commonly known food pathogens. Prophylactic as well as therapeutic action of cultures has been demonstrated in single of mixed culture. The different pathogens inhibited by probiotics include Staphylococcu aureus, Salmonella typhimurium, E. coli, Helicobacter pyori, etc. The mechanism of antibiosis of cultured milk products is attributed to metabolic products and byproducts like organic acids, hydrogen peroxide and productio of antibiotic like substances such as nisin.

Different probable mechanisms involved are

- Lowering of the intestinal pH
- Competition for nutrients.
- Adhesion to intestinal wall preoventing colonization by pathogens.
- Neurtralization of toxins.
- Production of antibacterial substances.

Lactose intolerance

The lactose intolerance arising due to deficiency in enzyme β-galactosidase results in the inability of an individual to digest the lactose present in milk. The undigested lactose in the large bowel cause osmotic diarrhoea. The fermentation in cultured milk products reduces the level of lactose by hydrolysing it. The contribution of bacterial β-galactosidase enzyme is also a major factor as this enzyme improves the digestibility of lactose in terminal ileum.

Prevention of different forms of diarrhoea

The cultured milk products are not only involved in prevention, but are effectively used in the treatment of different forms of diarrhoea like infantile, antibiotic associated and travellers diarrhoea. The major mechanism of action by probiotics present in cultured milks is enhancement of immune response along with restoration of mucosal barrier function. In case of antibiotic related diarrhoea, these restore the normal microbial flora of intestine disturbed due to prolonged exposure to antibiotics. These also provide relief from gastritis caused by Helicobacter pylori because of their high acid tolerance thereby persisting longer in stomach than the infective organisms. Alleviation of constipation is also an active aspect of cultured milk product.

Control of Serum Cholesterol

The enhanced risk of coronary heart disease is directly linked with hypercholesterolemic state of individual. Cultured milk products produce certain hypocholesterolemic agents like hydroxy methyl glutaric (HMG), orotic acid and uric acid which inhibit cholesterol synthesis (IDF: 1991). The bacterial cultures, part of cultured milk act on cholesterol in intestine which ultimately leads to its reduction in absorption. Some of the organisms have ability to assimilate cholesterol in significant amount, which is another factor in lowering of plasma cholesterol.

The deconjugation of bile acids like taurocholic acid and glycholic acid is another important mechanism as the deconjugated bile acids function poorly in supporting absorption of lipids from intestinal tract.

Anti-mutagenic and Anti-carcinogenic Activity

The mutagenicity and carcinogenicity of compounds are reflection of their cancer causing ability. The cultured milk products cause reduction in these mutagenic and carcinogenic activities. The probiotics show antimutagenic activity by producing different hydrophobic compounds while fermenting the milk. Broadly three different categories have been identified with their anticarcinogenic activity, viz :

- Tumor cell inhibition.
- Suppression of bacteria producing different enzymes responsible for release of carcinogens. These enzymes include β-glucosidase, β-glucuronidase, azoreductase.
- Saturation of carcinogenic compounds like nitrosamines with simultaneous suppression of enzymes.

Different mechanisms have been established to occur during prevention of cancer due to intake of cultured milk products:

a) Changes in the micro-ecology of intestine.

b) Normalized intestinal permeability.

c) Alteration in metabolic activity of intestine.

d) Increased immune response leading to intestinal immunity.

e) Strengthening of overall intestinal barrier mechanisms.

The involvement of cultured milk products in prevention of cancer is being accepted world over and advanced research is being done in this aspect.

Immuno-modulation

Recent findings have revealed that cultured milk products have potential to stimulate the immune system against a number of antigens and pathogenic microflora. The oral consumption of these products cause adherence of bacterial culture ot Gut Associated Lymphoid Tissued (GALT), hence strengthening the tissue, making it less prone to attack by antigens, bacteria and other exogenous compounds. The enhanced macrophage activity, increased T-helper cell mediated cytokines and inhibition of immuno-globulin E production, are some of the mechanisms which upregulate the immune system and cause potentiation in its battle against disease causing agents.

Certain other benefits derived from consumption of cultured milk products include synthesis of essential amino acids and vitamins like B_{12}, K and E which induce the overall nutritional status of the consumer.

Conclusion

The cultured milk products stand out with numerous nutritional as well as medicinal advantages. Their involvement in alleviation of certain present day ailments like coronary heart disease, cancer, makes them a most suitable food component of diet on regular basis. At present, research is being conducted on improvement of traditional cultured milk products including our own Dahi to make them more consumer friendly product, enriched with higher nutritive and therapeutic value in western countries , these products are being vigorously marketed under various trade names, like *bioghurt, yoghurt.* In India too, the consumption of cultured milk products is steadily increasing with present production levels standing at 4.5 million tones of total milk produced. Cultured milk products thus truly fits in with what Hippocrates said about foods "Let your food be the first medicine".

Chapter 17

FREEZE-DRIED STARTER CULTURES IN FERMENTED DAIRY PRODUCTS MANUFACTURE

Starter cultures play a key role in the preparation of fermented dairy products. They impart flavour, good body and texture to the products. Starters help in developing pleasant acidic taste, conferring protection against pathogens and providing a longer shelf life to the cultured milk products.

The preparation of contamination free lactic starters is the cornerstone for the successful manufacture of fermented dairy products. The present preparation of the liquid cultures in the factories is time consuming, laborious and sometime creates uncertainity in the fermentation processes. It needs the services of skilled persons. The freeze-dried starters are convenient and reliable to use as an ideal inoculum.

Freeze-drying of cultures

For freeze-drying of any starter culture or organisms, the cells must be grown in a growth medium such as tryptone dextrose broth. de Man Rogosa and Sharpe (MRS) broth or in skim milk based broth observing the optimum growth condition i.e. pH of the medium, rate of inoculum, temperature and period of incubation. The culture must give rapid and vigorous growth, since population density in the correct physiological state is necessary.

For the preparation of freeze-dried culture ampoule, broth culture (4x20ml) is centrifuged at 2500 rpm for minimum time and suitable cryoprotective agents/compounds are added to the cell content immediately. Approximately 0.2 ml. of this suspension is transferred rapidly to sterile ampoule and subjected to freeze-drying process in two steps i.e. primary and secondary drying in centrifugal freeze-drier. the ampoules are sealed under vacuum or nitrogen. In case of bulk freezedried starter culture, broth cultuture of 10 litre or more is centrifuged (16,000 rpm). The cell biomass is resuspended in a suitable cryprotective agents/compounds. The clumps of cells in suspension are broken and transferred into sterile stainless steel trays with lid. the open trays are loaded into the chamber at 15°C of the freeze-drier. The temperature of the chamber is allowed to lower to -30°C, whereas the condenser is maintained at -40°C, The vacuum pump is switched on and pressure is maintained at 0.01 mm Hg. After completing the primary drying, the refrigeration of the chamber is switched off and the temperature allowed to rise upto 10°C, slowly by switching on the heater and care is taken to prevent frothing. The instrument is switching on the heater and care is taken to prevent frothing. The instrument is switched off after observing complete dryness in the starter concentrate and the trays closed with lids are removed from the chamber. The dried culture concentrate powder is packed in sterilized laminated aluminium foil pouches in 25 gm quantity under aseptic conditions and sealed under vacuum of nitrogen. The Freeze-dries culture is stored at 40°C or at low temperature.

Use of Freeze-dried culture

The bulk freeze-dried cultures are convenient to use. The vat milk can be directly inoculated with the culture by simply cutting the sachet and transferring the content at predetermined level. There are many advantages with freeze-dried starter concentrates. The sub culturing is not require. This sliminates the need for bulk transfer facilities like equipment, space and skilled labour. The activity of the cultures is determined at the time of production, hence the rate of inoculum can be standardized. Use of pre-tested cultures results in more uniform quality in the products in all the batches. Strain balance is maintained in case of mixed cultures.

The cultures, freeze-dried in ampoules need to be revived to prepare bulk culture. The revival is done as per the following procedure :

Step I The outer surface of the ampoule is wiped with cotton previously soaked in 75% alcohol or/10 ppm solution of chlorine or iodophore and dried.

Step II A deep mark is made with a file about 0.25 cm long near the top of the ampoule.

Step III The ampoule is broken near the flame with a twist in opposite direction of the mark holding the ampoule by both the hands, This must be done with care to avoid rapid rush of air into the tube.

Step IV a) Add 4-5 drops of sterile skim milk/broth medium using fine tip pipette.

b) After scraping the contents, dissolve fully, the suspension is transferred into 3-4 sterile milk/broth tubes.

Step V The tubes are incubated in the incubator at recommended growth temperature after mixing thoroughly until coagulated/enough growth as avidenced by turbidity.

To avoid starter failure, precautions are to be taken while reviving, during maintenance and at the time of propagation for product preparation. Culture transfers should always be done under strict aseptic conditions. The milk or milk based media used should be of good bacteriological quality. They should be free from the residues of chemicals, pesticides and antibiotics. Proper heat treatment should be given while preparing the medium.

Maintainance and propagation of ampoule culture

The revived cultures are maintained in litmus milk/yeast dextrose litmus milk, stored at 4°C and transferred regularly once in month.

The cultures are activated by sub-culturing thrice in sterlised skimmed milk, inoculated with 1.0 percent culture and incubated for 10-12 hrs at the recommended temperature for fermented milk preparation. One culture can be propagated upto 25 times without any fear of losing its original characteristics. The culture is stored in the refrigerator.

Preparation of bulk culture

Take 500ml/1000 ml (or as per requirements) clean fresh milk in a metal or glass container with lid. Steam it in an autoclave or pressure cooker or heat it to a temperature of 900 for 30 minutes by placing the milk container in a gas heated boiling water container. After heating the milk, keep the container in tap/chilled water and cool it to 22/30/37°C and inoculate with 1.0 percent active culture. Incubate the inoculated milk at a temperature of 22/20/37°C for 12-14 hrs. The set culture may be used for the manufacture of fermented milk products. Use fresh bulk cultures for the preparation of products. In practice, starter culture from the incubator is used in Cheese, Yoghurt and Dahi making.

Defects of Starter Culture

	Defects	Reasons
1.	Insufficient acid development	Abnormal milk, high concentration of detergent and disinfectant residues, antibiotics, neautralisers, bacterial contamination, phageinfection.
2.	Insufficient flavour development	Loss of proper balance of cultures, high concentration of detergent and disinfectant residues, low citrate ion milk, overripening of failure to cool the culture.

3.	Hard and lumpy curd	Higher incubation temperature.
4.	High acidity	Higher incubation temperature, excessive inoculum or both.
5.	Wheying off	Low solids content in milk, over-ripening, agitation during incubation .
6.	Ropiness	Coliform contamination (some of the lactic cultures are ropy to provide heavier body)
7.	Gasiness	Coliform, yeast contamination.
8.	Bitterness	Spore farmers surviving in heat treated milk.
9.	Maltiness	Under ripening of the culture through a series of transfers.
10.	Green apple flavour	Repeated transfers of the culture before adequate development.

Quality control test for starter culture

1. Organoleptic test

i) Body — Smooth, firm, somewhat viscous but not very firm, complete absence of lumpiness, wheying off.

ii) Taste — Clean acidic but not malty, bitter, rancid, unclean, yeasty, fruity or putrid.

2. Acidity test

Weigh 10 gm of culture and titrate against N/NaoH using phenolphthalein as indicator. Express the result in terms of lactic acid. Note the proper acid development (more than 0.7 percent) in the culture.

3. Microscopic Examination

Use gram's staining technique to detect contamination. The starter cultures are gram positive.

4. Catalase test

Starter cultures are catalase negative.

5. Activity test

Add 3.0 percent culture in 100 ml autoclaved skimmed milk and titrate the acidity with N/9 NaoH using phenolphthalein as indicator after incubation for 3.5 hours at 37°C. Development of 0.40 percent titrate acidity indicates a culture of good activity.

Careful selection of starter culture and composition of lactic acid bacteria is important in maintaining the integrity of each fermented milk product. It is especially important that the milk should be fresh and free from flavours and odours The milk and other ingredients such as skimmed milk powder, cane sugar, stabilizer, colour, flavour, fruit and nut etc. should not contain large number of micro-organisms, some of which produce substances that interfere later with the growth of starter culture. The detergents and disinfectants should be used in proper concentration for cleaning and sanitization purpose for dairy utensils and packing material etc. The personnel and plant hygiene should be of good standard.

Annexure-I

Lactic Culture Use in Fermented Milk Products

(Available with National collection of Dairy Cultures at National Dairy Research Institute, Karnal)

	Single lactic cultures	Fermented milk products
1.	Lactococcus lactis ssp. cremoris	Single-cheese, dahi, component of mixed starter culture of dahi, lassi, butter milk, shrikhand, cheese (cottage, cheddar).
2.	Lc. lactis ssp. lactis	Single-cheese, dahi, component of mixed starter culture of dahi, lassi, butter milk, shrikhand, kumiss, karna drink, cheese (cottage, cheddar).
3.	Lc. lactis ssp. lactis biovar diacetylactis	Single-cultured butter, butter milk, dahi, lassi, shrikhand, cheese, Component of mixed starter culture of dahi, lassi, shrikhand, cheese (Cottage, cheddar).
4.	Streptococcus salivarius ssp. thermophilus	Component of mixed starter culture of dahi, yoghurt, cheese (Mozzarella, Swiss).
5.	Lactobacillus acidophilus	Single-acidophilus milk, whey beverages, added with mixed starters of dahi, yoghurt, bulgarian milk.
6.	L.B. delbrueckii ssp. bulgaricus	Single-bulgarian milk, component of mixed starter culture of yoghurt, whey beverages, karna

			drink, kumiss, dahi, cheese (Mozzarella & Emmenthal)
7.	Lactobacillus helveticus		Single-cheese (Mozzarella).
8.	Propionibacterium shermanii		Single-cheese (Swiss).
9.	Bifidobacterium bifidum		Added with mixed starter culture of dahi, yoghurt.
Mixed Starter cultures			
10.	NDRI Dahi Culture BD-1		Dahi, butter milk, lassi.
11.	NDRI Dahi Culture BD-4		Dahi, Lassi, Srikhand,
12.	NDRI Yoghurt Culture	YH-3	Yoghurt
13.	NDRI Cheese Culture	CH-3	Cheese (Cheddar)
		CH-4	Cheese (Cheddar)
		CH-8	Cheese (Cheddar)
		CH-9	Cheese (Cheddar)
		CH-11	Cheese (Cheddar)

(Please note : Single starter culture in practice is rarely used).

Annexure -II

Media

Media listed below are recommended for growing, propagation and maintenance of cultures. All media are sterilised at 15 lb pressure for 20 minutes. Media should be incubated for one week at 30°C/37°C to check for sterility before use.

1. Sterile milk

Steam/heat for few minutes fresh clean milk and separate when warm or 10.0 percent reconstituted skimmed milk powder (spray-dried). Distribute in test tubes/vials, plug with cotton and sterilise.

2. Yeast dextrose milk

Prepare as for sterile milk plus 1.0 percent dextrose and 0.3 percent yeast extract powder.

3. Litmus milk

To fresh skimmed milk or 10 percent reconstituted skimmed milk spray-dried powder, add 0.75 g/litre of litmus blue and thoroughly stir for 15-20 minutes. Distribute in test tubes vials and sterilise.

4. Yeast dextrose litmus milk

Prepare as for litmus milk plus 1.0 percent dextrose and 0.3 percent yeast extract powder.

Approx. 2.0 percent Ca CO_3 i.e. as a thin layer in the bottom of the test tube is added.

5. Yeast Dextrose Broth (for Streptococci)

Peptone	-	0.5 g
Yeast extract	-	0.5 g
Dextrose	-	1.5 g
Sodium acetate	-	1.5 g
Distilled water	-	100 ml

pH : 6.8±0.1

6. Tomato Juice Broth (for Lactobacilli)

Tomato Juice	-	30.0 ml
Papain Solution	-	3.0 ml
Dextrose	-	0.05 g

Distilled water		66.5 ml
pH : 6.8±0.1		

7. de Man Rogosa and Sharpe (MRS) Broth (for Lactobacilli)

Peptone	-	1.0 g
Meat extract	-	1.0 g
Yeast extract	-	0.5 g
K_2PHO_4	-	0.5 g
Ammonium acetate	-	0.5 g
Tween 80	-	0.1 ml
Salt A	-	0.5 ml
Distilled water	-	100 ml
pH : 6.8±0.1		

(Salt A : $MgSo_4.7H_2O$-11.5 g
$MnSo_4. H_2O$-2.4 g
(in 100 ml distilled water)

8. Skimmed milk based media

a) Skimmed milk	-	5.0 ml
Yeast autolysate	-	1.0 g
Dextrose	-	1.0 g
Distilled water	-	95 ml
pH : 6.5±0.1		
b) Skimmed milk	-	50.0 ml
Tryptone	-	1.0 g
Dextrose	-	0.1 g
Distilled water	-	50 ml
pH : 6.5±0.1		

Chapter 18

DAIRY PRODUCTS

Ghee

Ghee (clarified butter oil) is the most important indigenous dairy product of India. About 33% of the total milk produced in India is converted into ghee. It can be prepared either from butter or cream by direct heating to 110-120% C. Conversion of butter or cream into ghee is a convenient method for the preservation of fat in the absence of refrigerated storage. Ghee should have maximum moisture content of 0.3%.

Processed Cheese

Processed cheese is a product obtained by heating a blend of different lots of natural cheese of different ages with water, salt, colour and emulsifier into a homogenous plastic mass. It should not contain more than 47% moisture and less than 40% fate on dry matter basis.

Malted Milk Powder

The nutritive value. palatability and digestibility of this products made it an instant success. Malted milk is the product obtained by mixing whole milk or partially skimmed milk or milk powder with malt extract. It should not contain added sugars, foreign colours and preservatives. Malted milk powder shall contain not less than 7.5% milk fat and not more than 3.5% moisture. It is used as a beverage at home and in the confectionary industry.

Yoghurt

Yoghurt is a product manufactured from boiled concentrated whole milk or party defatted milk containing small amounts of skim milk powder by the use of suitable known cultures. The fat content in yoghurt may vary from 0.0 to 5% and the total solids from 9 to 20%

Coffee Complete

This product is formulated from soluble coffee, sugar and milk solids in a form ready-to-reconstitute into coffee by addition of hot water.

Composition

Moisture	22.0	25.00%
Milkfat	8.5	9.00%
Milk solids-not-fat	20.00	21.00%
Instant Coffee	7.5	8.00%
Sugar	39.0	40.00%

Tea Complete

Tea complete is prepared from extract of choise blends of tea, milk solids and sugar. The dried product obtained in light brown powder is readily reconstituted into tea by the addition of hot water. It is packed in tin cans under nitrogen.

Composition

Moisture	2.0	3.0%
Milkfat	12.0	13.0%
Milk solids-not-far	30.0	31.5%
Tea solids	12.0	13.0%
Sugar	40.0	41.5%

Dried Ice-Cream Mix

By using a ready-to-reconstitute dry ice-cream mix, containing all the necessary ingredients like cream, milk powder, stabilizer, sugar etc. much labour can be saved. The development of this product facilitates housewives and small scale Ice-Cream manufactures to prepare Ice-Cream at short notice.

Composition

Moisture	1.5	2.0%
Milkfat	30.0	31.0%
Milk solids-not-fat	28.0	29.0%
Stabilizer	1.0	1.5%
Sugar	35.0	37.0%

Dried Cheese Spread

Many consumers prefer a mild flavoured cheese spread for use with sandwiches and biscuits and hence a cheese spread with about 55.0% moisture, 25% fat and 20.0% milk solids-not-fat has been developed. It has also been possible to make this highly delicious product available in the form of a powder which can be reconstituted into cheese spread with water, or can be used as such in the preparation of soup, butter-toast etc. The spread can also be prepared with various flavours and spices.

Composition

Moisture	2.0	3.0%
Milk fat	46.0	50.0%
Total solids	97.0	98.0%

Srikhand Powder

Srikhand, a special dairy product popular in Maharashtra and Gujarat is made from Dahi-solids, intimately mixed with sugar and occasionally with butter. The ready-to-reconstitute Srikhand powder enables a housewive to obtain the product by adding lukewarm water in the ratio of 2-3 by wt. and add flavouring of her choice.

Compostion

Moisture	2.0	3.0%
Mil fat	15.0	17.0%
Total solids	97.0	98.0%
Sugar	40.0	45%

Protein-Rich Biscuits From Jowar-Soybean-Skim Milk (Weaning Food)

The method of manufacture consisted of pregelatinization of 30 parts of Jowar flour and dry mixing remainder 30 parts with 30 parts of full fat soyflour, 10 parts of skim milk powder, 0.5 parts CMC and 1.0 part baking soda. The vegetable fat (9.5 part for low fat and 24.0 parts for high fat biscuits) was rubbed with ground sugar (36.0 parts for low fat and 44 parts for high fat biscuits) to creamy consistency and mixed with pregelatinized Jowar flour and other dry ingredients. The dough was worked and then rolled to 3 milimeter thickness, cut into small pieces and baked at $170^0 \pm 5^0C$ for 15-20 minutes.

Approximate Compostion of Protein - rich JSM Biscuits

Characteristics	Type		ISI Specification
	High fat	Low fat	
Moisture%	4.58	4.47	6.0
Protein%	13.25	15.18	13.0 (minimum)
Fat %	19.50	12.50	12.0 (minimum)
Total Ash%	2.86	3.60	-
Total Carbohydrates%	59.81	64.25	-

Butter Powder From Buffalo Milk

The product having the most desirable characteristics is made by taking buffalo milk cream and mixing in it reconstituted skim milk powder so that the final total solids content including 1% each of sodium citrate and glycerol monostearate is 40% and contains 80% fat and 16.5% SNF (on dry basis). The mix (Optionally containing 0.015% BHA) is heated (to 65^{0}C), homogenized (141+35 kg/Cm^2), pasteurized (75^{0}C for 1 min), ripened with LF-40-a mixed lactic starter culture (at the rate of 1%) to obtain 0.12% to 0.16% lactic acidity and spray dried at 82^{0}C outlet and 175^{0}C inlet air temperatures. The butter powder should be immediately cooled to 50^{0}C and coarse sieved to break any lumps. The butter powder could be dry blended with 0.5% find sod. aluminium silicate to increase the flowability if desired. The finished butter powder contain 80% fat, 19.3% SNF and 0.7% moisture.

Weaning Food From Soybean and Cheese Whey

The weaning food was prepared by soaking, bleaching and grinding the soybean (in the presence of cheese whey), heating the mixture with the addition of vegetable oil, homogenizing and spray drying. The weaning food thus prepared was fortified with vitamins, iron and methionine. The average composition of the weaning food was : protein-22.85%, fat 21.23%, carbohydrates 49.97% (major component lactose), ash 4.49% moisture 1.36% and crude fibre-0.1%, The solubility index of the spray dried product was 7.33 ml and viscosity of 12% dispersion 2.029CP. The weaning food thus made met the Indian standards requirement for vegetable protein infant food with milk.

Spray Dried Mango Milk Powder

The product can be readily reconstituted into pleasant mango milk drink or used in Ice cream, custards, puddings etc. The product can easity be made in dairy plants manufacturing dried milk with some additional equipment.

Composition

Milk Fat	13.8%
Milk solids-not-fat	38.7%
Sugar	26.0%
Mango solids	18.0%
Emulsifiers and Stabilizers	1.0%
Moisture	2.5%

The raw material needed are (i) fresh concentrated skimmed milk (ii) fresh sweet cream (iii) fresh ripe mangoes (Chausa) (iv) refined sugar (v) glycerol monostearate as emulsifier and sodium alginate as stabiliser.

Improved Infant Formula

An industrial process has been developed that permits manufacture of an infant formula which resembles human milk in the ratio of protein : fat : carbohydrates. The protein content in formula is adequate to fulfill the entire nutritional requirements of infant during the first year of the life, but without overloading the renal functions (which the presently available formulae do). This also permits extension of available bovine milk for the manufacture of higher quantities of infant foods, as well as reduce costs. Further modification also permits adjustment of whey protein to casein ratio, thus simulating human milk more closely. The fat content has been modifeid so as to incorporate nutritionally superior middle chain glycerides from vegetable sources. Significantly this aspect has both nutritional and Cost advantage. Process has been also standardized for the manufacture of Malto dextrine through starch hydrolysis suitable for incorporation into the formula in order to adjust the ratio of calorie contributing nutrients.

Another outstanding feature of the formula developed relates to the bifidus stimulating property. Animal bio-assays as well as clinical studies carried out under medical supervision have demonstrated that Bifidobacterium bifidum can be implanted in the intestinal tract through feeding of formula developed. In this manner, the improved formulation is expected to favour superior utilisation of minerals, synthesise "B-complex" vitamins in intestine, play a detoxification role in chronic liver diseases and provide protection against intero-pathogenic infections.

Humanization of Buffalo Milk

In huminization of buffalo milk the following major steps are involved :

a) Removal of as-caseins : The first endeavour was to reduce the level of as-casein from buffalo milk, For that purpose, whole case in was fractionated by urea to selectively extract as-casein out of the mixture. The beta-K-casein thus obtained was reconstituted.

b) Buffalo milk was collected and skimming was done at room temperature within an hour of collection using Alfa-Felix Cream Separator or hand driven cream separator. This was then subjected to proteolysis by incubating with Trypsin (1.75 mg/ml) for half an hour at 37^{0}C. This was then pasterurised at 72.5^{0}C for 15 seconds in order to restrict the proteolysis.

Reconstitution of β-K-casein

Three approaches were made for reconstituting β-K-casein in milk with a view to bring down the concentration of as-casein in the finished product. For this purpose, both rennet whey and skim milk were used as the medium for redispersion of the casein.

a) **In Rennet whey** : Skim milk was first curdled with rennet and the rennet whey was recovered by filtering the coagulated milk thorugh cheese-cloth. The way thus obtained was reconsitituted with ß-K-casein in such a mannner that the total protein concentration in the casein fortified whey may not exceed as that in human milk. This was achieved by homogenizing that ß-K-casein in whey using a potter Elvejje, glass homogenizer.

b) **In Skim Milk** : Skim milk (buffalo) was diluted with water to bring down the concentration of protein near human milk. ß-K-casein was then homgeonized in the diluted skim milk in such a manner so that the final protein concentration became equivalent to human milk protein concentration.

c) **Buffalo skim milk** as such was subjected to proteolysis to have only ß-K-casein in the final product, because Trypsin being proteolytis enzymes reduces the as-casein when incubated with difinate concentration for a definite time period.

Lowering of calcium level and curd tension : Since buffalo milk has significantly higher level of calcium than human milk, the lowering of calcium was given distinct emphasis. This was achieved in two manners, namely (a) by electrodialysis and (b) by rennet coagulation. It was possible to reduce the calsium bny 50% by electrodialysis. By prolonging the rennet coagulation period, significant quantity of calcium could also be removed alongwith the milk clot. The reduction in calcium was finally ascertained by measurement of the curd tension which reduced significantly and gave a value as that of human milk.

Reconstitution with vegetable fat and carbohydrates : Human milk is considerably high in polyunsaturated fatty acids unlike cow and buffalo milk. Hence, the milk fat was partially replaced by vegetable fat. For this purpose, corn oil and coconut oil was used. The ß-K-casein fortified, electrodialyged milk and proteolysed milk was next mixed with adequate proportion of corn oil and coconut oil (2:1) and homogenized so that final fat level ranged between 2.50-3.00%.

Evaporated Milk

Lower heat stability of buffalo milk when it is heated after concentration has so far prevented the manufacturing of evaporated milk from it. Studies at NDRI revealed that addition of 0.5 to 1.0% acid casein to buffalo milk before its concentration increased its heat stability and enabled the manufacturing of evaporated milk. Conventional stabilizers (disodium phosphate and trisodium citrate) which are used in cow milk acted as destabilizing agents used in buffalo milk. However, the monosodium phosphate addition (0.05 to 0.10%) before concentration to buffalo milk caused a considerable increase in the heat stability of cocentrated buffalo milk and enabled it to withstand the sterilization treatmeet without coagulation. the stabilizing effect of monosodium phosphate was even better than acid casein.

Milk Powder

Drum Drying /Roller Drying :

Principle : Concentrated milk is applied in a thin film upon the smooth surface of a continuously rotating steam heated mental drum, roller of cylinder. The film or dried milk is continuously removed by a stationary knife/doctor blade/scraper. The drums/rollers are normally horizontal hollow cylinders 8-12 ft in length and 2-4 ft in diameter. They are heated internally by steam. In case of double drumps driers drums are mounted parallel and one drum is fixed on a moveable frame so that the gap between the drum could be adjusted as desired. The speeds of the drums are also adjustable. The average speed ranges between 12-20 r.p.m. The milk film is removed from the drum after nearly 3/4 of revolution of the drum has taken place. The product is in contact with the drum for about 3 sec. or less at a temperature of about 150°C.

Manufacturing Process

The concentrated milk (standardized concentrated milk in case of whole milk powder) concentrated skim milk (in case of skim milk powder) with about 18% t.s. is pumped in the reserviour between the two drums of roller drying equipment. The operating conditions are adjusted to regulate the capacity of the drier to control the moisture content in the milk powder. Under proper drying conditions a uniform thin sheet of dry milk is scraped from each drum. The film drops into a trough and a screw conveyer breaks the film into small pieces while transporting to the packaging station. Further reduction in particle size can be done in a hammer mill. The ground particles are sieved through a mesh and packed in 25 or 50 kg Kraft paper bags with a plastic liner in case of skim milk powder and gas packed in metal container in case of whole milk powder.

Spray Process

Principle

The basic principle consists in atomizing the concentrated milk to form a spary of very minute droplets (fog like mist) which are directed into large suitably designed drying chamber where they mix intimately with a current of hot air. Owing to the large surface area the milk particles surrender their moisture practically instantaneously and dry to a fine powder which is removed continuously.

Manufacturing Process

Concentrated milk (both standardized and skim milk) is atomized either with pressure type or centrifugal type atomizer. The atomized droplets of milk are dried within a chamber with inlet hot air at 150-230°C and outlet air at 75-100°C depending upon the drier characteristics. To reduce heat damage during dehydration and yet obtain the desired moisture in the powder a low exhaust air temperature is preferred. The atomized product is brought into intimate contact with heated air in the drying chamber for moisture removal. As the product is dried, it is necessary to separate the dried product from the air. Cyclone collector is most commonly used for powder collection. Multiple cycloned fo relatively smaller diameter increase the efficiency of powder recovery. The dried particles should be removed from the drying chamber as quickly as possible to reduce the heat damange to the product.

The dried product collected from cyclone separator is cooled and packaged. Skim milk powder is packed in kraft paper bags with a plastic liner and whole milk powder is gas packed in metal containers.

Dried Milk

Definition : Dried milk or milk powder is the product obtained by the removal of water from milk by heat or other suitable means to produce solid containing 5% or less moisture. Whole milk, skim milk or partially skimmed milk may be used for the purpose of drying.

Legal Standards (PFA Regulation)

Whole milk powder shall contain not more than 5.0% moisture and not less than 26% fat.

Partially skimmed milk powder shall not contain more than; 5% moisture and the fat content of the product shall be between 1.6-24.0%.

Skim milk powder shall not contain more than 5.0% moisture and note more than 1.5% fat.

The minimum solubility and solubility index shall be as follows :

	Roller Dried	**Spray Dried**
Solubility %	85.0%	98.5
Solubility index	15ml	2 ml

Flavoured milk

As per P.F.A. standard, the flavoured milk, by whatever name it may be called, may contain chocolate, coffee or any other edible flavour, edible food colours and cane sugar. Flavoured milk shall be pasteurised, sterilised or boiled.

1. Standardisation of milk

It should meet the standard of different ypes of milk from which it is made. The standards for different types of milk have been prescribed by P.F.A.

2. Addition of Sugar

The sugar should be added at the rate of 5-7% of milk.

3. Filtration

The milk is then filtered through a muslin cloth so as to remove any extraneous material.

4. Addition of colour and flavour

The edible flavour is added at the rate of 1 ml per litre of of milk and the colour should be added.

5. Pasteurization

Heating to a temperature of $63^{0}C$ for at least 30 minutes or $71.5^{0}C$ for 15 secs. and cooled to a temperature of $10^{0}C$ or less and shall be maintained at that temperature until delivery.

Chapter 19

PRODUCTS DIVERSIFICATION IN DAIRY INDUSTRY

Research work has been in progress at the National Dairy Research Institute to develop dairy products in a ready-to-reconstitute concentrated form having a reasonably long storage life under atmospheric conditions. Some of the developed products are enumerated below.

1. Banana Milk Powder

Milk is dehydrated, after mixing with fresh banana pulp sugar and stabilizers. This powder is suitable for the preparation of flavoured milk, custards, soups, pudding etc. The final prouduct contains :

Moisture	2.0	2.5%
Milkfat	18.0	20.0%
Milk solids non-fat	53.0	55.0%
Fruit Solids	13.0	15.0%
Sugar	10.0	12.0%

The product is marketed in gas packed tins.

2. Coffee Complete

Is formulated to contain soluble coffee, sugar and milk solids in a form ready-to-reconstitute into a cup of coffee beverage by the addition of hot water. It is ideally suited for use in large scale catering establishments and for meeting the demands of the travelling public.

The product has an approximate composition of :

Moisture	22.0	25.0%
Milkfat	8.5	9.0%
Milk solids-not-fat	20.0	21.0%

Instant Coffee	7.5	8.0%
Sugar	39.0	40.0%

3. Tea Complete

Prepared from extact of choice blends of tea, milk sclids and sugar, the dried product obtained as light brown powder is readily reconstituted into tea by the addition of hot water. It is packed in tin cans under Nitrogen.

Composition :

Moisture	2.0	3.0%
Milk fat	12.0	13.0%
Milk solids-not-fat	30.0	31.5%
Tea solids	12.0	13.0%
Sugar	40.0	41.5%

4. Dried Ice-cream Mix

Preparation of ice cream requires special efforts in the assembling of necessary ingredients like cream, milk powder, stabilizer, sugar etc. It is also necessary to mix the ingredients in definite proportions and process the same in special equipments to get a product of standard quality. By using a ready-to-reconstitute dry ice-cream mix containing all the necessary ingredients much labour can be saved. The development of this product has made it easy for the housewives and the small scale ice cream manufacturers to prepare ice cream for use at short notice.

Composition :

The spray dried ice-cream mix contains :

Moisture	1.5	2.0%
Milk fat	30.0	31.0%
Milk solids-not-fat	28.0	29.0%
Stabilizer	1.0	1.5%
Sugar	35.0	37.0%

5. Dried Cheese Spread

During recent years, processed cheese has become increasingly popular. Many consumers prefer a mild flavoured cheese spread for use with sandwiches and biscuits and hence a cheese spread with about 55% moisture, 25% fat and 20% milk solids not fat has been developed. It has also been possible to make this highly delicious products available in the form of a powder which can be reconstituted into cheese spread with water, or can be used as such in the preparation of soup, butter toast etc. It is also possible to prepare the spread with various flavours and spices.

Composition :

The approximate composition of the product is :

Moisture	2.0	3.0%
Milk fat	46.0	50.0%
Total Solids	97.0	98.0%

6. Dried Channa

Chhana (acid coagulated milk) is a popular milk base for a variety of Indian confections. Although easy to prepare, the product available in the market is not always of uniform quality and is often mixed with starch. It also requires some time for the base to be ready for use. Investigations have shown that Chhana could be made in the form of a powder for subsequent reconstitution and use. The technique developed permits the use of Chhana powder for the preparation of "Sandesh".

Composition :

Moisture	2.0	3.0%
Milk Fat	35.0	40.0%
Total Solids	97.0	98.0%

7. Srikhand-Powder

Srikhand is a special dairy product popular in Maharashtra and Gujarat. It is made from dahi solids intimately mixed with sugar and occasionally with butter. Its preparation is time consuming and requires special skill. Research work at the Institute has made it possible to have a ready to reconstitute Srikhand-powder. The housewife will only be required-to-reconstitute the powder with lukewarm water in the ratio of 2:3 by weight and add flavouring of her choice. Srikhand powder contains :

Composition :

Moisture	2.0	3.0%
Milk fat	15.0	17.0%
Total solids	97.0	98.0%
Sugar	40.0	45.0%

8. Edible Casein and Sodium Caseinate

Problems of inadequate milk production become more acute with inefficient utilization. In India where the present milk production is sufficient only to make available about 106 g of milk per head per day, a considerable quantity of milk (perhaps as much as 5% of total production in certain areas) is converted into industrial casein used for non-edible purpose. This situation is the result of inadequate transport facilities and high atmospheric temperature conditions resulting in lower keeping quality of milk. In the context of the crying need for the supply of proteins foods, it is imperative that all available milk is used as humand food. Techniques have been developed to isolate casein in an edible form or in the form of spray dried sodium caseinate suitable for admixture with cereal flours for the preparation of cakes, biscuits, etc. Apart from enabling the use of sub-standard milk for edible purposes, the technique makes it possible to get a higher return for such milk, thereby indirectly increasingly the farmers' income.

Composition :

Edible Caseine

Moisture	9.0	7.0%
Milk fat	1.4	1.5%
Milk proteins and ash	89.5	91.5%

Softy from Soyabean and Buttermilk

An increasing trend is evident in the consumption of frozen milk products such as icecream, softy etc. in the urban area of this country. However, the short supply and high cost of milk solids, from which these products are made are not within the reach of low-income families. Hence, a low cost softy yet of acceptable quality, is developed from soyabean and buttermilk.

Composition :

Fat	9.0% (Hydrogenated fat)
Solids-not-fat	12.0% (Soy-solids:buttermilk solids, 1.3:1.0)
Sugar	15.0%
Total solids	36.0%

Protein-Rich Biscuits from Jowar-Soybean-Skimmilk

The biscuits are versatile foods as they can be eaten by people of all age groups as snack or can be softened with water/milk to serve as a weaning food. Such a product, particularly high-protein biscuits can be useful means of supplementing the diet of any section of a community with protein-calorie malnutrition. Use of locally available inexpensive ingredients such as Jowar, a widely grown cereal and soybean, a source of high-quality protein, for the manufacture of protein-rich biscuits would be a healthy proposition using a simple technology for its manufacture.

Composition :

		High fat	Low fat
Mositure	%	4.58	4.47
Protein	%	13.25	15.18
Fat	%	19.50	12.50
Total ash	%	2.86	3.60
Carbohydrate	%	59.81	64.25

Lassi from soybean and buttermilk

Lassi a cultured drink made from dahi is very common in our country. It is not only refreshing, delicious but also nutritious and easily digestable, due to which it is quite popular amongst all age groups. Replacement of milk soilds in lassi, therefore, with vegetable proteins such as soybean in combination with buttermilk, will not only help in reducing the cost of the product considerably, but might also divert a large portion of liquid milk for direct consumption which is being used presently for this product.

Composition :

Protein	3.26%
Fat	1.57%
Ash	0.60%
Carbohydrates	15.53%
Total solids	20.96%

Frozen Yoghurt from Soybean and Buttermilk

Amongst various fermented milk products, yoghurt occupies important place and is gaining popularity every day all over the world. Popularizing frozen yoghurt "that too from soybean and buttermilk" in India will not only help to improve the nutritional status of Indian population but also would be a possible substitute for icecream which is a luxury item due to its high cost.

Composition :

Protein	4.50%
Fat	2.40%
Ash	0.48%
Carbohydrates	18.26%
Total solids	25.60%

Flavoured Type Milk Beverage from Cheese Whey

Cheese whey is an excellent source of protein "ranks high in nutritive value only next to egg protein", lactose, minerals and water soluble vitamins. Utilization of cheese whey for the manufacture of flavoured type milk beverage; a most logical use to return whey to the human food chain in a palatable form in the light of growing global food shortage. Therefore, a flavoured type milk beverage from cheese whey was developed having 3% protein, 6% sugar and synthetic flavour.

Soft Drink Type Beverage from Lactose Reduced Whey

Considering the availability of lactose reduced whey in abundent quantity especially in Western Countries, another approach to utilize cheese whey, could be converting it into soft drink type beverage.

The product was developed, which will not only be refreshing like any other soft drink but will also supply 1% protein and about 10% carbohydrates.

The Dairy Technology Division of the National Dairy Research Institute will be glad to assist any party, interested in the manufacture of the above products.

Chapter 20

COFFEE COMPLETE

Coffee Complete is a product ready for reconstitution into hot or cold coffee by the addition of water. It is formulated product incorporating Instant soluble coffee into a sweetened condensed full cream milk base. It has been developed at the National Dairy Research Institute during the course or Investigation on a major research project undertaken to standardise the conditions for production for sweetened condensed full cream buffalo milk.

Commercial instant coffee required milk and sugar to be added at the time of reconstitution for getting a cup of coffee. Coffee complete contains all the ingredient namely, milk, sugar and coffee. It is ideally suited for use in large scale catering establishments and for meeting the demand of the travelling public. Simplicity and convenience characterise the product which can be made available at competitive rates.

Approximate Composition

On hundred grams of the product contain approximately the following ingredients :

Instant Coffee	7.2 gms
Milk fat	8.1 gms
Non-fat milk solids	20.0 gms
Sugar	38.0 gms
Water	26.7 gms

Thr poduct is of deep coffee colour and has a smooth pasty consistency. It may not flow freely but when packed in tubes, could be extruded out as a ribbon. The flavour is typical of coffee concentrate.

Principle of Production

Production involves a two stage process. The first stage is preparation of sweetened condensed full cream milk corresponding to the composition of 9 per cent fat and 22 per cent solids-not-fat. This could be from either standardised cow or buffalo milk, The technique of production consists of the conventional treatment, namely, forewarming or preheating, condensing under vacuum with addition of sugar, inducing micro crystallisation of lactose, cooling, etc. However, when buffalo milk is used as raw material, considerable modifications are necessary in the conventional process to ensure the production of a suitable base. For the manufacture of sweetened condensed milk from buffalo milk all other conditions of manufacture are maintained as for those from cow's milk except the milk is flash heated to 115-116°C before condensing and mass crystallization carried out after seeding with finely ground lactose by holding for 3 hrs at 28-29°C.

The second stage in the prepartion of coffee complete consists of the incorporation of concentrated instant coffee into the sweetened condensed full cream milk. The coffee is added in the form of a concentrated solution made in boiling water, precooled before admixing with the tempered sweetened condensed milk base. The addition is to be carried out under as aseptic conditions as possible and is to be followed by proper mixing and cooling to avoid incomplete admixture, improper crystallisation, etc.

The product is to be finally packed either in lacquered tin plate cans for institutional use or in collapsible aluminium tubes for retails use.

Storage

The product when packed without any post-manufacture contamination could be expected to keep fresh for about 6 months at storage temperatures below 15°C. If the temperature of storage is higher, the shelf life is proportionately reduced. Under normal atmospheric conditions, the product could be expected to keep fresh for 2 months in a cool dry atmosphere.

Once opened, the tin of coffee complete should be used within two to three days, if the tin is not stored under refrigeration. The product requires to be handled and used in the same way as full cream condensed milk.

Instructions for use

(i) If packed in tin, open the tin and mix the contents thoroughly before use. When packed in collapsible tubes this is not necessary.

(ii) Use on tablespoonful of coffee complete (20-22ml) for a standard cup of about 140 ml.

(iii) Empty the spoon of coffee into cup. Add twice its volume of water and mix to form a paste.

Chapter 21

PANEER

Paneer is an important indigenous product. It is used as base material for preparation of large number of culinery dishes. It is prepared by the combined action of acid coagulation and heat treatment. As per PFA standards paneer is required to have a minimum of 50 percent fat on dry matter basis. This can be met by using milk containing 6 per cent fat. It is claimed that good quality paneer can be made from buffalo milk containing more than 5 per cent fat. However, or research has shown that acceptable quality paneer can be made from milk containing fat as low as 3.5 percent. Cow milk results in inferior product.

Manufacturing Technique

Coagulation of Milk

Buffalo milk is standardized to a minimum fat level of 5.5 to 6.0% to meet the legal standard. Milk is heated to 85-90°C for 5 min followed by cooling to 70°C. A1% solution of citric acid heated to 70°C is slowly added to milk with continuous agitation till clear greenish whey separates out.

Draining, Hooping & Pressing

When coagulation is complete, stirring is stopped and the curd is allowed to settle down, whey is drained out and the curd is scooped into a hoop lined with cheese cloth. The curd is wrapped in cheese cloth and is pressed for about 10 min by applying a pressure of about 0.6 lbs/sq inch.

Cooling and Packaging

The pressed paneer is then removed and immersed in potable tap water for cooling and absorption of moisture till its temperature reaches that of cooling water. Paneer is then transferred to chilled water to bring its temperature to 5-10°C. Deep chilling to low temperature is essential to prolong it shelf life. Chilled paneer is then removed from the water and allowed to drain till all the loose water is removed. The Paneer is then cut into convenient sized and packed in suitable packaging materials like polyethylene film and parchment paper, etc. It is stored at refrigeration temperature till disposal.

Preservation

The paneer is a highly perishable article. It cannot be stored for more than one day at room temperature. if it is prepared under sanitary conditions it can keep well for about a week at refrigeration temperature. Our research has shown that if paneer is dipped in sodium chloride brine solution (5%) prior to packaging it enhances the shelflife upto 22 days at refrigeration temperature. Almost the same result was obtained by dipping paneer in 0.2% hydrogen peroxide solution. When paneer was dipped in a fungicide solution (delvocid, 0.5%) following hydrogen peroxide treatment, its shelf life increased upto 32 days at refrigeration temperature.

Heat sterilization is the only effective method to improve the shelf life of paneer at room temperature. Paneer cubes packed in tins and sterilized in an autoclave at 15 psi for 15 min with a little added water can keep well over a period of 50 days at room temperature.

Yield and Composition

The yield of paneer ranged from 18-22% depending upon composition of milk. It contains about 46% total solids, 24% fat, 17% protein, 3.1% carbohydrates and 2% ash.

Chapter 22

CHEESE FROM BUFFALO MILK

Cheese is one of the most important dairy products in the world market. It privides one of the best methods of conserving and preserving milk solids. Its production in India has been relatively limited in the past, however, it is picking up quite fast in recent days. In broad sense, the two indigenous dairy products, namely, Paneer and Chhana could also be classified as cheese.

The manufacture of cheese originated and flourished in countries with relatively cold climate where cows are the main milch animals. Consequently, methods of cheese manufacture were standardized for cow milk and emphasis was given to those varieties for which cow milk happens to be more suitable. In contrast, in our country the major share of milk is from buffaloes. Buffalo milk differs markedly from that of cow milk both quantitatively and qualitatively. As a result, the most common variety, the cheddar cheese made in India does not develop proper flavour and body and texture when it is made from buffalo milk. The main problem is considerably faster rate of syneresis. which results in lower moisture content in finished cheese. This in turn, affects adversely the three most important biochemical reactions, i.e., glycolysis, proteolysis and lipolysis which constitute the cornerstone of cheese flavour. In order to overcome this problem attempt should be made to develop a manufacturing technique which would ensure greater retention of moisture and accelerated rate of of glycolysis, proteolysis and lipolysis.

The most popular variety of cheese in the world market has been cheddar. So is the case in our country. The other varieties made in India or which have good future prospects are Gouda and Mozzarella cheese. Buffalo milk is especially; suitable for Mozzarella cheese. However, when the techniques standardized for Cheddar and Gouda cheese from cow milk are applied to buffalo milk, it poses lot of problems and finally results in inferior products, Therefore, attempts have been made for about last two decades to modify the standard method of cheddar cheese manufacturing from cow milk so that it suits buffalo milk.

Scientific Basis of Cheese Manufacture

Cheese consists of a concentration of the constituents of milk, principally, fat, casein and insoluble salts, together with water in which small amounts of soluble salts, lactose and albumin are found. To retain these constituents in concentrated form milk is coagulated either by means of lactic acid produced by bacteria or by the addition of rennet or by both. A portion of water is removed by cooking, stirring or draining the curd or by mechanical application of pressure. The cheese may or may not be ripened, the nature of the process depends upon the particular variety of cheese.

The hundreds of varieties differ very much in size, shape, colour, hardness, texture, odour and taste. However, all cheeses irrespective of country of origin and method of manufacture possess following characteristics in common:

i) Chese is made from milk of certain mammals

ii) Addition of lactic culture,

iii) Clotting the milk, with rennet or similar enzyme preparations,

iv) Cutting or breaking the coagulum to release the whey,

v) Consolidation or matting of the curd,

vi) Salting the curd for taste as well as to control physicochemical changes and

vii) Ripening of the green cheese.

The above factors are common to all cheeses, but the conditions vary considerably. The chief factors responsible for differences in the final cheese are :-

i) The type of milk used,

ii) The degree of ripening of milk and ripening organisms,

iii) The temperature of renneting and subsequent cooking of the curd in whey,

iv) The milling and salting of the curd,

v) The pressure applied to the green cheese,

vi) The time, temperature, and relative humidity of ripeninng and

vii) The special treatments such as stabbing the cheese, bathing in the brine, and the surface treatment to produce a certain type of coat.

Steps in Cheddar Cheese Manufacture From Cow Milk

1. Selection of milk-Fresh, good quality milk, free from antibiotics and preservatives.

2. Selection of starter -A good, active and unifrom starter is essential.
3. Clarification and Standardization of milk-Casein/fat ratio (C/F)-0.7.
4. Pasterurisation - 63°C/30 min or 72°C/15 sec.
5. Cooling to 30°C.
6. Adding starter (LF-40) at 30°C-1% by wt.

7.	Adding rennent when titratable acidity of milk increased by 0.01 to 0.02% -2.5g/100 lit.	45-60 min.
8.	Cutting the coagulum, whey acidity 0.1%	30 min.
9.	Cooking start at 30°C	15 min.
10.	Cooking/stirring finish at 38°C	90 min.
11.	Draining, when whey acidity is 0.13-0.16% or about 0.02% higher than cutting acidity.	10 min.
12.	Packing the curd, after piling acidity of whey should be 0.17 to 0.20 %	10 min.
13.	Cheddaring, periodical turning of blocks and piling and repiling till whey acidity reaches 0.45 to 5%	2 hrs.
14.	Milling	10 min.
15.	Salting -2% by wt. of curd, in three applications	30 min.
16.	Hooping -After the salt has dissolved completely	10 min.
17.	Pressing - Max. pressure of 2 kg/cm^2 to be applied slowly,	30 min.
18.	Dressing the cheese-The hoops are removed from the press, cheese cloth is pulled to remove all the wrinkles and pressed again overnight.	10 min.
19.	Removing cheese from press. when the rind becomes free from openings.	12-24 hrs.
20.	Drying the cheese-Dry at 10-15°C till dry, clean and bright surface is obtained.	2-5 days
21.	Paraffining -Dip the cheese in paraffin heated to 220°F,	
22.	Ripening at 8-10°C	4-8 months

In the manufacture of Cheddar cheese from buffalo milk, the basic steps remain the same as applied to cow's milk, however, certain modifications have to be introduced to get desirable product.

Cheddar Cheese from Buffalo Milk

In India, around 1960, the first research project to study preparation of Gouda cheese from buffalo milk was launched by I.C.A.R. at Aarey Milk Colony, Mumbai. Systematic work to stadardize a method for manufacture of cheese from buffalo milk was taken up at N.D.R.I., Karnal in 1962. Later J. Czulak an Australian scientistis suggested a modified procedure for manufacture of Cheddar and Gouda cheese from buffalo milk. Recently, a method was standardised for the manufacture of cheddar cheese from Buffalo milk at N.D.R.I. Karnal. Thus basically there are three different approaches recommended for obtaining as satisfactory cheddar cheese from buffalo milk which may be designated as follows :

I. Czulak Method

II. Burde Method

III. Presalting Method

These three methods differ among other things mainly in the stage at which salt is added. In case of Burde method salt is added the same way as is done conventionally in cow milk cheese. In case of Czulak method 1.5-2% of salt W/V is added to the whey at the end of cooking after draining half of the whey. The curd is stirred for about 20 minutes followed by draining. In presalting method 1% salt is incorporated in milk itself before culturing. The basic premise of salt addition in the last two methods is to replace part of divalent calcium ions of casein micelle with sodium ions. This may cause lossening of the casein micelles and softening of the final cheese. The salient features of these methods are given in following section :

Main Distingushing Features of Czulak, Burde and presalting Methods

Steps	Czulak Method	Burde Method	Presalting Method
Standardization, C/F ratio	0.7	0.7	0.7
Pasteurization (°C/30 min.)	63	63	63
Salt addition (%)	—	—	1
Culturing temp. (°C)	30	31	28-29
Rate of starter	1.5	2.5	2.5
Ripening period (Min.)	10	10	10
Rate of rennet (g/100 lit.)	2.5	2.5	2.5
Setting time (Min.)	35	30	55
Whey acidity at cutting (%LA)	0.11	0.11	0.13

Final Cooking emp, (°C)	36.6	38	36
Interval between cutting and half whey draining (Min.)	50	—	—
Rate of salt addition (%)	1	—	—
Total cooking time (Min.)	60	50	45
Whey acidity at draining (%LA)	0.12	0.12	0.15
Cheddaring time (Min.)	210	185	180
Milling acidity (%LA)	0.4	0.44	0.45
Rate of Salting (%)	2	2	2
Yield of Green chese	12.60	12.65	13.22
Moisture in green cheese (%)	34.93	35.85	37.83

Remarks : The acid development, cheddaring characteristics and body and texture was superior in case or presalting method. Chicken breast character was visible only in case of cheese made by presalting method. The final flavour and body and texture of presalted cheese after ripening was of better quality than the other two methods.

Salient Features of Presalting Method

1. The standardized (C/F, 0.7) and pasteurized (63°C/30 min) Buffalo milk is cooled to 28°C followed by addition of common salt @ 1% with thorough mixing.
2. After 15 min an active starter culture (LF-40) is added @ 2.5 percent. Supplementation of regular culture with 0.5% L. case enhances flavour development. After about 10 min, Hansen's calf rennet powder (2.5g/100 lit) is dissolved in tap water (20 times) and added to milk with thorough mixing. Substitution of calf rennet with microbial rennet, viz, Modilase, Noury and Marzyme have stimulatory effect on flavour development.
3. After setting (50-55 min) the curd is cut with 1.4 cm knives. Precaution should be taken to judge the exact cutting time. Delay in cutting results in a tough coagulum which hamperes uniformiy of the cubes and higher losses in whey due to breaking up into small particle.
4. The stirring is started after 10-15 min of cutting and the curd is cooked to 35-36°C in 40-45 min. After proper cooking the curd is left in whey undisturbed for 5-10 min and then whey is drained. The curd expels moisture at a very fast rate and even a delay of 10 min.

in drainage of whey was found to result in excessive drying and hardening of cubes, which ultimately led to tough body and mechanical openness in the pressed cheese. Hence, draining has to be quick and cooking time of 1 hr. to be critically observed.

5. Higner piling during cheddaring helps obtaining good texture at the end. It is essential to develop a good texture resembling chicken breast type during cheddaring to ensure porper milling, salting, pressing and rind formation.
6. After pressing green cheese blocks are transferred to cold storage for drying. The temperature of cold storage should be maintained prederably between 10-15^{0}C. After proper drying generally in 2-3 days, the cheese blocks are paraffined. It is recommended to ripen the cheese at 15^{0}C for about 3 weeks followed by completion of curing at 8-10^{0}C.

Gouda Cheese

Gouda cheese was originally prepared in the vicinity of Gouda in the province of South Holland, Netherlands, but, is now prepared all over the world It is a semihard to hard, sweet curd, renneted cheese made from high pH curd (5.3 to 5.4) without much repressive action of the starter bacteria on the fault producing ones. It is a yellow, waxy and firm bodied cheese with a mild flavour and is characterized by the presence on a number of small shiny eyes. As per the legal limit in U.S.A., Gouda cheese should have at least 46% fat on dry matter (FDM) basis, while Davis reproted FDM of 48% in Netherlands.

Steps in Gouda Cheese Manufacture From Cow Milk

1. Selection of Milk-Fresh, good quality milk free from antibiotics and preservatives.
2. Selection of Starter -A good, Active and uniform starter is essential.
3. Clarification and Standardization of Milk-Casein/Fat ratio-0.65 to 0.7.
4. Pasteurization, 72^{0}C/16 sec.
5. Cooling to 30^{0}C.
6. Addtion of KNO_3 15g/100 lit. Milk, Annatto colour 22-25 ml/100 lit., starter 0.75% Rennet 3.5g/100 lit.
7. Cutting the coagulum after 25-30 min.
8. Cooking up to 38^{0}C.
9. Removal of 40% whey followed by addition of 15% wash water at about 72^{0}C to give final temp. of 36-38^{0}C.

10. Continuous stirring while hot water is added (15-20 min) and then for 20-30 min. after. The curd is then allowed to pitch.

11. Drain the whey. Fill the curd in cloth lined hoops and press for 6-8 hrs. at 10-15 psi. the whey acidity from the press is 0.35-0.40%.

12. Salting by immersing cheese in 20% brine at pH 4.8 for 3-5 days at 15^{0}C to give 1.5-1.8% salt.

13. Drying at 15^{0}C and 80% RH.

14. Ripening at 15^{0}C for 2-3 months, for rich flavour, 5-6 months.

15. For sale, cheese may be oiled (linseed oil) on the rind and packed in film. Some cheeses are waxed.

Steps in Gouda Cheese manufacture From Buffalo Milk

When standard method used for Gouda Cheese manufacture from cow milk are applied to buffalo milk, the resulting cheese tends to be hard, rough and rubbery in body. The typical Gouda flavour is completely lacking rather it has a definite bitter character. in order to imrprove the flavour development the following modified method has been recommended (Czulak, 1964) :

1. Stadardize buffalo milk to a C/F ratio of about 0.67.

2. Dilute milk with 10-15% of water and pasteurize at 163°F for 13-15 sec.

3. Cool the milk to 86°F and add about 1% of normal cheese starter.

4. After about 1 hr. add sufficient rennet to coagulate the milk in 30-40 min.

5. Cut the curd with a ½ inch curd knife.

6. As soon as free whey appears determine its titratable acidity.

7. Five min. after cutting start stirring the curd and at intervals check the titratable acidity of the whey. When acidity has risen 0.005% above that at cutting, stop stirring.

8. Draw off 1/3 of the whey and then scald the curd by adding slowly whilst stirring, clean, preferably pasteurized water heated to 160°F. The amount of the water needed equals 10% of the initial volume of the milk used. This treatment should raise the temperature of the curd to about 97°F.

9. Stir the curd for not longer than 5 min., then press it down under the whey for about 20 min.

10. Draw all the whey off, cut the curd into slabs, hoop it and press it for about 1 ½ hrs. Then dress the hoops and press the curd overnight.

11. Salt, wax and mature as for Gouda cheese from cow milk.

Mozzarella Cheese

Mozzarella cheese originated from buffalo milk in the Battipaglia region of Italy. It is a soft, white, unripened, plastic curd cheese with bland but mildly acid flavour. It has special melting and stretching characteristics. Due to its unique physical properties it is widely used in the preparation of bakery products mainly Pizza. Pizza is an Italian dish which has spread very fast and become an international dish. In recent years, the production of Mozzarella cheese is catching up rapidly in cosmopolitan cities of India, like Delhi, Mumbai and Kolkata etc.

Steps in Mozzarella Cheese Manufacture

1. **Selection of Milk** - Fresh, good quality milk, free from antibiotics and preservaties. Buffalo, cow or mixed milk can be used. Originally made from whole, raw milk, it can now be made from pasteurized milk, partially skimmed milk.
2. **Selection of Culture** - A good, active, uniform culture containing S. lactis, S. thermophilus and L. bulgaricus is often used. Also S. thermophilus and L. bulgaricus in the ratio of 1:1 can be used.
3. Clarification and standardization of milk to any desired fat level, mostly 3.2%.
4. Pasteurization, 72°C/16 seconds.
5. Cooling to 31-32°C.
6. Addition of starter at the rate of 0.5-2.0%.
7. Addition of rennct @ of 20 ml or 2.5g/100 lit. after the acidity has increased by 0.02% to give a coagulation time of 25-30 min.
8. The curd is cut and left undisturbed for 10-15 min. followed by cooking slowly upto 38-39°C for 30-45 min.
9. Whey is drained off and the curd is allowed to ripen to an acidity of 0.65 to 0.70%.
10. The curd is cut into pieces and stretched in hot water (82-85°C) for proper development of body and texture.
11. The curd is moulded by filling hot, plastic curd into hoops.
12. The moulded cheese is immersed in water at 10°C for ½ to 1 hr for hardening.
13. The cheese block is then transferred to a 16-20% brine solution at 8-10°C for sufficient time to allow 1.6% salt in cheese.
14. Dry off the cheese for about an hour and pack in PVDC film or laminted pouches (moisture and airtight) preferably under vacuum.

Cottage Cheese

Cottage cheese is a soft, unripened variety made from skim milk, to which cream and salt may be added. Since the cheese is made from skim milk and it is unripened, it is considerably cheaper. It has a pleasant, mild flavour which is compatible with variety of other foods. In addition, it is a good source of quality protein and low in calories which is highly suitable to those conscious of over weight and cardiovascular ailments.

Steps in Cottage Cheese Manufacture from Cow Skim Milk

1. Selection of milk-Fresh, good quality milk, free from antibiotics and preservatives.
2. Selection of starter-A good, active and uniform starter is essential.
3. Standardization of Milk- SNF of milk to 9.0% by fortifying with skim milk powder.
4. Pasteurization - 63°C/30 min., or 72°C/16 sec.
5. Cooling - 30±1°C.
6. Addition of calcium chloride @ 10g/100 lit.

7.	Addition of starter culture @ 6%.	0
8.	Addition of rennet @ 0.04g/100 lit.	75 min.
9.	Cutting of curd at whey acidity 0.5%	240 min.
10.	Cooking start	15 min.
11.	Cooking finish at about 55°C	60 min.
12.	Washing of curd	
	First wash Temp 27°C	10 min.
	Second Wash Temp 17°C.	10 min.
	Third Wash Temp. 8°C	10 min.
13.	Creaming of curd with dressing containing 18% fat.	45 min.

Preparation of dressing

Calculated quantity of cream and skim milk is mixed to give 18% fat in the mixture. The mix is preheated (60°C) and homogenised. The homogenised dressing is pasteurised at 75°C for 15 sec., cooled to room temperature and then stored at 7°C till use.

Steps in Cottage Cheese Manufacture from Buffalo Skim Milk

Step	Temperature	Time
Pasteurization of buffalo skim milk	63°C/30 min.	
Addition of sodium chloride @ 0.1%	30°C	5 min.
Addition of starter culture (BD) @ 5%	30°C	5 min.
Cutting of curd at an acidity of 0.7%	30°C	270 min.
Cooking start	30°C	15 min.
Cooking Finish	60°C	75 min.
Draining of whey	60°C	10 min.
First washing with water at 27°C	60°C	10 min.
Second washing with water at 17°C	-	10 min.
Third washing with water at 8°C	-	10 min.
Draining of water	-	45 min.
Creaming of curd with dressing containing 18% fat	8°C	-

Chapter 23

WHEY PROTEIN CONCENTRATE

Background Information

Whey contains nearly 50 percent of the nutritionally superior milk constituents. Whey proteins are of the best quality with high PER (3.6), biological value (104) and NPU (95). They possess almost all the essential aminoacids. The functional properties of whey proteins such as solubility, emulsifying, foaming, gelformation and waterbinding are excellent.

To meet the requirements of many feed industries whey protein concentrates (WPC) are mainly used as ingredients in non-dairy products, but also to some extent in dairy products like infants and weaning foods. They can also be utilized for designing speciality food products, such as health food, hospital feeding, fruit juices drink comibinations, etc. In order to derive maximum benefit from whey, a technology has been developed at this institute for the production of whey protein concentrates by employing ultrafiltration technology.

Method of Manufacture

The process of manufactrue of WPC involves, pretreatment and ultrafiltration of whey followed by spray drying of UF-retentate. The pH of whey obtained from buffalo milk cheddar cheese is adjusted to 7.2 prior to heating to 85°C/15 sec., the whey is cooled to 50°C and ultrafiltration is carried out to a level of 85 percent volume reduction. the retentate is spray dried using 180°C inlet and 80°C inlet and 80°C outlet temperatures. Whey protein concentrate powder thus obtained is cooled to room temperature, packaged in polythylene or metallized polyester packaging material.

Composition

The average chemical composition of whey protein concentrate is as follows :

Constituents (%)	Buffalo cheddar cheese whey protein concentrate
Moisture	3.75
Protein	43.46
Fat	4.45
Lactose	42.76
Ash	5.58

Shelf Life

The product remains good for more than six month at room temperature.

Chapter 24

PRODUCTION OF YOGHURT

Yoghurt is one of the most popular fermented dairy products all over the world. Its consumption has increased tremendously in the last few years mainly due to the introduction of wide variety of flavours/fruits ot the product, claims regarding its therapeutic value and also changes in the marketing trend.

Types of Yoghurt

Yoghurt is so popular that it has assumed different forms, e.g. stirred, set, frozen, and liquid yoghurt. Of all the varieties, set yoghurt is the most common with a rather firm body. The flavour of yoghurt irrespective of the type, is the same since the main flavour compound is acetaldehyde.

Starter Cultures for Yoghurt

Yoghurt is prepared by the combined fermentative activity of two specific lactic acid bacteria viz. Streptococus salivarius subs. thermophilus and Lactobacillus delbrueckii subsp. bulgaricus which are in symbiotic association in the starter. Selection of good quality starter is the corner stone in successful preparation of the product. The interaction between the component strains produces the characteristic body and texture as well as flavour in the product. Acetaldehyde alongwith volatile acids and lactic acid contribute to the flavour in yoghurt.

Preparation of Bulk Starter

For the preparation of yoghurt bulk culture, good quality milk (in respect of chemical and bacteriological qualities) preferably skimmed milk is taken in a container with lid. It is subjected to 45 min steaming in an autoclave or pressure cooker. The heat treated milk is cooled to 42°C and inoculated with an active yoghurt starter @ 1.0% by taking all aseptic precautions. After mixing the culture well, t is incubated at 42°C for about three and half hours. The curdled starter is removed and chilled at 5°C till use. Depending upon the availability, the starter may comprise of individual component strains or mixed culture. Separately maintained strains may be mixed at the time of product preparation.

Preparation of Yoghurt

Materials :

- Weighing balance.
- Whole/skim milk spray dried powder.
- Batch pasteurizer with provision for heating and cooling.
- Incubator at 42°C.
- Hand operated milk filter/dispenser.
- Cold store at 5°C.
- Sugar, sodium alginate, colour, fruits etc.

Method :

Yoghurt is prepared from good quality cow/buffalo/skim milk. The milk should be of normal composition and free from foreign matters including those imparting undesirable flavours. It should also not contain any preservative or neutralizers. Regarding bacteriological quality, it should have methylene blue reduction time of more than two hours.

The selected milk is standardized to 3% fat and then heated slowly to 60°C. Simultaneously skim milk powder upto 2 to 3% is also added. The mixture is continuously stirred to get maximum incorporation of milk powder. The insoluble skim milk powder is filtered off with the help of a fine quality muslin cloth.

In the production of sweetened Yoghurt, sugar in the form of syrup is added to the level of 5 to 6%. Sugar syrup is prepared by dissolving 1000 g of sugar in 250ml of tap water in a flask and sterilizing by steaming in three consecutive days. The quantity of sugar may be increased to 7%. However, beyond this concentration certain starter strains get slightly inhibited.

Most of the yoghurt cultures give fairly firm curd, typical of the product, or otherwise stabilizer (sodium alginate, gelatin or guar gum @ 0.2 to 0.3%) may be added to the milk mixture. Addition of higher quantities of stabilizer affect the refreshing taste of the product. The milk and mixture is then heated to 60°C and subjected to homogenization at 100 kg/cm^2. Homogenization prevents cream layer formation during setting and hence gives uniformity to the texture of the product.

The homogenized milk mixture is then heat treated at 90°C for 30 min after which it is cooled rapidly to 42°C without exposing it to atmosphere. Cooling is best effected by passing chilled water into the jacket of the vat.

The cooled milk is then inoculated with an active yoghurt starter @ 2 to 3%. Care must be taken to maintain the balance of the component cultures of yoghurt viz. Streptococcus sub sp. thermophilus and Lactobacillus delbrueckii sub sp. bulgaricus in the ratio of 1:1.

The inoculated milk is then distributed in 100ml quantities into plastic or glass containers with lid. The lids of containers should be simultaneously replaced.

The inoculated milk (with all additives inclduing cultures) is then kept for setting in an incubator maintained at 42°C. Storage at zero and sub-zero temperature adversely affects the body and texture of this product.

Defects in Yoghurt

- **Lack of uniformity** : This defect result due to improper mixing of various ingredients during its preparation.

- **Browning effect** : Due to excessive heating of milk, milk proteins may turn brown which may effect the colour of the final product.

- **Wheying off** : Wheying off in the product may result due to any one of the following reasons : (a) disturbance of the product, particularly at the time of setting, (b) incubation at higher temperature than the recommended one, and (c) prolonged incubation.

- **Thin body** : Thin body of yoghurt may be due to (a) drastic heat treatment (b) pre-ripened removal from the incubator, (c) lower SNF content and (d) imbalance in the proportion of the two starter bacteria.

- **High acidity** : Prolonged incubation and failure to cool the product promptly after setting cause development of high acidity.

- **Gassiness** : This defect is due to the contaminaiton of the product with either coliform bacteria or yeasts.

- **Yeasty flavour** : This is due to the contamination of product by acetic acid forming yeast getting access through sugar or fruits.

- **Unclean flavour** : Unclean flavour in the product is either due to poor quality of milk or contamination of product with unwanted bacteria especially of coliform type.

- **Cooked flavour** : Excessive heating of the milk during processing develops cooked flavour which is carried to the product also.

Standards for Yoghurt

Although at present no standards are prescribed for yoghurt except for those applicable to milk, yet it is necessary that yoghurt should be prepared, packaged and stored under good hygienic conditions.

Fruits and Artificial Flavours in Yoghurt

The flavour of yoghurt is mainly due to the acetaldehyde content in the product although volatile acids and diacetyl also contribute to some extent. However, quite often the product is flavoured with artificial flavours like pineapple, orange, rose, lime, mango etc. which is entirely the choice of the consumer. The level of artificial flavours is adjusted in the product in such a way that it does not give harshness and palatability of the product is maintained. Flavours are added at the time of addition of culture, prior to incubation.

There is also practice these days to prepare fruit yoghurt. The presence of fruits in yoghurt adds to the nutritive value of the products. Trials at NDRI have shown that strawberry, orange, pineapple etc. go well with yoghurt. Seed free pulp of various fruits is added at a rate of 10 to 15% prior to the stage of distribution and incubation. Care must be taken to distribute the pulp well in the packaging containers. Another thing to be borne in mind is that presence of fruit pulp causes a reduction in the shelf life of yoghurt, i.e. fruit yoghurt has only 2 to 3 days shelf life compared to that of plain yoghurt which keeps well for 7 days at 5°C.

Prospects of the Yoghurt

Being new to this country, yoghurt at present has only limited market but there are signs of healthy commercial competition, particularly in metropolitan cities. In the presence of assured outlets, returns are expected to be quite remunerative.

Nutritive Value of Yoghurt

Yoghurt is one of the most nutritive and refreshing fermented dairy products. The complex protein fraction of milk is changed to much similar form which can be easily digested and assimilated by the body. Free fatty acid and vitamin B complex contents of milk increase significantly during the process of yoghurt preparation. Compared to milk, yoghurt is also rich in essential and non-essential amino acids. The therapeutic value of yoghurt is unique which is mainly due to L. delbrueckii su sp. bulgaricus included in the starters. Consumption of yoghurt has stimulative effect on the secreting glands of the digestive system. Yoghurt starter bacteria exert inhibitory effect on the putrificative and pathogenic bacteria present in the bowel. Finally, the yoghurt is said to be beneficial to the patients of heart diseases, arteriosclerosis, hypertension and chronic inflammation of liver. There are reports that yoghurt bacteria exert an inhibitory effect in the cancerous tissues too.

Chapter 25

TEA COMPLETE

1. This product is readily reconstituted into tea by the addition of boiling water. It is formulated to contain choice blends of tea, milk solids and a limited quantity of sugar, in the form of powder. Tea Complete has been developed at the National Dairy Research Institute, Karnal, during the course of investigation on the development of new products from milk.

2. Physical characteristics and approximate composition

2.1 The product is in the form of fine powdered tea, brown in colour, and is gas packed in tins.

2.2 One hundred gram of product contains approximately; the undermentioned ingredients :-

Milk fat	13.0 g
Milk solids-not-fat (SNF)	31.5 g
Sugar	39.5 g
Tea solids	14.0 g
Moisture	2.0 g

3.Principles of Production

The following are the major steps in its production :

3.1 **Preparation of milk concentrate**; Milk is standardised to correspond to a fat : SNF ratio of 9:22. This is to be carried out as per standard procedure from the knowledge of the compostion of milk used.

3.2 The standardised milk is concentrated to 46-48% solids in a single or double effect vacuum evaporator. The concentrated milk is rapidly cooled to below 8^0C and stored at that temperature till used.

3.3 **Preparation of tea infusion** : An extract of tea from the blended leaves is to be made for admixture with milk concentrate prior to drying. The quantity of tea leaves required for each batch is calculated on the basis of 2.5 kg of tea leaves for every 7 kg of milk concentrate (refer 3.2). The extraction of tea from the leaves could be done in any conventional extractor by passing boiled water at 90^0-92^0 C over the layer of tea. Extraction can be rendered more complete by providing for recirculation of the tea extract over the leaf in a closed system for 8-10 minutes. The extract must be cooled to below 8^0C immediately after extraction.

3.4 **Admixing of concentrated milk, sugar and tea extract** : High grade refined sugar in the proportion of 3.5 kg of sugar for each 7 kg of concentrated milk is dissolved in the tea brew when hot, and before cooling. This brew with sugar is mixed when cold with the concentrated milk. Alternatively, half the required quantity of sugar can be dissolved in the tea brew and the other half can be finely ground and dry blended with the spray dried product, avoiding post contamination.

3.5 **Drying of tea milk-concentrate** : The mixture of tea infusion, concentrated milk and sugar is dried in a spary drier with a disc type atomiser under conditions which lead to low heat powder production.

3.6 **Packing** : The powder, immediately after production, is filled into tin plate containers and double gassed at intervals of 24 hours before final closing. Retails packaging of powder in moisture proof polythene bags for consumption within a month is also possible.

4. Storage

4.1 The product is very hygroscopic and is to be stored in a cool dry place and the lid is to be replaced on the tin immediately after use. As per present indication, the product could be expected to retain its freshness for a period of 6 months when stored at ambient temperatures.

5. Reconstitution

5.1 The product is reconstituted into 'tea' by dissolving about one and a half tea spoons of the powder with about 7-8 spoons of hot water to be followed by make-up water to fill the cup (140 ml). Sugar is to be added according to taste.

Chapter 26

CASEIN FROM MILK

Casein is an important bye-product of milk, that can be manufactured very easily. After the extraction of butter, the residue is usually thrown off. This can be utilised in making casein.

Casein made from butter separated milk "Skim Milk". In order to obtain the protein from the milk rapidly, a little quantity of acid is added. By doing so, the milk will coagulate and water will be separated.

Casein is sold in granular or powder form. It is an essential raw material by which a number of items are produced. In the past few years, the plastic was prepared from casein which was known as casein plastic. In recent years there have, however, been absolute by other durable cheap and better plastics made from synthetic material.

MANUFACTURE OF CASEIN

If we want to make better quality of casein the fat content of the skim milk, from which it is made, should be minimum. Therefore it is necessary, the cream may be again separated from skim milk so that its fat content is minimum.

After separating the last trace of cream from the skim milk it is heated 350°C and filled in the wooden tank equipped with a hand agitator or mechanical agitator. For co-agulation of casein 150 ml of dilute hydrochloric acid (1 part of acid into 1 parts water) and is added by spray pump slowly and stirring is continued. Milk starts coagulating as the acid is added and coagulated man settles down at bottom. When complete coagulation has taken place, the mass is allowed to settle for half an hour. Now the stop coke is opened and the whey is drained over a draining cock made of wire cloth fixed in wooden frame, so that the coagulated mas is retained over it. The coagulated mass is again dropped into the tank for washing.

Now-a-days a different types of filter is using to separate whey.

Washing is done in the tank by adding dilute acid water (8 C.C. acid in 50 ltr. of water). The acid is added sufficient quantity so that coagulation is completely under water. After ten minutes, the water is drained out. Two such type of required more. It should be remembered that washing should be such type that there should be leaving no whey.

The coagulation is hanged in a cloth so that water tickles down. Even after this process there is sufficient water present necessity squeezing and processing. For this the cloth fieled with coagulation is put under two wooden frames and pressed by putting some weight.

A screw press may be used for the same purpose as it makes the pressing very easy. The casein is now form of a cake.

Now the cake should be cut in the pieces. Then the pieces are rubbed on over a 10 mesh more cloth fixed in a wooden frame. Granules of casein are obtained below the sieve.

The next step is to dry the granules. If the production is 5-10 kg. casein per day and it is shiring run that the charging can be done in open by spreading the granules over white sheets on a coat, but if larger production is required a tray dryer will be needed.

Tray dryer is a almirah which is heated inside with electric elements. Granule is placed in trays which are put in place over the sacks provided in the almirah. The heating can also be done with coal.

The granules are next ground to powder. Different types of grinding machines are available including driven. If powder is available that it is casein to run the grinder in the keep of 1/2 H.P. motor. The powder is packed in polythene bags which are placed in card board boxes. Indian standard institution has prescribed the requirement for edible quality casein code No. IS : 1167-1965.

NOTE

1. Skim milk should not have any cream.
2. Spray should be slower.
3. Complete coagulation of whey should be.
4. Moisture contents should be minimum.
5. For grinding purpose, a pulveriser should be used.
6. Drier temperature should not be more than 100°C.
7. Moisture content should be minimum.

The process can be completed in the following steps.

1. Cream separation.
2. Coagulation of whey.
3. Washing with water acid solution.
4. Removal of water from casein.
5. Pressing.
6. Granulation or powder.

7. Drying.
8. Grinding.
9. Testing.
10. Packing.

PLANT ECONOMICS

Rated Plant capacity	=	160.00 KGS/day
LAND & BUILDING	=	Rs. 1,68,500.00
(Land 100 sq.mt.)		

PLANT & MACHINERY

1. Cream Separator
2. Wooden tank
3. Spray press
4. Screw Press
5. Oscillating granulator
6. Tray dryer
7. Grinding m/c.
8. Misc. Accessories

FIXED CAPITAL

1.	Land & Building	Rs.	1,68,500.00
2.	Plant & Machinery	Rs.	51,300.00
3.	Other Fixed Assets	Rs.	31,000.00
	TOTAL	Rs.	2,50,800.00

RAW MATERIALS

1. Skim Milk
2. HCL

TOTAL WORKING CAPITAL/MONTH

1.	Raw Material	Rs.	4,00,700.00
2.	Salary & Wages	Rs.	35,160.00
3.	Utilities & Overheads	Rs.	10,000.00
	TOTAL	Rs.	4,45,860.00

TOTAL CAPITAL INVESTMENT

Total Fixed Capital	Rs.	2,50,800.00
Total Working Capital for 2 Months	Rs.	8,91,720.00
TOTAL	Rs.	11,42,520.00

TURN OVER/ANNUM

By selling 48000 Kg. of Casein	Rs.	67,20,000.00

PROFIT SALES RATIO = Profit / Sales x 100 = 16.30 %
RATE OF RETURN = Operating profit / T.C.I x 100 = 95.88 %
BREAK EVEN POINT (B.E.P) = 30.95 %

Chapter 27

DAIRY FARM

The domesticated water buffallo is one of the gentiest of all farm animals. Despite an intimidating appearance it is more like a house hold pat-sociable, gentle, and serve. In rural Asia the care of buffalloes is after turned over to small boys & girls aged about 4 to 9.

Another belief is that the buffallo is exclusively a tropical animal. River type buffalloes, However, have been used to pull snow plows during Bulgarian winter.

Buffallo milk has a higher content of both butter fat and non fat-solids than cows milk does. Throughout much India it is in such demand that Cow's milk is sometimes hard to sell.

Breeds: The major genetic division of the buffallo are the swamp Buffallo of the eastern half of the Asia, which has swept back horns and the river buffalo of the western half of Asia which usually has the curled horns. There is also the mediterranean buffalo, which is of the river type but has been isolated for so long that it has developed some unique characteristics.

Although there is only one breed of swamp buffallo, certain sub-groups seem to have specific inherited characteristics. Swamp buffalloes range from 250 kg for some small animals in China, 200-300 kg in Berma and 500-600 kgs in Laos. Only in India and Pakistan are there well defined breeds with standard qualities. There are eighteen (18) river buffallo breeds in south asia which are further classified as the Murrah, Gujrat, Uttar Pradesh, Central Indian & South Indian breeds.

COMPOSITION OF CATTLE FEED

There is no definite composition to Buffalo feed compound but in general practice the following composition is followed :-

Ground nut Cake	25%
Wheat bran	27%

Grain Husk	15%
Maize	30%
Mineral	1%
Salt	2%

MANUFACTURING PROCESS

The manufacturing process for Dairy milk is started with the milking buffaloes by hand (at small scale) & milking buffaloes by machine (at large scale).

The detailed process is given here with :-

MILKING BUFFALOES BY HAND

The profitable operation of a dairy herd depends in a large part upon how well you milk your buffaloes. You can do everything else carefully and well, but if you do not milk your buffaloes properly, you can never be successful in dairying. Poor milking habits cause low production, mastitis, & poor quality milk. An important part of milking buffaloes is to produce the cleanest possible milk. Milk must be low in sediment.

Although machine milking is rapidly replacing hand milking, many dairymen still use the latter. In milking by hand, buffaloes must be carefully prepared to produce high quality milk.

COOLING & STORING MILK

The careless handling of milk between milking & delivering to the plant can cause high bacteria counts to develop in the milk thus a mechanical cooler is employed for the purpose. Whole of the milk should be stored at 50^{0}F to prevent spoilage. Storage Tanks made of stainless steel are employed for storing the raw milk.

FILTERATION :

The cold raw milk is filtered, however, it can be filtered before cooling & storing in tank, but the precaution is to be taken at this stage so that no foreign matters or undesired materials may be carried on.

HOMOGENIZATION:

Filtered milk is fed into homogeniser. Homogenization is the process by which the milk is emulsified and are further divided to produce a more stable emulsion that will not separate on standing. The fat is emulsified with liquid part of milk that are water mostly. Hence, to prevent sedimentation or fat in milk. This homogenization process is done. By this way high quality homogenized milk is produced.

After feeding the milk into homogenizer, the pressure of the homogenizer is increased about 2500 psi. However, if this pressure does not produce milk that meets the standard, it may be necessary to use a pressure as high as 3000 to 3500 Lb.

CLASSIFICATION:

The milk is passed through a clarifier as it leaves the homogenizer. Cold milk clarification is preferred to hot milk. This clarification operation can be performed before homogenization. But the complete clarification can be achieved at this stage.

Clarifier can be replaced by cream separator but since the separator bowl is not designed to hold a large amount of sediment and consequently is not efficient for clarifying a large volume of milk. However, This operation can be omitted to get high quality milk.

PASTEURIZATION:-

In this process, the clarified milk is fed to pasteurizer and heated to the required temperature & held there during the holding period (usually at 145°F & for at least 30 minutes). Vat pasteurizer with jackets & agitators is employed for the pasteurization.

The milk is heated by hot water or steam passing into the space between the two tanks. In this process, excessive heating of any part of the milk & a consequent "cooked" flavour is prevented.

At the end of the holding period, the cold water is circulated through the jacket or coil of the pasteurizer, Temperature of the milk may be quickly lowered 10° to 15°, & at this point the heated flavour will not continue to develop. This is done to destroy all pathogenic bacteria.

REFRIGERATION OR FREEZING SYSTEM

After the complete processing of milk it is to be stored in a cold upto chilling condition so that no unwanted micro-organisms/pathogenic organism can be developed in the processed milk. It is stored until delivered for distribution i.e. for packing in Cans or pouches.

PLANT ECONOMICS

Rated Plant capacity	=	DAIRY FARM (1200 LTR./DAY)
LAND & BUILDING (Land required 2000 sq.mt.)	=	Rs. 21,80,000.00

PLANT & MACHINERY

1. Steam boiler
2. Homogenizer complete with accessory
3. Refrigeration system consists of air compressor, refrigerants & cerenlating tube tank
4. Pasteurizer with cooling arrangement
5. Filter (ordinary)
6. Pouch making, filling & sealing Machine complete automatic with printing arrangement
7. Milk reception tank
8. Milk Cans (Aluminium)
9. Dies different capacity
10. Buffalloes Kundi 100 Nos.
11. Misc. other equipments such as Laboratory & testing equipments

FIXED CAPITAL

1.	Land & Building	Rs.	21,80,000.00
2.	Plant & Machinery	Rs.	17,17,000.00
3.	Other Fixed Assets	Rs.	4,20,000.00
	TOTAL	Rs.	43,17,000.00

RAW MATERIALS

1. Raw Material for Buffaloes feed green fodder/Cattle feed
2. Health expenses (medicines) etc.
3. Raw material i.e. pouch, Polythene sheet etc.
4. Misc. other items such as printing ink etc.

TOTAL WORKING CAPITAL/MONTH

1. Raw Material	Rs.	59,500.00
2. Salary & Wages	Rs.	38,750.00
3. Utilities & Overheads	Rs.	15,200.00
TOTAL	Rs.	1,13,450.00

TOTAL CAPITAL INVESTMENT

Total Fixed Capital	Rs.	43,17,000.00
Total Working Capital for 3 Months	Rs.	3,40,350.00
TOTAL	Rs.	46,57,350.00

TURN OVER/ANNUM

By sale of 1200 x 365 litres of Milk	Rs.	52,56,000.00

PROFIT SALES RATIO = Profit / Sales x 100 = 45.14 %

RATE OF RETURN = Operating profit / T.C.I x 100 = 50.94 %

BREAK EVEN POINT (B.E.P) = 42.88 %

Chapter 28

FLAVOURED MILK

The freezing of fluid milk and concentrated milk is not being practical on any large commercial scale, but since there is a growing demand for this product, the industry should develop into a sizeable one. At the present time, frozen milk is of value only in those places where fresh milk is scarce, expensive or not available. There has long been a demand for milk that would retain its natural flavour on shipboard during long voyages; like wise in the tropical countries where cows are few and good milk is very scarce.

B. I. S. SPECIFICATIONS

1. SCOPE:-

1.1 This code prescribes the techniques used in the manufacture and the methods of sampling and test for pasteurized milk.

2. Terminology:-

2.0 For the purpose of this code, the following definitions shall apply.

2.1 Milk-milk shall include cow's or buffalo's, whole or skimmed, standardized, toned, double toned and recombined milk or other kind of milk as defined under the prevention of food adulteration Rules, 1955 as amended from time to time.

2.2 Milk plant or Dairy-it shall be taken to include the building, machinery, equipment and appliances necessary for the collection, pasteurization, cooling bottling or filling in other containers and storage of milk.

2.3 Pasteurization - It shall refer to:-

a) The process of heating every particle of milk at a specified temperature;

b) Holding the milk at such temperature continuously for a specified period in a standard and properly;

c) Immediate cooling after heating.

2.3.1 The milk shall be heated to at least 63°C and held at 63°C continuously for at least 30 minutes, or it shall be heated to at least 71.5°C and held at 71.5°C continuously for at least 15 seconds. Other temperature and time combinations that enable the pasteurized milk to meet the requirements.

2.3.2 The holding the milk, it should be cooled immediately in the standard and properly operated equipment to a temperature not exceeding 5°C.

2.3.3 The pasteurized milk should be maintained at a temperature not exceeding 10°C until it leaves the milk plant for distribution.

3. General Requirements:-

3.1 Milk plant- The building where the milk is received, processed, bottled and stored and the equipment and containers are cleaned and sterilized, shall be constructed according to approved design (see IS:2491-1972). The floors, walls and ceilings, doors and windows, arrangement for lighting and ventilation, toilet and hand washing facilities for protection of milk and cleaned equipment from contamination in the building shall conform to the requirements specified in IS: 2491-1972.

3.2 Water supply:- The water supply shall conform to the tolerances specified for water for dairies (see IS: 4251-1967) and shall be easily accessible and adequate.

3.3 Sanitary piping:- All piping used to conduct milk shall be sanitary milk piping of a type which can be easily cleaned and sanitized (See IS:3382-1965).

3.4 Equipment and Containers:- Milk receiving equipment, storage tanks pasteurizing and cooling equipment, cans, bottles, aluminium foils and other packing materials with which milk comes into contact shall be of smooth impervious, non-corodiable, non-toxic material and so constructed as to be easily cleaned and sanitized. Milk bottles, cans, tanks and other items of equipment shall conform to relevant Indian standards prescribed for this purpose.

3.5 Cleaning and Sanitisation of Plant Equipment and Containers:- The pasteurization plant and other equipment used for receiving, processing storage and bottling, and milk cans and bottles used for filling milk, shall be cleaned and sanitized according to the method prescribed in IS: 5253-1969.

3.5.1 After sanitization and during usage or storage, the equipment and containers shall be protected from contamination.

3.6 Surroundings and Waste Dispoal:- The immediate surroundings shall be kept in a neat and clean condition and proper arrangements made for the disposal of waste.

3.7 Personnel, Health and Cleanliness:- All employees and other persons handling milk or equipment in the plant shall be examined periodically by a competent authority and certified to be physically be competent fit and free from infections with the organisms of typhoid, paractyphoid fever or other communicable diseases. All persons working in the milk plant shall wear clean garments preferably white suits and caps, and strictly adhere to rule of personal hygiene.

4. Raw Milk

4.1 Chemical Requirements for milk-milk shall satisfy the standards prescribed for the corresponding raw milk under the prevention of Food Adulteration Rules, 1955.

4.2 Bacteriological Requirements:- As far as possible raw milk with methylene blue reduction time of not less than one hour in summer and not less than two hours in winter should be accepted for pasteurization.

5. Pasteurization

5.1 The pasteurization of milk shall be performed according to the procedure specified under 2.3. The pasteurizing vat or pasteurizer shall be equipped with accurate temperature indicating and recording devices. High temperature short time plants shall should be provided with automatic flow diversion valve.

6. Hygienic Requirements:-

6.1 The pasteurized milk in dairy plant shall conform to the requirements.

7. Bottling and packing:-

7.1 Bottling, capping of bottles and packaging of pasteurized milk shall be done in standard equipment. The caps shall be made of aluminium foil.

7.2 Bottles shall be of standard quality (See IS:1392-1971) and shall be cleaned and sterilized in standard equipment using standard procedure.

8. Marking

8.1 The following information (full or abbreviated) shall be marked legibly on the container;

a) Pasteurized milk,

b) Cow/buffalo/standardized/skimmed/tonned/double toned milk,

c) Name and address of the plant,

d) Date of manufacture, and

e) Net content.

9. Sampling

9.1 Representive samples of pasteurized milk for testing conformity to this code shall be drawn as described in Appendix F of IS: 4238-1967.

10. Tests

10.1 The tests shall be carried out as prescribed in appropriate clauses of Indian Standards given in Table-1.

10.2 Quality of Reagents:- Unless specified otherwise, pure chemicals and distilled water (See IS:1070-1977 shall be used).

Flavouring Essence

Strawberry Essence:-

Straw berries, fresh	-	16 ounces,
Angelica (california)	-	6 fluid ounces
Brandy (california)	-	6 ounces
Alcohol	-	8 ounces
Water	-	Q.S.

Mash the berries to a pulp in a mortar or bowl, and transfer to a flask, along with the Angelica, brandy, alcohol and about 8 ounces of water, let macerate over night then distil off until 32 ounces have passed over. Colour strawberry red. The addition of a little essence of vanilla and a pint of lemon improves this essence.

Vanilla Essence

Vanilla beans chopped fine	-	30 parts
Potassium Carbonate	-	1 parts
Boiling water	-	1,450 parts
Alcohol	-	450 parts
Essence of musk	-	1 part

Dissolve the potassium carbonate in the boiling water, add the vanilla, cover the vessel, and let stand in a moderately warn place until cold. Transfer to a wide mouthed Jar, add the Alcohol, Cork, and let macerate for 15 days; than decant the clear essence and filter the remainder. Mix the two liquid and add the essence of musk.

PROCESS OF MANUFACTURE

Treatment Before pasteurization:-

Adequate storage capacity for raw milk is necessary for efficient operation of a plant. Many plants hold the current days receipts in storage tank at 40°F or below, so that once the next days operation has been started no shot downs will be necessary. Delays during the pasteurization process result in bum on of milk in contact with heating surfaces, as well as waste of labour, heat-and refrigeration.

The process steps usually taken before pasteurization are:-

1. Filtering or clarifying,
2. Separating,
3. Standarizing,
4. Vitaminizing,
5. Homogenizing.

PLANT ECONOMICS

LAND & BUILDING (Land area 500 sq. mts.) = Rs. 6,25,000.00

PLANT & MACHINERY

1. Milk processing unit complete with cream extraction machines, pasturization unit, cooling unit etc.
2. Packing unit, complete with filling machine, sealing machine etc.
3. Milk storage tank
4. Other miscellaneous

FIXED CAPITAL

1.	Land & Building	Rs.	6,25,000.00
2.	Plant & Machinery	Rs.	13,12,000.00
3.	Other Fixed Assets	Rs.	83,000.00
	TOTAL	Rs.	20,20,000.00

RAW MATERIALS

1. Raw Milk
2. Flavouring saffron, cashewnut (four pieces), pista, Almonds, Elachi etc.
3. Empty Bottles
4. Miscellaneous

TOTAL WORKING CAPITAL/MONTH

1.	Raw Material	Rs.	46,11,000.00
2.	Salary & Wages	Rs.	52,750.00
3.	Utilities & Overheads	Rs.	41,000.00
	TOTAL	Rs.	47,04,750.00

TOTAL CAPITAL INVESTMENT

Total Fixed Capital	Rs.	20,20,000.00
Total Working Capital for 2 Monhs	Rs.	94,09,500.00
TOTAL	Rs.	1,14,29,500.00

TURN OVER/ANNUM

1. By sale of flavoured milk, 1500 Ton (75,00,000 Bottles of 200 ml each)
2. By sale of 80,000 kgs. of Ghee

TOTAL Rs. 6,21,00,000.00

PROFIT SALES RATIO = Profit / Sales x 100 = 4.43 %

RATE OF RETURN = Operating profit / T.C.I x 100 = 24.07 %

BREAK EVEN POINT (B.E.P) = 54.84 %

Chapter 29

DAIRY FARM TO PRODUCE MILK

There are different kinds of milk obtained from different animals, like cows, buffalow, goat, camel and many others. But generally we use goat milk, cow milk, and buffalow milk. The following gives analysis of milk from goat and cow.

INGREDIENTS	COW MILK	GOAT MILK
Water	87.40	87.54
Solids	0.75	0.85
Casein	3.00	3.00
Albumen	0.40	1.00
Fats	3.75	4.50
Sugar	4.70	4.50

People with very low vitality have to live on milk products for some times, with fruit to supplement, it. In some foreign countries, milk obtained from animals like vama selue Hippopotamies, Gluens, pig and Blue whole etc. is used.

CATTLE FEED

The success of the development project depends largely on the availability of well - balanced feed in respect of carbohydrates, proteins vitamins & minerals. Therefore the need for balanced cattle feed as an addition to the green fodder & hay for the general improvement of the cattle health forms an essential part of the intensive cattle development programme.

In general practice the following coposition is followed for cattle feed.

Groundnut Cake	25%
Wheat bran	27%
Grain Husk	15%
Maize	30%
Mineral	1%
salt	2%

Some more formulations are as folows: -

A.	Wheat or rice bran	55%
	Soya Bean or Groundnut cake	35%
	Molasses	8%
	Mineral Supplement	2%
B.	Wheat or rice bran	26%
	Coconut	65%
	Molasses	8%
	Mineral Supplement	2%
C.	Citrus Pulp	27%
	Coconut Cake	63%
	Molasses	8%
	Mineral Supple	2%

MANUFACTURING PROCESS

The manufacturing process for Dairy milk is started with the milking cows by hand (at small scale) & milking cows by machine (at large scale).

The detailed process is given here with :-

MILKING COWS BY HAND

The profitable operation of a dairy herd depends in a large part upon how well you milk your cows. You can do everything else carefully and well, but if you do not milk your cows properly, you can never be successful in dairying. Poor milking habits cause low production, mastitis, & poor quality milk. An important part of milking cows is to produce the cleanest possible milk. Milk must be low in sediment.

Although machine milking is rapidly replacing hand milking, many dairymen still use the latter. In milking by hand, cows must be carefully prepared to produce high quality milk.

COOLING & STORING MILK

The careless handling of milk between milking & delivering to the plant can cause high bacteria counts to develop in the milk thus a mechanical cooler is employed for the purpose. Whole of the milk should be stored at 50°F to prevent spoilage. Storage Tanks made of stainless steel are employed for storing the raw milk.

FILTERATION :

The cold raw milk is filtered, however, it can be filtered before cooling & storing in tank, but the precaution is to be taken at this stage so that no foreign matters or undesired materials may be carried on.

HOMOGENIZATION:

Filtered milk is fed into homogeniser. Homogenization is the process by which the milk is emulsified and are further divided to produce a more stable emulsion that will not separate on standing. The fat is emulsified with liquid part of milk that are water mostly. Hence, to prevent sedimentation of fat in milk. This homogenization process is done. By this way high quality homogenized milk is produced.

After feeding the milk into homogenizer, the pressure of the homogenizer is increased about 2500 psi. However, if this pressure does not produce milk that meets the standard, it may be necessary to use a pressure as high as 3000 to 3500 Lb.

CLARIFICATION:

The milk is passed through a clarifier as it leaves the homogenizer. Cold milk clarification is preferred to hot milk. This clarification operation can be perform before homogenization. But the complete clarification can be achieved at this stage.

Clarifier can be replaced by cream separator but since the separator bowl is not designed to hold a large amount of sediment and consequently is not efficient for clarifying a large volume of milk. However, This operation can be omitted to get high quality milk.

PASTEURIZATION:-

In this process, the clarified milk is fed to pasteurizer and heated to the required temperature and held there during the holding period (usually at 145°F & for at least 30 minutes). Vat pasteurizer with jackets & agitators is employed for the pasteurization.

The milk is heated by hot water or steam passing into the space between the two tanks. In this process, excessive heating of any part of the milk and a consequent "cooked" flavour is prevented.

At the end of the holding period, the cold water is circulated through the jacket or coil of the pasteurizer, Temperature of the milk may be quickly lowered 10° to 15°, & at this point the heated flavour will not continue to develop. This is done to destroy all pathogenic bacteria.

REFRIGERATION OR FREEZING SYSTEM

After the complete processing of milk it is to be stored in a cold upto chilling condition so that no unwanted micro-organisms/pathogenic organism can be developed in the processed milk. It is stored until delivered for distribution i.e. for packing in cans or pouches.

TESTING:-

The testing of milk is an essential for the quality control purposes. However, testing may be done prior to storage under freezing condition. But it is better to test the final product before packing. When product is cleared from testing or quality control section then it is ready for packing & distribution and sent to packing section.

PACKING:-

There are two methods adopted from packing milk. Firstly packed or stored in aluminium milk cans for distribution. Secondly, milk packed in plastic pouches of capacity 1/2 kg, 1 kg, & 2 kgs packs.

Milk is stored in milk cans. There will no difficulty. It is traditional. But, in pouches filling of milk is to be performed with a great care and skilled operator is to be employed for this purpose. Automatic pouch making, milk filling & pouch sealing machine is available with printing provision.

Milk filled & sealed in pouches is now ready for despatch and distribution for marketing.

PLANT ECONOMICS

Rated Plant Capacity	=	700.00 LTS/Day
LAND & BUILDING (Land 1 Acre)	=	Rs. 27,87,500.00

PLANT & MACHINERY

1. Steam Boiler
2. Homogenizer
3. Refrigeration
4. Pasteurizer with cooling arrangement
5. Filter (ordinary)
6. Pouch making, filling and sealing Machine complete automatic with printing
7. Milk reception tank (stainless steel make)
8. Milk can (aluminium)
9. Dies
10. Misc. other equipments such as laboratory and testing equipment

FIXED CAPITAL

1.	Land & Building	Rs.	27,87,500.00
2.	Plant & Machinery	Rs.	5,12,500.00
3.	Other Fixed Assets	Rs.	10,60,000.00
	TOTAL	Rs.	43,60,000.00

RAW MATERIALS

1. Raw material for cattle feed.
   Green Fodder/cattle feed
2. Health expenses
3. Raw material for pouch polythene sheet

TOTAL WORKING CAPITAL/MONTH

1.	Raw Materials	Rs.	57,187.50
2.	Salary & Wages	Rs.	28,560.00
3.	Utilities & Overheads	Rs.	32,000.00
	TOTAL	Rs.	1,17,747.50

TOTAL CAPITAL INVESTMENT

Total Fixed Capital	Rs.	43,60,000.00
Total Working Capital for 2 Months	Rs.	2,35,495.00
TOTAL	Rs.	45,95,495.00

TURN OVER/ANNUM

By sale of 252000 litres milk (Homogenized and pasteurized)	Rs.	37,80,000.00

PROFIT SALES RATIO = Profit / Sales x 100 = 40.10 %

RATE OF RETURN = Operating profit / T.C.I x 100 = 32.98 %

BREAK EVEN POINT (B.E.P) = 42.97 %

Chapter 30

ICE CREAM & ICE - CANDY

Ice - Cream is a frozen dairy product food product made by freezing a pasteurized mix with agitation to incorporate air and insure uniformity of consistency. The mix is composed of a combination of milk products, sugar, dextrose corn syrup in dry or liquid form, water or other optional ingredients, with or without eggs or eggs products with harmless flavoring and with or without added stabilizer or emulsifier and all of wholesome edible material.

Ice - candy is the hardened ice cream without emulsifier. In ancient times, sugar must have been a highly valued consumption item. Therefore, there was no candy that used sugar as liberally as we do in the present age. But a complete change occurred in the picture. Anyone can now enjoy the sweet state of candy. Today, there is a great varieties of candies, which meet the desires of children.

Ice - cream must have evolved from Ice beverages and water ices that were popular in the early medical period. Wires & fruits juices were cooled with ice and show brought from mountains by runners to the court of New, Emperor of Rome in the first century. Early plants were established in western countries in cities like New York, Chicago.

FORMULATIONS

CANDY PRODUCTS AND CONFECTIONERY CHOCOLATE

PEANUT BARS

Sugar	3 Lb.
Corn Syrup	3 Lb.
Water	1 Pt.

Cook to 240°F. Then cold and pours of washed peanuts and cook for 10 minutes. Remake from fire and in chocolate.

Fruit Jelly Candies

Fruit Juice	2 qt.
Sugar	3 Lb.
Corn Syrup of Invert Syrup	3 Lb.
Commercial Pectin Syrup	1 qt.

Mix fruit juice and pectin syrup. Add the sugar and corn, or invert, syrup. Boil to 222-223°F Remove from fire. Put into starch molds or oiled pans, about 1/2 inch deep. Allow to burden 24 hours. Remove from molds and dust with powdered sugar or dip in chocolate.

Sugar Coating for Candy

Cocoa Butter Substitute	35 lb.
Powdered Skin milk	15 lb.
Powdered Sugar	50 lb.
Salt	2 oz.
Vanillin	1/2 oz.

This may be coloured and flavored with oil soluble colors. After melting the cocoa butter substitute, add the other materials gradually in a dough mixer and finally run over finishing rolls at a temperature of 110°F. In using, run an enrober at 104°F.

French Chewing Candy

Mixture No. I

Corn Syrup	25 lb.
Albumen - Dissolved in	3 lb.
Nulomoline	25 lb.
Water	6 lb.

Boil the corn syrup to 245°F. Add the Nulomoline and stir until it is melted. Place the batch into a heater. Start the beater. Then gradually add the aqueous albumen solution and heat until light.

Mixture No. 2

Sugar	30 lb.
Cream (20% butter fat)	10 lb.
Numbomoline	5 lb.
Coconut Oil (76°F m.p.)	7 lb.
Corn Syrup	25 lb.

Ice-Cream Preparation

Albumen	10 oz.
Sugar	80 oz.
Whole dried milk	10 oz.

Indian Gum	5 oz.
Vanillin	1.5 oz.

Or

Dried Milk	50 oz.
Sugar	50 oz.
Cream of Tartar	4.4 oz.
Sodium	2 oz.
Vanillin	0.06 oz.

Chocolate Ice Cream

Milk	32 oz.
Sugar	16 oz.
Flour	2 oz.
Salt	1/8 oz.
Eggs	4 oz.
Cream	32 oz.
Vanillin	1/4 oz.
Unsweatened	5 oz.

MANUFACTURING PROCESS

PREPARATION OF THE MIX

A very important process involved in the manufacture of ice cream is preparing the mix. Preparing the mix involves, assembling the ingredients from storage area to the preparation zone, weighing or metering and mixing ingredients and the pasteurization, homogenization, cooling and storage of the mix.

According to the recent studies on ice cream manufacturing plant methods, equipment, and layout it is found that four methods are in for processing mix.

1) The bulk ingredients and continuous high temperature short time pasteurization.

2) Ingredients in cans and high temperature short time pasteurization

3) Bulk in gradients and batch pasteurization.

4) Ingredients in cans and batch pasteurization

The lowest cost method for preparing mix is the can and batch pasteurization method due to the low cost of requirement involved.

ORDER OF ADDING INGREDIENTS

All liquid ingredients (cream, milk, condensed milk, syrup etc.) are placed in the vat and the agitation and heating shorted at once. the dry ingredients including MSNF, dried eggs, cocoa, sugar, and stabilizer are added while the liquid material is agitated and before the temp. reaches 120°F. It gelatin is the stabilizer used, it is best to and it after it is thoroughly mixed with an equal volume of sugar and before the liquid reaches 120oF. When butter plastic cream, frozen cream are added they should be cut into fairly small pieces and added in time to allow complete melting before the pasteurizing temp. is reached.

PASTEURIZATION OF MIX

Pasteurization of all mixes is compulsory because this process destroys all pathogenic or decease producing bacteria, thereby safe guarding the health of the consumer. Pasteurization requires only slight additional expense, since the mix is usually heated to facilitate solution, and since the homogenization process can be accomplished best at the pasteurization temperature level.

Proper pasteurization consists in rapidly heating to a definite temperature, holding at that temp. for a definite minimum of time, and then rapidly cooling to below 40°F.

Reasons for high temperature pasteurization result in (1) Greater bacterial kill resulting in lower bacterial count in ice cream (2) Suitable temperature and time of pasteurization result in (a) Better body and texture

(b) Better flavour.
(c) Protection against
(d) Saving of stabilizer
(e) Increased capacity

For maximum benefits the mix probably should be processed at 210° - 220°F.

HOMOGENIZING OF THE MIX

Homogenization is usually accomplished by forcing the mix thro's small crifice under suitable conditions of temperature and pressure, using a positive displacement plunger pump to furnish the pressure. The orifice consists of a value and seat in which the two adacent surfaces are parallel and lapped smooth and is surrounded by an impact ring against which the mix impringes as it leaves the valve. The break up of fat particles is caused by the shear forces set up in a thin stream of mix traveling at high velocity between the closely adjacent surfaces of the value and seat and then by a sheltering effect as it imprages on the impact ring upon leaving the valve.

COOLING THE MIX

Cooling the mix immediately after homogenization to 32° - 40°F is essential after which it should be held in aging tanks until used, unless the mix is cooled to a temperature of 40°F or lower it will become very viscous and the ice cream will not melt down smoothly. Also temp. below 40°F retard the growth of bacteria coolers of the surface or cabinet types are generally used for ice cream mix.

AGING THE MIX

Experimental work shows that appreciable benefits result from an aging period although little is gained by aging longer than 4 hr.

Aging mix before freezing has been practical since the in addition of the ice cream industry. The changes which undoubtly occur during aging are (1) The fat is solidified (2) If gelatin has been used as a stabilizer it swells and combines with Water (3) The proteins of the mix may change slightly.

(4) The viscosity is increased, largely due to the previously mentioned changes. The aging temp. should not exceed 40°F. When the mix has been properly aged, it is ready for the freezing process which generally follows immediately.

THE FREEZING PROCESS

Freezing the mix is one of the most important operations in the making of ice-cream for upon it depends the quality, palatability and yield of the final product.

ICE CREAM PREPARATION (FREEZE IT)

Albumen	10 oz.
Sugar	80 oz.
Whole Dried Milk	10 oz.
Indian Gum	5 oz.
Vanillin	1.5 oz.
Dried Milk	50 oz.
Sugar	50 oz.
Cream of Tartar	4.4 oz.
Sodium	2 oz.
Vanillin	0.06 oz.

Package 4.5 ounces = 127.5 grams.

Stir contents of the package into 1/2 pint. (one cup) cold milk. Stir until dissolved. Whip 1/2 pint (one cup) chilled whipping cream. Add the dissolved freeze. It to the whipped cream and mix freeze.

Chocolate Ice Cream

Milk	32 oz.
Sugar	16 oz.
Flour	2 oz.
Salt	1/8 oz.

Eggs	4 oz.
Cream	32 oz.
Vanillin	1/4 oz.
Unsweatened	4 oz.

CHOCOLATE

Eat milk and add flour, salt the sugar. Stir thoroughly in double boiler for 20 minutes after batches brought to a boil. After the mass thickness add the beaten eggs and cook for 5 minutes longer with content stirring. Cool, add cream which has been whipped into a stiff paste and then add the flavouring add the melted chocolate which was previously mixed with a little sugar and warm milk to form a paste. Put in a refrigerator or pack in ice and salt until frozen.

PROCESS DESCRIPTION

The process here describes is roughly divided into two units, namely are to concentrate the material and the other to form hard candies. The former consists of an automatic dissolving machine, receiving tank, automatic vacuum concentrator, cooling table, kneeling machine and hot table, while the latter requires machines described in the latter half beginning from the batch roller, of the plant layout.

The process of the vacuum concentrator unit is to evaporate material under low temperature with reduced pressure. How to carry this process and what machines should be used for this process are very important factors because they decide the taste and colouring of the final product.

Vacuum concentrators widely employed now in Japan are highly automated to make the processing time as short as possible. The candy materials taken out of the concentrators are then mixed with various additives, spius or unique flavours according to the desires of candy makers. The mixing process requires sufficient kneading to obtain excellent products.

After kneading is sufficiently carried out, the candy is drawn in rope shape of determined newsier by the batch roller (set with sizing roller). The machine employed in this plant is designed to make a drawing of 50 m of rope per minute.

The drawn candy is then put into the hard candy forming unit. Where candies are made, formed by the plastic forming machine.

The forming machine will not a only perform at high speed but also, provided with a number of die permit various kinds of forming.

The formed candies are finally cooled down to normal temperatures and charged to the packaging machine. The process for cooling down is carried out by a cooling conveyer, where it is also possible to check and adjust ill formed candies.

PLANT ECONOMICS

Rated Plant capacity	=	500.00 LIT/Day
LAND & BUILDING (Land 400 sq.mt.)	Rs.	3,30,000.00

PLANT & MACHINERY

1. Milk Storage S.S. Tank
2. Freon compressor
3. Brine tanks
4. Homogenizer (Churner)
5. Blending tank
6. Lab. Equipment
7. Baby Boiler
8. Mis. Equipments & Accessories

FIXED CAPITAL

1.	LAND & BUILDING	Rs.	3,30,000.00
2.	PLANT & MACHINERY	Rs.	2,24,500.00
	TOTAL	Rs.	5,54,500.00

RAW MATERIALS

1. Fresh Milk
2. Fat Cream
3. Sugar
4. Stabilizer, colour essences, Chemicals dry fruits
5. Containers
   Big Cup
6. Small Cup
7. Stocks for bar
8. Ice blocks for trolleys

TOTAL WORKING CAPITAL/MONTH

1.	Raw Material	Rs.	3,05,625.00
2.	Salary & Wages	Rs.	26,040.00
3.	Utilities & Overheads	Rs.	45,000.00
	TOTAL	Rs.	3,76,665.00

TOTAL CAPITAL INVESTMENT

Total Fixed Capital	Rs.	5,54,500.00
Total Working Capital for 2 Months	Rs.	7,53,330.00
TOTAL	Rs.	13,07,830.00

TURN OVER/ANNUM

1. By sale of Big cup 6,00,000
2. Small Cup 9,00,000
3. Ice Cream bars 4,50,000
4. Ice Candy bar 4,50,000

TOTAL	Rs.	74,25,000.00

PROFIT SALES RATIO = Profit / Sales x 100 = 35.24 %

RATE OF RETURN = Operating profit / T.C.I x 100 = 200.09 %

BREAK EVEN POINT (B.E.P) = 19.38 %

Chapter 31

PROCESSED CHEESE

Cheese is the product made from the curd obtained from whole or skimmed milk, with or without added cream, by coagulating the casein and further treatment, of the separated curd by ripening ferments, special molds or seasoning. Cheese has not been the popular item of food in India mainly because animal rennet is used in the its preparation. Preparation such as surti paneer, bandal and Ducca Cheese, which are popular in certain parts are allied to cheese.

Composition of Cheese

The composition of cheese depends upon the variety. All cheese contain the same constituents of milk but in varying proportions. The most variable constituents are fat and water.

MANUFACTURING PROCESS

Cheese is a often made from milk which has been subjected some heat treatment but not enough to qualify pasteurised milk as measured by the phosphate test. Temperatures from 145-150°C and an exposure time of a about 15 seconds may be used. This heat exposure destrous many bacterial capable of causing difficulty in cheese making and ripening. The treatment is not enough to destroy all the enzymes of milk and some bacterial of value in cheese ripening probably sourning. Cheese made from milk heated in this fashion develops more flavour than does cheese made from pasteurized milk such cheese must be egged for 60 days before sale unless it is to be used for manufacturing purposes, when it will be given an additional heat treatment. Cheese made from pasteurised milk may be solid at any time after its manufacture.

Curd Formation

A characteristic of all cheese making is the formation of a cured or the coagulation of the milk coagulation is brought about by means of the action of lactic acid produced by fermentation, by the action of rennet or pepsin or by a combination of lactic acid and rennet.

In either case, it is the casein of milk which is congealed to form the cured. Casein is coagulated readily by acids, and by enzymes, such as rennet and pepsins. The chemical changes involved in the case of acids coagulation of and enzymes coagulations and distinctly different. When milk is coagulated by lactic acid, the calcium of calcium casenate probably units with the lactic acid to form calcium lactate. The casein is bet free and from a firm"gel" or cured. This change in milk is brought about by other acids.

The rate of rennet coagulation is influenced by several factors, such as the temperature and the acidity of the milk. In the case of the hard variety of cheese, sufficient rennet in added to the milk to bring about a complete coagulation is 15 to 20 minutes. After adding and mixing, rennet to milk the fist signs of coagulation may be observes in 8 to 10 minutes. It will be observed that there is slight thickening of the milk, flocculant cured particles will become visible to the age, and finally, the casein will form a firm gel.

When the coagulation is dependent upon the action of lactic acid produced by the bacterial fermentation of lactose, form 5 to 16 hours, may be required before sufficient acid is produced to bring about coagulation. After comlete coagulation when is separated by passing coagulated milk through press when cheese being formed a rectangular block. Now these cheese will pass through fitting machine and packing machine. Then Packaged cheese is kept at 10°C for 6 months for ripening . Then it is marketed.

PLANT ECONOMICS

Rated Plant capacity = 290.00 KGS/Day

PROCESSED CHEESE 220 KGS/DAY

CREAM 70 KGS/DAY

LAND & BUILDING (Land 500 sq. mtrs.) Rs. 10,30,000.00

PLANT & MACHINERY

1. Cheese Vat (Jacketed)
3. Cream Separator
4. Milk Cans
5. Cheese cutting table
6. Cheese knives
7. Cheese Hoops
8. Cheese Press
9. Cheese Grinder
10. Ghee kettle
11. Weighing balance platform type
12. Weighing balance,

13. Deep freezer large vertical, multidoor
14. S.S. Pump
15. Bulk Cooler
16. Plastic Vats
17. Centrifuge for fat test
    (both electrically/manually tested)
18. Boiler
19. Cheese filling and packaging Machine
    automatic type.
20. Processed cheese kettle
21. Pipe fittings, Pumps, valves and other

FIXED CAPITAL

1.	LAND & BUILDING	Rs.	10,30,000.00
2.	PLANT & MACHINERY	Rs.	10,21,500.00
3.	OTHER FIXED ASSETS	Rs.	2,00,000.00
	TOTAL	Rs.	22,51,500.00

RAW MATERIALS

1. Milk
2. Starter
3. Colour, salt etc.
4. Packaging material with labels

TOTAL WORKING CAPITAL/MONTH

1.	Raw Material	Rs.	5,06,250.00
2.	Salary & Wages	Rs.	47,125.00
3.	Utilities & Overheads	Rs.	22,750.00
	TOTAL	Rs.	5,76,125.00

TOTAL CAPITAL INVESTMENT

Total Fixed Capital	Rs.	22,51,500.00
Total Working Capital for 2 Months	Rs.	11,52,250.00
TOTAL	Rs.	34,03,750.00

TURN OVER/ANNUM

1. By sale of 90000 Packs of 400 gms each Processed cheese
2. By sale of 1,50,000 Packs of 200 gms each of processed cheese
3. By sale of 21000 kgs of cream

TOTAL	Rs.	1,05,00,000.00

PROFIT SALES RATIO = Profit / Sales x 100 = 24.67 %

RATE OF RETURN = Operating profit / T.C.I x 100 = 76.11 %

BREAK EVEN POINT (B.E.P) = 33.95 %

Chapter 32

MILK POWDER & GHEE

Milk Powder is the milk that has been dried or desiccated. This is usually done by heating the milk. The final product contains less than three percent water. Milk powder can be prepared from whole milk. Milk from which fat has been partially removed, or from skim milk.

There are a number of advantages in converting milk into milk powder. Milk contains eighty-seven percent water and because of this it gets spoilt quickly. It also needs special and bulky containers for transport. On the other hand, milk-powder takes up only one-eight of the space of the original milk. Besides, milk in powder form can keep for a long period as much as six to eight months under tropical conditions.

There are three main types of plant for producing milk powder or dried milk.

i) Roller driers
ii) Spray driers
iii) Vacuum roller driers.

PROPERTY OF MILK POWDER

The most of important practical property of milk powder is its "solubility", which is measured by the proportion which can be reconstituted into solution or colidal suspension in water. Spray powder usually gives figures of about 99 percent, while roller powders give figures of about 90 percent. It should be noted, however, that the solubility of a powder may be increased considerably neutralization of the milk, since the excess sodium irons bring more protein and phosphate into solution.

Milk for spray powder is not commonly neutralized, but for roller powder milk is frequently neutralized down to a lactic and acidity of 0.12 percent or even less. When considering solubility figures of powders, therefore, consideration must be given to

i) The method of testing

ii) The degree of neutralization

Unfortunately there is no official method of measuring solubility, and slight differences in technique can easily lead to considerable differences in results.

It is often difficult to get agreement between laboratories for this reason.

The amount and nature of the sediment when the two types of powder are reconstituted are highly characteristic and together with the odour and taste usually enable the reconstituted milk to to readily identified.

In concentrates of 50 percent, total solids ageing and crystallisation of the lactose may result in from 10 to 90 percent. If fat becoming free on foam drying (extractable) by carbon tetrachloride). This excess can be prevented by heating the concentrate immediately before drying, a free fat value of less than 10 percent, being possible. Free fat can be decreased by increasing homogenisation pressure, and it increases with decreased powder particle size. Dispersibility is slightly decrease by increasing free fat.

The properties of the dry milk are due largely to the constituents of the milk from which it is made.

COMPOSITION OF MILK-POWDER

The average composition of milk powders:-

	Whole Milk powder percent	**Skim Milk** powder percent
Water	3.5	3.5
Fat	26.5	1.0
Protein	25.5	52.0
Ash	6.0	8.0

PROCESS OF MANUFACTURE OF MILK POWDER

There are mainly two process:

i) Roller drying

ii) Spray drying

Although Roller drying is widely preferred:-

ROLLER DRYING:-

The basic type is the just-Hatmaker, and consists of two steam heated rollers about 5 feet long by 2- 1/2 feet in diameter. They have a clearance of about 0.02 inch. Which may vary according to the conditions of processing.

ii) Spray Drying:

This method consists essentially in directing a spray of hot, precondensed milk into a current of hot air. There are three main types:-

i) Simple spray
ii) Revolving sprinklers
iii) Revolving disc.

Spray drying plant much bulkier than roller drying for given output, and spray powder costs more to produce. The product is, however, so much better, that it can only be a matter of time before nearly all milk powder is produced by the spray process. The confectionery and other industries will doubtless continue to accept roller powder.

The stages in spray drying are essentially the following :

i) Reception

ii) Clarification or filtration

iii) Cooling

iv) Storage

v) Preheating (160° to 190°F)

vi) Precondensing at about 110°F to about 42 percent total sides.

vii) Atomising in chamber, hot air entering at about 330° and leaning at about 200°F.

viii) Separation of powder

ix) Packing

MANUFACTURING PROCESS OF GHEE

Butter (unsalted) is dumped in the butter melter, which is a vertical jacketed stainless steel cylindrical tank fitted with an agitator (provided with reduction gear to work on variable speeds). If the butter is very cold and hard, it should be cut into small pieces before heating. Then a steam inlet to the jacket is opened and the agitator run at low speed.

The tipping tank, which is jacketed at the bottom, is filled with clean water and heated to 77-79°C (170 - 174°F) by opening the steam inlet of the jacket. The centrifugal oil separator is then started and when it has attained full speed, the hot water from the tipping tank is run into it. When the water has completely run out, the discharge valve of the butter melter is gradually opened to allow the melt to enter into the oil separator. The rate of the flow of the melt is so regulated as to avoid overflow. The melt is now separated into oil and serum.

The oil flows into the float-controlled balance tank and thence into the vacuum pan due to suction. Here it is dehydrated at 56-63°C (133-145°F) under a vacuum of 57-62 cm. of mercury. At the end of the operation, the vaccum is broken and butteroil allowed to flow by gravity into the receiving kettle for subsequent cooling, packaging and storage at room temperature.

PLANT ECONOMICS

Rated Plant capacity	=125000.00 KGS./Day
LAND & BUILDING (Land Area 4 Acre)	Rs. 1,26,25,000.00

PLANT & MACHINERY

1. Storage Tanks
2. Feed Pump with motor
3. Preheater, Jacketted Type with all accessories
4. Plate heat exchanger with all accessories
5. Spray Drier with atomizer & complete accessories
6. Cream Separator
7. Boiler
8. Chilling Plant
9. Milk Powder filling/Sealing unit (Automatic)
10. Cream Heating tank with jacket System
11. Pouch weighing filling sealing Machine for Ghee packing
12. Pumps, Valves, Pipe Lines & other tanks, water pumps etc.
13. Laboratory Testing Equipment
14. D.G. Set

FIXED CAPITAL

1.	LAND & BUILDING	Rs. 1,26,25,000.00
2.	PLANT & MACHINERY	Rs. 1,37,80,000.00
3.	OTHER FIXED ASSETS	Rs. 47,75,000.00
	TOTAL	Rs. 3,11,80,000.00

RAW MATERIALS

1. Milk
2. Citric Acid
3. Magnesium Oxide
4. Misc. Chemicals, NaCl, $CaCo_3$ etc.
5. Tin Containers
6. Pouches for Ghee & Milk

TOTAL WORKING CAPITAL/MONTH

1. RAW MATERIAL	Rs.	4,56,45,375.00
2. SALARY & WAGES	Rs.	7,13,900.00
3. UTILITIES & OVERHEADS	Rs.	4,65,000.00
TOTAL	Rs.	4,68,24,275.00

TOTAL CAPITAL INVESTMENT

Total Fixed Assets	Rs.	3,11,80,000.00
Total Working Capital for 1 Month	Rs.	4,68,24,275.00
TOTAL	Rs.	7,80,04,275.00

TURN OVER/ANNUM

1. By Sale of 1500000 Kgs. of Skimmed Milk Powder
2. By Sale of Ghee 2250000 Kgs.
3. By Sale of Milk 8125000 Lts.

TOTAL Rs. 61,37,50,000.00

PROFIT SALES RATIO = Profit / Sales x 100 = 6.15 %

RATE OF RETURN = Operating profit / T.C.I x 100 = 48.41 %

BREAK EVEN POINT (B.E.P) = 34.34 %

Chapter 33

SOYA MILK AND PANEER

Soyabeans are very much popular as food crop in most of the countries all over the world where a large number of food products are prepared from soyabean seeds. As edible oil milk and milk products giving sources crop the soyabeans are getting wide acceptance. In India too since last few decades. Soyabean seeds have a high nutritional composition; and can be converted in to various states, tastes, colours, flavours and other quality substances.

As far as the use of soyabean is concerned it has taken a place from soap industry to food industries like. The soya milk, in particular has been developed like a boon for human beings as large. The speciality lies in the fact that in the reasons when traditional cow milk buffalo milk is not available in sufficient quantity, this milk serves the purpose almost equitably to other animal milk type.

PROCESS OF MANUFACTURE

Soyamilk has a good storage stability. Pasteurized soyamilk could be stored for about one week at 5°C. The milk could be stored in bottles, plastic sachets or in bulk containers.

Basic raw material for processing of soyamilk is soyabean.

From 1 Kilogram of good quality soyabean about 10 litres of soyamilk is produced.

Soyabean is air dried and spread on floor for picking up stove pieces, debars, and other unwanted material. The prepared soyabean is then fed to Dalralaing, Machine. The shell mixed Dal is separated for Dal & husk. The Dal is further removed of contaminated shell be air blanching method. The soyabean Dal is now put to a blancher for steam heating where the dal is sufficiently cooked for 2-3 hours. It should not be overcooked. The cooked Dal is removed from the blancher and fed to a nut grinder and ground very fin. The ground soyabean is diluted to desired milk consistency. The milk is stirred & mixed in a storage can. It in this diverted to homogenizer. After it is homogenised it is diverted to be pasteurized where it is subjected to steam heating as will as ice cooling in succession. After it is pastwrind the material is stored in milk tanks. Flavour & sweating agents are also mixed as required & suitably homogenised.

The soyamilk is paced in suitable containers & sent to cold room for storage.

PREPARATION OF PANEER

Attempts have been made to prepare paneer from blended soya milk with mixed milk. Soyamilk is prepared form 'Hardea' variety of soya seeds by the illinois process. The milk standardized to 3.5% fat blended with soy milk and modified milk at 10% 15% and 35% soyasolid levels is used.

Citric acid is used as a coagulatic. Paneer prepared from modified milk having 20% milk soya it found acceptable. In the form of raw paneer, the product is soft compared to lower levels of soy solids.

MOISTURE:-

The ordinary moisture determination, by drying to constant weight at 10°C really measure all volatile matters as well as water. Aldehyde, Ketones acids alcohols etc. are the volatile matters which are not measured separately in paneer but as moisture content. Production of soyamilk paneer consists of the following steps:-

Milk Preparations:-

The milk intended to be converted in to paneer is strained through a muslim cloth in a vat. Thoroughly mixed/blended with morning evening collects. The temperature of the milk is raised to 85% by circulating hot water in the vat jacket.

Ripening:-

Milk is then ripened with a suitable starter. The required quantity of a good lacto stirred is strained through a muslin cloth in to the milk and mixed thoroughly.

Renneting:-

The required sennet quantity is diluted in water and mixed thoroughly with the milk.

Setting Time:-

The coagulation time is altered without any more of stirring still the curd is properly precipitated and set.

Whey extraction:-

After whey removed the curd is make at one and of the vat and cut into lumps of convenient and uniform sizes and turned over to facilitate removal of remaining whey as well as imprethe compactness of body and texture. The lumps are placed one above the other till the desired acidity body and texture is obtained.

Milling:-

When the acidity has reached 0.8 to 0.9% and the texture is like the chicken meat, the paneer is ready formilling. Hot iron test should give 3/4 to 1 1/4 length of threads Aeration, salting (if required) and hooping is done hereafter pressing:-

Pressing:-

So prepared paneer is placed under press platens kept horizontal in pain & parallel to each other (Face wise) the pressure is increased gradually. This lot is altered to remain under pressure for a few hours.

Hot bath after taking form the press it is given hot bath at about 140°CF for a few seconds.

There after the paneer is dressed and kept in the churning room at 55°F to 60°F. Here after the paneer can be kept in refrigerator for damp together before it is finally sold to the retailers.

PLANT ECONOMICS

Rated Plant Capacity = 1000 Ton/Year

LAND & BUILDING (Land Area 2000 sq.mts.)Rs. 23,95,000.00

PLANT & MACHINERY

1. SOYA MACHINERY:-
   Wet Grinder
2. Dry Roller Grinder
3. Husk Separator
4. Air blower fan
5. Blancher
6. Homogeniser
7. Pasteuriser
8. 10 M-que Tanks
9. Ice Plant
10. Packing Plant
11. Circulator
12. Lab. equipments & fittings
13. Water softener
14. PANEER:- Storage tank
15. Transfer/transportation cans
16. Cans
17. Double jacketed vat
18. Blending/mixing vessel
19. Coal fired small industrial Boiler
20. Hydraulically operated press
21. Centrifnge
22. Strainers, Hair sieve knives dry & wet bulb thermometer Thermometers, Lactomet. Pans, para. weight Machine

FIXED CAPITAL

1.	LAND & BUILDING	Rs.	23,95,000.00
2.	PLANT & MACHINERY	Rs.	21,43,500.00
3.	OTHER FIXED ASSETS	Rs.	2,25,000.00
	TOTAL	Rs.	47,63,500.00

RAW MATERIALS

1. Soyabean
2. Lactic Acid
3. Salt, Acid and Sugar
4. Coal
5. Lubricating oil, & packaging etc.

TOTAL WORKING CAPITAL/MONTH

1.	RAW MATERIAL	Rs.	7,45,000.00
2.	SALARY & WAGES	Rs.	52,250.00
3.	UTILITIES & OVERHEADS	Rs.	29,750.00
	TOTAL	Rs.	8,27,000.00

TOTAL CAPITAL INVESTMENT

Total Fixed Capital	Rs.	47,63,500.00
Total Working Capital for 2 Months	Rs.	16,54,000.00
TOTAL	Rs.	64,17,500.00

TURN OVER/ANNUM

1. By sale of 600 tons of soyamilk
2. By sale of 400 MT of soyapaneer

TOTAL Rs. 1,50,00,000.00

PROFIT SALES RATIO = Profit / Sales x 100 = 20.21 %

RATE OF RETURN = Operating profit / T.C.I x 100 = 47.24 %

BREAK EVEN POINT (B.E.P) = 44.57 %

Chapter 34

LACTOSE AND BY-PRODUCTS PROCESSING FROM MILK

Properties of Lactose

MOLECULAR FORMULA = $C_{12}H_{22}O_{11}H_2O$

It is white, hard, crystalline mass or white powder. It is sweetness, odorless. It is stable in air. Soluble in water, insoluble in ether and chloroform; very slightly soluble in alcohol. It's specific gravity 1.525. It decomposes at 203.5°C mp. It is nontoxic.

Grades :- Crude, Fermentation, spray dried, edible, U.S.P.

Lactose is the only sugar available commercially that is derived from animal rather than plant sources. It is available in the varying degrees. The fermentation grade is 98 wt.% pure, whereas USP lactose is refined to 99.8 wt.% purity. This not very soluble in water (20 gms/100 gms water at 25°C), nor is it varysweet (less than one third the sweetening power of sucrose). Typically, lactose, which is a reducing sugar, reacts with amines and amino compounds with resultant browning.

The concentration of lactose in milk products ranges from 4.8 wt.% in whole milk to 73.5% in sweet driedwhey.

Lactose (milk sugar) is the only sugar available commercially that is derived from animal rather than plant sources. The concentration of lactose in milk products ranges from 4.8 wt% in whole milk to 73.5 wt% in sweet dried whey, a by products from the manufacture of cheese. Lactose is prepared commercially from whey as the crystalline monohydrate. It is available in varying degrees of purity. The fermentation grade is 98 wt 5 pure, whereas VSP lactose is refined to 99.8 wt% purity. Although the monohydrate is the commercially available form of lactose, the sugar can be crystallised at high temperature to give the B - anhydride.

PROCESS OF MANUFACTURE

First, milk is taken and filtered to remove suspended impurities like straw or anything. Then it is slightly warmed. The milk is then passed through a cream separator cream separated milk is then passed through a plate heat exchanger where the skim milk is pasteurised at 70.6°C in 15 seconds. The present pathogen will be killed at that temperature in plate heat exchanger.

The milk coming out from plate heat exchanger is heated in a vacuum pan evaporator. Where it concentrates. The concentrated milk is now passed through a spray dryer where the removal of moisture takes place leaving behind 3% moisture in the milk powder. The milk powder so manufactured is packed automatically by automatic filling sealing and packaging machine in the can. The product so filled in the can is in nitrogen atmosphere, so that it will remain as usual in the can for longer period.

LACTOSE MANUFACTURING

Production

Generally cheese sweet_ whey or casein (acid) whey(Cheese, Processed Cheese and Whey is used as raw material for production of lactose. Today, permeates from the ultrafiltration of milk or sweet whey are also coming into consideration. With all types of raw materials precaution have to be taken regarding the minerals prest; calcium salts may give rise to deposition in evaporators.

The liquid whey (ca.6.5% dry matter content) is clarified (a) and concentrated in falling film evaporators (b) to 55-65% total solids. Upon cooling (c), the greater part in the lactose crystallizes as lactose monohydrate. The crystal slurry is transferred to a line of decanters and centrifuges and washed several times. Thus, after drying, milling and fractionation, yellowish lactose (edible grade) of different pamele size is obtained.

After the washing stage the raw product can be redissolved(i), treated with activatedcarbon(j) and recrystallized to refiner or pharmaceutical grades of lactose. From 1000 kg liquid whey 32.5 kg lactose and 32.5 kg delactosed wheypowder are obtained.

Environmental Protection : To avoid pollution the dryer should be provided with a cyclone to remove the powder from the exhaust air. Fluid cleaning streams must be purified by simple aerobic or anaerobic digestion before entering a public sewage treatment.

PLANT ECONOMICS

Rated Plant Capacity	=	22.62 MT./day
LACTOSE	=	*1638 MT/ANNUM.*
CASEIN	=	*1638 MT/ANNUM.*
WHEY POWDER	=	*1638 MT/ANNUM.*
GHEE	=	*1872 MT/ANNUM.*
LAND & BUILDING (Land Area 20 Acre)	Rs.	1,50,70,000.00

PLANT & MACHINERY

1. Milk Storage Tank
2. Ordinary Filter
3. Milk Pasteuriser
4. Milk Cream Seperator
5. Cream Storage Tank
6. Refrigeration Systems for Milk Chilling
7. **For Casein** : Acid treatment Tank (S.S)
8. Washing Tank
9. Oscillating Granulator
10. Fluidised bed dryer
11. Micropulveriser
12. Automatic Casein Powder in Pouches
13. Whey Storage Tank
14. Candle filter
15. Falling film Evaporator
16. Crystallisation Tank
17. Dryer
18. Micro-pulveriser
19. Redissolving tank
20. Filter
21. Automatic Sieving machine
22. Automatic Pouch filling Weighing, Sealing machine.
23. Centrifuge
24. Ghee receiving kettle
25. Automatic Pouch Weighing, filling, sealing for Ghee.
26. Water Softener
27. Boiler
28. Pipes, Pumps, Valves, Fittings and
    Other accessories.
29. Laboratory equipment
30. Miscellaneos

FIXED CAPITAL

1.	LAND & BUILDING	Rs.	1,50,70,000.00
2.	PLANT & MACHINERY	Rs.	2,72,60,000.00
3.	OTHER FIXED ASSETS	Rs.	1,06,00,000.00
	TOTAL	Rs.	5,29,30,000.00

RAW MATERIALS

1. Milk
2. Chemical Preservative etc.
3. Hydrochloric Acid
4. Pouches, Tins, Cartons, Labels and other packaging materials.

TOTAL WORKING CAPITAL/MONTH

1.	RAW MATERIAL	Rs.	2,78,72,000.00
2.	SALARY & WAGES	Rs.	3,03,840.00
3.	UTILITIES & OVERHEADS	Rs.	5,03,000.00
	TOTAL	Rs.	2,86,78,840.00

TOTAL CAPITAL INVESTMENT

TOTAL FIXED CAPITAL	Rs.	5,29,30,000.00
TOTAL WORKING CAPITAL FOR 2 MONTHS	Rs.	5,73,57,680.00
TOTAL	Rs.	11,02,87,680.00

TURN OVER/ANNUM

1. By Sale Casein 1638 MT
2. By sale of Lactose 1638 MT
3. By Sale of Whey Powder 1638 MT
4. By Sale of Ghee 1872 MT

TOTAL Rs. 59,20,20,000.00

PROFIT SALES RATIO = Profit / Sales x 100 = 36.49 %

BREAK EVEN POINT (B.E.P) = 14.19 %

Chapter 35

CONDENSED MILK (SWEETENED)

The basic principle in the process of preserving unsweetened condensed milk by heat-sterilization was introduced by John B. Meyenberg, a Swiss, who was an operator in the original plant of the Anglo-Swiss Condensed Milk Co., Switzerland. He migrated to the U.S.A. in 1884, and in the same year was granted a basic patent on his invention of a sterilizer. Later in 1884 and in 1887, he was granted patents on his process of preserving milk. His process patents provided sterilization by steam under pressure at a temperature not exceding 116°C (240°F), while the sealed cans were continuously agitated by the revolving reel.

Definition

Condensed milks are the products obtained by evaporating part of the water of whole milk, or fully or partly skimmed milk, with or without the addition of sugar. The term 'condensed' milk is commonly used when referring to 'full-cream sweetened condensed milk', while the term 'evaporated milk' is commonly used when referring to 'full cream unsweetened condensed milk'. Skimmed milk products are known as 'sweetened condensed skim milk' and 'unsweetened condensed skim milk' respectively. The ratio of concentration of mlik soilds is about 1:2.5 for full-cream products and 1:3 for sweetened condensed skim milk.

SPECIFICATIONS

Definition under the Prevention of Food Adulteration (PFA)

Rules 1955

Condensed Milk Sweetened

It is the product obtained from cow or buffalo milk or a combination thereof or from standardised milk, by the partial removal of water after addition cone sugar. It may contain added refined lactase, permitted flavour, calcium chloride, sodium citrate, sodium salts of orthophospheric acid (as linear phosphate with a degree of polymerisation upto 6 units) not exceeding

0.3 percent by weight of the finished product. Such additions need not be declared on the label condensed milk sweetened shall not contain less than 9.0 % milk fat, not less than 31.0 % total milk solids and not less than 40 % cane sugar.

Milk - Unsweetened (Evaporated Milk)

The product obtained from cow or buffalo milk or a combination thereof or from standard milk by the partial removal of water. It may contain added calcium chloride, citric acid and sodium citrate sodium salts of orthophospheric acid and polyphospheric acid (as linear phosphate with a degree of polymerisation upto 6 units) not exceeding 0.3 % by weight of the finished product such addition need not be declared on the label. Condensed milk unsweetened shall not contain less than 8.0 % milk fat and not less than 26 percent milk solids.

Skimmed milk, Sweetened

The product attained from cow or buffallo skimmed milk or a combination thereof by the partial removal of water and after addition of cane sugar. It may contain added refined lactose, calcium chloride, citric acid, and sodium citrate, sodium salts of orthophosphoric acid and polyphosphoric acid (as linear phosphate with a degree of polymerisation upto 6 units) not exceding 0.3 % of by weight of the finished product such addition need not be declared on the label. Condensed skimmed milk sweetened shall contain not less than 26% of total milk solids not less than 40% sugar. The fat content shall not exceed 0.5 % by weight.

Skimmed milk unsweetened (Evaporated Skimmed milk)

The product obtained from cow or buffalo skimmed milk or their combination by partial removal of water. It may contain added calcium chloride, citric acid and sodium citrate, sodium salts of orthophosphoric acid and polyphosphoric acid (as linear phosphate with polymerisation degree upto 6 units. Condensed skimmed milk unsweetened shall contain not less than 20 % total milk solids not more than 0.5 % by weight of fat content.

Composition and Standards

(a) The gross composition of condensed milks, sweetened or unsweetened, whole or skim

METHOD OF MANUFACTURING, PACKAGING AND STORAGE OF CONDENSED MILK

Details of manufacture:-

Basic principle. The basic principle in the production of condensed and evaporated milks is that high quality milk is filtered/clarified, standarised, forewarmed and condensed/evaporated to the desired level. The concentrated product is preserved by the addition of sugar for condensed mlik and by heat-sterilization for evaporated milk.

Receiving milk. The quality of the incoming milk is one of the indispensable corner-stones upon which rest the quality and marketability of every form of concentrated milk. It is well known that the sanitry quality of the milk on the receiving platform depends on its background on the farm, viz.,healthy cows, clean milk production, clean utensils, freedom from colosrum, prompt cooling and refrigerated transport. However, all milk supplies must be systematically and thoroughly inspected each day.

When milk is received at the plant, its temperature should be at 10oC (50°F) or below. The milk should be clean sweet, free from off-flavours and odours and reasonably free from extraneous material. Contamination by antibiotics, pesticides and other chemical residues and metals is highly undesirable.

No abnormal milk should be accepted. Acid development is objectionable, for not only does this indicate an excessive bacterial count, but it also reduces the heat-stability of milk.,

Among the various platform and laboratory test usually performed on the intake milk to determine its acceptance/rejection, much reliance is placed on alcohol (Ethanol) and Clot-On-Boiling (COB) test to determine its acceptance for condensing. These tests are discussed below:-

i. **Alcohol (Ethanol) test** :- To make this test, 5 ml. of milk is placed in a test tube and an equal amount of a solution with 68 percent alcohol added. The mixture is shaken and any formation of clots or flakes denotes a positive test, i.e. the milk is susceptible to heat-balance in the same manner as heat-coagulation. The alcohol test is especially important for the manufacture of evaporated milk, as it detects the tendency of the milk to curdle during sterilization. This test detects: abnormal milk (including colostrum) which is high in mineral salts; developed acidity in milk; mastitis milk likely to result in sweet curdling; etc. It is more sensitive than the COB test.

ii. **Alcohol Index (AI)** :- Determined by placing absolute alcohol in the burette and 10 ml. milk in a beaker. The number of ml. of alcohol required for flake formation is known as the Alcohol Index (AI). An AI of 7 is indicative of good stable milk for acceptance, while 3 or less shows that milk is fit for rejection.

iii. **Alcohol-Alizarin Test** :- This test not only determines the heat-stability of milk but also the pH. (Milk is coagulated if the pH is 5.6 or below).

Under Indian conditions today, where any developed acidity in milk is invariably neutralized by the addtion of sodium bicarbonate by unscrupulous dealers resulting in a disturbed salt balance, acceptance of milk on the basis of Alcohol Tests alone may prove impractical since the bulk of the daily milk supply may then have to be rejected.

iv. **Clot-On-Boiling test** :- In this test, 5 ml. of milk is placed in a test tube and kept in a boiling water-bath for 5 minutes. Afterwards it is removed and examined for precipitation. If curd is observed, the milk is said to fail the COB test and should be rejected.

After the milk has been accepted on the basis of the above tests, it is weighed, sampled and tested for fat, NSF, etc.

Filtration/Clarification.

This is done in order to remove visible foreign matter, which is unsightly and may cause consumer complaints, from the milk. The milk is generally pre-heated (in warm milk clarifiers) to 35-40°C to increase the efficiency of the operation. Afterwards, it is cooled so as to preserve its quality.

Standardization.

This is done so as to conform to legal standards in the finished product. The standardization of raw milk is normally carried out in three stages:

(a) the first standardization, which establishes the desired ratio of Fat: SNF (usually 1 : 2.44);

(b) the second, which establishes the desired ratio of added sugar to the total milk-solids;

(c) the third, which adjusts the concentration of the finished condensed milk to the desired percentage of total solids.

Forewarming/pre-heating.

This refers to the heating of milk before it is condensed, and serves the following purpose:

(i) To ensure that the finished product is free from micro organisms and enzymes;

(ii) to ensure uninterrupted boiling in the vacuum pan;

(iii) to provide an effective means of controlling objectionable age-thickening in the finished product.

The temperature-time of forwarming/pre-heating extends over a wide range, such as 82 to 93°C (180 to 200°F) for 5 to 15 minutes; or 116 to 149°C for 0.5 to 5 minutes. The modern trend is towards high-temperature short-time heating, such as 115 to 118°C (239 to 248°F), for No.Hold/flash. The exact temperature time of heating is so controlled as to provide optimum viscosity in the manufactured product without inducing excessive thickening or thinning during storage.

Tubular heat exchangers are commonly used for forewarming; either double-tube or shell-and-tube heat-exchangers are preferred.

Addition of sugar

(a) Purpose.

Sugar is added for the purpose of preserving the condensed milk without resorting to sterilization by heat.

(b) Kind.

Generally sucrose is added as it has proved most suitable. It is either highly refined cane or beet sugar. Other sweetening agents, such as corn syrup solids, glucose and dextrose, have been used to replace sugar by 5 to 25 percent. The disadvantages of these sweetening agents are their reduced sweetening capacity compared to sucrose and their adverseeffects on colour and the rate of thickening in storage.

(c) Amount.

This ranges from 40 to 45 percent in the finished product,which requires 18 to 20 percent sugar on milk basis.

Hunziker advocated a Sugar Ratio (sugar-in-water concentration) of 62.5 to 64.6 percent; this amount not only ensures proper protection against microbial growth, but also prevents sugar crystallization.

(d) Quality

Sucrose in granulated or syrup form must be of good quality. Liquid sugars (approximately 65 percent sucrose) should be subjected to a high pasteurizing temperature to destroy the micro-organisms before they are added to condensed milk

(e) Method

The temperature and time at which sugar is added to the milk in the batch have a definite effect on the keeping quality and physical stability (age-thickening) of the finished product. Sugar is added at the end of the condensing process. The dry sugar is dissolved in the least possible quantity of water. If added before condensing, an increase in viscosity and greater difficulty in the evaporation of moisture result. Further, the presence of added sugar in the fresh milk during forewarming increases the heat-resistance and survival capacity of the micro-organisms, thereby adversely affecting keeping quality. In order to ensure freedom from extraneous material, the sugar syrup may be passed through a pressure filter or a centrifugal clarifier.

(f) Condensing.

The basic priciple consists in the removal of water from the standardized milk by boiling it under partial vacuum at a low temperature till the desired concentration is reached. This operation is carried out in an evaporator, which should preferably be of the single-effect type (also known as a vacuum pan). The chief advantages of condensing milk in vacuum are: economy of operation, rapidity of evaporation and protection of milk against heat damage. Vacuum condensing achieves the object of obtaining a finished product which is free from any cooked flavours and can be readily reconstituted into the original milk.

4(a) Description of a vacuum pan

The vacuum pan or evaporator is the heart of the milk condensary. It is used in the manufacture of every type of concentrated milk product. It consists essentially of five major parts and numerous accessories

PLANT ECONOMICS

LAND & BUILDING (Land 750 sq.mts.) Rs. 10,15,000.00

PLANT & MACHINERY

1. MILK RECEVING SECTION:
   Milk weighing machines,milk receni-
   ning tanks chian conveyors etc.
2. PASTEURISING SECTION:Milk tanks,
   milk tanks,pumps,plate pasteurisers
   milk filers, water heaters- Cont..
3. hot water pumps chilled water pumps temp. recorders, etc.
4. MILK STORAGE SECTION: Stainless- steel milk tanks, milk, pumps, stainless steel pipes etc.
5. REFRIGERATION SECTION: Refrigeration plant, compressors condensers,electric motors- Cont.
6. Ammonia pipes etc.
7. BABY BOILER: Vertical multi tubular
   boiler,steam & water mixing batteries
8. Vacuum pan Evaporator (stainlessbody, jacketed) with
   vacuum pump, condenser & other accessories
9. Mixer and Homogenizer (s.s.body)
10. Can washing machine with accessories,
11. Automatic can drying machine with hot air blowing arrangement
12. Automatic can weighing, filling &
    double seaming machine with conveyors
13. Automatic label pasting machine
14. Carbon sealing machine
15. Laboratory equipments complete
16. Water softening plant

FIXED CAPITAL

1.	LAND & BUILDING	Rs.	10,15,000.00
2.	PLANT & MACHINERY	Rs.	26,00,000.02
3.	OTHER FIXED ASSETS	Rs.	3,50,000.00
	TOTAL	Rs.	39,65,000.02

RAW MATERIALS

1. Milk
2. Sugar
3. Cans
4. Chemicals, Preservatives etc.
5. Cartons with strips

TOTAL WORKING CAPITAL/MONTH

1.	RAW MATFRIAL	Rs.	10,27,300.00
2.	SALARY & WAGES	Rs.	74,250.00
3.	UTILITIES & OVERHEADS	Rs.	1,40,600.00
	TOTAL	Rs.	12,42,150.00

TOTAL CAPITAL INVESTMENT

TOTAL FIXED CAPITAL	Rs.	39,65,000.02
TOTAL WORKING CAPITAL FOR 2 MONTHS	Rs.	24,84,300.00
TOTAL	Rs.	64,49,300.02

TURN OVER/ANNUM

Receipts from sale of condensed milk (200 gm pack tin) Quantity- 1800000 tin.	Rs.	2,25,00,000.00

PROFIT SALES RATIO = Profit / Sales x 100 = 24.15 %

RATE OF RETURN = Operating profit / T.C.I x 100 = 84.26 %

BREAK EVEN POINT (B.E.P) = 37.00 %

Chapter 36

BUTTER MILK

Fermented milks refer to those milks which have been made by employing selected micro-organization to develop the characteristics flavour and/or body and texture.

Fermentation has been defined as the metabolic process in which chemical charges are brought about on an organic substratum, whether protein, carbohydrate, or fat through the action of enzymes whether protein carbohydrate or fat through the action of enzymes, liberated by specific living micro-organism.

The fermented milks are natural Butter milk, cultured butter milk, Acidophilus milk, Bulgarian butter milk, kumiss, kefer, yoghurt and Dahi.

The by-product obtained from the churning of sweet cream is essentially the same in composition as skim milk. As a beverage, buttermilk owes its flavour to the lactic acid and other substances present in small amount which differ in excellence according to the nature of the organism.

Much of the so called buttermilk at the present times consist of skim milk artificially soured by the addition of a suitable culture, which may be of the ordinary lactic acid bacillus or the similar B. bulgaricus whole milk, as skim milk, is thus treated so called acidobhilus milk is a produce prepared by careful sterlization and inoculation with a pure culture.

In certain countries, fermented milk food, are favoured over fresh, fluid milk for reasons safety better flavour and texture, and possible beneficial therapeutic effect where inadequate transport pasteurization, and refrigeration facilities exist inparticularly in hot climates, many authorities prefer to sour the milk first; in this manner the presence of enormous number's of harmless lactic acid bacteria and their metabolic and products discourage and growth of food poisoning and disease producing bacteria. The traditional flavour and texture quality are not necessarily retained, but economically and from a lowered calorie point of view low fat, cultured butter milk made with starters has more allure.

PROPERTIES & CHARACTERISTICS OF BUTTER MILK

1. Much more palatable than milk.
2. Nutritine value usually increased.
3. It is more easily assimilated by the human system than milk.
4. It contain beneficial antibiotics.
5. It possess therapeutic properties.
6. The regular consumption of butter milk claimed to increase longevity of human beings.

MANUFACTURING PROCESS OF BUTTER MILK

Natural Butter Milk : This is a by-product of churning cream for butter making. Ripened cream which has undergone a clean, lactic fermentation is usually preferred. Also included, under Indian condition, is country butter milk obtained as a by product of churning whole milk curd for production of country butter.

Cultured Butter Milk : This is obtained by inoculation and incubation of Pasteurized skim milk with lactic starter.

Details of manufacture :

Preparation : For the manufacture of cultured butter milk, fresh skimmed milk is preferable. The solids content should range from 9 to 10 percent. The skimmed milk should be free from antibiotics and inhibitory substances. If milk containing an appreciable amount of fat is used. It should be homogenized. If cream or butter fat is desired in the product, it may be added to the cold, butter milk when the curd is broken up. Manufacturing milk is heated in a holder pasteurizer vat to 82-88°C (180°-190°F) for thirty minutes with frequent stirring and then cooled to 22°C (72°F) one percent bulk lactic starter is added and mixed thoroughly in the milk and then allowed to incubate at 21-22°C (70-72°F) without further agitation until coagulation occurs and an acidity between 0.80 and 0.85 percent is reached. The curd is broken up by slow agitation to give a smooth consistency and cooled to 5-10°C. It is then packed and stored at 5-10°C until distribution.

Creaming : Creaming imparts a rich flavour to the butter milk and has the effect of decreasing the viscosity (viscosity can also be decreased by adding 20 to 25 percent of pasteurized sweet whole milk during break up of the curd).

Salting : Salt at 0-1 percent may be added to the finished product to increase its flavour.

Adding Butter Granules : Butter granules or flakes are sometimes added to cultured butter milkmade from skimmed milk to simulate an old fashioned churned butter milk appearance.

Wheying-off or Whey Separation :

The water content of normal milk is about 87 percent; that of skim milk is about 91 percent. When the milk forms a curd in the manufacture of cultured butter milk, this water remains but it is loosely held by the protein as a sponge holds moisture. Part of it may be expelled from the protein and appears as a watery layer or in pockets. This condition is called "wheying-off" or "whey separation". The free liquid is actually whey, not water, and it contains soluble minerals, proteins, lactose, and vitamins.

Too Much Viscosity :

Many cultured butter milks are so thick that they appear more like custards than fluids, and in this condition it becomes difficult to empty the container. The lack of fluidity, ideal for yogurt but not butter milk, also decreases its refreshing qualities. The most important cause is excess acidity. As the acidity increases, the butter milk body thickens.

PLANT ECONOMICS

Rated Plant Capacity	=	200.00 Kg./Day
LAND & BUILDING (Area reqd. 1500 sq.mt)	Rs.	48,00,000.00

PLANT & MACHINERY

1. Homogenizer
2. Filteration unit
3. Pasteurization unit
4. Incubator
5. Refrigerattion unit
6. Storage tank for skimmed milk made of stainless steel
7. D.G.Set
8. Material Handling equipments Viz Conveyor belt, Bucket elevator etc.
9. Pouch filling & Sealing Machine
10. Laboratory & Milk Testing Equipments
11. Boiler
12. Misc. pipe fitting, pumps,motor, Valve viz., fixture,tools etc.

FIXED CAPITAL

1.	LAND & BUILDING	Rs.	48,00,000.00
2.	PLANT & MACHINERY	Rs.	32,00,000.00
3.	OTHER FIXED ASSETS	Rs.	4,00,000.00
	TOTAL	Rs.	84,00,000.00

RAW MATERIALS

1. Skimmed milk
2. Lactic starter
3. Misc. Cream, Salt, Butter granules etc.
4. Flexible Pouches

TOTAL WORKING CAPITAL/MONTH

1.	RAW MATERIAL	Rs.	5,76,500.00
2.	SALARY & WAGES	Rs.	1,18,375.00
3.	UTILITIES & OVERHEADS	Rs.	1,11,200.00
	TOTAL	Rs.	8,06,075.00

TOTAL CAPITAL INVESTMENT

Total Fixed Capital	Rs.	84,00,000.00
Total Working Capital for 2 Months	Rs.	16,12,150.00
TOTAL	Rs.	1,00,12,150.00

TURN OVER/ANNUM

Received By sale of Butter milk
(600000 kgs) in pouch of 200 ml (3000000) Rs. 1,50,00,000.00

PROFIT SALES RATIO = Profit / Sales x 100 = 18.16 %

RATE OF RETURN = Operating profit / T.C.I x 100 = 27.20 %

BREAK EVEN POINT (B.E.P) = 57.64 %

Chapter 37

TONED MILK

There are different kinds of milk obtained from different animals, like cows, buffalow, goat, camel and many others. But generally we use goat milk cow milk, and buffalow milk. The following gives analysists of milk from goat and cow.

INGREDIENTS	COW MILK	GOAT MILK
WATER	87.40	87.54
SOLIDS	0.75	0.85
CASEIN	3.00	3.00
ALBUMEN	0.4	01.00
FATS	3.	754.50
SUGARS	4.	704.50

People with very low vitality to live on milk products for some time, with fruit to supplement it. In some foreign countries, milk obtained from animals like vama salue Hippopotamies, Gluens pig and Blue whole etc. is used.

Buffalo milk contains more sugar and more casein. it's analysis is as under.

Water	-	82.2%
Protein	-	4.75%
Minerals	-	0.80%
Casein	-	4.45%
Calcium	-	0.203%
Vitamin A	-	0.162%
Fats	-	7.10%
Phosphorus	-	0.125%
	Total	99.890%

India posses an enormous cattle (180 million) and buffaloes (61 million) population but the annual milk production has reached only about 30 million tonnes. The low milk production is primarily due to the low-potential of animals and lack of adequate nutrition.

MANUFACTURING PROCESS OF TONED MILK

Frist of all skimmed milk powder is procured from the market. For the Production of 100 kgs of tonned milk, 9 kgs of skimmed milk powder is taken in a stainless steel vessel fitted with agitator and motor.

Now in this stainless steel vessel calculated quantity of Butter oil (2 kgs) is added.

Calculated quantity of Hot water (89 liters) is added at 60°C for the preparation of toned milk and the entire mass is homogenised.

The toned milk thus formed is sent for pasteurization to kill the germ. It is further tested and packed in pouches and sent for marketing.

STANDARDISATION

Milk is standardised according to ISI (now B.I.S.) specification or according to requirements by wholesaler.

HOMOGENISATION

Fioteted milk is fed into homogenizer. Homogenization is the process by which the milk is emulsified and are further divided to produce a more stable emulsion that will not separate on standing. The fat is emulsified with liquid part of milk that are at water mostly. Hence to prevent sedimentation of fat in milk that homogenization process is done. But this way high quality homogenized milk is produced.

After feeding the milk into homogenizer, the pressure of the homogenizer is increased about 2500 psi. However, of this pressure does not produce milk that meets the standard, it may be necessary to use a pressure high as 3000 to 3500 LB.

A uniform, steady pressure is necessary to secure satisfactory homogenization. The milk should have a slight, positive pressure. Otherwise air may be drawn into the pistons which causes the needles of the pressure gauge to vibrate. Such a result indicates irregular presssure.

Sediment may appear in the operation which is undesirable. To reduce sediment, clarification is done.

CLARIFICATION

The milk is passed through a clarifier is it leaves the homogenizer.

Cold milk clarification is preferred to hot milk. This clarification operation can be perform before homogenization but the complete clarification can be achieved at this stage clarifier can be replaced by cream separator but since the separator bowl is not designed to hold a large amount of sediment and consequently is not efficient for clarifying a large volume of milk. However, this operation can be omitted to get high quality milk.

PASTEURISATION

The milk after clarification is passed through a plate heat exchanger for pasteurisation. In plate heat exchanger (P.H.E.) the milk is pasteurized by UHT method. It is modern method of pasteurisation of milk and used where large volumes of milk are handled. The UHT pasteuriser gives a continuous flow of milk which is fully pasteurised and free from pathogens.

After complete processing, milk is stored in cold upto chilling conditions so that unwanted micro organisms/pathogenic micro organism can not be developed in the processed milk. It is sacred until delivered for distribution to wholesalers.

Testing

The testing of milk is an essential for the quality control purposes however may be done prior to storage under freezing condition.

Distribution

After Complete processing, the toned milk is checked for proper pasteurisation by quality controller. Then the milk at 1 or 2°C is supplied to the wholesalers present at distant places by the tanker or by filling in the big stainless steel cans. Under chilling conditions Temp may rise to 7 to 8°C during transportation.

PLANT ECONOMICS

Rated Plant Capacity	= 50000.00 LTS/Day
LAND & BUILDING (Land 20000 sq.mts.)	Rs. 1,21,00,000.00

PLANT & MACHINERY

1. Complete Plat & Machineries with erection & commissioning
2. Laboratory equipments

FIXED CAPITAL

1.	LAND & BUILDING	Rs.	1,21,00,000.00
2.	PLANT & MACHINERY	Rs.	2,45,00,000.00
3.	OTHER FIXED ASSETS	Rs.	54,00,000.00
	TOTAL	Rs.	4,20,00,000.00

RAW MATERIALS

1. Skimmed Milk Powder
2. Butter oil
3. Chemicals for laboratory & process
4. Pouches

TOTAL WORKING CAPITAL/MONTH

1.	RAW MATERIAL	Rs.	80,54,500.00
2.	SALARY & WAGES	Rs.	3,19,200.00
3.	UTILITIES & OVERHEADS	Rs.	21,70,000.00
	TOTAL	Rs.	1,05,43,700.00

TOTAL CAPITAL INVESTMENT

TOTAL FIXED CAPITAL	Rs.	4,20,00,000.00
TOTAL WORKING CAPITAL FOR 2 MONTHS	Rs.	2,10,87,400.00
TOTAL	Rs.	6,30,87,400.00

TURN OVER/ANNUM

By sale of pouch of milk (500 ml) Rs. 19,80,00,000.00

PROFIT SALES RATIO = Profit / Sales x 100 = 27.39 %

RATE OF RETURN = Operating profit / T.C.I x 100 = 85.96 %

BREAK EVEN POINT (B.E.P) = 34.99 %

Chapter 38

DAIRY PRODUCTS & MILK PACKAGING IN POUCHES GHEE, BUTTER, PANEER AND CASEIN, FLAVOURED MILK, CHEESE, YOGHURT AND ICE CREAM

Milk is an Important human food. It is palatable, easy to digest and highly nutritives. It contains proteins, fat, sugar, minerals and a liberal quantity of different kinds of vitamins.

In World milk production, India ranks next only to the United States of America and the U.S.S.R. But the milk produced in India is far from adequate for its vast population as the daily average consumption per head comes to even less than half of the optimum requirement of about 310 grams.

Unlike rich countries like the U.K. and the U.S. dairying in India is a subsidiary occupation of almost all the farmers. More than 60 per cent of the families involved in dairying belong to the small or marginal farmers or even agricultural labourers.

In the first half of the 1900 dairying in the country was largely unorganised, except for military farm which were established and largely stocked with the european breeds. In the plantation areas, pure breed exotic bulls were randomly crossbred with local cows. Apart from the "pockets" of improved animals thus created, dairying was largely left in the hands of traditional producers, middle man, product makers and vendors.

MANUFACTURING PROCESS

COOLING AND STORING MILK:

The careless handling of milk between milking and delivering to the place can cause high bacteria counts to develop in the milk, a mechanical cooler is employed for the purpose. Whole of the milk should be started at

50°F to prevent spoilage. Storage tanks made of stainless steel are employed for storing the raw milk.

FILTERATION:

The cold raw milk is filtered, however, it can be filtered before cooling and storing in tank, but the precaution is to be taken at this stage so that no foreign matters or understand materials may be carried on.

STANDARDISATION:

Milk is standardised according to ISI specification or according to requirements by wholesaler.

HOMOGENISATION:

Filtered milk is fed into homogenizer. Homogenization is the process by which the milk is emulsified and are further divided to produce a more stable emulsion that will not separate on standing. The fat is emulsified with liquid part of milk that are at water mostly. Hence to prevent sedimentation of fat in milk that homogenization process is done. But this way high quality homogenized milk is produced.

After feeding the milk into homogenizer, the pressure of the homogenizer is increased about 2500 psi. However, of this pressure does not produce milk that meets the standard, it may be necessary to use a pressure high as 3000 to 3500 LB.

A uniform, steady pressure is necessary to secure satisfactory homogenization. The milk should have a slight, positive pressure. Otherwise air may be drawn into the pistons which causes the needles of the pressure gauge to vibrate. Such a result indicates irregular presssure.

Sediment may appear in the operation which is undesirable. To reduce sediment, clarification is done.

CLARIFICATION :

The milk is passed through a clarifier is it leaves the homogenizer. Cold milk clarification is preferred to hot milk. This clarification operation can be perform before homogenization but the complete clarification can be achieved at this stage clarifier can be replaced by cream separator but since the separator bowl is not designed to hold a large amount of sediment and consequently is not efficient for clarifying a large volume of milk. However, this operation can be omitted to get high quality milk.

PASTEURISATION :

The milk after clarification is passed through a plate heat exchanger for pasteurisation. In plate heat exchanger (P.H.E.) the milk is pasteurized by UHT method. It is modern method of pastedurisation of milk and used where large volumes of milk are handled. The UHT pasteuriser gives a continuous flow of milk which is fully pasteurised and free from pathogens.

After complete processing milk is stored in cold upto chilling conditions so that unwanted micro organisms/pathogenic micro Organism can not be developed in the processed milk. It is sacred until delivered for distribution to wholesalers.

Testing:-

The testing of milk is an essential for the quality control purposes however may be done prior to storage under freezing condition.

Distribution:-

After Complete processing, the processed milk is checked for proper pasteurisation by quality controller. Then the milk at 1 or 2°C is supplied to the wholesalers present at distant places by the tanker or by filling in the big stainless steel cans. Under chilling conditions Temp may rise to 7 to 8°C during transportation.

MANUFACTURE OF CASEIN

If we want to make better quality of casein the fat content of the skimed milk, from which it is made, should be minimum. Therefore it is necessary, the cream may be again separated from skimed milk so that its fat content is minimum.

After separating the last trace of cream from the skim milk it is heated 350°C and filled in the wooden tank equipped with a hand agitator for mechanical agitator. For coagulation of casein 150 ml of dilute hydrochloric acid (1 part of acid into 1 parts water) and is added by spray pump slowly and stearing is continued. Milk starts coagulating as the acid is added and coagulated mas settles down at bottom. When complete coagulation has taken place, the mass is allowed to settle for half an hour. Now the stop coke is opened and the whey is drained over a draining cock made of wire cloth fixed in wooden frame, so that the coagulated mas is retained over it. The coagulated mass is again dropped into the tank for washing.

Now-a-days a different types of filter is using to separate whey.

Washing is done in the tank by adding dilute acid water (8 C.C. acid is 50 list of water). The acid is added sufficient quantity so that coagulation is completely under water. After ten minutes, the water is drained out. Two such type of required more. It should be remembered that washing should be such type that there should be leaving no whey.

The coagulation is hanged is a cloth so that water tickles down. Even after this process there is sufficient water present necessiry squeezing and processing. For this the cloth filled with coagulation is put under two wooden frames and pressed by putting some weight.

A screw press may be used for the same purpose as it makes the pressing very easy. The casein is now from of a cake.

Now the cake should be cut into pieces. Then the pieces are rubbed on over a 10 mesh more cloth fixed in a wooden frame. Granules of casein are obtained below the sieve.

The next step is to dry the granules. If the production is 5-10 kg. casein per day and it is stirringly run that the charging can be done in open by spreading the granules over white sheets on a coat, but if larger production is required a tray dryer will be needed.

Tray dryer is a almirah which is heated inside with electric elements. Granul is placed in trays which are put in place over the sacks provided in the almirah. the heating can also be done with coal.

The granules are next ground to powder. Different types of grinding machines are available including driven. If powder is available that it is casein to run the grinder in the keep of 1/2 H.P. motor. The powder is packed in polythene bags which are placed in card board boxes. Indian standard institution has precized the requirement for edible quality casein code No. IS: 1167-1965.

YOGHURT FROM MILK

It is an indisputable fact that the enormously increasing popularity of yoghurt, now becoming available throughout the world, is primarily based on the cultural and biochemical performance of lactic cultures, namely, Streptococcus thermophilus and Lactobacillus bulgaricus. These are the corner stones upon which the success or failure of yoghurt processing hinges.

Although our knowledge regarding the growth and biochemical performance of yoghurt lactic cultures in cow milk has been well established, there is paucity of informtion on this aspect in milk of other species like buffalo. Attempts have been made to obtain information on the ability of lactic cultures in the preparation on three types of yoghurt; namely, plain yoghurt, fruits yoghurt and sweetend yoghurt by the procedure indicated in the flow sheet.

Processing:-

Cow and buffalo milk samples are individually steamed for 30 min., cooled to a temperature of 43°C then inoculated at 3% level with Str. thermophilus and Lb. bulgaricus in equal proportions (1:1). The contents are mixed thoroughly and filled in glass bottles covred with lids or aluminium foil caps, transferred to water bath maintained at 42°C±0.5°C. After incubation for 3.0-3.5 hrs. when the coagulum is formed, the bottles are removed from waterbath, cooled at 30oC for 1/2 hr. and transferred to refrigerator for overnight storage.

PLANT ECONOMICS

Rated Plant Capacity = 3390.00 KGS/day
(Milk Processing = 10000 litres/day)

LAND & BUILDING (Land 8553.mts.) Rs. 1,16,51,500.00

PLANT & MACHINERY

1. Centrifuge or Cream separator
2. Pasteuriser with cooling arrangements and accessories
3. Refrigeration system consists of air Compressor, refrigerator and brine circulating tank
4. Filter ordinary
5. Milk reception tank (stainless steel)
6. Water softener unit
7. Steam boiler
8. Miscellaneous equipments as laboratory testing equipments
9. Automatic Pouch filling & sealing machine.
10. Vacuum Pan Evaporator
11. Vertical Storage Tank with stirrer
12. Vertical storage tanks
13. Neutralisation tank
14. Pasteurisation Unit
15. Fermenting tank
16. Churner
17. Ghee receiving kettle
18. Pipe fitting, pumps, motor, valve and other miscellaneous machinery
19. Screw Press
20. Oscillating Granulator
21. Tray Dryer
22. Grinding Machine
23. Wash Water Storage tank,

FIXED CAPITAL

1.	LAND & BUILDING	Rs.	1,16,51,500.00
2.	PLANT & MACHINERY	Rs.	98,30,000.00
3.	OTHER FIXED ASSETS	Rs.	33,00,000.00
	TOTAL	Rs.	2,47,81,500.00

RAW MATERIALS

1. Milk
2. Chemicals for butter paneer, cheese flavoured milk etc.
3. Hydrochloric Acid
4. Cans, Polyethene, packets, Corrugated boxes etc.
5. Culture or Innoculum

TOTAL WORKING CAPITAL/MONTH

1.	Raw Material	Rs.	45,05,800.00
2.	Salary & Wages	Rs.	2,75,310.00
3.	Utilities & Overheads	Rs.	6,32,500.00
	TOTAL	Rs.	54,13,610.00

TOTAL CAPITAL INVESTMENTS

Total Fixed Capital	Rs.	2,47,81,500.00
Total Working Capital for 2 Months	Rs.	1,08,27,220.00
TOTAL	Rs.	3,56,08,720.00

TURN OVER/ANNUM

1. Paneer 60,000 Kgs.
2. Butter 300000 Kgs.
3. Ghee 372000 Kgs.
4. Casein 42,000 kgs.
5. Milk 600000 litres in pouches
6. Cheese 60000 kgs.
7. Ice cream 210000 Kgs.
8. Yoghurt 180000 kgs.

TOTAL Rs. 10,26,60,000.00

PROFIT SALES RATIO = Profit / Sales x 100 = 28.64 %

RATE OF RETURN = Operating profit / T.C.I x 100 = 82.56 %

BREAK EVEN POINT (B.E.P) = 30.09 %

Chapter 39

SOYMILK AND TOFU

SOYAMILK

It is a creamy, milk-like product made by soaking and grinding soybeans in water. Soymilk has been known in mainland China for centuries. Hot soymilk is used as a breakfast beverage in mainland China, Japan, Taiwan and Thailand. The product is generally popular with the local Chinese population. During the last few decades soymilk has been introduced in other parts of the world also.

Besides being rich in protein, vitamins and minerals. soymilk is a very economical, lactose free, highly digestible and nutritious alternative of dairy and meat centered diet. It can do almost everything that bovine milk could do. It is cholesterol free product, has a very low fat content and is rich in polyunsaturated fatty acids of phospholipids especially lecithin and also linolenic acid. Generally soymilk contains around 7-8% total solids in it. Adding 3-4% sugar and about 0.05% salt brings it to a sugar, salt and total solid level approximately identical to toned (2% fat) cow's milk, i.e. about 12-13% total solids. This can be consumed as such or after sweetening and diluting. Alternatively, it can be made into yogurt (curd) or tofu (paneer) or used directly in cooking. Soy food chart, gives an idea about various products made from soymilk, tofu and okara. In addition to that blends of the soymilk with cow/buffalo milk have been successfully tried for the preparation of "Rasogolla", a chana (coagulated product similar to the silken tofu in texture) based very popular Indian sweet. Flavoured soymilk is available in bottles and also in loose packing at some places in the market.

Soybean contains some anti-nutritional constituents also in it but its careful processing in proper scientific ways during soymilk and other product manufacturing makes it suitable for human consumption.

TOFU

Tofu is the most popular among all soy products. Also called soy paneer (in India) and been curd it is a tasty and very nutritious product made by coagulating hot soymilk with some food grade chemicals such as calcium chloride, magnesium chloride, calcium sulphate, acetic acid and citric acid etc. It is a versatile food that can be converted into a variety of value-added products. Tofu is the perfect and least expensive substitute of milk cheese or paneer Nutritionally its protein is as good as protein derived from animal sources.

Tofu is a very porous product and absorbs the flavour of the food with which it is cooked, Generally three types of tofu viz. firm, soft and silken tofu are available in the market. The basic method of making tofu of the above three varieties is the same. Different types of tofu are suited for different kinds of dishes. Tofu is an extremely perishable food. It should be kept in water under proper refrigeration. The water should be changed daily. It keeps tofu fresh for a week or more, depending on the refrigeration condition. Preferably tofu should be used as fresh as possible. Vacuum packed tofu is also available in the market.

OKARA

This is the undissolved residual portion left after extracting soymilk from soybeans during the process of making soymilk. Okara is rich in protein and fiber and is mainly used in the preparation of biscuits and other bakery items and for the thickening of soup and gravy etc. Its sun drying after mixing it with some spices and other ingredients makes traditional type of Indian badi (not nugget) which is used as a protein source to prepare curry. Some traditional Indian dishes like Halwa and Laddu are also prepared from it. Okara is also used as a main protein source in cattle feed. It is a highly perishable product with a very limited shelf life in normal conditions. Proper refrigeration can preserve it for a week or more.

SOYMILK POWDER

This is concentrated and dried form of soymilk that is prepared after its evaporation and spray drying. This powdered soymilk is used to prepare baby food and nutritious bakery and confectionery items. It retains its nutritional properties after reconstitution and soymilk thus obtained could be converted into instant beverages. tofu and yogurt (curd) etc.

NUTRITIONAL VALUE

As per the American Journal of Clinical Nutritional "It can be concluded that soy protein can serve as a sole protein source in all human beings except premature infants" It is low in fat and contains no cholesterol. It is an excellent food for babies, children, elderly people and pregnant and lactating women. In a most recent development US Department of Food and Drug Administration (USFDA) has authorised a health claim saying that "25 grams of soy protein a day, as part of a diet low in saturated fat and cholesterol, may reduce the risk of heart disease".

For most people in India and in the West soymilk is not palatable as such in spite of the fact that nutritionally it is almost as good as cow's milk Soymilk typically has 3.5-4% protein and 7-8% total solids.

About 50% of the Indain adult population is lactose intolerant Drinking milk causes illness, bloating, abdominal pain and gas to them. In human beings this lactose intolerance is because of the loss of the ability to digest lactose, the carbohydrate portion of cow/buffalo milk. Most of the people suffering from this problem cannot recognize symptoms upon eating dairy products. They simply reject consuming milk. Soymilk is the only alternative for the children and adults having lactose intolerance or allergy to bovine milk. Besides being a healthy nutrition for the general mass, soy protein in a proven cholesterol lowering agent. This protein is kidney friendly and causes calcium to be better utilized to avoid the conditions of osteoporosis.

Recent studies have shown that some of the nutrients of soymilk are potential cancer fighters. A good protein is relatively free from fat so that the protein intake does not ruin one's overall health. Protein should be inexpensive, appetizing, available in natural form, bulk or fiber, and should contain as many other nutrients as possible. Soybean absolutely fits in this category. Soy is one of the few plant foods that contain the proper balance of eight essential amino acids. Particularly soy is abundant in lysine, an amino acid that is usually scarce in plant food.

SOYACOW PROJECT

This project is concerned with the production of soymilk - a high nutritious alternative to dairy milk. It is based on a new patented process technology implemented in the so called SoyaCow System.

This project was started in India in 1991 jointly by Child Haven International, CHI a Canada based international NGO (follower of the Gandhian philosophy) working in India and Nepal, and Prosoya Inc. of Canada, a leading name in soymilk technology. Initially the project was granted substantial funding from CIDA (Canadian International Development Agency). Its main objective is to provide low cost nutrition to the general Indian population in the form of soymilk and its derivatives. SoyaCow Centre was established in India jointly by Child Haven International and Prosoya in the year 1993, and this patented technology of manufacturing table top soymilk machines suitable for the cottage industry in India was transferred to SSP Ltd., a Faridabad (Haryana) based well known dairy, food processing and pharmaceutical equipment manufacturing company. Now these machines are being manufactured at SSP under the guidance of the SoyaCow Centre. This centre is providing all kinds of assistance from making busines plan to installation of the machine, operator's training, developing recipes suitable to the local taste, helping the users of this machine in marketing of soy products, providing all the know-how on soymilk to the general people. In association with the American Soybean Association this center has developed the technology to give 4-6 months shelf life to soymilk in bottles without any refrigeration. Also, vacuum packaging technology is provided to pack tofu for a longer shelf life. This technology is given free to the soyacow users. Sites using this technology are doing very well.

SOYACOW

SoyaCow is a table-top, batch processing machine that yields high quality soymilk at the cottage industry level. This machine produces 5 litres of soymilk every half an hour (using 2 kg. of soybean in one batch costing about Rs. 15/- per kg). This 15 litres of milk could then be converted into 30 litres of flavoured drink, 15 kg of yogurt (curd) or approx. 3 kg of tofu. The production cost of soymilk and tofu comes to around Rs. 5.84/- per litre and Rs. 33.70/- per kg respectively gives an idea of the economic viability of this project on a commercial scale.

The machine includes accessories for making tofu (soy paneer) also. It requires only 5-10 m area with domestic power supply for its installation (1 HP single phase, 220 V) A skilled operator and one helper are enough for operating the machine.

The soymilk produced with Prosoya's advance technology has a mild cereal like flavour and a smooth mouth feel with excellent soluble protein without any "beany-off flavour". This is achieved in the processor by cold grinding of properly soaked soybeans in water without air, pressure cooking the resulting slurry with culinary steam and separating the soymilk from the undissolved solids (okara) in a filter press. The basic soymilk thus obtained is absolutely free from any chemical impurity and can be easily formulated into tasty cold or hot drinks, or further processed to produce tofu, yogurt, forzen desserts and a variety of other products.

Many companies, have tried introducing soymilk and other derivatives in India, but have failed primarily due to the presence of a "beany-off flavour" in the milk, high price of the products due to high cost of the equipment, and poor quality of the resultant products.

keeping in view the aspects of the above failure the "SoyaCow" machine has been developed by Prosoya to produce a "non-beany" (without off-flavour) soymilk at the cottage industry level in India and other developing counting. Based on its patented technology Prosoya also offers larger size plants to produce soymilk and its powder.

Cost Benefit Analysis for SoyaCow

A.	**Equipment"**	**SoyaCow SC-20 System**
B.	**Capacity**	**301itres/hr**
C.	**Capital Investment**	
C.1	Cost of Machine including taxes & duties	130,152.00
C.2	Freezer	15,000.00
C.3	Pre-Operational Expenses	5,000.00
C.4	Total Capital Investment (C.1+C.2+C.3)	150,152.00
D.	**Monthly Expenses @16 batches/day/shift**	
D.1	Interest on Loan @ 18% pa	2,177.28
D.2	Other Expenses	1,000.00
D.3	Sub-Total (D.1+D.2)	3,177.28
D.4	Manpower Cost 2 Workers @ Rs. 2000/month	4,000.00
D.5	Soy Beans @ Rs. 15/kg	12,000.00
D.6	Cost of Electricity @ Rs. 3.5/KW	1,680.00
D.7	Water, Sewer & Maintenance	2,000.00
D.8	Fuel-LPG @ Rs. 12.5/batch	5,000.00
D.9	Rent	1,000.00
D.10	Contingency	5,000.00
D.11	Depreciation @ 10% pa	1,209.60
D.12	Sub-Total (D.4 to D.11)	31,889.60
D.13	Total Expenses (D.3 + D.12)	35,066.88
E.	**Additional Production Expenses (/month)**	
E.1	Flavoured & Sweetened Milk @ Rs. 1.5/litre	9,000.00
E.2	Tofu @ Rs. 5/batch	2,000.00
F.	**Net Cost of Production**	
F.1	Soy Milk (Plain) (Rs./litre)	5.84
F.2	Flavoured Soy Milk (Rs./litre)	7.34
F.3	Curd (Rs./kg)	7.31
F.4	Tofu (Rs./kg)	33.70
G.	**Monthly Income**	
G.1	Soy Milk (Plain) 6000 litre/month @ Rs. 8/litre	48,000.00
G.2	Soy Milk (flavoured & sweetened) 6000 litre/month @ Rs. 12/litre	72,000.00
G.3	Curd 4800 kg/month @ Rs. 12/kg	57,600.00
G.4	Soy Paneer (Tofu) 1200 kg/month @ Rs. 45/kg	54,000.00
G.5	Okara (by-product) 1000 kg/month @ Rs 3/kg	3,000.00
H.	**Net Profit/Month**	
H.1	Soy Milk (Plain)	12,933.12
H.2	Flavoured Soy Milk	27,933.12
H.3	Curd	22,533.12
H.4	Tofu	16,933.12
I.	**Payback Period (Month)**	
1.1	Soy Milk (Plain)	11.61
1.2	Flavoured Soy Milk	5.38
1.3	Curd	6.66
1.4	Tofu	8.87

Soya milk and related Food Products are becoming popular throughout the World due to their good nutritional value and medicinal qualities. Soya milk is high in protein, low-in fat and carbohydrate and contains no cholesterol. It is an excellent food for babies, children, elderly people and pregnant and lactating women since it contains Vegetable Protein which is very nutritious and easy to digest.

Besides possessing high nutritional value, soyamilk is best for people suffering from diabetes and lactose-intolerance. Recent studies show that some of the nutrients of soyamilk are potential cancer fighter. Its regular consumption reduces blood cholesterol level and improve kidney functions.

Soya milk and its derivatives are the cheapest source of protein than any of the animal or plant protein. Soya milk produced by 'SOYA COW' machine is free of beany off-flavour and can be converted into Tofu, Curd, Hot and Cold Drinks, Ice-Cream, Fruit Shakes, etc.Tofu (soya paneer) makes tasty dishes like 'Matar Paneer', 'Palak Paneer' etc. and snacks like Soya Burgers, Patties, Sandwiches, Pakoras, etc. It is also used for Western style main dishes and desserts.

Many companies have tried introducing soya milk, Tofu and other soya dairy products, but have failed primarily due to the presence of beany off-flavour in the milk, high price of the product due to high cost of equipment and poor quality of other products. Keeping an eye of these aspects of failure, 'Soya Cow' has been developed to produce high quality soya milk and Tofu with an investment of about Rs. 1.3 lakh in plant & machinery inclusive of taxes & duties.

'Soya Cow' SC-20 is a table top machine that yields high quality soya milk at the cottage industry level using a break-through Candadian technology. A 'Soya Cow' produces 13-14 litres of soya milk every half an hour (using 1.75 kg of soya beans costing about Rs. 10/- per kg) at a cost of Rs. 2/- to 3/- per litre. The machine includes accessories for making Tofu (soya paneer) also. The machine requires 5-10 sq. m area with domestic power supply for its installation (1 HP single phase 220 V). A skilled operator and one helper are enough for operating the machine.

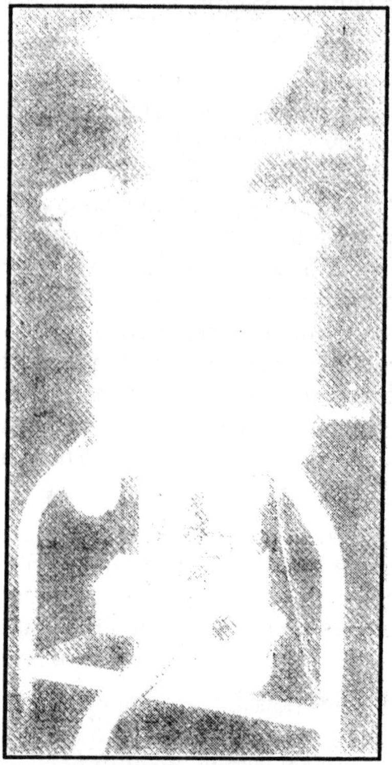

GRINDER / COOKER

FILTER PRESS

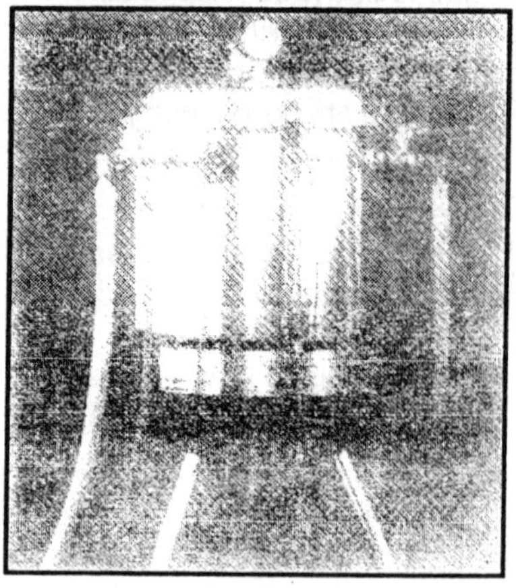

MANUAL BOILER

TOFU BOXES

"SoyaCow" Machine for Soymilk/Tofu(Soy Paneer) Production

SoyCow is a small and economical batch processor for producing highly nutritious non-beany Soymilk without chalkiness and with excellent soluble protein yiled.

Produces 15L of Soymilk in one batch by using two Kilograms of soybean.

Uses Prosoya's Patented "air less cold grinding" technology.

Made of Stainless Steel which meets Sanitary Standards.

Available with manual and electric boiler option.

Uses any quality of Soybean without de-hulling and still makes an excellent Soymilk base.

No chemical treatment or additive is required.

The machine includes tofu making system also.

Chapter - 40

DETAILS OF MACHINERIES USED IN DAIRY FARM & PRODUCTS

ALUMINIUM ALLOY MILK CAN

Manufactured: Under Licence from ALFA LAVAL (INDIA) LTD. One Piece hygienic construction no spillage, easy draining, built in durability, corrosion proof, sturdy handles, precision engineered, maintained quality, ISI Marked.

1.1	W-40	ALUMINIUM ALLOY MILK CANS WITH LID 40 LITRE CAPACITY
1.2	MC-50	ALUMINIUM ALLOY MILK CANS WITH LID 50 LITRE CAPACITY
1.3	MC-30	ALUMINIUM ALLOY MILK CANS WITH LID 30 LITRE CAPACITY
1.4	MC-20	ALUMINIUM ALLOY MILK CANS WITH LID 20 LITRE CAPACITY
1.5	MC-10	ALUMINIUM ALLOY MILK CANS WITH LID 10 LITRE CAPACITY
1.6	MC-5	ALUMINIUM ALLOY MILK CANS WITH LID 5 LITRE CAPACITY
1.7	MCCA	ALUMINIUM ALLOY MILK CAN LIDS MUSHROOM TYPE

ALUMINIUM ALLOY MILK CAN WITH INTERLOCKING ATTACHED LID

Rubber gasket for assured sealing and to avoid leakage. One piece hygienic construction, Easy draining, built in durable, corrosion proof, sturdy handle.

1.11	MC140	ALUMINIUM MILK CAN WITH INTERLOCKING ATTACHED LID 40 L CAP
1.12	MC150	ALUMINIUM MILK CAN WITH INTERLOCKING ATTACHED LID 50 L CAP
1.13	MC130	ALUMINIUM MILK CAN WITH INTERLOCKING ATTACHED LID 30 L CAP
1.14	MC120	ALUMINIUM MILK CAN WITH INTERLOCKING ATTACHED LID 20 L CAP
1.15	MC11O	ALUMINIUM MILK CAN WITH INTERLOCKING ATTACHED LID 10 L CAP
1.16	MCIR	RUBBER GASKET FOR ABOVE INTERLOCKING CAN

STAINLESS STEEL MILK CANS 304 QUALITY

Stainless Steel Milk Cans, hygienic construction strong and sturdy body, corrosion proof and crack resistance, easy to clean well finished with mushroom type lid.

1.20	MCS-40	STAINLESS STEEL MILK CAN WITH LID 40 LITRE CAPACITY

1.21	MCS-30	STAINLESS STEEL MILK CAN WITH LID 30 LITRE CAPACITY
1.22	MCS-20	STAINLESS STEEL MILK CAN WITH LID 20 LITRE CAPACITY
1.23	MCSC	SS MILK CAN LID MUSHROOM TYPE

MILK BUCKETS OF STAINLESS STEEL WITH LID HYGIENIC CONSTRUCTfON

1.31	MBS-2	2 LITRE CAPACITY
1.32	MBS-3	3 LITRE CAPACITY
1.33	MBS-5	5 LITRE CAPACITY
1.34	MBS-8	8 LITRE CAPACITY
1.35	MBS-12	12 LITRE CAPACITY
1.36	MBS-15	15 LITRE CAPACITY

PLASTIC MILK CAN

1.41	MCP-40	Plastic seamless double wall Milk Cans made from virgin FDA approved polyethylene in Mufti-Layers construction with built in handles 40 LITRE CAPACITY
1.42	MCIP-40	**INSULATED PLASTIC MILK CANS** having above features but with P U. F insulation for long distance transportation and enhancement of shelf life. 40 LITRE CAPACITY
		PLASTIC MILK CAN LIDS
1.43	CLP	Plastic Can Lids Mushroom type for Sintex plastic can
1.44	CLP4	Plastic Milk Can Lid 400 Grams ± 10 Grams
1.45	CLP5	Plastic Milk Can Lid 500 Grams ± 10 Grams
1.46	CLP54	Plastic Milk Can Lid 540 Grams ± 10 Grams
1.47	RH	CAN HAMMER (RUBBER)
1.48	ICA	ICE CHAMBER ALUMINIUM FOR MILK CANS

CAN SCRUBBER

1.50	CSSS	Capacity 425 Litre S.S. Immersion Bath with Nylon Brushes, All welding joints are ground smooth. All the surfaces are polished to 150 Grits. Complete with electric motor 1 H.P, 1440 R. PM., 3 phase, 1 P55, Gear Box and Driving Chain-1
1.51	CSMS	.... As above but Mild Steel body.
1.52	BS	Spare Brushes Set for Can Scrubber
1.53	CS13	**CAN STEAMING BLOCK** Can Steaming Block used to rinse and sterilize inside of 40 L Milk Cans using hot water followed by live steam at 3 Kg./ Cm Sq. Pressure, Manual, Foot operated.

CAN TROLLEY FOR 40 L & 20 L CAN

1.54 CTNO Can Trolley for 20L /40 L Can hand driven, made from Mild Steel. The Wheels are made of Polymer Non Virgin Nylon as per NDDB Specification

1.55 CTO **Can Trolley** ordinary

1.56 CRTII - Crate Trolly to hold one stack of 11 Crates as per N.D.D.B Specification

MILK TESTING CENTRIFUGES HAND OPERATED CENTRIFUGES

Original Milktesting Machine, hand driven, solid construction, covered, strong and sturdy, perfect alignment, ball bearing, smooth running, pan covers made from CRCA sheets, highly finished colour special powder coated english/ international model, ISI Marked dynamically balanced.

2.1	MC8	....	-Do-	For 8 Tests
2.2	MC12	....	-Do-	For 12 Tests
2.3	MC 24	....	-DO-	For 24 Tests

GH SERIES

2.4 As above with extra housing cover & brake for safe operation three Piece construction best quality for 12/24 Test hand operated.

GC SERIES

Original Milktesting machine hand operated features as MC series but with heavy gear box for extra long life.

2.5	GC 8	....	-Do-	For 8Tests
2.6	GC 12	....	-Do-	For12 Tests
2.7	GC 24	....	-DO-	For 24 Tests

GB SERIES

Milk testing machine hand driven features as MC series but with Aluminium die cast base and non breakable plastic clamp to hold plastic holders. Centrifuge has high finishing and smooth operation.

2.8	GB-8	....	-Do-	For 8Tests
2.9	GB-12	....	-Do-	For12 Tests
2.10	GB-24	....	-DO-	For 24 Tests

2.11 UH-8 Umbrella type head with hand operated base for 8 test only.

SPARES

2.21 UHS Umbrella type head for 8 test (Top only) to be fitted on JT Series base or UH-8

2.22	WRM	Vertical spindle for milk testing centrifuges (Tempered)
2.23	MCG	C. 1. Gear for above (Tempered)
2.24	MCH	Handle complete with knob
2.25	AT	Aluminium tube holder for butyrometers
2.26	PT	Plastic tube holder for Butyrometer (Fresh Quality)

ELECTRICAL CENTRIFUGES
ECT SERIES

Milktesting' Machine, Electrically Operated AC-50 Cycles, 1/4 H.P Attractive Indicator Lamp, Chord Plug-Pin, Fitted in Heavy Cast Iron Base Pan Cover of CRCA Sheets, White/ Blue Colour with Plastic Clips/ Metal Clips, Dynamically Balanced.

2.31	EC12	....	as above	For 12 Tests
2.32	EC 24	....	as above	For 24 Tests
	As above but complete with timer, brake and reverse switch			
2.33	ECT 12	....	as abov~	For 12 Tests
2.34	ECT 24	....	as above	For 24 Tests

NOVA SAFETY CENTRIFUGES

Small Centrifuge for butyrometer with acid resistance coating, plexiglass cover, special motor, rapid braking, angle head with 0-5 minute timer, easily can be placed on laboratory table.

2.35	NSC 8	....	as above for 8 Tests
2.36	NSC 12	....	as above for 12 Tests
2.37	NSS 12	....	as above NSC 12 but with SS top for 12 tests
2.38	NS18	Nova Safety Multi purpose Centrifuge having operation for 8 GerberTest or 4x50 ml solubility Index tubcs.	
2.39	NSI-12	Nova Safety Multi purpose Centrifuge having operation for 12 Gerber Test or 12x50ml solubility index tubes.	
2.40	S150	Solubility Index tube for above machine	

JT SERIES

Electrical Centrifuge "JANTA" MODEL having features of ECT series but with light cast base with standard pan cover economy model.

2.41	JT 8	....	as above :	For 8 Test
2.42	JT-12	....	as above	For 12 Test
2.43	JT-24	....	as above	For 24 Test
2.44	JT B	Electrical Centrifuge Janta Model Base only.		
2.45	JT U8	Electrical Centrifuge Janta Model with Umbrella type top for 8 Test only.		

GS-3 SERIES

Milk testing machine, electrically driven having features with extra housing cover and brake of ECT series but for safe operation, Three piece construction

2.46 GET-24 .... as above For 24 Test

2.47 GEI-24 .... as above GET 24 with speed indicator

2.48 GES-24 .... as above GEI-24 in stainless steel construction.

2.49 SQC24 **SUPER SQUARE CENTRIFUGE FOR GERBER TYPE**
Absolutely new Centrifuge Automatic lid Interlocking Square Housing with Acrylic lid electric Operated AC-50 Cycles, 1/4 H.P Single Phase 220 Volts, dynamically balanced, timer and speed Indicator

2.50 SQT24 **SUPER SQUARE PILOT CENTRIFUGE FOR GERBER TEST**
Absolutely new centrifuge to have best results. having swing head. The Centrifuge will be **Electronically Controlled** having electronic display for speed, temperature and time. Special automatic thermostatic controlled hot air heater are provided to maintain the temperature at 65° C constant in the centrifuge to have the better results as per Gerber requirements, having other features i.e. automatic lid interlocking, automatic brake, electric motor A.C. 50 cycles and dynamically balanced. The super square pilot centrifuge is must for Dairy Laboratory for perfect test and calibration purpose.

BUTYROMETERS

3.1 MBIS Milk Butyrometer Corning Glass 0-10% Flat Scale ISI Marked, Red-Acid Proof Permanent Marking. - _

3.2 MBS Milk Butyrometer Corning Glass 0-10 % Flat Scale ISI Marked, Silver Screen Super Grade, Acid Proof Permanent Marking.

3.3 MBEX Milk Butyrometer Corning Glass 0-10% Original Lakshmi Flat scale ISI marked Silver Screen/Red Acid Proof Permanent marking, Export Grade Best Quality

3.4 MB2 Milk Butyrometer Corning Glass-0-10% Flat Scale Bunty Marked, Silver Screen permanent marking

3.5 MBSS Milk Butyrometer Corning Glass 0-10% Flat Scale Super Grade. Acid Proof, permanent marking

j3.6 MBS Milk Butyrometer Coming Glass 0-8% Flat Scale Super Grade, Acid Proof Permanent Marking.

3.7 MB6 Milk Butyrometer Corning Glass 0-6% Flat Scale Super Grade, Acid Proof Permanent Marking Suitable for Cow Milk

3.8 MB4 Milk Butyrometer Corning Glass 0-4% Flat scale permanent marking for standardized milk

3.9 ICRB Cream Butyrometer Corning Glass As Per ISI Specification 0-70% volumetric 5 ml cream

3.10 CR135 Cream Butyrometer Corning Glass As Per ISI Specification 0-70 % with cup and rubber stopper weighing method 5gm cream

3.11	ICBV5	Cream Butyrometer Corning Glass 0-50% volumetric
3.12	CBC50	Cream Butyrometer Corning Glass 0-50% with cup & rubber stopper
3.13	CBVS7	Cream Butyrometer Corning Glass 50% - 70% volumetric
3.14	BBCS7	Cream Butyrometer Corning Glass 50% - 70% with cup & rubber stopper.
3.15	BBR8	Butter Butyrometer 0-80% Corning Glass As per ISI Specifications volumetric
3.16	BBC8	Butter Butyrometer Corning Glass 0-80% with cup & rubber stopper.
3.17	BBC9	Butter Butyrometer Corning Glass 0-90% with cup & rubber stopper.
3.18	BBCI	Butter Butyrometer Corning Glass 0-100% with cup & rubber stopper.
3.19	ISMB	**Skim Milk Butyrometer** for Double Quantity 0-0.5%
3.20	CHB4	Cheese Butyrometer Corning Glass 0-40% As Per ISI specification weighing method 3gm. with cup & rubber stopper
3.21	CHBV4	Cheese Butyrometer corning Glass 0-40% volumetric
3.22	MPB 35	Milk Powder Butyrometer 0-35% Corning Glass Flat Scale Weighing System with cup & rubber stopper
3.23	MPBV	Milk Powder Butyrometer 0-35% Corning Glass Volumetric.
3.24	ICBV	Ice Cream Butyrometer 0-20% Volumetric
3.25	ICBC	Ice Cream Butyrometer 0-20% with cup & rubber stopper
3.26	CMBV	Condensed Milk Butyrometer 0-20% corning Glass Volumetric.
3.27	CMBC	Condensed Milk Butyrometer 20% corning glass with cup & rubber stopper.
3.28	CLBV	**Chocolate Butyrometer** 0-20% corning glass, volumetric.
3.29	CLBC	Chocolate Butyrometer 0-20% corning glass with cup & rubber stopper.

BUTYROMETER WATER BATH (ELECTRICAL)

Stainless Steel Basin, Infinitely Variable Temperature Control. from 25°C to 100 °C Thermostat, one Drain Cock, Complete with Rack, Cable with Pin Plug and ON/ OFF Switch 220 Volt/50 cycle with cover

3.30	WB12	..............as above	for 12 Tests
3.31	WB 24	..............as above	for 24 Tests
3.32	WBJ16	Water Bath plain with rack of aluminium, it require separate heat source i.e. hot plate, Bunsen burner etc. for 16 Test	
3.33	HPWB	Hot plate with temperature control suitable for above.	

LOCK STOPPERS'

4.1	LSBISI	Lock Stoppers 'Original Lakshmi' ISI Marked Gerber Type (Brass cap) Workmanship Guaranteed, Packed in One Dozen Boxes.
4.2	LSG	Lock Stopper GerberType Ginni. (Metal Cap) Packed in one Dozen boxes
4.3	SCR	Single Conical Rubber Stopper Made From Acid Proof And Soft Quality.
4.4	LPA	Regulating Pins for Lock Stoppers Aluminium Die casted.
4.5	LPP	Regulating Pins for Lock Stoppers Plastic.
		PIPETTES
5.1	MPCH	Milk Pipette 10.75 ml Glass with Heavy wall thickness

5.2	MPCG	Milk Pipette 10.75 ml. Clear Glass Super Grade
5.3	MPISI	Milk Pipette 10.75 ml. ISI marked
5.4	MPSG	Glass Pipette for Milk 10.75 ml Super Grade ISI marked.
5.5	CP5	**Cream Pipette** 5 ml
5.6	AP11	Amyl Alcohol Pipette 1 ml with One Safety Bulb
5.7	SAP10	Acid Pipette 10 ml with Two Safety Bulb
5.8	PG1	Pipette 1 ml graduated in 1/100
5.9	PG2	Pipette 2 ml graduated in 1/50
5.10	PG5	Pipette 5 ml graduated in 1/20
5.11	PG10	Pipette 10 ml graduated in 1/10
5.12	PG25	Pipette 25 ml graduated in 1/25
5.13	PPUM	**Pipette pump** for easy usage

STANDS

6.1	BS1	Butyrometer Stand- Cum- Shaking for 12 Butyrometer (Wooden)
6.2	BS2	Butyrometer Stand- Cum- Shaking for 12 Butyrometer (Plastic)
6.3	BS3	Butyrometer Stand- Cum- Shaking for 12 Butyrometer (Aluminium)
6.4	BS4	Butyrometer Stand- Cum- Shaking for 24 Butyrometer (Wooden)
6.5	BS5	Butyrometer Stand-Cum- Shaking for 24 Butyrometer (Plastic)
6.6	BS6	Butyrometer Stand- Cum- Shaking for 24 Butyrometer (Aluminium)
6.7	BSX7	Butyrometer Stand without shaking Superior 12 Test unbreakable made of PP
6.8	SBS24	A Sample Bottle Stand (Aluminium) for 24Bottles 0.275 ± 5 Grm.
6.9	SBS12	A Sample Bottle Stand (Aluminium) for 12 Bottles
6.10	SBSP12	Sample Bottle stand plastic for 12 bottles
6.11	SBSP24	Sample Bottle stand plastic for 24 bottles
6.12	PSA	Pipette Stand Round shape for 12 Pipettes (Aluminium)
6.13	PS	Pipette Stand (Plastic) for 12 Pipettes
6.14	TP-12	Test tube stand 12 test

BRUSHES

7.1	BBR	Brushes for cleaning Butyrometers made from nylon bristles
7.2	BBS	Brushes for cleaning Butyrometers scales made from nylon bristles
7.3	BBB	Brushes for cleaning Butyrometers bodies from nylon bristles
7.4	BBFB	Brushes for cleaning Butyrometer having full line of nylon bristles
7.5	BRS2	Brushes for cleaning Milk Pipettes made from nylon bristles best quality
7.6	BRS3	Brushes for cleaning Sample Bottle made from nylon bristles best quality
7.7	BB1	Milk Bottle Brushes made of nylon bristles.
7.8	TT3	Test: Tubes brushes made of nylon bristles
7.9	BRS5	Milk Can Brushes made of Jute bristles.
7.10	CBN	Milk Can Brushes made of nylon bristles.
7.11	BPLS	Brushes for cleaning Pipe Line small size made from nylon bristles
7.12	BPLL	Brushes for cleaning pipe line large size made from nylon bristles

TILT MEASURES

8.1	TME1	Tilt Measures 1 ml for Acid Lakshmi make Superior quality with cork No.4 Export Quality (CORNING GLASS)
8.2	TMA	Tilt Measure 1 ml for Acid with Rubber Cork No. 4 (PLASTIC)
8.3	TMGA	Tilt Measure 1 ml for Acid with Rubber Cork No. 4 (GLASS)
8.4	TML1	Tilt Measure 1 ml for Acid Lakshmi Make with Nylon Cork No.4 Best/ Heavy Quality (PLASTIC)
8.5	TME10	Tilt Measure 10 ml for Alcohol Lakshmi make Superior quality with cork No-4 Export Quality (CORNING GLASS)
8.6	TMPI	Tilt Measure, 10 ml for, Alcohol with Rubber Cork No 4 (PLASTIC)
8.7	TMGI	Tilt Measure, 10 ml for Alcohol with Rubber Cork No 4 (GLASS)
8.8	TMLO	Tilt measure, 10 ml for Alcohol Lakshmi make with Rubber Cork No 4 Best/ Heavy Quality (PLASTIC)
8.9	CR	Cork No. 9 (25mm) for above tilt measure in place of cork No. 4 (18mm)
8.10	GBTM	Glass bottle for Tilt measure for cork No .4 and cork No .9
8.11	AD 2/1	AUTOMATIC PERMANENT DISPENSER with stopper having two measuring chamber of 10 ml and 1 ml for laboratory purpose to have best results, Complete with base and stand

DAIRY THERMOMETERS

9.1	T02A	Dairy Thermometer 0-220° F Alcohol filled Stem Type
9.2	T02M	Dairy Thermometer 0-220° F Mercury filled Stem Type
9.3	T01A	Dairy Thermometer - 10-110°C Alcohol filled Stem Type
9.4	T01 M	Dairy Thermometer -10-110° C Mercury filled Stem Type
9.5	TD2A	Dairy Thermometer 0-220° F Alcohol Deluxe Quality
9.6	TD2M	Dairy Thermometer 0-220° F Mercury Deluxe Quality
9.7	TD1A	Dairy Thermometer -.10-110° C Alcohol Deluxe Quality
9.8	TD1 M	Dairy Thermometer -10-110° C Mercury Deluxe Quality
9.9	TZ2A	Dairy Thermometer 0-220° F Alcohol Zeal Type Best Quality
9.10	TZ2M	Dairy Thermometer 0-220° F Mercury Zeal Type Best Quality
9.11	TZ1A	Dairy Thermometer -10-110° C Alcohol Zeal Type Best Quality
9.12	TZ1 M	Dairy Thermometer -10-110° C Mercury Zeal Type Best Quality
9.13	DFT	**Dairy Floating Thermometers** 0-220° F/ 0-110° C multiple scale , mercury filled approx 11 " long.
9.14	TP110	Thermometer for Plate Heat Exchangers -10° to 110° C mercury filled
9.15	TPSS	Thermopockets complete for PHE made of SS AIS 304 quality
9.16	DFT	Handy Electronic Thermometer, fast in reaction, measuring range -50° C to + 360° C, with stainless steel 304 sensor.

AMYL ALCOHOL FOR GERBER TEST

10.1	AM400	" MILFANOL" A GRADE, 20 glass bottles of 400 ml packed in cardboard case

10.2	AMIL	"MILFANOL" A GRADE. 12 plastic bottles of 1 Litre packed in cardboards case
10.3	AM200	"MILFANOL" A GRADE, 200 Litre in plastic barrel bulk packing
10.4	AF200	"FAMINOL" B GRADE, 200 Litre in plastic barrel bulk packing
10.5	AB200	"BRAJINOL" B GRADE, 200 Litre in plastic barrel bulk packing

SAMPLING APPLIANCES

11.1	DS50	**Milk Sampling Dipper** Stainless Steel 50 ml capacity
11.2	DS160	Milk Sampling Dipper stainless steel 100 ml capacity
11.3	DS250	Tanker Dipper Stainless Steel 250 ml capacity
11.4	DA35	Milk Sampling Dipper Aluminium 35 ml capacity
11.5	DA50	Milk Sampling Dipper Aluminium 50 ml capacity
11.6	DA100	Milk Sampling Dipper Aluminium 100 ml capacity
11.7	DA250	Milk Sampling Dipper Aluminium 125 ml capacity
11.8	CTSS	**Cheese Trier** Stainless Steal overall length 155 mm
11.9	BTSS	ButterTrier Stainless Steel overall length 215 mm
11.10	SB35	Sample Bottle Plastic with capacity 35 ml
11.11	SB50	Sample Bottle Plastic with capacity 50 ml
11.12	SB85	Sample Bottle Plastic with capacity 85 ml
11.13	SB100	Sample Bottle Plastic with capacity 100 ml
11.14	SB125	Sample Bottle Plastic with capacity 125 ml
11.15	SB200	Sample Bottle Plastic with capacity 200 ml with screw cap
11.16	SB300	Sample Bottle Plastic with capacity 300 ml with screw cap
11.17	SBSS 1	Sample Bottle Stainless Steel 304 quality 100 ml. capacity
11.18	SBSS50	Sample Bottle Stainless Steel 304 quality 50 ml. capacity
11.19	SMS4	SS Measure set of 1000 ml, 500 ml, 200 ml, 100 ml
11.20	SMS	SS Measure of 1000 ml
11.21	SMS.5	SS Measure 500 ml
11.22	SMS.2	SS Measure 200 ml
11.23	SMS.1	SS Measure 100 ml
11.24	WB250	**Wash Bottle** Polyethylene 250 ml.
11.25	WBP	Wash Bottle Polyethylene 500 ml.
11.26	WB1250	Wash Bottle Polyethylene with inbuilt dropper 250 ml
11.27	WB1500	Wash Bottle Polyethylene with inbuilt dropper 500 ml

STRAINER / FUNNEL

12.1	ST 101	Milk Strainer Aluminium Anodized (Conical Type) with Brass Mesh
12.2	MS 101	Milk Strainer Aluminium Anodized (Conical Type) with Stainless Steel Mesh
12.3	MFSS	Milk funnel / strainer stainless steel Superior made from AISI 304 quality having Top dai: 320 mm; Bottom Dia 127 mm, height 190.mm. approx. weight 1 kg. as per NDDB specification.
12.4	SSB	Spare Mesh for Above (Brass)

12.5 MSS Spare Mesh for Above (Stainless Steel)
12.6 SMSS Spare Mesh for above (Superior stainless steel complete)
12.7 FCL Filter Cloth Nylon

MILK STIRRER / PLUNJAR

13.1 PA36 Milk Can Plunger Aluminium 36"
13.2 PA30 Milk Can-Plunger Aluminium 30"
13.3 PS36 Milk Can Plunger Stainless Steel 36"
13.4 PS30 Milk Can Plunger Stainless Steel 30"
13.5 P LT Milk Tanker Plunger Stainless Steel with Three Supports.

MILK COLLECTION TRAYS

14.1 MCTA Milk Collection Tray G.I. Sheet 600 mm x 450 mm x 65 mm.
14.2 MCTS Milk Collection Tray Stainless Steel Sheet 600 mm x 450 mm x 65 mm. SS 304, one piece construction approx. weight 2.0 Kg. Regulars
14.3 MCSS Milk collection tray made from SS 304 quality stainless steel sheet, one piece construction 600mm x 450 mm x 65 mm, approx. weight 5.0 kgs, Outlet of 38 mm dia pipe, with spoon type fixing 150 mm long terminated with 38 mm SMS union as per NDDB specification

CERTIFIED INSTRUMENTS FROM SHRIRAM INSTITUTE FOR INDUSTRIAL RESEARCH, NEW DELHI.

15.1 SRB Sri Ram Institute Tested and Certified Milk Butyrometer 0-10%
15.2 SRP Sri Ram Institute Tested and Certified Milk Pipettes 10.75 ml.
15.3 SRT Sri Ram Institute Tested and Certified Thermometers
15.4 SRL Sri Ram Institute Tested and Certified Lactometers

16.1 RTKH RECOMMENDED FAT TESTING KIT GERBER METHOD
Recommended Testing Kit **Hand Operated** consisting of fat testing Gerber Centrifuge 12Test,handoperated-No1, Milk Butyrometer ISI 0-10%-2 Boxes, Lock Stopper ISI marked -4 dozen, Lock Stopper key-5 nos, Milk Pipette ISI marked-12 nos, Tilt measure Plastic 1 ml-4 nos, Tilt measure Plastic 10 ml-4 nos, Sample Bottle 100 ml -50 nos, ButyrometerStandaluminum 12T-1nos, Pipette stand aluminium 1-nos, Sample bottle stand12Test-inos, ButyrometercleaningBrush-1gross, Pipette Brush-1 gross, Sample Bottle Brush-1 gross, SS. Sample dipper 100ml -1 nos Wash bottle -10 Nos. Thermometer 0-110°C Alcohol Deluxe-10 nos, Lactometer 0-40 ° 841 F Zeal -1 doz, Lactometer jar small size - 2nos, Amyl Alcohol "MILFANOL" A grade -5litre, S.S. Can Plunger -1 No, Milky sure urea testing-1 pack.

16.2 RTKE Recommended testing kit Electrical operated for 12 Test consisting of above assessories but with electrical Testing centrifuge Nova 12 Test

16.3 RKKGE Recommended testing kit electrical operated for 24 Test consisting of electrical centrifuge GE3 series 24Test.

17.1 RS Richmond Scale for S.N.F. Calculation

18.1 ATK AcidityTesting Kit

LACTOMETERS
ZEAL TYPE

19.1 LLC84 Lactometer 0-40° Graduation at 84^{0} F Zeal Type

19.2 LLC60 Lactometer 0-40° G raduation at 60° F Zeal Type

19.3 LMS84 Original Lakshmi Lactometer 0-40° Graduation at 84^{0} F Metal Scale Mercury polished Zeal type

19.4 LMS60 Original Lakshmi Lactometer 0-40° Graduation at 60° F Metal Scale mercury polished Zeal type

19.5 LCS84 Chadha Lactometer 0-40° Graduation at 84^{0} F with coloured scale Zeal type

19.6 LCS60 Chadha Lactometer 0-40°, Graduation at 60° F with coloured scale Zeal type

19.7 LCOZ Original Zeal Lactometer 0-40° made by G.H. Zeal England.

QUEVENE TYPE

19.8 LQ040 LakshmiLactometerQuevenetype, 0-40° Graduation at 60° F, 1/2 calibrated.

19.9 LQ1540 Lakshmi LactometerQuevenetype, 15-40° Graduation at 60° F, 1/2 calibrated.

19.10 1Q2040 Lakshmi LactometerQuevenetype, 20-40° Graduation at 60° F,1/2 calibrated.

19.11 LQ1535 LakshmiLactometerQuevenetype, 15-35° Graduation at 60° F, 1/2 calibrated.

19.12 LOL5040 Lakshmi Lactometer Quevene type, 0-40° Graduation at 60° F,1/2 calibrated.

19.13 LIS Lactometer 20-35 As per ISI Specification at 270 ^{o}C temperature

19.14 LIST Lactometer Star make ISI marked 20-35 at 27° C temperature Best Quality

DESCO TYPE

19.15 LDT80 Lactometer Desco type 0-40 at 80° F temperature 6" overall height

19.16 LDT60 Lactometer Desco type 0-40 at 60° F temperature 6" overall height

19.17 LID 2/4/60 Lactometer Desco type 20-40 at 60° F temperature 6" overall height

LACTOMETER WITH INBUILT THERMOMETER

19.18 LDGL Lactodensimeter for milk large model, 1,020-1,040, with thermometer 0 ^{o}-40° C in stem., Graduated at 20° C temperature

19.19 LDGS Lactodensimeter for milk small model 1,020-1,035, with thermometer 0-40° C, Graduated at 20° C temperature

19.20 LD60 F Lactodensimeter for milk small model 1,000 - 1,040, with thermometer 0-110° C Graduated at 60° F temperature

HYDROMETER

20.1 HYDAA Hydrometer for Amyl Alcohol 0.800-0.850: 0.001 g/ml. on Temp 20° C

20.2 HYDSA Hydrometer for Sulphuric Acid, 1.800-1.850: 0.001 g/ml on Temp 20° C

LACTOMETER JARS

21.1 LJ Lactometer Aluminium Jar big size with round base anodized with spout & bottom for Quevene type

21.2 LJA Lactometer Aluminium Jar small size for zeal type with round base anodized with spout & bottom for Zeal type

21.3 LJBP Lactometer Plastic Jar big size with round base for Quevene type base

21.4 LJBP Lactometer Plastic Jar small size with round base for Zeal type base

21.5 LJBSS Lactometer Jar Stainless Steel AIS1304 Big Size with round base anodized with spout and bottom for Quevene type

21.6 LJSSS Lactometer Jar Stainless Steel AIS1304 Small Size with round base anodized with spout and bottom for Zeal type

22.1 EMT-88 **NETCO ELECTRONIC MILK FAT TESTER**
Manufactured at highly equipped plant with latest available technology as per NDDB specification instant read out, amazing speed of 130-150 Tests/ Hrs., Easy operating cost measuring up to 13% fat with accurate results and repeatability.

22.2 8611 **NETCO Milkotester Model 8611**
Electronic Milk Fat Tester Model 8611 Pillar Type Display

22.3 8622 NETCO Milkotester Model 8622
Electronic Milk Fat Tester Model No. 8622 PillarType Display with reading in both Sides

MILKO MUNEEM
ELECTRONIC MILK FAT TESTER WITH INBUILT DATA PROCESSOR

22.4 MM-I Having all features of electronic milk fat tester and in addition it has provision to feed member code No, and weight of milk through key pad, Instant display of member code No., weight, fat and amount (value) of milk on 7 segment display, provision for interfacing of electronic weighing scale for automatic transfer of weight to the system, Instant print out on 80 column Printer, Print out slip, shift report, Payment slip and monthly report

22.5 MMP-1 Printer for above

NETCO ELECTRONIC MILK TESTER REAGENTS

22.6 SP Sachet EDTA

22.7 EA Emulsifier 100 Ml.

22.8 AA Antifoaming agent 100 Ml.

22.9 CB3 — Combination of 3 in One Sample
22.10 BKM — Beaker for Mllkotester

22.11 MCC — **AUTOMATIC MILK COLLECTION CENTER CONSISTING OF**

1. Computer, Pentiun with 64 MB Ram
2. 1.2 GB Hard Disk.
3. VGA Mono Monitor
4. 101 Keys Key Board
5 80 Col. Dot Matrix Printer
6. 100 KG Electronic weighing Scale
7. Dairy Thermometer
8. IBMPC Compatible EMT
9. Computer Stationery
10. Key Skin Cover for Key Boards
11. Dust Cover for the Computer
12. Guarantee for One Year

Salient Features

1. Instant Automatic Processing of weight, fat and Value of Milk.
2. All Data in Print as well as Digital Display.
3. Complete Summary Print out of the Day.
4. Each Members Monthly Report.
5. Tri- Monthly (Period Optional) Total Printout Summary.
6. Tri- Monthly (Optional Period) Summary of Each Day.
7. Print out Headed by Collection Centre Name.

ULTRASONIC MILK ANALYZER

22.12 U3-1 — Ultrasonic Milk analyzer 3 in 1 for analyses of FAT, SNF and DENSITY in a sample of whole freshly drawn milk or preserved milk

22.13 U4-1 — Ultrasonic Milk Analyzer 4inl for analyses of FAT, SNF, DENSITY and PROTEIN in a sample of whole freshly drawn milk or Preserved milk. Must for dairy Laboratory and milk collection centers.

22.14 U5-1 — Ultrasonic Milk Analyzer 5 in 1 for analyzer of FAT, SNF DENSITY, PROTEIN, TEMPERATURE and Percentage of ADDED WATER in a sample of whole freshly drawn milk or preserved milk. Must for dairy laboratory & collection centers.

LABORATORY INSTRUMENTS

23.1	SL 100	Spirit Lamp 100ml
23.2	SDT4	Sediment Tester Bench Mounting Hinch Aluminium Bottle Cap 400 mm, Filtering Surface Dia 18 mm,GerberType, DischargeTube with filters and comparative Chart.
23.3	SD24	Sedimentation Disc 28 mm
23.4	AG	Acidity Gun of Stainless Steel Double Pipe.
23.5	RFA	Abbe Refractometer with Refractive Index & Sugar Scale
23.6	RFB	**Butyro Refractometer (Oil + Sugar Refractometer)**
23.7	RF32	Hand Refractometer O.32% Erma Type
23.8	RF28	Hand Ref ractometer 28.62% Erma Type
23.9	RF58	Hand Refractometer 58.92% Erma Type

23.10	RF30	Hand Refractometer 0.30%, 0-50% (B&S Type) Erma Type
23.11	RF40	Hand Ref ractometer 40.85% (With Imported Optics)
23.12	I M85	Infra Red Moisture Balance (5 gm. Capacity)
23.13	I MB10	Infra Red Moisture Balance (10 gm. Capacity)
23.14	I MB20	Infra Red Moisture Balance (20 gm./ 25 gm Capacity)
23.15	MPA	Melting Point Apparatus
23.16	CCO	Colony Counter Ordinary
23.17	CCD	Digital Colony Counter 3 Digit
23.18	MF1000	Muffle Furnace Fiber 1000° C size 10"x 5"x5"
23.19	MF1200	........as above 1200° C size 10" x 5" x 5"
23.20	HMR250	Heating Mantle with Energy Regulator 250 Ml.
23.21	HMR500	........as above 500 Ml.
23.22	ACV	Autoclave (Vertical) Inner Chamber of S.S with Gasket. Gauge & Safety Valve size H= 450 mm, x 250 mm Dai
23.23	ACH	Autoclave (Horizontal) size -450 mm dia x 250 mm
23.24	OV250	Oven Universal (MemmertType)temp range 0-250° C SS size 300x300x300mm
23.25	IB	Bacteriological Incubator size 300 x 300 x300 mm
23.26	OVDW	Vacuum Oven Double Walled S.S 250 x 300 mm.
23.27	WABR	Water Bath Rectangular Single Walled S.S. 300 x 250 x100 mm.
23.28	WABS	Serological water Bath S. S. 300 x 250 x175 mm Temp Control System
23.29	WABB	**Water Bath with water suction Device for B.R.Test**
23.30	TD 12	Tray Dryer SS to Accommodate 12 Trays with forced air Circulation fan temp Controller System
23.31	TD 24	.... as above For 24 Trays
23.32	IBOD6	B.O.D. Incubator S.S Automatic 6 Cu Ft.
23.33	IBOD10	.... as above 10 Cu. Ft.
23.34	WS2	Water Still Automatic wall type Cap. 2 Ltrs.
23.35	WS4	.... as above Cap. 4 Ltrs.
23.36	HP12	Laboratory hot plate (with Rotatory Switch) size 12"/ 10"
23.37	CH450	Humidity Cabinet Double wall forced air Circulation SS size 450 x450 x700 mm.
23.38	M22	Lab Microscope complete with 2 Objective and 2 eyes Pieces
23.39	M1500	Laboratory Advance Microscope Mag.1500
23.40	P-HM	Digital Ph Meter (Lab Model)
23.41	PHP	Ph Meter Pocket Type
23.42	PH	Ph Paper 10x20 Leaves Ph 3.5-6.0
23.43	COND	Lab Conductivity Meter
23.44	COPH	Photoelectric Colorimeter Analog type with S. Filters
23.45	COPHD	Digital Photoelectric Colorimeter

LABORATORY BEAKER, FLASK & TEST TUBES

23.46	GB50	Glass Beaker 50 ml
23.47	GB100	Glass Beaker 100 ml
23.48	GB250	Glass Beaker 250 ml

23.49	GB500	Glass Beaker 500 ml
23.50	CF1L	**Conical Flask** 1 liter
23.51	CF500	Conical Flask 500 ml
23.52	CF250	**Conical Flask** 250 ml
23.53	TT1	**Test tube** Glass 10 mm x 75 mm
23.54	TT2	Test tube Glass 12 rim x 75 mm
23.55	TT3	Test tube Glass 12 mm x 100 mm
23.56	TT4	Test tube Glass 15 mm x 125 mm
23.57	TT5	Test tube Glass 15 mm x 150 mm
23.58	TT6	Test tube Glass 16 mm x 100 mm
23.59	TT7	Test tube Glass 18 mm x 150 mm
23.60	TT8	Test tube Glass 25 mm x 100 mm
23.61	TT9	Test tube Glass 25 mm x 150 mm
23.62	TT10	Test tube Glass 25 mm x 200 mm
23.63	TT11	Test tube Glass 32 mm x 200 mm
23.64	TT12	Test tube Glass 38 mm x 200 mm
23.65	GMP11	Test Tube All Graduated 11 ml. (10 mm. Dia) for measuring milk pipette.
23.66	MC100	**Measuring Cylinder** 100 ml Borosilicate Glass
23.67	CSG	**Laboratory Safety Goggles.**

MILK PRESERVATIVES FOR LABORATORY USE

23.68	FML	Formalin (400 grm. Bottle)
23.69	MBT50	Methylene Blue tablet (pack of 50 tablets)
23.70	RT100	Resazurine tablets (pack of 100 tablets)
23.71	PDT	Potassium Dichromate Tablets (Pack of 1000 tablets)

LABORATORY CHEMICALS

23.72	LCACC	Accetone 500 ml Bottle
23.73	LCDIA	Diastix (50 Sticks Pack)
23.74	LCRES	Resorcinol (250 gms. Bottle)
23.75	LCPHS	Phenolphthalein solution (125 ml Bottle)
23.761	LCSH	Sodium Hydroxide N/10 (500ml Bottle)
23.77	LCLM	Leishman Methanol (500m1 Bottle)
23.78	LCLA	Lactic Acid (500 grm. Bottle)
23.79	LCSCH	Starch 250 grm.

SEALING ACCESSORIES

23.80	LSD	Lead Seal 1/2" size
23.81	SEW	Sealing Wire Twisted Commercial Quality 20/33.
23.82	SEP	Sealing Pincer with mark of the Customer

23.83	AC	Aluminium Hand Bottle Capper.
23.84	ACW	Spare Rubber Washers for Hand Bottle Capper.
23.85	AC38	**Aluminium Foils Caps** 38 mm for Milk Bottles

CREAM SEPARATORS

CREAM SEPARATORS CAP. 60 LPH.

24.1	RS7	Cream Separator RS-7 Hand Driven Table Model 60 Ltr. Capacity Per Hour (Lister Model) with Stainless Steel Bowl Discs.
24.2	SSS7	As Above SSS-7 Complete with Stainless Steel Bowl, Stainless Steel Receiving Tank & Stainless Steel Spout set.

CREAM SEPARATOR CAP 60 LPH ELECTRIC

24.3	ES7	Electrically Operated with stainless steel bowl discs and bowl stainless steel receiving tanks & stainless steel spout set. Table model. Power consumption AC 220 volts 50 Hz.

CREAM SEPARATORS CAP. 100 LPH.

24.4	RS 8	Cream Separator RS-8 Hand Driven Table Model, Capacity 100 Ltr. Per Hour (Lister Model) with Stainless Steel Bowl Discs (Ball Bearing).
24.5	SSS8	As Above SSS-8 with Complete Stainless Steel Bowl, Stainless Steel Spout set and Stainless Steel Receiving Tank

CREAM SEPARATORS CAP. 165 LPH.

24.6	RS 9	Cream-Separator RS-9 Hand Driven Table Model Capacity 165 Ltr. Per Hour (Lister Model) with Stainless Steel Bowl Discs (Ball Bearing)
24.7	SSS9	As Above SSS-9 with Complete Stainless Steel Bowl, Stainless Steel spout set & Stainless Steel Receiving Tank.
24.8	EA 9	Electric Attachment with motor 1/4 H.P Single Phase A.C. for RS-9 or SSS-9 Complete with Heavy Base Plate & Auto Speed Pulley.

CREAM SEPARATORS CAP. 225 LPH.

24.9	RS 10	Cream-Separator RS-10 hand Driven Table Model Capacity 225 Litres Per Hour (Lister Model) with Stainless Steel Bowl Discs & Spouts set (All Ball Bearing)
24.10	EA10	Electric Attachment with motor 1/4 H.P Single Phase A.C. for RS-10 Complete with Heavy Base Plate & Auto Speed Pulley.

CREAM SEPARATORS CAP. 325 LPH.

24.11	RS 11	Cream-Separator RS-11 hand Driven Table Model Capacity 325 Litres Per Hour (Lister Model) with Stainless Steel Bowl Discs & Spouts set (All Ball Bearing)
24.12	SSS11	As Above SSS-11 Complete with Stainless Steel Bowl, Stainless Steel spouts set & Stainless Steel Receiving Tank.
24.13	EA 11	Electric Attachment with 1/2 H.F Single Phase A.C. for RS-11 or SSS-11 Complete with Heavy Base Plate & Auto Speed Pulley.

CREAM SEPARATORS CAP. 425 LPH.

24.14	RS 12	Cream-Separator RS-12 Hand Driven Table Model Capacity 425 Litres Per Hour (Lister Model) with Stainless Steel Bowl Discs & Spouts Set (All Ball Bearing)
24.15	SSS12	As Above SSS-12 Complete with Stainless Steel Bowl, Stainless Steel spouts Set & Stainless Steel Receiving Tank.
24.16	EA 12	Electric Attachment with 1/2 H.P. Single Phase motor A.C. for RS-12 or SSS-12 Complete with Heavy Base Plate & Auto Speed Pulley

CREAM SEPARATORS CAP. 550 LPH.

24.17	RS 13	Cream- Separator RS-13 Hand Driven Table Model, Capacity 550 Litres Per Hour (Lister Model) with Stainless Steel Bowl Discs & Spouts set (All Ball Bearing)
24.18	SSS13	As Above SSS-13 Complete with Stainless Steel Bowl, Stainless Steel Spouts Set & Stainless Steel-Receiving Tank.
24.19	EA13	Electric Attachment with 1/2 H.P Single Phase motor A.C. for RS-13 or
24.20		SSS-13 Complete with Heavy Base Plate & Auto Speed Pulley.
24.21	A108	Lakshmi 108 All Electric Cream Separator (Alfa Model) Capacity 550 Litres Per Hour. All Milk Contacting parts Made From Stainless Steel with 1/2 H.P Single Phase Electric Motor
24.22	L108	As Above Capacity 550 Litres per Hour with Stainless Steel Bowl Discs and Stainless Steel Spout Set with 1/2 H.P Single Phase Motor

CREAM SEPARATORS CAP. 750 LPH.

24.23	A109	Lakshmi 109 All Electric Cream Separator, (Alfa Model) Capacity 750 Litres Per Hour. All Milk Contacting Parts Made From Stainless Steel with 1/2 H.P. Single Phase A.C. Motor
24.24	SSS14	Lakshmi 109 Cream Separator, Hand Cum-Electric Operated Table Model Capacity 750 Litres per Hour. (Alfa Model) All milk contacting parts made from Stainless Steel, Complete with 1/2 H.P Single Phase A.C. Motor

CREAM SEPARATORS CAP. 1000 LPH.

24.24 AE1 Lakshmi AE-1 All Electric Cream- Separator Capacity 1000 Litres Per Hour. All Milk contacting Parts made from Stainless Steel (Alfa Model). with 1 H.P Three Phase A.C. Motor (Crompton)

24.25 AEO 2 **ORIGINAL LAKSHMI ON LINE CREAM SEPARATOR CAP.2000 LPH.** Cream Separator 2000 LPH Hermetic type . The Separator will be tripurpose on line with built-in feed pump and will be fitted with standardizing device all milk contacting parts will be of SS-304 with 5 H.P. 3 Phase Electric Motor

24.26 AEG5 **ORIGINAL LAKSHMI GHEE CLARIFIER CAPACITY 500 LPH** Lakshmi All Electric Ghee Clarifier Centrifuge having capacity 500 LPH, Complete Bowl, Bowl Disc and Spout set will be made from Stainless Steel 304 Quality with 1.H.P three phase A.C. Motor.

24.27 AEG1K **ORIGINAL LAKSHMI GHEE CLARIFIER CAPACITY 1000 LPH** Lakshmi All Electric Ghee Clarifier Centrifuge having capacity 1000 LPH, Complete Bowl, Bowl Disc and Spout set will be made from Stainless Steel 304 Quality.

24.28 GF800 **GHEE FILTER** Microfined Ghee filtration unit to filter ghee up to 5 micron having capacity of 800 to 1000 kg / hour power consumption 1 HP 3 Phase 50 cycles, complete body will be of SS 304 Quality.

SPARES FOR CREAM SEPARATORS

25.1 OR10 'O' Rings for RS. 7/8/9/10/11/12

25.2 OR13 'O' Rings for RS. 13 to 108, 109 & AE-!

25.3 NS9 Neck Spring for RS 7/8/9

25.4 NS10 Neck Spring for RS 11/12/13/Lakshmi 109

25.6 BN10 Bowl Nut S.S. for RS 7/8/9 /10/11

25.7 BN13 Bowl Nut S.S for RS 12/131108/109

Gasket Kit for Cream Separators

25.8 GK911 Gasket for Model RS 7, RS 8, RS9, RS10 and RS. 11 Cream Separator

25.9 3K1 2 Gasket for Model RS. 12, RS. 13 Cream Separator

BUTTER CHURNERS

BUTTER CHURNERS CAP. 5 LTR.

26.1 BC5 Butter Churner Stainless Steel Hand Driven, Barrel Capacity 5 Ltr. with M. S. Base for Home Use and Laboratory Purpose.

BUTTER CHURNER CAP. 20 LTR.

26.2 BC20 Butter Churner Stainless Steel Hand Driven, Barrel Capacitv 20 Ltr with

Input/output Door, Sight Glass, Air Discharge Nipple, Drain outlet and Mounted on M.S. Stand

26.3 BCE20 .... as above but with electrical attachment

BUTTER CHURNER CAP. 60 LTR.

26.4 BC60 Butter Churner Stainless Steel Hand Driven, Barrel Capacity 60 Ltr with Input/output Door, Sight Glass, Air Discharge Nipple, Drain outlet and Mounted on M.S. Stand

26.5 BCE 60 .... as above but with electrical attachment

BUTTER CHURNER CAP. 90 LTR.

26.6 BC100 Butter Churner Stainless Steel Hand Driven, Barrel Capacity 90 Ltr with Input/output Door, Sight Glass, Air Discharge Nipple, Drain Outlet and Mounted on M.S. Stand

26.7 BCE100 .... as above but with electrical attachment

BUTTER CHURNER CAP. 150 LTR.

26.8 BC150 Butter Churner Stainless Steel Electrically Driven, Having 150 Ltr Capacity SS Barrel of AISI 304 Quality with Input/Output Door, Sight Glass, Air Discharge Nipple, Drain Outlet Complete with Water Spray Rod, Variable Speed Gear Box Mounted on Mild Steel Strong Frame AC 220/440 Volts 1 H.P Single/Three Phase.

BUTTER CHURNER CAP. 250 LTR.

26.9 BC250 Butter Churner Stainless Steel Electrically Driven, Having 250 Ltr Capacity SS Barrel of AISI 304 Quality with Input/Output Door, Sight Glass, Air Discharge Nipple, Drain Outlet Complete with Water Spray Rod, Variable Speed Gear Box Mounted on Mild Steel Strong Frame AC 220/440 Volts 2 H.P Single/Three Phase.

BUTTER CHURNER CAP. 500 LTR.

26.10 BC500 Butter Churner Stainless Steel Electrically Driven, Having 500 Ltr Capacity SS Barrel of AISI 304 Quality with Input/Output Door, Sight Glass, Air Discharge Nipple, Drain Outlet Complete with Water pray Rod, Variable Speed Gear Box Mounted on Mild Steel Strong Frame AC 440 Volts 3 H.P Three Phase

BUTTER CHURNER CAP. 1000 LTR.

26.11 BC1000 Butter Churner Stainless Steel Electrically Driven, Having 1000 Ltr Capacity SS Barrel of AISI 304 Quality with Input/Output Door, Sight Glass, Air Discharge Nipple, Drain Outlet Complete with Water Spray Rod, Variable Speed Gear Box Mounted on Mild Steel Strong Frame AC 440 Volts 5 H.P Three Phase.

26.12 BT250 **ButterTrolley** 250 Kg capacity having drain outlet & sand blasted from inside

26.13 BT 150 **ButterTrolley** 150 Kg capacity having drain outlet & sand blasted from inside

OPTIONAL FEATURES FOR ABOVE BUTTER CHURNERS

27.1 INCH Optional Control Panel with additional inching.facility can be connected with any of the above Electrical Butter Churners

27.2 ACDC Optional-AC/DC Drive with three speed control functions with control panel which can be connected with any of the above electrical Butter Churner

27.3 BCSPL Optional Fixed Speed Gear Box having fixed gears on RPM. 4,8,16 and 32 for Best Results forTable Butter.

BUTTER MAKING ACCESSORIES

28.1	BWW	Wooden Butter Worker made of Teak Wood with Suitable Stand Capacity of 5Kg
28.2	BW10	Wooden Butter Worker made of Teak Wood with Suitable Stand Capacity 10 Kg
28.3	BW14	Wooden Butter Worker made of Teak Wood with Suitable stand capacity 12.5/14 Kg
28.4	BPT9	Butter PrintTable Paddle Operated Suitable for Making 9 Cakes of 25Gms at a time
28.5	BPT24	.... as above for 24 cakes of 25 Grms at a time
28.6	BPT36	.... as above for 36 cakes of 25 Grms at a time
28.7	BPT9-50	.... as above for 9 cakes of 50 Grms at a time
28.8	BPT4	.... as above for 4 cakes of 100 Grms (Amul Shape) at a time.
28.9	BPT2	.... as above for 2 cakes of 500 Grms (Amul Shape) at a time.
28.10	BP5T5	Butter Print table, Paddle Operated of 4 Cavity Block Suitable for Making Cakes from 50 Grm. to 500 Grms.
28.11	BP250	Butter Print Table, Paddle Operated Suitable for Making 250 Grms Cakes.
28.12	BP 500	Butter PrintTable, Paddle Operated Suitable for Making 500 Grms Cakes.
28.13	BM	Butter Moulds of Rectangular Shape Made of Teak Wood.
28.14	BS1	Butter scotch hand teak wood 10"x3"
28.15	BS2	Butter scotch hand teak wood 12"x3"
28.16	BS3	Butter scotch hand teak wood 14"x3"
28.17	BS4	Butter scotch hand teak wood 12"x4"
28.18	BSP1	Butter scoop perforated 10"x4"
28.19	BSP2	Butter scoop perforated 12"x5"
28.20	BSP3	Butter scoop perforated 14"x6"
28.21	BB1	Butter board teak wood 12"x8"x1

28.22 BK12 Butter Knife teak wood 12"x3"
28.23 BK15 Butter Knife teak wood 15"x4"
28.24 BB18 Butter beater 18"x3"
28.25 BP15 **Butter cream sieves** teak wood frame with nylon filter
28.26 BL15 Butter ladle plain type 15"x3"
28.27 BL18 Butter ladle plain type 18"x3"
28.28 BSPW Butter Salt pure white colour 450 gm
28.29 BCASL Butter colour Annato grade 5 litre jar
28.30 MB1 Butter moisture balance complete with all accessories of 0.1 % complete with melting cup, wire holder for cup butter scoop, spirit lamp. Butter wt. **small rider and large rider.**
28.31 BSSS **Butter Scotch of stainless steel** size 175 x 75 mm thickness 12 mm complete with handle non stick surface.
28.32 BS40 **Butter Shovels of stainless steel** having blade thickness 3 mm, size 270 x 240 mm handle, 38 mm pipe grip, sand blasted.

SEALING AND FILLING MACHINES
SEALING MACHINE HAND OPERATEDTABLE MODEL available in

29.1 SMH8 8" sealing length
29.2 SMH10 10" sealing length
29.3 SMH12 12" sealing length

SEALING MACHINE PADDLE OPERATED STANDING MODEL

29.4 SMP10 10"sealing length
29.5 SMP16 16"sealing length
29.6 SMAT **AUTO CONTINUES SEALING MACHINE TABLE MODEL** motor operated having special feature of Auto Jaw sealing on variable speeds, suitable for fast & easy operation for pre-pouch having 12" sealing length.
29.7 PPFMS **POLY PIPE FILLING & SEALING MACHINE SEMI AUTOMATIC** The poly pipe is converted into pouch having sealing both the sides. The machine fill and seal 300 to 400 pouches per hour The tube has to be manually fed in one length. The operation of filling, sealing and cutting is done in one operation. The machine will have 20 Litre float balance tank .
29.8 SHF **Poly pipe sealing and mannual filling machine.** The liquid is been measured and filled in to the hopper. Sealing and tube cutting operation will be paddle operated in one shot.
29.9 PFMS **POUCH FILLING & SEALING MACHINE SEMIAUTOMATIC** Semi Automatic Pouch Packing Machine for Milk. This Machine fill and seal 300 to 400 Pouches per hour. The preformed pouches are to be manually fed however the operation of the filler and sealer are by pressing separate levers. The machine will have SS construction.
29.10 PFMA **POUCH FILLING MACHINE AUTOMATIC** To fill and seal 1200 Packs per Hour. The cabinet is built on a stainless steel chassis. All Milk contact parts made from stainless steel complete

automatically controlled by electronic circuits.

29.11 LCFS **YOGHURT/LIQUID FILLING & SEALING MACHINE SEMI AUTOMATIC**
Semi Automatic Yoghurt/liquid Packing Machine for Milk. This Machine fill and seal approx. 300 cups per hour. The cups are to be manually fed and the filling will be done automatically, manually cups has to be taken under the sealer for sealing operation. Tolerance ± 2%.

MILK PUMPS

The motor will be directly coupled to the pump having 2900 RPM and TEFL design reputed make suitable for operation on Single/ 3 phase. 50 Hz 400/440 Volts. A.C. Supply. All the parts of the pump coming into direct contact with milk will be of stainless steel of AISI 304 quality and will be finished to dairy standards. The motor portion will- be S.S shrouded.
The shroud will have air circulation holes and cable entry. The pumps will be fitted over 3 nos. SS legs

30.1 MP1 .... as above but with Milk Pump 1 HP
30.2 MP2 .... as above but with Milk Pump 2 HP
30.3 MP3 .... as above but with Milk Pump 3 HP

BATCH PASTEURIZER

The Batch Pasteurizer will be triple walled. The inner shell fabricated from stainless steel 304 Quality sheet. Sufficient insulation will be provided to ensure no heat loss. One reduction gear box attached with electric motor fitted on the top. Agitator SS 304 with shaft and blade will be provided on the top.

31.1 BP500 .... Same as above in 500 Ltrs
31.2 BP250 .... Same as above in 250 Ltrs
31.3 BP100 .... Same as above in 100 Ltrs
31.4 BP40 .... Same as above in 40 Ltrs

32.1 BS480 **BATCH TYPE MILK BOTTLE STERILIZER**
Batch Milk Sterilization unit made of 6 mm M.S Sheet rolled welded construction, horizontal with M.S Frame for placing bottle
Crate Cap. 480 x 200 ml bottle per batch. The sterilizer is supplied with quick closing/ opening screw type door and steam spraying device on the top and bottom. It is supported on four MS Pipe for floor mounting.
The following Accessories supplied with sterilizer
1 No. Steam Trap
1 No. Pressure Gauge
1 No. Safety Valve
1 No. Blow off Cock

1 No. Dial Thermometer

33.1 MSMP9 **PASTEURIZATION UNIT CONTINUOUS MSMP 900 LPH**

The plate pasteurization unit is well suited for pasteurization of Milk

STANDARD DESIGN

1. Balance Tank is stainless steel, inside and outside polished, equipped with S.S. Float and loose cover.
2. Stainless steel centrifugal pump for product, complete with electrical motor.
3. Plate heat exchanger with frame cladded with stainless steel. The plate pack is clamped between frame head and follower by means of stainless steel tie bars placed along the edge of the frame.
4. External Holding time : 20 seconds.
5. Stainless steel electrical water heating set
6. Set of temperature regulating equipment consisting of Control panel for controlling and recording of the pasteurization and outlet temperature.
7. Set of internal stainless steel pipes, fittings and base frame for mounting of the equipment.

The equipment is assembled on base frame and tested in our factory.

MILK COOLING

34.1 DF5K **COOLING CABINET 500 LTRS. CAPACITY**

For Milk having Double compartment of 250 ltrs. Complete with suitable one no. compressor and Refrigeration system. The outer and inner shell both will be of Stainless Steel. The input door will be provided on the top and stainless Steel Ball Valve will be fitted at the bottom,

34.2 DF1OK **COOLING CABINET 1000 LTRS. CAPACITY**

For Milk having four compartments of 250 ltrs. Complete with suitable two nos. compressor and Refrigeration system. The outer and inner shell both will be of Stainless Steel. The input door will be provided on the top and Stainless Steel Ball Valve will be fitted at the bottom.

35.3 BCT 450 **MILK COOLING TANK (BULK COOLERS) 450 Litres**

Direct expansion Cooling Tank (Open Tank) Capacity 450 Ltrs. Has large opening lids for easy access and rounded internal corners, to facilitate thorough cleaning. Tank insulation is provided by factory injected polyurethene foam of 50 mm. All control system, integral condensing units (Hermetic Type) with R22 refrigerant.

Having Features of :-

★ Low Running Cost
★ High Standard of Milk Hygiene
★ Reduced Electricity Consumption
★ Agitator On/ Off
★ 35°C to 4°C within 3 Hours
★ wing Unit Hermetic, 220Vofts Single Phase and 3 Phase, 50 HZ Supply,
★ Two Milking tank Design

★ Cooling On/Off
★ Digital Temperature Display
★ All SS 304

35.2 IBT1850 **MILK COOLING TANK !CE BANK TYPE 2000 Ltrs.**

(Minimal Capacity 1850 Ltrs.)

Ice Bank Tank is constructed from three layers of Stainless Steel. The inner most tank hold the milk, then comes the chilled water tank and the ice bank itself, finally the outer layer, packed with high quality, non setting fiberglass insulation, fully tested copper cooling coils are at the heart of the chilling system, with spray rails distributing iced water spray maximum capacity, wide radius corners, easy cleaning as do self supporting inspection lids. The tank come complete with handy calibrated measuring Rod.

Having Features of :

★ Agitator for gentle, even distribution
★ Easy to read thermometers
★ Ice Welter Spray Rails
★ Self supporting Lids
★ Wide Radius comers for Easy Cleaning.
★ Available in a range of size to suit all farm needs
★ High Capacity non corrosive water pump
★ Removable cover for easy access to mechanical parts
★ Three S.S. Tanks for lasting Hygienic and Service
★ 1 X 3.00 H.P. Compressor Unit

INSTANT MILK CHILLING UNITS (IMCU)

36.1 IMCU10 **INSTANT MILK CHILLING UNIT (IMCU) 10000 Litres Per Day**
IMCU WILL WORK ON 1000 LPH INSTANT CHILLING BASIS

Milk will be cooled from 30 Deg C to 8 Deg. C in first run and further temperature is lowered to 4 Deg C by recirculation.

The package includes :

* 1 No. Balance tank 100 Litre
* 1 No. Milk Pump 1 HP
* 1 No. In line Milk Filter
* 1 No. Plate Heat Exchanger 1000 litre Per Hour Capacity
* 1 No. Milk Storage Tank Double Compartment 10000 Litre having inner Shell of S.S and outer Shell will be of MS construction.
* 2 No. Semi Hermetic Compressor of 7.5 TR. with instant chiller, spray pound and control panel.
* 1 Each Chilled water pump and Condenser water pump.
* 1 Lot SS/MS/GI Pipeline and fittings.
* 1 Lot Electrical panel and cabling.

36.2 IMCU5 **INSTANT MILK CHILLING UNIT (IMCU) 5000 Litres Per Day**
IMCU WILL WORK ON 500 LPH INSTANT CHILLING BASIS

Milk will be cooled from 30 Deg C to 8 Deg. C in first run and further temperature is lowered to 4 Deg C by recirculation.

The package includes :

* 1 No. Balance tank 100 Litre
* 1 No. Milk Pump 1 HP
* 1 No. In line Milk Filter
* 1 No. Plate Heat Exchanger 1000 litre Per Hour Capacity
* 1 No. Milk Storage Tank Double Compartment 5000 Litre having inner Shell of S.S and outer Shell will be of MS construction.
- ★ 1 No. Semi Hermetic Compressor of 7.5 TR. with instant chiller, spray pound and control panel.
- ★ 1 Each Chilled water pump and Condenser water pump.
- ★ 1 Lot SS/MS/GI Pipeline and fittings.
- ★ 1 Lot Electrical panel and cabling.

pound and control panel.

- ★ 1 Each Chilled water pump and Condenser water pump.
- ★ 1 Lot SS/MS/GI Pipeline and fittings.
- ★ 1 Lot Electrical panel and cabling.

36.3 IMCU10 **INSTANT MILK CHILLING UNIT (IMCU) 2000 Litres Per Day**
IMCU WILLWORK ON 350 LPH INSTANT CHILLING BASIS

Milk will be cooled from 30 Deg C to 8 Deg. C in first run and further temperature is lowered to 4 Deg C by recirculation.

The package includes:

- ★ 1 No. Balance tank 100 Litre
- ★ 1 No. Milk Pump 1 HP
- ★ 1 No. In line Milk Filter
- ★ 1 No. Plate Heat Exchanger 500 litre Per Hour Capacity
- ★ 1 No. Milk Storage Tank Double Compartment 10000 Litre having inner Shell of S.S and outer Shell will be of MS construction.
- ★ 1 No. Sealed Hermetic Comnressor of 5 TR. with instant chiller, spray pound and control panel.
- ★ 1 Each Chilled water pump and Condenser water pump.
- ★ 1 Lot SS/MS/GI Pipeline and fittings.
- ★ 1 Lot Electrical panel and cabling.

PLATE COOLERS/CHILLERS

FROM 500 LPH TO 3500 LPH

The Most Highly Efficient and Cost-Effective Method to Pre cool Milk. 4 Instant Milk Cooling. © Reduces Energy Costs. © Wide range Enables the Most Cost Effective Size to be Used. 0 Virtually Maintenance Free © Expandable to Meet future Increase in your Milk Production.

Herringbone Plate	Bright annealed Stainless Steel 630x145
End Plates	Grade 304 Stainless Steel.

Gaskets	Food Grade Rubber.
Connections	Milk 32 mm. O. D. Water 1" Bspt Male
Water Flow	Minimum-Equal to Milk Flow. Maximum 2.5 Times Flow
water or milk Pressure :	Maximum 2 Bar (29PSI)

Balance Tanks A Range of Balance tank are Available to Maximize the Plate Cooler Pertormance

37.1	M100	.....................as above	having capacity of 500 LPH
37.2	M200	.....................as above	having capacity of 1000 LPH
37.3	M300	.....................as above	having capacity of 1500 LPH
37.4	M400	.....................as above	having capacity of 2000 LPH
37.5	M500	.....................as above	having capacity of 2500 LPH
37.6	M600	.....................as above	having capacity of 3000 LPH
37.7	M700	.....................as above	having capacity of 3500 LPH

DUMP TANK

Dump Tank receiving tank of 2mm. S.S. 304. Dump tank will be rectangular shaped, open top with 1.6 mm S.S. cover on 4 nos. S.S. tubular legs with S.S. plug cork 38 mm dia of SMS type.

38.1	DT1K..................	as above	having capacity 1000 Litre
38.2	DT5..................	as above	having capacity 500 Litre.
38.3	DT250..................	as above	having capacity 250 Liter.

39.1 FB20 FLOAT BALANCE TANK Capacity 20 Ltrs.
Balance Tank will be of stainless steel 304 quality, inside and outside polished, equipped with SS 304 Float and loose cover.

39.2 F8250 FLOAT BALANCE TANK Capacity 250 Ltrs.
Balance Tank will be of stainless steel 304 quality inside and outside polished, equipped with SS 304 Float and loose cover.

MILKING MACHINES

MILKING MACHINE MODEL CS-1

40.1 CS1 Milking Machine with one can and cluster assembly, floor mounted, with imported components Like pulsator. set of liners, set of teat cups, milk claw and vacuum controller

MILKING MACHINE MODEL CS-1T (TROLLY MOUNTED)

40.2 CS1T Milking Machine with one can and cluster assembly, trolley mounted, with imported components Like pulsator, set of liners, set of teat cups, milk claw and vacuum controller

MILKING MACHINE MODEL CS-2

40.3 CS2 Milking Machine with two can and cluster assembly, floor mounted, with imported components Like pulsator, set of liners, set of teat cups, milk claw and vacuum controller

MILKING MACHINE MODEL CS-2T (TROLLY MOUNTED)

40.4	CS2T	Milking Machine with two can and cluster assembly, trolley mounted, with imported components Like pulsator, set of liners, set of teat cups, milk claw and vacuum controller

MILKING MACHINE MODEL CS-3

40.5	CS3	Milking Machine with three can and cluster assembly, floor mounted, with imported components Like pulsator, set of liners, set of teat cups, milk claw and vacuum controller

MILKING MACHINE MODEL CS-4

40.6	CS4	Milking Machine with four can and cluster assembly, floor mounted, with imported components Like pulsator, set of liners, set of teat cups, milk claw and vacuum controller

MILKING MACHINE MODEL CS-5

40.7	CS5	Milking Machine with five can and cluster assembly, floor mounted, with imported components Like pulsator, set of liners, set of teat cups, milk claw and vacuum controller

MILKING MACHINE MODEL CS-6

40.8	CS6	Milking Machine with six can and cluster assembly, floor mounted, with imported components Like pulsator, .set of liners, set of teat cups. milk claw and vacuum controller

Additional accessories if required Kero/Petrol engine of reputed make suitable for above machine with necessary fittings will be quoted on request.

MILKING MACHINE SPARES ACCESSORIES

41.1	MMSCA	Strip Cup Assembly
41.2	MMDB	Drinking Bowl
41.3	MMET	Ear Tag for Cows or Buffalos
41.4	MMTA	Ear Tag Applicator
41.5	MMDC	Dip Cup
41.6	MMBS	Brush set (set of 4 Brushes)
41.7	MMTB	Milk Tube Brush with connector
41.8	MMLB	Liner Brush
41.9	MMCB	Claw Brush
41.10	MP%/1XB	Extensions for tube brush (Set of 3 mm)
41.11	MMCL	MS Clamp for PV.C Pipe
41.12	MMOIL	Special CAS Oil for Vacuum Pump 1 Ltr.

MILK CAN ASSEMBLY & PARTS

41.13	MMASSE	Milk Can Assembly to fit with any make with complete Milk Can, Can Cover Assembly, Pulsator, Cluster set and Vacuum Tube
41.14	MMCA	Cluster Assembly
41.15	MMTC	Teat Cup Stainless Steel (set of 4Nos)
41,16	MMPUL	Pulsator SAC Uniflow (oil free & adjustable)
41.17	MMPN	Nipple for pulsator SS (Required to fit S.A.C. Pulsator on other make)
41.18	MMPS	Spring for Pulsator
41.19	MMMC	Milk Claw
41.20	MMNRRV	Non return valve
41.21	MMCC	Can Cover of stainless steel
41.22	MMCSR	Can Seal Ring
41.23	MM3WC	Plastic clamp for T.RT & M.T. (Set of 2 Nos)
41.24	MMPTC	Plastic Support for twin pulsator tube (set of 2 Nos)

RUBBER PIPES AND TUBES

41.25	MMVH	Vacuum Hose Long
41.26	MMTPT	PVC Transparent Milk Tube
41.27	MMSPT	Short Pulsation Tube (set of 4 Nos).
41.28	MMTPT	Twin PulsatorTube
41.29	MMVR	VACUUM REGULATOR

VACUUM PIPE LINE

41.30	MMPL	PVC Rigid pipe length 3meter
41.31	MMCU	PVC coupler (set of 2 Nos)
41.32	MMBND	PVC Bend
41.33	MMTEE	PVC Tee (set of 2Nos)
41.34	MMEL	PVC End Cap (set of 2Nos)
41.35	MMVL	Vacuum Cock
41.36	MMTVL	Tee set for Vacuum Cock
41.37	MMTVG	Tee set for Vacuum Guage
41.38	MMVG	Vacuum Guage

KHOA MACHINES (Milk Condensing Unit)
KHOA MACHINE 15 LTR. CAPACITY
Gas Operated Model

42.1	KM15	It Prepare Khoa of 10 Litre of Milk, It takes around 55 Minutes and Consumes about 0.8 Kg. of Gas, Motor -1 /4 H.P (1 No), Weight -150 Kg. Approx. Size - L 1066mm x B 760mm x H 1066mm, Volume of Container:- 55 Litre with S.S. Side Cover

42.2 KM15C ....as above with M.S. side covers

*** Diesel Operated Model:**

42.3 KM10D It Prepare Khoa of 10 Litre of Milk, in around 45 Minutes and consume about 1.4 Litre of diesel, Motor -1/4 H.P, Weight -180 Kg. Approx. Size - L 1066 mm x B 762 mm x H 1055 mm. Volume of Container 105 Litre with S.S. Side Cover

42.4 KM10DC ....as above with M.S. side covers

KHOA MACHINE 30 LTR. CAPACITY

Gas Operated Model

42.5 KM30G It prepare Khoa of 20 Litre of Milk in around 55 Minutes and Consumes about 1.5 Kg. of Gas. Motor - 1/4 H.F (1 No.), Weight - 180 Kg. Approx. Size - L 1220 mm x B 760mm x H 1066. Volume of Container 105 Litre S.S. Side Cover

42.6 KM30GC as above . M.S. side covers

Diesel Operated Model

42.7 KM20D It Prepare Khoa of 20 Litre of Milk, It takes around 45 Minutes and Consumes about 2.5 Litre of Diesel, Motor -1/2 H.F, Weight -260 Kg. Approx Size - L 1372mm x B 915mm x H 1055mm Volume of Container 105 Litre with S.S. Side Cover

42.8 KM20DC .... as above with M.S. side covers

KHOA MACHINE 60 LTR. CAPACITY

- Gas Operated Model

42.9 KM60G It Prepare Khoa of 30 Litre of Milk in around 45 Minutes and Consumes about 2.5 Kg. of Gas. Motor 1 H.P, Approx. Weight - 280 Kg. Approx. Size L 1375 mm x B 1066 mm x H 1145 mm. Volume of Container :225 Litre with S.S. Side Cover

42.10 KM60GC .... as above with M.S. side covers

- Diesel Operated Model

42.11 KM 30D It Prepare Khoa of 30 Litre of Milk, in around 40 Minutes and Consumes about 3.5 Litre of Diesel, Motor -1 H.P, Weight -345 Kg. Approx. Size - L1525mm x B1066mm x H 1145mm. With S.S. Side Cover

42.12 KM30DC as above . vN M.S. side covers

AUTOMATIC MILK VENDING MACHINES FOR LOOSE MILK

43.1 3FRC1K **THREE DELIVERY-FIXED- REFRIGERATED-CIP -1000L**

3Faucet FRP insulated front panel, Mounted on the front wall of the milk Booth, 1000 ltrs, capacity, insulated S.S.Tank, fitted with suitable refrigeration system, S.S milk pump & Agitator mounted on M.S. Stand, insulated S.S. milk line, C.I.R System, Balance tank and Electronic Control Panel Board.

43.2 3FRC7.5 **THREE DELIVERY- FIXED-REFRIGERATED- CIP- 750L**

.... as above but tank capacity 750 Litre

43.3 3FRC5 **THREE DELIVERY- FIXED-REFRIGERATED-CIP-500L**

.... as above but tank capacity 500 Litre

43.4 2SRC 7 **TWO DELIVERY- SS-REFRIGERATED- CIP- 700L**

All S.S. Body, movable on wheels, 700 Litres. S.S. Tanks, insulated with PUF, with suitable refrigeration system, Two delivery point, S.S. milk pump, Agitator, insulated S.S. milk line, C.I.F System, Balance tank and Electronic Control panel Board.

43.5 2SRC 5 **TWO DELIVERY- SS-REFRIGERATED- CIP- 500L**

.... as above but tank capacity 500 Litre

43.6 2SRC 2 **TWO DELIVERY- SS-REFRIGERATED- CIP- 200L**

.... as above but tank capacity 200 Litre

43.7 1SRC2 **SINGLE DELIVERY - SS - REFRIGERATED -CIP - 200L**

All S.S. Body, movable on wheels, 200 ltrs. S.S. Tanks, insulated with PUF with suitable refrigeration system, Single delivery point, Agitator, S.S. milk pump, insulated S.S. milk line, C.I.F System Balance tank and Electronic Control panel Board.

43.8 1 SRC1 **SINGLE DELIVERY - SS - REFRIGERATED -CIP -100L**

.... as above but tank capacity 100 Litre

43.9 FF2 **SINGLE DELIVERY - FRP - ELECTRONIC- 200L**

200 Ltrs. capacity FRP light weight insulated tank, with coin operated Electronic single delivery point.

43.10 FE-2 **SINGLE DELIVERY- FRP- ELECTRONIC-PUSH BUTTON 200L**

200 Ltrs, capacity FRP light weight insulated tank, with Electronic push button operated, single delivery point, can be placed in dealer/ agent shop

43.11 RM-2 **SINGLE DELIVERY - FRP - MECHANICAL- 200L**

200 Ltrs. capacity FRP light weight insulated tank, with mechanically operated single delivery point, and suitable for mounting on cycle Rickshaw.

43.12 RM-1 **SINGLE DELIVERY - FRP - MECHANICAL- 100L**

100 Ltrs. capacity FRP light weight insulated tank, with mechanically operated single delivery point, and suitable for mounting on cycle Rickshaw.

INSULATED PLASTIC CARTS for vending of ice cream & pouch milk or milk products consisting of an insulated box of polyethylene and

PUF as insulation material, Insulated cart can be supplied with or without trolley and is ideal for vending of ice creams, shrikhand, sweetened milk etc.

43.13 S-15-03 150 Litre insulated box only with additional small openable lid and drain hole.

43.14 S-22-02 225 Litre insulated box only moulded with special projections for keeping two ice pads, available with additional small openable lid and drain hole.

SPARE PARTS OF MILK VENDING SYSTEMS

44.1	VMBM5	Measuring Beaker only for Mechanical vending 500 ml	
44.2	VMBM1	Measuring Beaker only for Mechanical vending 1000 ml	
44.3	VMBES5	Measuring Beaker only for Electronic vending 500 ml	
44.4	VMBES1	Measuring Beaker only for Electronic vending 1000 ml,	
44.5	V3PM	Three port valve for mechanical beaker.	
44.6	V3FE	Three port valve for electronic beaker.	
44.7	VMVS	Mechanical Vending set complete with beaker 500 ml, three port valve, lever & filling tube.	

S.S. VALVES & FITTINGS - SMS - AISI 304 QUALITY

45.1	DFU25	S.S. UNION COMPLETE	25 MM
45.2	DFU38		38 MM
45.3	DFU51		51 MM
45.4	DFU63		63.5 MM
45.5	DFU76		76 MM
45.6	DFU101		101 MM
45.7	DFT25	S.S.TEE PLAIN	25 MM
45.8	DFT38		38 MM
45.9	DFT51		51 MM
45.10	DFT63		63.5 MM
45.11	DFT76		76 MM
45.12	DFT101		101 MM
45.13	DF2W25	S.S.TWO WAY VALVE COMPLETE	25 MM
45.14	DF2W38		38 MM
45.15	DF2W51		51 MM
45.16	DF2W63		63.5 MM
45.17	DF2W76		76 MM
45.18	DF3W25	S.S.THREE WAY VALVE COMPLETE WITH UNION	25 MM
45.19	DF3W38		38 MM
45.20	DF3W51		51 MM
45.21	DF3W63		63.5 MM
45.22	DF3W76		76 MM
		S.S. TWO WAY VALVE COMPLETE WITH UNION AND COUNTER FLANGE	
45.23	DF2C25		25 MM
45.24	DF2C38		38 MM
45.25	DF2C51		51 MM
45.26	DF2C63		63.5 MM
45.27	IS38	S.S. INLINE STRAINER/ FILTER	38 MM

45.28	IS51		51 MM
45.29	IS63		63.5 MM
15.30	DFPC25	S.S. PIPE CLAMPS	25 MM
45.31	DFPC38		38 MM
45.32	DFPC51		51 MM
15.33	DFPC63		63.5 MM
65.34	DFPC76		76 MM
15.35	DFBL25	S.S. BLANKS FROM PLATES	25 MM
15.36	DFBL38		38 MM
15.37	DFBL51		51 MM
15.38	DFBL63		63.5 MM
15.39	DF5C	S.S. SAMPLE COCK	1/2" BSP 3/4"
45.40	DFB25	S.S. BEND PLAIN	25 MM
45.41	DFB38		38 MM
45.42	DFB51		51 MM
45.43	DFB63		63.5 MM
45.44	DFB76		76 MM
45.45	DFB101		-101 MM
45.46	DFBU25	S.S. BEND WITH UNION	25 MM
45.47	DFBU38		38 MM
45.48	DFBU51		51 MM
45.49	DFBU63		63.5 MM
45.50	DFBU76		76 MM
45.51	DFBU101		101 MM
45.52	DFRM1	S.S. REDUCER MALE FROM SOLID BAR	76 x 63.5 MM
45.53	DFRM2		76 x 51 MM
45.54	DFRM3		76 x 38 MM
45.55	DFRM4		76 x 25 MM
45.56	DFRM5		63.5 x 51 MM
45.57	DFRM6		63.5 MM x 25
45.58	DFRM7		63.5 MM x 38
45.59	DFRM8		51 x 38 MM
45.60	DFRM9		38 MM x 25 MM
45.61	DFRLI	S.S. REDUCER LINER FROM SOLID BAR	76 x 63.5 MM
45.62	DFRL2		76 x 51 MM
45.63	DFRL3		76 x 38 MM
45.64	DFRL4		76 x 25 MM
45.65	DFRL5		63.5 x 51 MM
45.66	DFRL6		63.5 x 38 MM
45.67	DFRL7		63.5 x 25 MM
45.68	DFRL8		51 x 38 MM
45.69	DFRL9		51 x 25 MM

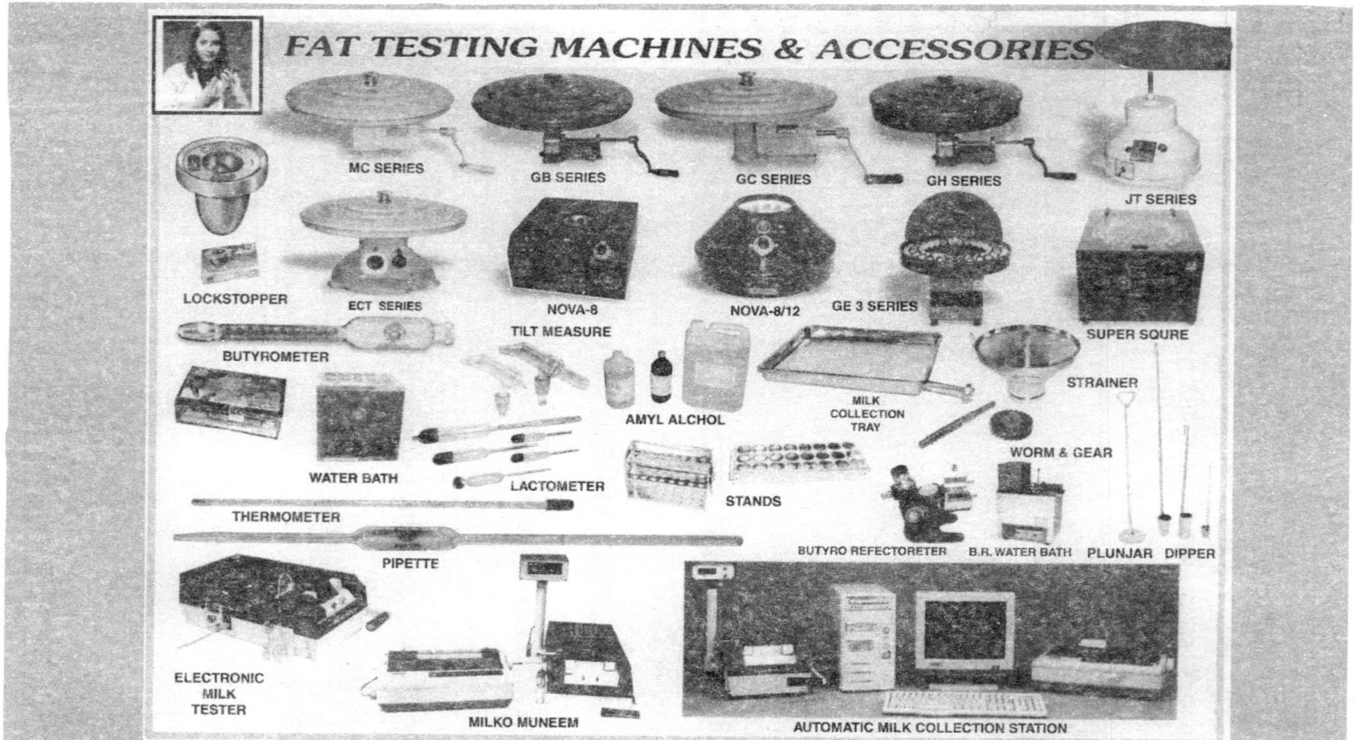

FAT TESTING MACHINES & ACCESSORIES
MC SERIES
GB SERIES
GC SERIES
GH SERIES
JT SERIES
LOCKSTOPPER
ECT SERIES
NOVA-8
NOVA-8/12
GE 3 SERIES
SUPER SQURE
TILT MEASURE
BUTYROMETER
AMYL ALCHOL
MILK
COLLECTION
TRAY
STRAINER
WORM & GEAR
WATER BATH
LACTOMETER
STANDS
THERMOMETER
PIPETTE
BUTYRO REFECTORETER
B.R. WATER BATH
PLUNJAR
DIPPER
ELECTRONIC
MILK
TESTER
MILKO MUNEEM
AUTOMATIC MILK COLLECTION STATION

MILK COOLING
BULK COOLER
PLATE CHILLERS
CHILLED MILK STORAGE TANK
RAW MILK
INSTANT WATER COOLER
PLATE CHILLER
MILK PUMP
BALANCE TANK
INSTANT MILK CHILLING UNIT
MILK PASTURIZERS & HEAT EXCHANGERS
BATCH BOILER/ PASTURIZER
PLATE PACK
MILK PASTURIZATION PLANT

CREAM SEPARATORS
SSS-7
SSS-9
ES-7
SSS-13
A-108
AE-1
AEO-2
BUTTER CHURNERS
BC-20
BC-60
BC-500
BUTTER TROLLEY
BP5T5

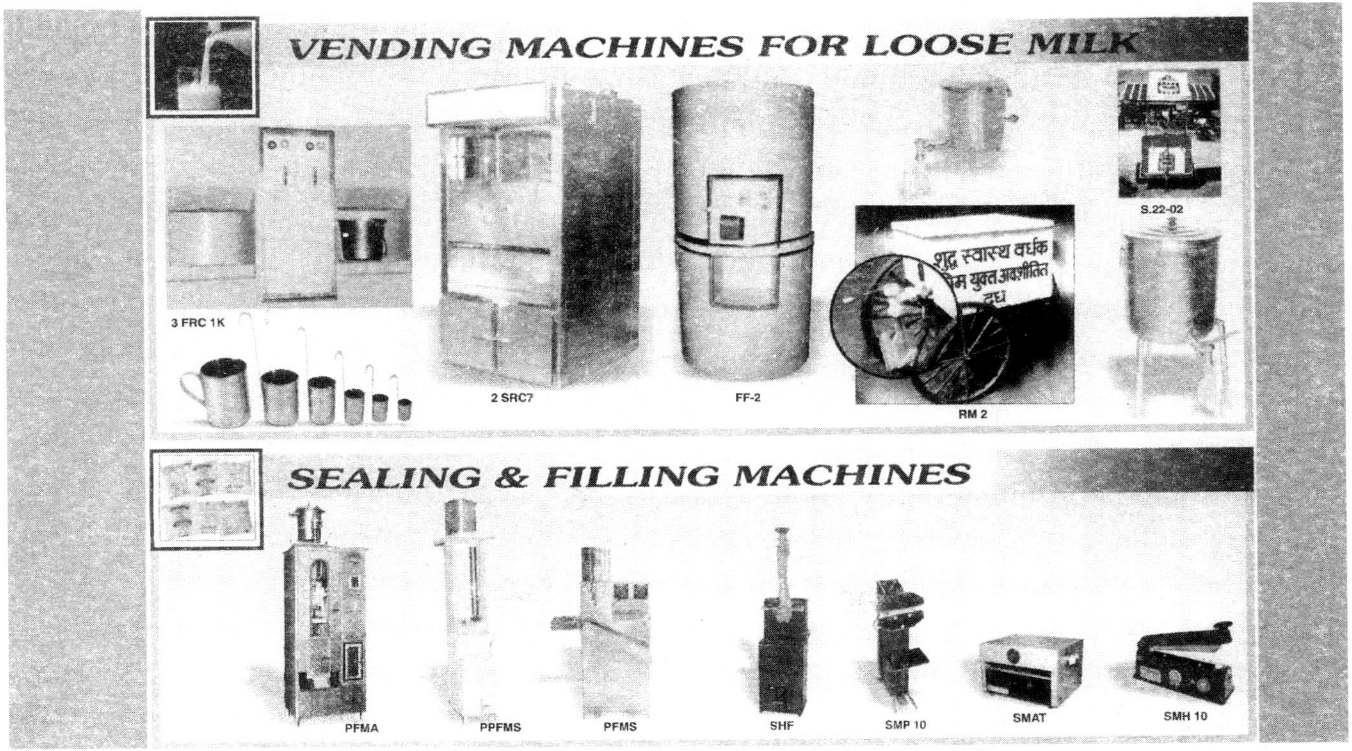
VENDING MACHINES FOR LOOSE MILK
3 FRC 1K
2 SRC7
FF-2
शुद्ध स्वास्थ्य वर्धक
RM 2
S.22-02
SEALING & FILLING MACHINES
PFMA
PPFMS
PFMS
SHF
SMP 10
SMAT
SMH 10

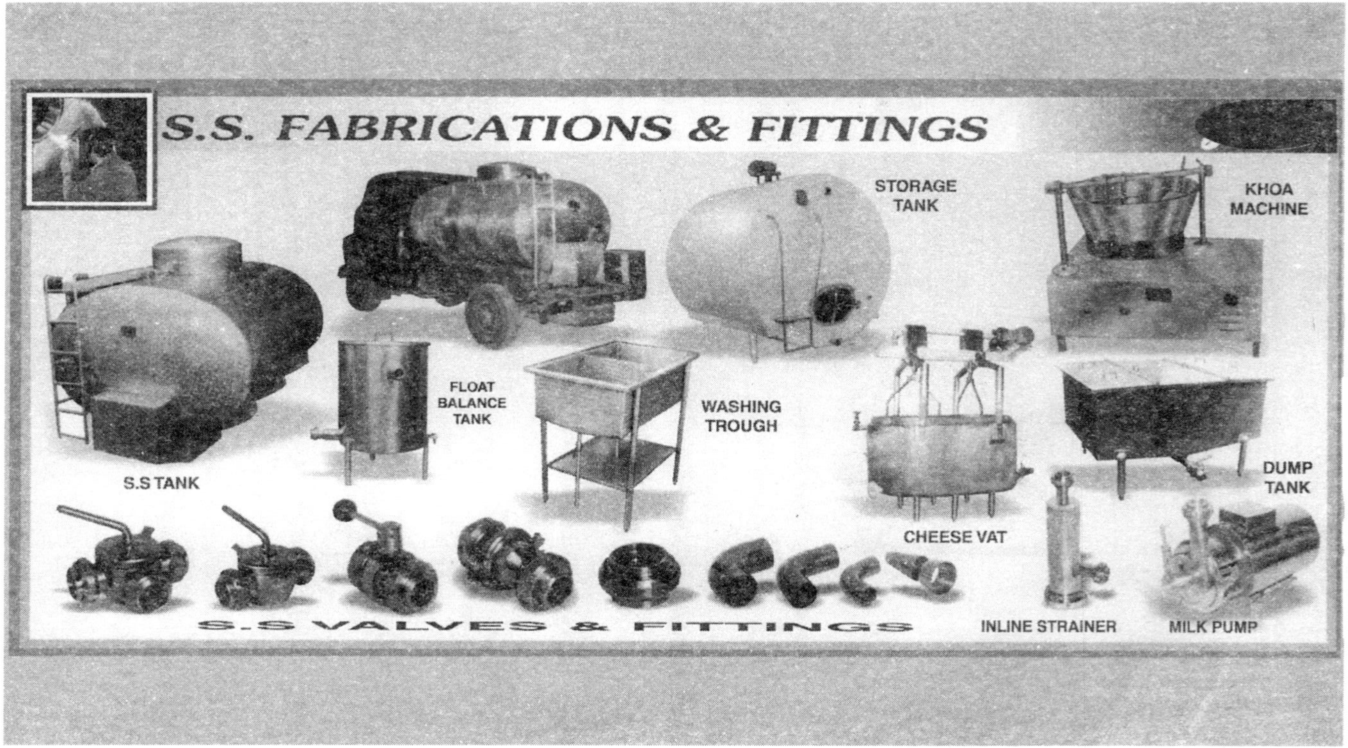
S.S. FABRICATIONS & FITTINGS
STORAGE TANK
KHOA MACHINE
FLOAT BALANCE TANK
WASHING TROUGH
S.S TANK
DUMP TANK
CHEESE VAT
S.S VALVES & FITTINGS
INLINE STRAINER
MILK PUMP

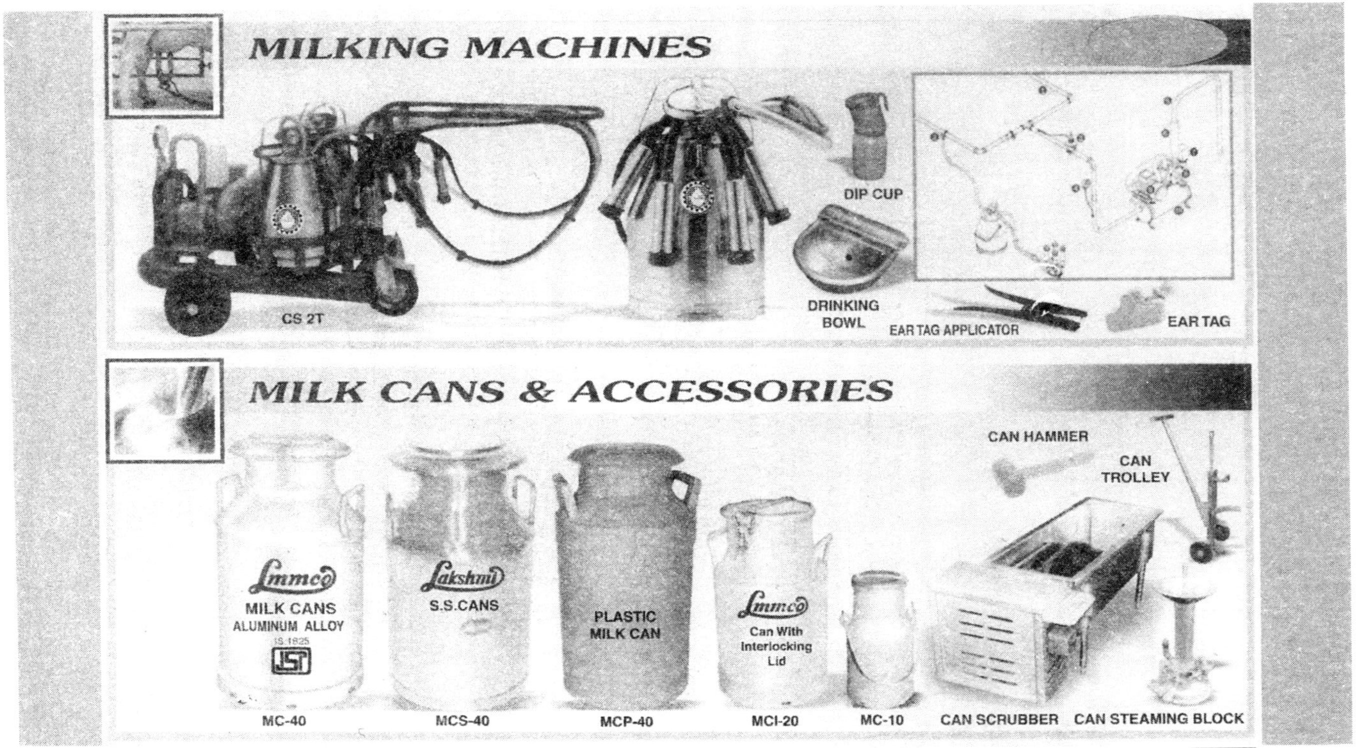
MILKING MACHINES
CS 2T
DIP CUP
DRINKING BOWL
EAR TAG APPLICATOR
EAR TAG
MILK CANS & ACCESSORIES
Lmmco
MILK CANS
ALUMINUM ALLOY
IS:1825
MC-40
Lakshmi
S.S.CANS
MCS-40
PLASTIC MILK CAN
MCP-40
Lmmco
Can With Interlocking Lid
MCI-20
MC-10
CAN HAMMER
CAN TROLLEY
CAN SCRUBBER
CAN STEAMING BLOCK

45.70 DFRL10 38 MM x 25 MM

S.S. FLOW REGULATING VALVE COMPLETE WITH UNION

45.71	FR51		51 MM
45.72	FR63		63.5 MM
45.73	FR76		76 MM
45.74	NRV38		38 MM
45.75	NRV51		51 MM
45.76	NRV63		63.5 MM
45.77	DFAV38	ANGLE VALVE WITH UNION	38MM
45.78	DFAV51		51 MM
45.79	DFAV63		63.5MM

WEIGHING BALANCES/SCALES

MILK RECORDING

46.1 25-MR Milk recording scale mechanical hanging type, "Salter make" tubular type weighing capacity 25 Kg division in 100 gm.

46.2 50-MRD Milk recording scale mechanical hanging dail type reading "Salter make" weighing capacity available in 25 Kg or 50 kg division in 100 gm.

LABORATORY SCALES

46.3 002-W Weighing Capacity 200 gms, Least Count 10 mg, Platform Size 107 mm Dia, with SS Platform, Having LCD Double Display with Battery Backup.

46.4 06-W Weighing Capacity 6KG, Least Count 0.5 Gram, Platform Size 345 x 225 mm, Having S.S. Platform with single FIP Display with Battery Backup.

ECONOMY MODELS

46.5 02-W Weighing Capacity 2 KG, Least Count 1 Gram, Having S.S. Platform of 170 x 150 mm. with Single LED Display with Adaptor.

46.6 05-W Weighing Capacity 5KG,Least Count 2Gm, Having Plastic Platform of 240 x 190 mm. with Single LED Display with Adaptor.

46.7 10-W Weighing Capacity 10 Kg, Least Count 5 Gm, Having Plastic Platform of 240 x 190 mm. with Single LED Display with Adaptor.

INDUSTRIAL TABLE TOP SCALES

46.8 12/30-W Weighing Capacity of 12/30 Kg, Least count 2/5 Gm, Having SS Platform of 345 x 225 mm. with Single FIP Display.

HANGING SCALES

46.9 150-W Weighing Capacity 150 KG,Least Count 50Gm, Having Hook with LCD Single Display

INDUSTRIAL PLATFORM SCALES .

46.10 125W Weighing Capacity 125 Kg. Least Count 50 Grams, Having M.S. Platform of 600 x 500 mm. with Single LED Display

46.11 60/120 Weighing Capacity 60/120 Kg, Least Count 10/20 Gm, Having SS Platform of 600 x500mm.with Single LCD Display, Having Battery Backup

Courtesy : Chaddha Sales Pvt. Ltd., Delhi.

Chapter 41

SUPPLIERS OF PLANT AND MACHINERIES

Mahesh Eng. Works
Supplying of extracting machinery, oil extractor machines, dryer-de-hydrator oil extractor machines, dairy machinery, butter making machinery, milking machine, bucket milking machine, mobile milking machine, dairy milking equipment, bulk milk cooler, etc.
Address: No. 1, Modi Estate,
Near Mahakali Temple, Dudheswer Road,
Ahmedabad - 380 004, India
Phone: +(91)-(79)-25626688
Fax: +(91)-(79)-25626688
Mobile: +(91)-9825336443
Website: www.milkycreamseparator.com

Master Food Tech
Supply and manufacture of food processing plants, ice cream plant machinery, ice plant machinery, brine chilling plant equipment, deep freezer plant equipment, cold storage plant, mushroom plant, dairy plant and industrial food processing plant.
Address: S. No. 232/2, Pune Nasik Road,
Atlas Compound, Opposite Rupee,
Co.Op.Bank, Bhosari, Pune - 411 039, India
Mobile: +(91)-9822027910

Shreya Engineering Works
Deals in manufacturing and supplying automatic filling machine, liquid fillers, filling machines, ice cream plant and dairy machinery, ice cream cup filling machine, ice cream filling machine, ice cream cup filling machine.
Address: Zone E-3, Shed No. C1/309,
Opposite Old Telephone Exchange,
Vitthal Udyognagar, Anand - 388 121, India
Phone: +(91)-(2692)-232185
Fax: +(91)-(2692)-232185
Mobile: +(91)-9427004851
Website: www.shreyaengineering.co.in

Swaraj Industries, India
Manufacturer and supplier of machinery such as weigh bowl horizontal milk storage tanks, stainless steel horizontal milk storage tanks, weigh bowl dairy tanks, leakage proof dairy tanks and steel dairy tanks.
Address: Gat No. 53, A/ P, Chimbli, Tal.
Khed, Pune - 412 105, India
Mobile: +(91)-9921691005
Website: www.swarajindustries.com

Triveni Engineering
Supplying and manufacturing chemica machinery, dyes machinery, dye intermediate machinery, industrial dyrer, ro system, we cake dryer, paste dryer, herbal products machinery, food products machinery nutraceutical machinery, dairy produc machinery.
Address: Plot No. 62, Yamuna Estate, GIDC,
Phase- II, Vatva, Ahmedabad - 382 445,
India

Phone: +(91)-(79)-25830411
Fax: +(91)-(79)-25830411
Mobile: +(91)-9825095243/9879476859

Aaryavrat Engineering & Technologies
Engaged in manufacturing and exporting a range of weighing scales, electronic weighing scales and electronic weighing scale platform type. Also supply industrial process machinery, industrial process equipment, dairy equipments etc.
Address: 8, Renuka Royal, Plot No. 52, CTS 6258, Near Master Bakery, Ajmera Colony, Pimpri, Pune - 411 018, India
Fax: +(91)-(20)-30622073
Mobile: +(91)-9923087879/9370787980

Four Brothers Ex-imp Private Limited
Engaged in exporting and manufacturing of food processing machines, bakery machinery, candy machines, dairy equipments, popcorn machines, vermicelli machines, peanut butter making machine and dry fruit cutting machines.
Address: Old No. 123 New No. 255, Linghi Chetty Street, Chennai - 600 001, India
Phone: +(91)-(44)-42163224
Fax: +(91)-(44)-42167724
Mobile: +(91)-9940166232

Maruti Machines Pvt. Ltd.
Supplier of food processing equipments, bakery machinery, biscuit making machines, candy machines, confectionery machines, dairy processing plants, fruit processing equipments, mineral water plants, snack machines and vegetable dehydration plants.
Address: B - 23, Ambica Industrial Estate, Ambica Nagar, Odhav, Ahmedabad - 382 415, India
Phone: +(91)-(79)-22975760/22874026
Fax: +(91)-(79)-22874026
Mobile: +(91)-9879599554/9879798821

SS Engineers & Consultants
Manufacturing and supplying of food processing equipments that includes sterilizers, industrial sterilizers, bottle sterilizers, food sterilizers and dairy equipments. Also offers dairy plant and machinery, food processing equipments and dairy equipments.
Address: D. No. 11-49/2, Morumpudi Junction, Rajahmundry - 533 103, India
Phone: +(91)-(883)-2426845/2426846/2426847
Fax: +(91)-(883)-2430819
Mobile: +(91)-9440868551/9346144644

Laxmi Gas Services
Deals in supplying and manufacturing of bakery equipments, commercial bakery equipments, digital bakery equipment, bakery machinery, dairy equipments and steel dairy equipments.
Address: Mumbai Pune Road, Opposite Formaica Company, Akurdi, Pune - 411 035, India
Phone: +(91)-(20)-27692121
Mobile: +(91)-9822089812/9881370626

Sunrise Process Equipments
Manufacturing and supplying of food processing machinery like dairy tanks, diary storage tanks, food product storage tanks, metal food product storage tanks, steel storage tanks, stainless steel storage tanks and mild steel storage tanks etc.
Address: A -102, Shree Rameshwar Tower, Shimpoli Road Borivali West, Mumbai - 400 092, India
Phone: +(91)-(22)-28993705/28993706/28993707
Fax: +(91)-(22)-28993705
Mobile: +(91)-9821226682

BAAF Engineers Private Limited
Deals in manufacturing and supplying of industrial machinery that includes milk spray drying plants, milk evaporating plants, milk pasteurization plant and dairy milk pasteurization plants.
Address: E-48, Site-B, UPSIDC Surajpur Industrial Area, Dadri Road, Greater Noida - 201 306, India
Phone: +(91)-(120)-2560783
Fax: +(91)-(120)-2560784
Mobile: +(91)-9868565403

Delta Engineering, Pune
Engaged in manufacturing chemical processing machinery like pharmaceutical agitators, chemical agitators, chemical

reactors, industrial reactors along with pressure vessel, heat exchanger, dairy bag filters and stainless steel bin wash.
Address: W- 100, S- Block, MIDC, Bhosari, Pune - 411 026, India
Mobile: +(91)-9850329333

D-Mech Engineers
Deals in manufacturing of industrial machinery, milk pasteurizer, cleaning crate washer, can washer, crate washer, semi automatic can washer, processing can washer, electrical can washer and dairy can washer.
Address: Plot 4, Krishna Nagar, Sector 25, Faridabad - 121 001, India
Phone: +(91)-(129)-2441688/4150884
Fax: +(91)-(129)-4150884
Mobile: +(91)-9891267870/9756205100

AKAR MACHINERY CORPORATION
Manufacturer of paneer-press, cream separator, dairy machinery, deep fat fryer and atta kneading machine.
Address: Plot No. G-105, M.I.D.C. Gokul Shirgaon, Kolhapur - 416234, India
Phone: +(91)-(231)-2672008
Mobile: +(91)-9890207989/9326699999

Ashapuri Engineering Works
Deals in manufacturing and exporting of dairy cquipments and dairy machinery parts.
Address: Chhagaji Compound, Opposite Pumping Station, Mehdikuva, Ahmedabad - 380 004, India
Phone: +(91)-(79)-25630715
Mobile: +(91)-9924243099

Milk - Tech Engineers
Engaged in production of dairy machinery like evaporator, pasteurizer, spray dryer, milk pump, khoa making machine, ghee ,aking machine and food processing machinery.
Address: No. 80, 3rd Floor, Lavanya Apartment, 13th Cross, Ganga Nagar, Bengaluru - 560 024, India
Mobile: +(91)-9448694666

Airtemp Refrigeration
Engaged in manufacturing and selling ice cream plant, hotel kitchen equipments, pourlour equipments, dairy machinery and refrigeration eqipments.
Address: No. 4, Kotadiya Estate, Opposite Raj Rani Beda Works, Near Corporation Gardan, Ambica Nagar, Odhav, GID, Ahmedabad - 380 024, India
Phone: +(91)-(79)-22977999
Fax: +(91)-(79)-22748743
Mobile: +(91)-9426014765

Shree Vishwakarma Engineering Corporation
Manufacturing and exporting all kinds of dairy equipments and dairy machinery.
Address: 2001/3, GIDC Vunagar, Vadodara - 388 121, India
Mobile: +(91)-9824019031

AKAR MACHINERY CORPORATION
Manufacturer of paneer-press, cream separator, dairy machinery, deep fat fryer and atta kneading machine.
Address: Plot No. G-105, M.I.D.C. Gokul Shirgaon, Kolhapur - 416234, India
Phone: +(91)-(231)-2672008
Mobile: +(91)-9890207989/9326699999

Eon Trading, LLC Delaware Usa
Exporters of cheese production machinery dairy machinery and plants.
Address: T20. 3rd Floor, Super Mall, Salunke Vihar wanowrie, Pune - 411 040, India
Phone: +(91)-(20)-26837606
Fax: +(91)-(20)-26837606
Mobile: +(91)-9823468885/9850244437

Sonus International
Engaged in manufacturing of all kinds of food machinery moulds, dairy machinery moulds chemical machinery moulds, confectioner machinery moulds and distillery machiner moulds.
Address: F-12, Rangoli Complex, Opposite V. S. Hospital, Ashram Road, Ellisbridge, Ahmedabad - 380 006, India
Phone: +(91)-(79)-26578116
Mobile: +(91)-9898181626

Kaival Engineers & Technology Systems
Manufacturers of a range of dairy machiner

Address: No. 101, Shreeji Complex,
Plot No. 81, G. I. D. C., Makarpura,
Vadodara - 390 010, India
Phone: +(91)-(265)-2359752
Fax: +(91)-(265)-2637423
Mobile: +(91)-9879063551

Sneha Dairy Consultancy
Leading manufacturer of dairy machinery.
Address: Green Avenue, Opposite TGB Restaurant, Adajan, Surat - 395 009, India
Phone: +(91)-(261)-2746240
Fax: +(91)-(261)-2746240
Mobile: +(91)-9825116239

Milk - Tech Engineers
Engaged in production of dairy machinery like evaporator, pasteurizer, spray dryer, milk pump, khoa making machine, ghee ,aking machine and food processing machinery.
Address: No. 80, 3rd Floor, Lavanya Apartment, 13th Cross, Ganga Nagar, Bengaluru - 560 024, India
Mobile: +(91)-9448694666

The National Engineering Co.
Manufacturer and supplier of spice grinding machinery, dairy machinery, noodles making machinery and pulverizer machine.
Address: 22, Netaji Subhas Road, Kolkata - 700 001, India
Phone: +(91)-(33)-22206910
Fax: +(91)-(33)-22104973
Mobile: +(91)-9903976834

S. Y. M. Engineers
Suppliers of dairy machinery especially homogenizers and spares.
Address: W 72, M. I. D. C., Kolhapur - 416 234, India
Phone: +(91)-(231)-2671439

Vivek Engineering Works, Anand
Manufacturer of dairy machinery.
Address: Lambhvel Road, Near Indira Statue, Anand - 388 001, India
Phone: +(91)-(2692)-250663
Mobile: +(91)-9879859577

Nutec Food & Dairy Consulting
Suppliers of dairy machinery.
Address: Road No. 11, East Patel Nagar, Patna - 800 023, India
Mobile: +(91)-9835267011/9334318997

Srikar Refrigeration
Manufacturer of dairy machinery.
Address: No. 7-1-246/45, Balkampet, Hyderabad - 500 016, India
Mobile: +(91)-9394760979/9505457795

Castech (Uk) Limited
Engaged in supply polyurethane mouldings, precision aluminium castings, investment castings, stainless steel investment castings for instrumentation, food processing industry, dairy machinery etc.
Address: Unit 10 Manor Farm Astwood, Bucks - Mk16 9JS, United Kingdom
Phone: +(44)-(1234)-391973
Fax: +(44)-(1234)-391185

N.T. F.-Aalborg A/S
Deals in all kinds of dairy plants and dairy machinery.
Address: Hagensvej-17, Stovring - DK9 530, Denmark
Phone: +(45)-(9837)-3766
Fax: +(45)-(9837)-3751

Caseartecnica Bartoli Srl
Authorized dealer of mixers, dairy machinery and dairy equipments.
Address: 26, V. Bernini, Parma - 43100, Italy
Phone: +(39)-(521)-982381
Fax: +(39)-(0521)-994866

L. P. Kolding A/S
Deals in all types of dairy machinery.
Address: Egtvedvej-2, Kolding - DK6 000, Denmark
Phone: +(45)-(7552)-4177
Fax: +(45)-(7553)-2351

Hojer Orbaek A/S
Deals in all types of dairy plants and dairy machinery.
Address: Langemosevaenget-3-5, Post Box 21, Orbaek - DK5 853, Denmark
Phone: +(45)-(6533)-1566
Fax: +(45)-(6533)-1668

Ingvald
Deals in all kinds of food processing machines like dairy articles, dairy plants, dairy machinery, fish industry machinery and food industry machines.
Address: Jeppe Aakjaers Alle-14,
Post Box-659, Odense
N. V. - DK5 210, Denmark
Phone: +(45)-(0)-66118211
Fax: +(45)-(0)-66118250

A. B. C. Hansen A/S
Dealing in all kinds of dairy plants and dairy machinery.
Address: Mollestensvej-13, Post Box 73,
Randers - DK8 900, Denmark
Phone: +(45)-(8642)-6488
Fax: +(45)-(8641)-3622

Shree Vishwakarma Engineering Corporation
Manufacturing and exporting all kinds of dairy equipments and dairy machinery.
Address: 2001/3, GIDC Vunagar,
Vadodara - 388 121, India
Mobile: +(91)-9824019031

Srikar Refrigeration
Manufacturer of dairy machinery.
Address: No. 7-1-246/45, Balkampet,
Hyderabad - 500 016, India
Mobile: +(91)-9394760979/9505457795

Milk - Tech Engineers
Engaged in production of dairy machinery like evaporator, pasteurizer, spray dryer, milk pump, khoa making machine, ghee ,aking machine and food processing machinery.
Address: No. 80, 3rd Floor, Lavanya
Apartment, 13th Cross, Ganga Nagar,
Bengaluru - 560 024, India
Mobile: +(91)-9448694666

AKAR MACHINERY CORPORATION
Manufacturer of paneer-press, cream separator, dairy machinery, deep fat fryer and atta kneading machine.
Address: Plot No. G-105, M.I.D.C. Gokul
Shirgaon, Kolhapur - 416234, India
Phone: +(91)-(231)-2672008
Mobile: +(91)-9890207989/9326699999

Parikh Udyog
Engaged in manufacturing steel investment castings, alloy steel investment castings, industrial investment castings and stainless steel investment castings for food processing industry, dairy machinery, artificial limbs and packing equipment.
Address: C-14, M I D C Gokul Shirgaon,
Kolhapur - 416234, India
Phone: +(91)-(231)-2672269/2672438
Fax: +(91)-(231)-2672520
Mobile: +(91)-9822044892

S. Y. M. Engineers
Suppliers of dairy machinery especially homogenizers and spares.
Address: W 72, M. I. D. C.,
Kolhapur - 416 234, India
Phone: +(91)-(231)-2671439

Kaival Engineers & Technology Systems
Manufacturers of a range of dairy machinery.
Address: No. 101, Shreeji Complex, Plot No. 81, G.I.D.C., Makarpura,
Vadodara - 390 010, India
Phone: +(91)-(265)-2359752
Fax: +(91)-(265)-2637423
Mobile: +(91)-9879063551

The National Engineering Co.
Manufacturer and supplier of spice grinding machinery, dairy machinery, noodles making machinery and pulverizer machine.
Address: 22, Netaji Subhas Road,
Kolkata - 700 001, India
Phone: +(91)-(33)-22206910
Fax: +(91)-(33)-22104973
Mobile: +(91)-9903976834

Eon Trading, LLC Delaware Usa
Exporters of cheese production machinery, dairy machinery and plants.
Address: T20, 3rd Floor, Super Mall,
Salunke Vihar wanowrie,
Pune - 411 040, India
Phone: +(91)-(20)-26837606
Fax: +(91)-(20)-26837606
Mobile: +(91)-9823468885/9850244437

Vivek Engineering Works, Anand

Manufacturer of dairy machinery.
Address: Lambhvel Road, Near Indira Statue, Anand - 388 001, India
Phone: +(91)-(2692)-250663
Mobile: +(91)-9879859577

Keshari Agro & Dairy Consultant
Wholesaler and trader of dairy machinery.
Address: Govrnment. Milk Scheem, Civil Line, Near W C L, Nagpur - 440 001, India
Mobile: +(91)-9890807179

Sneha Dairy Consultancy
Leading manufacturer of dairy machinery.
Address: Green Avenue, Opposite TGB Restaurant, Adajan, Surat - 395 009, India
Phone: +(91)-(261)-2746240
Fax: +(91)-(261)-2746240
Mobile: +(91)-9825116239

Ashapuri Engineering Works
Deals in manufacturing and exporting of dairy equipments and dairy machinery parts.
Address: Chhagaji Compound, Opposite Pumping Station, Mehdikuva, Ahmedabad - 380 004, India
Phone: +(91)-(79)-25630715
Mobile: +(91)-9924243099

Avedemil
Wholesale dealers of dairy machinery.
Address: Z. I. Rn 10, Ruffec - 16700, France
Phone: +(33)-(545)-891148

A. B. C. Hansen A/S
Dealing in all kinds of dairy plants and dairy machinery.
Address: Mollestensvej-13, Post Box 73, Randers - DK8 900, Denmark
Phone: +(45)-(8642)-6488
Fax: +(45)-(8641)-3622

Handing ApS
Deals into all types of dairy plants and dairy machinery.
Address: Nordkranvej-5-9, Lynge - DK3 540, Denmark
Phone: +(45)-(481)-60166
Fax: +(45)-(481)-60165

Scandinavian Production & Processing Company A/S
Deals in all kinds of dairy plants, dairy machinery and ice cream machines.
Address: Sams?vej-30E, Hinnerup - DK8 382, Denmark
Phone: +(45)-(8691)-1499
Fax: +(45)-(8691)-1833

Fullwood Limited
Deals in robotic milking machines and dairy machinery.
Address: Grange Road, Ellesmere - SY129DF, United Kingdom
Phone: +(44)-(1691)-627391
Fax: +(44)-(1691)-627361

Ingvald
Deals in all kinds of food processing machines like dairy articles, dairy plants, dairy machinery, fish industry machinery and food industry machines.
Address: Jeppe Aakjaers Alle-14, Post Box-659, Odense N. V. - DK5 210, Denmark
Phone: +(45)-(0)-66118211
Fax: +(45)-(0)-66118250

L. P. Kolding A/S
Deals in all types of dairy machinery.
Address: Egtvedvej-2, Kolding - DK6 000, Denmark
Phone: +(45)-(7552)-4177
Fax: +(45)-(7553)-2351

Ganesh Engineers, Mumbai
Manufacturer, exporter and supplier of diary machinery spare parts and dairy equipment.
Address: No. 13/14, Jaybharat Industrial Estate, Opposite Virwani, Industrial Estate, Near Wester Express Highway, Goregaon East, Mumbai - 400 063, India
Phone: +(91)-(22)-28740962

Finix India Equipments
Suppliers of dairy equipments and food machinery.
Address: Sect. 7, Plot No. 55, P.c.n.t.d.a. M. I. D. C., Bhosari, Pune - 411 026, India
Phone: +(91)-(20)-66303168/27125155
Fax: +(91)-(20)-27125155

Mahesh Process Equipments Private Limited
Engaged in manufacturing of food processing machinery and dairy equipment.
Address: Plot No. 408, Savli DIDC, Manjusar, Vadodara - 391 775, India
Phone: +(91)-(266)-7264408/3253183
Mobile: +(91)-9377587898

Kims Engineers Private Limited
Manufacturing and exporting dairy processing machinery, food processing machinery and dairy equipment.
Address: Plot No. 39, Phase-II, Kasba Industrial Estate, Kolkata - 700 001, India
Phone: +(91)-(33)-24428622
Fax: +(91)-(33)-24431181

Shree Sai Projects, Saharanpur
Manafacturers and exporters of food processing equipments, dairy equipments like milk silo, bulk milk cooler, amcs, milk storage tanks, ghee boiler, butter churn, spray dryer, evaporators, chemical and distillary plant and machinery.
Address: Trade Centre, Pratap Market, Saharanpur - 247 001, India
Phone: +(91)-(132)-2766355
Fax: +(91)-(132)-2766355
Mobile: +(91)-9258077752

Intoto Marketing
Exporters of all kinds of packaging machineries for dairy, food industries, rotary band sealers etc.
Address: Off. 4, Commerce Centre Paud Road, Kothrud, Pune - 411 038, India
Phone: +(91)-(20)-25412389/25412390
Fax: +(91)-(20)-25461824

E. I. Daggoy Trading Company
Exporter of all type of machineries like soap cutting, embossing, candy plant, pouch machinery, tallow bleaching plant, salt milling, dairy milk plant & machinery, stone crusher machine, wheat silo plant etc.
Address: Mata Ramabai, Ambedkar Nagar, Mumbai - 400 076, India
Phone: +(91)-(22)-25786345
Mobile: +(91)-9820251944

Devi Exim Private Limited
Exporters of food processing machinery such as dairy equipment etc.
Address: 20, Barakhamba Road, New Delhi - 110 001, India
Phone: +(91)-(11)-23314786/23310815
Fax: +(91)-(11)-23315405

Ess Pee Sales Agency, Delhi
Exporters of Dairy Plants, dairy Equipments, Food Processing Machinery, float balance tank, ghee boiler, milk storage tank, soft drink plants, plate heat exchangers, htst pasteurization plant etc.
Address: 71, Kundan Nagar, Laxmi Nagar, Delhi - 110 092, India
Phone: +(91)-(11)-22413437

Suruchi Consultants
Manufacturers of dairy and food industry plants and machineries
Address: A 661, Sector 19, Noida - 201 301, India
Phone: +(91)-(120)-2523845/4320845
Fax: +(91)-(120)-2523845 / 2553033
Mobile: +(91)-9810315831

3A Technik
Merchant trader of food processing machinery and dairy food machines.
Address: Landstrasse 60, Vaduz - 9490, Switzerland
Phone: +(41)-(77)-2534375
Fax: +(41)-(77)-2534375
Mobile: +(41)-772534375

Beigi Enterprises Limited
Sellers of used packaging, processing dairy equipments and machineries.
Address: 1500 Marine Drive, North Vancouver - V7P1T7, Canada
Phone: +(1)-(604)-9041213
Fax: +(1)-(604)-9041213
Mobile: +(1)-604-762-2266

Hammerum Stainless A/s
Dealing in all kinds of dairy equipments and slaughterhouse machinery.
Address: Dunsbjergvej-20, Rudkobing - DK5 900, Denmark
Phone: +(45)-(6333)-1800

Fax: +(45)-(6333)-1801

Yemen Dairy & Juice Industries Syc
manufacturers of machinery for juice and dairy products.
Address: P. O. Box 333, Hodeidah, Sana Road, Al-Hudaydah - 3337, Yemen
Phone: +(967)-(3)-228801
Fax: +(967)-(3)-228825

Kanters Gilze B. V.
Exporters of milking machinery and dairy cooler tanks.
Address: Lange Wagenstraat 11 A, Gilze - Nl5126 Ba, The Netherlands
Phone: +(31)-(161)-459797

A. P. V. Canada, Inc.
Manufacturer of all kinds of food processing machinery and dairy processing equipments.
Address:3280, Langstaff Road, Concord - L4K 4Z8, Canada
Phone: +(1)-(905)-7601852
Fax: +(1)-(905)-7601879

Millerbernd Manufacturing Co.
Engaged in manufacturing and supplying plant machinery, metal fabrication equipment and dairy processing equipment.
Address:622, 6th Street South, Winsted - 55395-772, United States Of America
Phone: +(1)-(320)-4852685
Fax: +(1)-(320)-4853900

Agmachine.com Limited
Engaged in supplying of all types of agricultural machinery such as farm equipments, tractors, sowing machinery, grain harvesting machinery, crop drying machinery, chemical spraying machinery, chemical fertilising machinery and dairy farming machine.
Address: 25 Roman Road, Steyning, Sussex - BN443FN, United Kingdom
Phone: +(44)-(1903)-810263

Jaya Industries, Kolkatta
Suppliers of food processing equipment, dairy equipment, road milk tanker, storage tanks, milk product chillers, milk product pasteurizes, aging tanks, equipment of manufacturing and packing butter/ghee, milk powder conveying systems, milk cans etc.
Address: No. 543, Jessore Road, Kolkata, West Bengal - 700 028, India
Phone: +(91)-(33)-25600361/25513568 Fax: +(91)-(33)-25799337
Mobile: +(91)-9231694285/9433005594
Website: http://www.jaya-industries.com

Nu-tech Dairy Engineers Private Limited
Exporter and manufacturer of industrial machinery such as material handling machinery, bagging machinery, khoya making machinery, post harvest machinery and food processing machinery.
Address: Plot No. 34, H S I I D C Food Park Saha, Ambala - 133 104, India
Phone: +(91)-(171)-2822700
Fax: +(91)-(171)-2822699
Mobile: +(91)-9354706554/9896067779

Yash Pharma Machineries
Deals in exporting and manufacturing of dairy products such as cream manufacturing plants, jacketed cream plants and automatic cream manufacturing plants.
Address: 110, Pushpak Industrial Estate, Nika Tube Compound, Phase-1, G.I.D.C., Vatva, Ahmedabad - 382 445, India
Phone: +(91)-(79)-25895872
Fax: +(91)-(79)-25895872
Mobile: +(91)-9376148872/9426040661

Indian Dairy Equipment Co.
Engaged in manufacturing and supplying of industrial machinery, milking machine with single cluster, power operated industrial machinery and electrical power operated industrial machinery.
Address: No. 364, Azad Market, Delhi - 110 006, India
Phone: +(91)-(11)-23615823
Fax: +(91)-(11)-23682900
Mobile: +(91)-9313824222

Kadam Dairy Equipments Private Limited
Manufacturer and supplier of food processing plants, food processing machinery, milk cooler, drip saver, can scrubber, cheese making

equipment, chillers, milk packing machinery, ice cream plants, ghee boilers, milk storage tanks and much more.
Address: 612, Vakil Nagar, Erandwana, Pune - 411004, India
Phone: +(91)-(20)-25448796
Fax: +(91)-(20)-25448796
Mobile: +(91)-9371311709

Gimret & Co.
Manufacturer and suppliers of food processing equipment, food processing machines, food treatment machines, dairy product processing machine, mixing machine, dispersing machine, heating, creaming system and cooling machine.
Address: 403, Rohit House, Tolstoy Marg, New Delhi - 110 001, India
Phone: +(91)-(11)-43586381/23314422
Fax: +(91)-(11)-23314377

Maxcare Marketing & Technical Services
Manufacturers and exporters of plant machinery for diary and food processing plants
Address: J-188, Saket, New Delhi - 110 017
Phone: +(91)-(11)-29555273/29552464
Fax: +(91)-(11)-29552464
Mobile: +(91)-9810819225

Krishna Dairy Machinery Corporation
Manufacturers of dairy, food processing equipments.
Address: A-23, Haridarshan Park Shopping Centre, Near Shankar Estate, Sureliya Road, Amraiwadi, Ahmedabad - 380 026, India
Fax: +(91)-(79)-25860857
Mobile: +(91)-9426048845

Pray Dairy Machinery Corporation
Manufacturer and dealer of chemical equipment.
Address: No. A/21, Revabhai Estate, Near Ishwarkrupa Kanta, Opposite Shankar Estate, CTM, Amraiwadi, Ahmedabad - 382 445, India
Mobile: +(91)-9998329938

Thompsons Food Machinery
Exporters of quality used food processing machinery.
Address: Unit K. G., Business Centre, Dallington, Northampton - NN5 7QS, United Kingdom
Phone: +(44)-(1604)-655400

Westney International Limited
Dealing in all kinds of agricultural machinery such as cultivators, dairy machinery, disc harrows and fertiliser spreaders.
Address: The Old Granary New Street, Sudbury - CO101JB, United Kingdom
Phone: +(44)-(1787)-379600
Fax: +(44)-(1787)-372846

Shanghai Pilotech Instrument
Manufacturer of all kinds of milk processing equipments and dairy machines.
Address: Building B No. 521, South Wanpinglu, Wanping Nan Road, Xuhui District, Shanghai - 200 032, China
Phone: +(86)-(21)-51082915
Fax: +(86)-(21)-54243425

Dairy Engineers & Consultants
Manufacturer and exporter of dairy machines and ice cream machines.
Address: No. 601, Satkrut Tower, Parth Sarthi Avenue, Near Shyamal Row House-2, Satellite, Ahmedabad - 380 015, India
Phone: +(91)-(79)-26760252
Mobile: +(91)-9825243624

Remi Process Plant And Machinery R. P. P. M. L
Manufacturer and exporter of emulsifiers, portable agitators, dairy, breweries and top entry agitators.
Address: Remi House, Plot No.11, Cama Industrial Estates Walbhat Road, Goregaon East, Mumbai - 400 063, India
Phone: +(91)-(22)-40589800
Fax: +(91)-(22)-26852335

Rupesh Equipments
Manufacturers of dairy equipment, chemical equipment and food processing equipment.
Address: Plot No. 29, Sector No. 10, P. C. N. T. D. A., Near Times Of India, Bhosari, Pune - 411 026, India
Phone: +(91)-(20)-25730743/27119972

ALL FOLLOWING PROJECT REPORTS ARE READILY AVAILABLE

- Calcined Petroleum Coke
- Calcining Of Magnesite & Dead Burnt Magnesite
- Calcium Aluminate
- Calcium Based Grease
- Calcium Carbide
- Calcium Carbonate
- Calcium Carbonate (Precipitated) From By Product (Lime Slurry & Carbon Dioxide)
- Calcium Carbonate (Activated & Precipitated)
- Calcium Chloride
- Calcium Gluconate
- Calcium Nitrate
- Calcium Silicate Bricks
- Calcium Stearate By Fusion Process
- Camphor Powder (Synthetic)
- Construction Chemicals (With Detailed Market Survey And Formulae Etc.)
- Carbon Dioxide
- Carbon Black From Fertilizer Waste
- Carbon Black (Petroleum Based)
- Carboxy Methyl Cellulose (Cmc)
- Casein And By Products
- Casein From Milk
- Cationic Softner (Stearic Acid Based)
- Caustic Soda
- Caustic Soda From Soda Ash By Soda Lime Process
- Caustic Soda (Liquid) By Electrolytic Process
- Caustic Soda From Trona
- Caustic Soda, Chlorine And Hydrogen Gas By Electro-Lysis Of Brine Solution
- Cellulose Acetate Moulding Powder
- Cellulose Powder & Micro Crystalline Cellulose Powder
- Cement Admixture
- Cement Colour
- Cement Water Proofing Compound
- Cement From Fly Ash & Lime
- Cement Tiles (Glazed)
- Chlorinated Paraffin Wax (Cpw)
- Citric Acid From Lemon
- Citric Acid From Molasses
- Double Firing (Heating)
- Chelated Zinc (Zn Edta)
- Chemicals From Prawn Head
- Chitin & Chitosan From Prawn Shell Waste
- Chloral Hydrate
- Chloramphenicol
- Chromic Acid (With Pollution Control)
- Chromic Acid (Oxide) & Blue Oxide
- Chlorinated Paraffin Wax (Cpw)
- Chromic Acid
- Cement Paint & Distemper
- Citric Acid From Lemon
- Citric Acid From Molasses
- Cleaning Of Cooling System And Boiler
- Coal Tar Distillation
- Coal Washing Plant
- Cobalt Octoate
- Compost For Mushroom
- Construction Chemicals
- Copper Oxychloride
- Coolant (Engine)
- Copper Phthalocyanine Blue & Green
- Correction Fluid
- Cupric Chloride
- Crude Oil Bleaching For Petroleum Jelly
- Cutting Oil
- Cyanuric Chloride
- Cyanoacrylate Adhesive
- Cutting Oil
- Defoaming Agent For Paper Industry
- De-Nickeling (Electrolytic Process)
- Detergent Cake & Powder
- Detergent Powder
- Detergent Concentrate (Idet 10)
- Dextrose Monohydrate & Dextrose Anhydrous Powder From Tapioca Starch
- Di-Basic Lead Stearate
- Di Calcium Phosphate
- Diclofenal Sodium Slow Release (Sr) Tables 100mg.
- Di Ethyl Oxalate
- Di Methyl Orthophthalate
- Di-Methyl Phthalate
- Diclofenac Gel
- Dioctyl Phthalate (Dop)
- Di Phenyl Glycerine
- Di Phenyl Oxide
- Dinitro-Chloro Benzene
- Distillery
- Distilled Water
- Dodecyl Benzene Sulphonate
- Dustless Chalk
- Edta & Its Salts
- Electroless Nickel Plating On Plastics
- Electrolyte (Like Sulphuric Acid) For Lead Acid Dry Rechargable 5.5.Ah. Battery
- Electropolishing On Gold Jewellery
- Electropolishing On Various Metals
- Endosulfan
- Enzyme Based Detergent Powder
- Ephedrine Hydrochloride
- Epoxy Resin Based Compound
- Ethanol (Biofuel)
- Ethyl Alcohol From Molasses
- Ethyl Acetate
- Ehtyl Ether
- Ethyl Alcohol (Potable Liquor)
- Ethyl Hexanol
- Extra Temperature Lubricating Grease
- Extraction Of Essential Oils By Sugar Critical Fluid (Carbon Dioxide) Method From Flowers, Herbal & Spices
- Fabric Stain Remover
- Fatty Acid
- Ferric Alum
- Ferric And Non Ferric Alum (Aluminium Sulphate)
- Ferro Chrome Ligno Sulphonate
- Ferro Manganese
- Ferro Silicone

Contact

EIRI

for required Project report apart from this list.

- Ferro Vanadium From Vanadium Sludge
- Ferrous Silicate
- Ferrous Sulphate
- Ferrous Sulphide
- Fertilizer From Animal Blood & Leather Waste
- Fluorescent Tube Light Powder
- Foamed Pvc Compounding & Its Products
- Formaldehyde
- Food Grade Grease Or Lubricant
- Fractional Distillation Of D.M.O (Dementholized Oil)
- Fractional Distillation Of Essential Oil & Medicinalplant Extract
- Friction Dust (Liquid & Powder) From Cnsl
- Fruit Flavours
- Furfural From Rice Husk
- Fumaric Acid
- Gas Filling Of Lpg Cylinder
- Garlic Acid
- Ginger And Garlic Paste
- Ginger Processing
- Gasket Shellac Compound
- Gear Oil
- Gibberellic Acid
- Glass Putty
- Gluconic Acid
- Glucose D- Powder
- Glycerine
- Gossypol (Poly Phenol) From Cotton Seed Oil
- Greases (Lithium Based)
- Guar Gum Powder
- Hair Fixer (Hair Gel Type)
- High Temerature Grease
- Hard Grease
- H - Acid
- Henna Paste Making
- Henna Powder Repackaging
- Heptal Dehyde
- Herbal Beer
- High Carbon Ferro Chrome
- Humid Acid
- Hydrated Calcium Silicate Brick
- Hydrated Lime From Sea Shell
- Hydrochloric Acid
- Hydro Fluoric Acid
- Hydrogen Peroxide (By Auto-Oxidation Process)
- Ice Packs (Solutions Type, White Gel Type, Violet Semi Solid Polymer Type)
- Improving Drop Point Paraffin Wax From 45-50°c To 75-80°c
- Industrial Alcohol

Market Survey Cum Detailed Techno Economic Feasibility Report on all Projects are available Contact.
"ENGINEERS INDIA RESEARCH INSTITUTE", 4449, Nai Sarak (D), Main Road, Delhi-110006 (India)
Ph. : 09811437895, 9811151047, 91-11-23918117, 23916431, 23947058, 64727385, 45120361
E-mail : eiriprojects@gmail.com, eiribooks@yahoo.com • website: www.eiri.in, www.eiriindia.org • www.eiribooksandprojectreports.com

ALL FOLLOWING PROJECT REPORTS ARE READILY AVAILABLE

PAINT, ENAMEL, SOLVENTS, THINNERS, INKS & VARNISH

PAINT, ENAMEL, SOLVENTS, THINNERS, INKS & VARNISH

- Acrylic Emulsion Paints
- Acrylic Cement Paint (Dry Powder)
- Aluminium Paint
- Automobile Paints
- Ball Point Pen Refill Ink
- Bituminious Road Emulsion
- Bitumen
- Bituminious Felts For Water & Damp Proofing
- Bituminious Road Emulsion Rapid Medium & Slow Setting
- Buffing & Polishing
- Cement Paint For White & Grey Cement
- Dispersant
- Dry Distemper
- Dry Distemper & Cement Paint
- Duplicating Ink Black For Gestner Duplicator
- Emulsion Paints (Water Based)
- Hammertone Paint
- Insulating Varnish & Wire Enamel
- Iron Oxide Pigments
- Insulating Varnish (Poly Vinyl Butyral Based, Ffc Grade)
- Lime Colour (Cement Colour)
- Synthetic Red Oxide For Floorings
- Solvent & Thinners
- Marking Inks (Water Proof)
- Metal Naphthanate (As Drier For Paints)
- N.C.Putty
- Offset Printing Ink
- Oil Bound Distemper Paint
- Paint Brushes
- Paint Manufacture For Rolling Coating Of Aluminium And Steel Coil
- Paint Removers
- Paint Industry
- Paint & Varnish
- Picture Varnish
- Powder Coating Paint
- Printing Inks (Offset,Flexo & Roto Gravure)
- Primer Paint & Enamel Paint
- Putty & Water Proofing Paint
- Printing Inks (Flexo-Graphic Ink)
- Putty (Metal Casement)
- Red Oxide Primer (Anti Corrosive)
- Refrectory Paint (Graphite Based)
- Screen Printing Inks
- Silk Screen Printing Ink Formulation For Plastic, Paper, Cloth
- Stamp & Pad Ink
- Stoving Paint
- Spirit Soluble Maleic Resin
- Texture Paint
- Thinners And Its Allied Products
- Toner Ink
- Varnish Thinner (Solvent)
- Vacuum Metallizing Lacquers
- Wood Primer

PHARMACEUTICAL, DRUGS, AYURVEDIC/HERBAL COSMETICS & MEDICINES, HOMOEOPATHIC MEDICINES, HOMOEOPATHIC MEDICINES, DISPOSABLE SYRINGE, DENTAL COLLEGE & FINE CHEMICALS ETC.

MEDICINES, HOMOEOPATHIC MEDICINES, DISPOSABLE SYRINGE, DENTAL COLLEGE & FINE CHEMICALS ETC.

- Aromatic Pills
- Alumina From Bauxite
- Aspirin
- Ayurvedic Pain Balm Ointments
- Ayurvedic Churan And Tablets
- Ayurvedic Tablets (Hajmola Type)
- Ayurvedic/Herbalpharmacy
- Ayurvedic Sherbats
- Ayurvedic Products
- Bulk Drugs (E.O.U)
- Blood Bags
- Calcium Gluconate
- Capsule, Tablet & Injection With Modern Instruments
- Cashew Feni
- Chloroquinone Phosphate (Bulk Drugs)
- Clinical Thermometer
- Dental Clinic
- Dental College
- Dental Grade Eugenol
- Dextrose Monohydrate, Liquid Glucose
- Dehydrated Onion & Onion Powder
- Dextrose Powder (Anhydrous From Starch)
- Dextrose Saline Solution
- Distillery (I.M.F.L)
- Disposable Needles For Syringes
- Disprin
- Distilled Water
- Empty Hard Gelatine Capsules
- Fairness Cream
- Filling & Packing Of Capsules
- Glucose - D - Powder
- Glycerine
- Hair Colour Mate (Formulations And Process Only)
- Herbal Cosmetics
- Herbal Shampoo
- Herbal Shampoo And Cream
- Herbal Hair Oils (Ayurvedic)
- Homoe & Bio-Medicines With Mother Tincture
- Homoepathic Medicines
- Hypodermic Needles
- I.V. Fluids
- Ibuprofen
- Infusion & Transfusion Sets (I.V. Set)
- Injectable For Pharmaceuticals
- Injection Ampoules Packaging Box
- Integerated Surgical Cotton
- Ice Making Plant
- Ice & Cold Storage
- Lactose & By Products Processing From Milk
- Lichen (Jatamansi Charila)
- Liquid Glucose And Its By-Products
- L-Lysine Monohydro Chloride
- Liquid Glucose From Potatoes
- Medical College
- Methanol (Hpcl Grade)
- Nicotine From Tobacco Waste
- Ointment-Ayurvedic (Yellow & White)
- Pharmaceutical And Food Grade Gelatine
- Pharmaceutical Industry (Tablets, Capsules, Liquid, Gel, Ointment Powder Injectable)
- Pharmaceutical Unit (Eou) With Formulations, Injectables, Etc. Pyridine & Derivatives
- Salt (Iodized Salt)
- Saline & Injection Water
- Saline Water & Dextrose Solution (I.V.Fluid In Plastic Bottles)
- Sorbitol
- Starch (Maize)
- Surgical Adhesive Plaster
- Surgical Bandages
- Surgical Gloves
- Surgical Cotton
- Surgical Cotton And Bandage
- Synthetic Camphor Powder
- Tablets & Capsules
- Tissue Culture
- Tincture From Rectified Spirit
- Trimethopime
- Veterinary College With Hospital
- Veterenary Medicines (Only Formulations)
- Vitamin 'C', Sorbitol' Anhydrous Dextrose, Starch

Market Survey Cum Detailed Techno Economic Feasibility Report on all Projects are available Contact.
"ENGINEERS INDIA RESEARCH INSTITUTE", 4449, Nai Sarak (D), Main Road, Delhi-110006 (India)
Ph. : 09811437895, 9811151047, 91-11-23918117, 23916431, 23947058, 64727385, 45120361
E-mail : eiriprojects@gmail.com, eiribooks@yahoo.com • website: www.eiri.in, www.eiriindia.org • www.eiribooksandprojectreports.com

ALL FOLLOWING PROJECT REPORTS ARE READILY AVAILABLE

- Polyester Resin
- Polyester Yarn From Waste
- Polyester Zip Fasteners
- Power Loom
- Printing On Saree
- Readymade Garments & Hosiery
- Readymade Garments Merchandise
- Readymade Garments & Covers
- Readymade Garments & Embroidery Of Gowns, Shirts, Blouses, T-Shirts Etc. (Only Ladies)
- Readymade Salwar Suit
- Ready Made Garments
- Recovery Of Nylon From Nylon Waste
- Rotary Printing And Dyeing On Cotton, Synthetic Textile
- Sanitary Napkins
- Screen Printing On Cotton Cloth
- Sewing Thread Reels & Balls Making Industries
- Screen Printing On Cotton, Polyester & Acrylic
- Shawls (Woollen)
- Shoe Laces
- Silk Fabrics On Handloom
- Socks Knitting
- Spinning, Doubling Dyeing, Mercerising & Bleaching Of Cotton Yarn
- Spinning & Carding Of Wool Into Yarns
- Starch Book Binding Cloth
- Surat Jari
- Surgical Cotton & Bandage
- Synthetic Textile Industry (Suiting, Shirting, Sarees) Terry Cloth
- T-Shirts
- Towels, Bed Sheet Covers
- Terry Towel
- Terry Fabrics Weaving Unit
- Textile Auxilliaries & Chemicals
- Textile Bleaching, Dyeing & Finishing & Printing Of Cotton Fabrics
- Textile And Finishing Agent
- Textile (Hosiery)
- Textile Mill
- Textile Dyeing & Printing
- Textile Printing (Job Work)
- Textile Pigment Printing Binder
- Towel (Terry)
- Velvet Cloth By Flocking Process
- Viscose Staple Fibre
- Wadding Oil (100%) For Wadding Of Cotton Hosiery Cloth In The Dyeing Process
- Weaving Of Dasuti Cloth With Printing, Dyeing, Embroidery & Finishing
- Washing Of Jeans & Other Garments
- Worsted Woollen Yarn Cloth
- Zari Glitter Salma Sitara Of Plastic Film

INFOTECH/IT, HOSPITALITY, HOSPITAL, COLLEGE, SCHOOL, MEDICAL, ENTERTAINMENT, CLUB, WARE HOUSING & REAL ESTATE PROJECTS.

- Amusement Park
- Aided School
- Amusement Park Cum Water Park
- Banquet Hall
- B.Ed And Law College
- Business Process Outsourcing (Bpo)
- Call Center (Domestic)
- Call Center (International)
- Children Recreation Centre
- Cold Storage
- Community Hall
- Community Centre
- Computer Education Institute
- Computer Software
- College
- Club
- Cyber Café
- Data Processing Centre
- Dental Clinic
- Dental College
- Diagonostic Centre
- E-Commerce/Business
- E-School (Rs. 10,000/-)
- Engineering College
- Entertainment Club
- Entertainment Club, Holiday Resort, 4 Star Hotel, Amusement Park Cum Water Park, Mushroom & Its Products, Fish Farming, Lake For Boating, Deer Park
- Fashion Technology Institute
- Fast Food Parlour
- Five Star Hotel
- Food Parlour
- Franchise Training Programme For Iit & Engineering Entrance Exams.
- Golf Course
- Health Club, Beauty Parlour
- Health Club And Fitness Center
- Health Resorts
- Holiday Resorts
- Holiday Resort Cum Entertainment Club With 4 Star Hotel
- Hospitals
- Hospital Cum Research Centre
- Hospital (400 Beds)
- Ice Cream Parlour
- Internet Service Provider (I.S.P.)
- I.T. Park (Infotech Park)
- Maternity Nursing Home
- Medical College
- Medical College, Hospital & Research Institute
- Medical Transcription Centre
- Mental Retardation Hospital & Cerebral Palsy
- Motel/Small Hotel
- Multistorey Commercial Complex
- Multistorey Residential Complex
- Multiplex Cum Entertainment Centre
- Nursery School
- Nursing School/College
- Nature Care Centre
- Nursing Home
- Old Age Home
- Online Shopping Mall (Rs. 10,000/- Report)
- Portal
- Pre-Fabricated Building
- Prenursery School
- Rehabilitation Centre For Aged & Needy Persons
- Residential Cum Commercial Complex
- Restaurant
- Restaurant With Pub
- Senior Secondary School
- Special Economic Zone (Sez)/Industrial Park
- School (Primary)
- School (Higher Secondary)
- School With Hostel
- School Of Nursing
- Three Star Hotel
- Township
- Tourist Club
- Training Institute For Medical Transcription
- Video Film Studio
- Vetenary College With Hospital
- Ware House
- Website Design & E-Mail Registering

POTATO AND POTATO BASED PRODUCTS

- Alcohol From Potatoes
- Dextrose Powder From Potatoes
- Frozen Finger Chips
- I M F L (Whisky) From Potatoes
- Liquid Glucose From Potato
- Potato Chips/Waffers
- Potato Powder (Automatic Plant)
- Potato Starch
- Potato Chips (Automatic Plant)
- Potato And Onion Flakes
- Potable Beer (Alcoholic) Based On Potato & Barley/Malt
- Potato Powder
- Sago Seeds (Saboo Dana)
- Vodka From Potatoes

Market Survey Cum Detailed Techno Economic Feasibility Report on all Projects are available Contact.
"ENGINEERS INDIA RESEARCH INSTITUTE". 4449, Nai Sarak (D), Main Road, Delhi-110006 (India)
Ph. : 09811437895, 9811151047, 91-11-23918117, 23916431, 23947058, 64727385, 45120361
E-mail : eiriprojects@gmail.com, eiribooks@yahoo.com • website: www.eiri.in, www.eiriindia.org • www.eiribooksandprojectreports.com